# GED
# MATHEMATICS
# WORKBOOK

DAVID ALAN HERZOG

*Dedicated to the memory of Henry Smolinski*

Third Edition

Macmillan General Reference
A Simon & Schuster Macmillan Company
1633 Broadway
New York, NY 10019

An Arco Book

MACMILLAN is a registered trademark of Macmillan, Inc.
ARCO is a registered trademark of Prentice-Hall, Inc.

**Library of Congress Cataloging-in-Publication Data**

Herzog, David Alan.
　GED mathematics workbook / David Alan Herzog.
　　p.　cm.
　At head of title: ARCO.
　ISBN: 0-02-860589-6
　　1. Mathematics—Examinations, questions, etc.　2. General
educational development tests—Study guides.　I. Arco Publishing.
II. Title.
QA43.H413　1996
513'.14'076—dc20　　　　　　　　　　　95-37213
　　　　　　　　　　　　　　　　　　　　　　　CIP

Manufactured in the United States of America

10　9　8　7　6　5　4　3　2　1

# Contents

# *About the GED Test*

## *WHAT IS THE GED?*

GED stands for General Educational Development Tests. The GED examination consists of five separate tests covering important subjects taught in high school. The five GED tests are:

1. Writing Skills
2. Social Studies
3. Science
4. Interpreting Literature and the Arts
5. Mathematics

The GED Testing Program started in 1942 when the United States was at war, and many young men dropped out of high school to join the armed services. The test was designed to provide a way for returning veterans to earn a high school diploma so that they could qualify for employment or further education. The purpose of the GED has not changed. It still offers adults who did not complete high school (for whatever reason) a chance to earn a diploma.

## *WHO TAKES THE GED TESTS?*

Anyone who left high school without graduating is probably eligible to take the GED. Every year nearly 800,000 adults take the GED test — and about 450,000 of them are awarded GED diplomas. In fact, one out of every seven high school diplomas issued in the United States each year is a GED diploma.

## *WHERE ARE THE GED TESTS GIVEN?*

The tests are given in all 50 states, the District of Columbia, the U.S. territories, most Canadian provinces, and the Canadian territories. There are more than 3,000 official GED Testing Centers in the United States and Canada. To locate a convenient testing center, contact your state, territorial, or provincial department of education. A list of addresses for all GED Administrators is provided on pages *xii* to *xviii*.

## *WHAT SUBJECTS ARE TESTED IN THE GED BATTERY?*

The English-language GED battery consists of five individual tests. Four of the tests are made up of all multiple-choice questions. The Writing Skills test, however, contains both a multiple-choice and an essay section. A brief description of each GED test follows.

**Test 1. Writing Skills.**   The Writing Skills test has two parts. Part I contains 55 multiple-choice questions that require you to correct and revise sentences that are presented in a writing selection. You will be asked to identify and correct errors in sentence structure, usage, capitalization, punctuation, and spelling. Part II asks you to write an essay on an assigned topic. The topics used for this test are all issues of general interest that require no special or technical knowledge.

**Test 2. Social Studies.**   The Social Studies test contains 64 multiple-choice questions drawn from the areas of history, economics, geography, political science, and behavioral sciences. Most of the questions refer to information provided in the form of reading passages, cartoons, graphs, or charts. The questions ask you to use, analyze, or evaluate the information provided. There are different U.S. and Canadian versions of the Social Studies test.

**Test 3. Science.**   The GED Science test contains 66 multiple-choice questions drawn from the areas of biology, earth science, physics, and chemistry. Some of the questions require specific knowledge, but most test for an understanding of basic scientific principles and ideas. Information may be provided in the form of reading passages, graphs, charts, maps, or figures. The questions require you to demonstrate your understanding of the information provided or to use the information to solve a problem.

**Test 4. Interpreting Literature and the Arts.**   This test contains 45 multiple-choice questions based on excerpts from classical and popular literature and commentaries about literature and the arts. The passages may be drawn from newpapers, magazines, novels, short stories, poetry, and drama. The questions test your ability to analyze and understand what you read.

**Test 5. Mathematics.**   The Mathematics test consists of 56 questions testing your ability to solve problems from the areas of arithmetic, algebra, and geometry. Most of the problems are presented as word problems. Many questions involve a real-life situation or ask you to interpret information presented in graphs, charts, tables, or diagrams. You are not allowed to bring a calculator to the test, but you will be given a page of important formulas to help you solve some of the problems on the exam.

## WHAT IS THE BEST WAY TO PREPARE FOR THE GED?

Some people prepare for the GED by enrolling in special classes. Many local school districts, colleges and community organizations sponsor GED programs. To find out about programs in your area, contact your local high school adult education program or community college. Check the yellow pages of your telephone directory under the heading of "Schools." GED programs may be listed as "Adult Education," "Continuing Education," or "GED."

Many GED candidates choose to study on their own. Libraries, schools, and bookstores offer a wealth of study materials to improve your skills. ARCO publishes three helpful GED study guides:

- *GED: High School Equivalency Examination*: a complete home-study course with subject area reviews and three full-length practice exams
- *GED Writing Skills Workbook*: a comprehensive review of English grammar and usage with sample GED Writing Skills questions and step-by-step guidelines for the GED essay
- *GED Mathematics Workbook*: everything you need to know about arithmetic, algebra, and geometry for the GED Mathematics test with two, full-length sample tests

## FORMAT OF THE GED TEST BATTERY

| Subject | Number of Questions | Time Allowed |
| --- | --- | --- |
| **Test 1. Writing Skills** | | |
| Part I. Multiple-choice<br>Sentence Structure (25%)<br>Usage (25%)<br>Capitalization (10%)<br>Punctuation (20%)<br>Spelling/Possessives/<br>Contractions (20%) | 55 multiple-choice | 75 minutes |
| Part II. Essay | 1 essay | 45 minutes |
| **Test 2. Social Studies** | 64 multiple-choice | 85 minutes |
| History (25%)<br>Economics (20%)<br>Geography (15%)<br>Political Science (20%)<br>Behavioral Science (20%) | | |
| **Test 3. Science** | 66 multiple-choice | 95 minutes |
| Life Science (50%)<br>  Biology<br>Physical Science (50%)<br>  Physics<br>  Chemistry<br>  Earth Science | | |
| **Test 4. Interpreting Literature and the Arts** | 45 multiple-choice | 65 minutes |
| Popular Literature (50%)<br>Classical Literature (25%)<br>Commentary (25%) | | |
| **Test 5. Mathematics** | 56 multiple-choice | 90 minutes |
| Measurement (30%)<br>Algebra (30%)<br>Geometry (20%)<br>Numeration (10%)<br>Statistics (10%) | | |

## WHAT TEST-TAKING STRATEGIES CAN HELP IMPROVE GED SCORES?

There are several test-taking strategies you should keep in mind as you take your GED test.

1. **Read the directions for each section carefully** before you start to answer questions. Make certain that you understand how you are to answer each different type of question.
2. **Read every question carefully.** Pay particular attention to any words that are underlined or printed in capital letters.
3. **Answer every question.** There is no penalty for wrong answers on the GED, so even when you have no idea which answer is correct, you still have a 20 percent chance of guessing the right answer.
4. **Don't look for trick answers.** GED questions are not trick questions, so don't waste your time looking for trick answers.
5. **Don't spend too much time on any one question**. If you really can't choose an answer, cross out the answers you know are wrong and choose from the ones that are left.
6. **Mark your answer sheet carefully.** Make sure that you answer each question by completely filling in the circle that matches both the question number and the answer choice you have selected. If you skip a question, you must remember to skip the corresponding answer space as well.

## WHAT IS A PASSING SCORE ?

GED scores are reported as standard scores ranging from 20 to 80 for each test. The raw score (or number of questions answered correctly) is converted to a standard score so that all tests and all forms of the GED can be evaluated similarly.

Passing scores for the GED tests are established by each state, province, or territory. To be successful in passing the GED in most states, a candidate must get a total minimum standard score of 225 on the five tests, with no score of less that 35 on any single test. In general, that means that a candidate who answers 60 percent of the questions in each test correctly will get a passing score.

The table on page *xi* indicates the minimum passing scores currently in effect in each state, territory, and province. For example, when the minimum standard score is given as 35 *and* 45, this means no test score can be less than 35 and an average score can be no lower than 45 for all five tests in the battery for a total standard score of 225. When the minimum standard score is given as 35 *or* 45, this means no test score can be less than 35. If one or more scores are less than 35, an average of 45 is required for all five tests in the battery.

To be certain of earning a GED certificate, you should aim to score above the minimum score on as many tests as possible. However, if you fall short of passing a single test or several tests, you can retake only those sections on which you failed to attain a passing score. Information on retaking the GED test battery is available from the Education Department of each state.

## MINIMUM PASSING SCORES

| State | Minimum Scores | Canadian Jurisdictions | Minimum Scores |
| --- | --- | --- | --- |
| Alabama | 35 and 45 | Alberta | 45 each test |
| Alaska | 35 and 45 | British Columbia | 45 each test |
| Arizona | 35 and 45 | Manitoba | 45 each test |
| Arkansas | 40 and 45 | New Brunswick | 45 each test |
| California | 40 and 45 | Newfoundland | 40 and 45 |
| Colorado | 35 and 45 | Northwest Territories | 45 each test |
| Connecticut | 35 and 45 | Nova Scotia | 45 each test |
| Delaware | 40 and 45 | Prince Edward Island | 45 each test |
| District of Columbia | 40 and 45 | Saskatchewan | 45 each test |
| Florida | 40 and 45 | Yukon Territory | 45 each test |
| Georgia | 35 and 45 | | |
| Hawaii | 35 and 45 | **Other Jurisdictions** | |
| Idaho | 40 and 45 | American Samoa | 40 each test |
| Illinois | 35 and 45 | Guam | 35 and 45 |
| Indiana | 35 and 45 | Kwajalein | 35 and 45 |
| Iowa | 35 and 45 | Marshall Islands | 40 or 45 |
| Kansas | 35 and 45 | Micronesia | 35 and 45 |
| Kentucky | 35 and 45 | Northern Mariana Is. | 40 or 45 |
| Louisiana | 40 or 45 | Panama Canal Area | 40 and 45 |
| Maine | 35 and 45 | Puerto Rico | 35 and 45 |
| Maryland | 40 and 45 | Republic of Palau | 40 and 45 |
| Massachusetts | 35 and 45 | Virgin Islands | 35 and 45 |
| Michigan | 35 and 45 | | |
| Minnesota | 35 and 45 | | |
| Mississippi | 40 or 45 | | |
| Missouri | 40 and 45 | | |
| Montana | 35 and 45 | | |
| Nebraska | 40 or 45 | | |
| Nevada | 35 and 45 | | |
| New Hampshire | 35 and 45 | | |
| New Jersey | 42 on Test 1, 40 on Tests 2–4, 45 on Test 5, and Total score of 225 | | |
| New Mexico | 40 or 50 | | |
| New York | 40 and 45 | | |
| North Carolina | 35 and 45 | | |
| North Dakota | 40 or 50 | | |
| Ohio | 35 and 45 | | |
| Oklahoma | 40 and 45 | | |
| Oregon | 40 and 45 | | |
| Pennsylvania | 35 and 45 | | |
| Rhode Island | 35 and 45 | | |
| South Carolina | 35 and 45 | | |
| South Dakota | 40 and 45 | | |
| Tennessee | 35 and 45 | | |
| Texas | 40 or 45 | | |
| Utah | 40 and 45 | | |
| Vermont | 35 and 45 | | |
| Virginia | 35 and 45 | | |
| Washington | 40 and 45 | | |
| West Virginia | 40 and 45 | | |
| Wisconsin | 40 and 50 | | |
| Wyoming | 35 and 45 | | |

# GED Administrators

ALABAMA
GED Administrator
GED Testing Program
State Department of Education
Gordon Persons Building
50 N. Ripley
Montgomery, AL 36130
(205) 242-8182 Fax: (205) 242-9708

ALASKA
Administrator
GED Testing Program
Alaska Department of Education
801 W. 10th Street, Suite 200
Juneau, AK 99801-1894
(907) 465-8727 Fax: (907) 463-5279

ARIZONA
GED Administrator
Arizona State Department of Education
1535 W. Jefferson
Phoenix, AZ 85007
(602) 542-5281 Fax: (602) 542-1849

ARKANSAS
GED Test Administrator
Arkansas Department of Education
Luther S. Hardin Building, #601
Three Capitol Mall
Little Rock, AR 72201-1083
(501) 682-1970 Fax: (501) 682-1982

CALIFORNIA
GED Administrator
California State Dept. of Education
560 J Street, Suite 290
Sacramento, CA 95814
(916) 324-7116 Fax: (916) 323-2597

COLORADO
GED Administrator
Colorado Department of Education
201 E. Colfax Avenue, Room 100
Denver, CO 80203
(303) 866-6612 Fax: (303) 830-0793

CONNECTICUT
Bureau of Adult Education and Training
State Department of Education
25 Industrial Park Road
Middletown, CT 06457
(203) 638-4151 Fax: (203) 638-4156

DELAWARE
State Supervisor
Adult and Community Education
Department of Public Instruction
Townsend Building
P.O. Box 1402
Dover, DE 19903
(302) 739-4681 Fax: (302) 739-3092

DISTRICT OF COLUMBIA
GED Administrator
Adult Basic Education Office
Penn Center, Administrative Unit
1709 Third Street, NE, Room 215
Washington, DC 20002
(202) 576-6308 Fax: (202) 576-7899

FLORIDA
Chief, Bureau of Adult and Community
    Education
Department of Education
325 W. Gaines
F.E.C. Room 1244
Tallahassee, FL 32399-0400
(904) 487-4929 Fax: (904) 487-6259

GEORGIA
Director, Assessment and Evaluation
Georgia Department of Technical and
    Adult Education
1800 Century Place, NE
Atlanta, GA 30345-4304
(404) 679-1644 Fax: (404) 679-1630

HAWAII
Administrator
Community Education Section
595 Pepeekeo Street, H-2
Honolulu, HI 96825
(808) 395-9451

IDAHO
Chief, Bureau of Instruction
State Department of Education
L.B.J. Building
Boise, ID 83720
(208) 334-2165 Fax: (208) 334-2228

ILLINOIS
Administrator, GED Testing Program
Adult and Continuing Education
    Section
Illinois State Board of Education
100 N. First Street
Springfield, IL 62777
(217) 782-3370 Fax: (217) 782-9224

INDIANA
GED State Administrator
Div. of Adult and Community
    Education
Indiana Department of Education
State House, Room 229
Indianapolis, IN 46204
(317) 232-0522 Fax: (317) 232-9121

IOWA
Adult Education Section
Bureau of Area Schools
Department of Public Education
Grimes State Office Building
Des Moines, IA 50319-0146
(515) 281-3636 Fax: (515) 242-5988

KANSAS
GED Administrator, Adult Education
State Department of Education
Kansas State Education Building
120 E. 10th Street
Topeka, KS 66612
(913) 296-3191 Fax: (913) 296-7933

KENTUCKY
State GED Administrator
Dept. of Adult and Technical Education
Office of Adult Education
Capitol Plaza Tower, 3rd Floor
500 Metro Street
Frankfort, KY 40601
(502) 564-5117 Fax: (502) 465-5316

LOUISIANA
Director, Adult Education
Louisiana Department of Education
626 N. 4th
P.O. Box 94064
Baton Rouge, LA 70804-9064
(504) 342-3510 Fax: (504) 342-7316

MAINE
Bureau of Applied Technology and
    Adult Learning
State Department of Education
State House Station #23
Augusta, ME 04333
(207) 287-5894 Fax: (207) 287-5894

MARYLAND
GED Administrator
Maryland State Dept. of Education
200 W. Baltimore Street
Baltimore, MD 21201
(410) 333-2280 Fax: (410) 333-8435

MASSACHUSETTS
GED Administrator
Bureau of Adult Education
MA Department of Education
350 Main Street
Malden, MA 02148-5023
(617) 388-3300 ext. 651
Fax: (617) 770-7332

MICHIGAN
Supervisor, Adult Basic Education and
    High School Completion
State Department of Education
608 W. Allegan
P.O. Box 30008
Lansing, MI 48909
(517) 373-8439 Fax: (517) 335-3630

MINNESOTA
GED Administrator
998 Capitol Square Building
550 Cedar Street
St. Paul, MN 55101
(612) 296-2704 Fax: (612) 297-5695

MISSISSIPPI
GED Administrator
State Board for Community/Junior
  Colleges
3825 Ridgewood Road
Jackson, MS 39211
(601) 982-6338 Fax: (601) 982-6365

MISSOURI
Director, Adult Education
State Department of Elementary and
  Secondary Education
205 Jefferson
P.O. Box 480
Jefferson City, MO 65102
(314) 751-1249 Fax: (314) 751-1179

MONTANA
GED Administrator
Office of Public Instruction
State Capitol Building
Helena, MT 59601
(406) 444-4438 Fax: (406) 444-3924

NEBRASKA
Director of Adult and Community
  Education
State Department of Education
301 Centennial Mall South
Lincoln, NE 68509
(402) 471-4807 Fax: (402) 471-0117

NEVADA
Education Consultant
Adult and Continuing Education
Department of Education
Capitol Complex
400 W. King Street
Carson City, NV 89710
(702) 687-3133 Fax: (702) 687-5660

NEW HAMPSHIRE
Office of Adult Basic Education
New Hampshire Department of
  Education
State Office Park South
101 Pleasant Street
Concord, NH 03301
(603) 271-6699 Fax: (603) 588-7893

NEW JERSEY
Manager, Div. of Adult Education
GED Testing
CN500
240 W. State Street, 10th Floor
Trenton, NJ 08625-0500
(609) 292-5543 Fax: (609) 633-9825

NEW MEXICO
Director, State Dept. of Education
Assessment and Evaluation
Education Building
Room 124
300 Don Gaspar
Santa Fe, NM 87501-2786
(505) 827-6524 Fax: (505) 827-6696

NEW YORK
GED Administrator
GED Office
Room 774
EBA
New York State Education Department
Albany, NY 12224
(518) 474-8741 Fax: (518) 474-2801

NORTH CAROLINA
Coordinator of Adult High School
  Programs
State Board of Community Colleges
The Caswell Building
200 W. Jones Street
Raleigh, NC 27603-1337
(919) 733-7051 ext. 307
Fax: (919) 733-0680

NORTH DAKOTA
Director
Adult Basic and Secondary Education
Department of Public Instruction
Capitol Building
Bismarck, ND 58505
(701) 224-3600 Fax: (701) 224-2461

OHIO
GED Administrator
State Department of Education
65 S. Front Street, Room 812
Columbus, OH 43215
(614) 466-9217 Fax: (614) 752-3956

**OKLAHOMA**
Administrator
Adult/Community Education Services
State Department of Education
2500 N. Lincoln Boulevard
Oklahoma City, OK 73105-4599
(405) 521-3321 Fax: (405) 521-6205

**OREGON**
Director
Office of Community College Services
255 Capitol Street, NE
Salem, OR 97310-0203
(503) 378-8648 ext. 359
Fax: (503) 378-8434

**PENNSYLVANIA**
GED Administrator
Adult Basic and Literacy Education
State Department of Education
333 Market Street
Harrisburg, PA 17126-0333
(717) 787-5532 Fax: (717) 783-6672

**RHODE ISLAND**
GED Administrator
Department of Elementary and
   Secondary Education
Vocational and Adult Education
   Division
22 Hayes Street, Room 222
Providence, RI 02908
(401) 277-2681 Fax: (401) 277-2537

**SOUTH CAROLINA**
GED Coordinator
State Department of Education
212 Rutledge Building
1429 Senate Street
Columbia, SC 29201
(803) 734-8347 Fax: (803) 734-8624

**SOUTH DAKOTA**
Adult Basic Education
Department of Education and Cultural
   Affairs
700 Governor's Drive
Pierre, SD 57501-2291
(605) 773-4463 Fax: (605) 773-6139

**TENNESSEE**
GED Administrator
State Department of Education
1130 Menzler Road
Nashville, TN 37210
(615) 741-7054 Fax: (615) 532-4899

**TEXAS**
Assistant Commissioner for
   Compliance
Texas Education Agency
William B. Travis Building
1701 N. Congress Avenue
Austin, TX 78701
(512) 463-9292 Fax: (512) 305-9493

**UTAH**
Director, GED Testing Program
Utah State Office of Education
250 East 500 South
Salt Lake City, UT 84111
(801) 538-7844 Fax: (801) 538-7521

**VERMONT**
Career and Lifelong Learning Division
State Department of Education
120 State Street
Montpelier, VT 05620
(802) 828-3131 Fax: (802) 828-3140

**VIRGINIA**
Associate Specialist
Virginia Office of Adult Education
Department of Education
P.O. Box 2120
Richmond, VA 23216-2060
(804) 371-2333 Fax: (804) 371-8593

**WASHINGTON**
GED Administrator
State Board for Community and
   Technical Colleges
319 7th Avenue
P.O. Box 42495
Olympia, WA 98504-2495
(206) 753-6748 Fax: (206) 664-8808

WEST VIRGINIA
Assistant Director
Bureau of Vocational, Technical, and
    Adult Education
1900 Kanawha Boulevard East
Building 6, Room B230
Charleston, WV 25305-0330
(304) 558-6318 Fax: (304) 558-0048

WISCONSIN
Wisconsin High School Equivalency
    Program
Department of Public Instruction
P.O. Box 7841
125 S. Webster Street
Madison, WI 53703
(608) 267-9448 Fax: (608) 267-1052

WYOMING
GED Administrator
Wyoming Department of Education
Hathaway Building
Cheyenne, WY 82002
(307) 777-6265 Fax: (307) 777-6234

DANTES
Attn: Code 12
6490 Saufley Field Road
Pensacola, FL 32509-5243
(904) 452-1089 Fax: (904) 452-1160

FEDERAL PRISONS
GED Administrator
Federal Bureau of Prisons
Department of Justice
320 First Street, NW
Washington, DC 20534
(202) 724-3022 Fax: (202) 638-1428

MICHIGAN PRISONS
Education Director
Michigan Department of Corrections
Grand View Plaza
P.O. Box 30003
Lansing, MI 48909
(517) 373-3605 Fax: (517) 373-2628

VETERANS ADMINISTRATION
Rehabilitation Planning Specialist
Department of Veterans Affairs
Room 548 (Teck World)
810 Vermont Avenue, NW
Washington, DC 20420
(202) 535-7273 Fax: (202) 535-7487

ALBERTA
Assistant Director, Student Evaluation
    Branch
Alberta Education
11160 Jasper Avenue, Box 43
Edmonton, AB T5K OL2
(403) 427-0010 Fax: (403) 422-4200

BRITISH COLUMBIA
Director, Examinations Branch
Ministry of Education
Parliament Buildings
617 Government Street
Victoria, BC V8V 2M4
(604) 356-7269 Fax: (604) 387-3682

MANITOBA
Acting Director
Distance Education Program Unit
The Independent Study Program
555 Main Street
Winkler, MB R6W IC4
(204) 474-1482 Fax: (204) 325-4212

NEW BRUNSWICK
English Language Edition
Director, Curriculum and Evaluation
    Branch
Advanced Education and Labour
416 York Street
P.O. Box 6000
Fredericton, NB E3B 5H1
(506) 453-8227 Fax: (506) 453-7913

NEWFOUNDLAND
Manager, High School Certification
Division of Program Development
Department of Education
Confederation Building, 3rd Floor
P.O. Box 8700
St. John's, NF A1B 4J6
(709) 729-2999 Fax: (709) 729-5896

NORTHWEST TERRITORIES
GED Administrator
Department of Education, Culture, and
Employment Programs
Government of the N.W. Territories
Lahm Ridge Tower, 3rd Floor
Franklin Avenue
Yellowknife, NT X1A 2L9
(403) 920-6218 Fax: (403) 873-0338

NOVA SCOTIA
Assistant Director
Testing and Evaluation
N.S. Department of Education
2021 Brunswick Street
P.O. Box 578
Halifax, NS B3J 2S9
(902) 424-5805 Fax: (902) 424-0614

PRINCE EDWARD ISLAND
Director, Educational Services
Department of Education and Human
Resources
P.O. Box 2000
Charlottetown, PE C1A 7N8
(902) 368-4690 Fax: (902) 368-4663

SASKATCHEWAN
Program Support Services Unit
Department of Education, Training, and
Employment
2220 College Avenue
Regina, SK S4P 3V7
(306) 787-5637 Fax: (306) 787-9178

YUKON TERRITORY
GED Administrator and Examiner
Yukon College
P.O. Box 2799
White Horse, YT Y1A 5K4/YK
(403) 668-8741 Fax: (403) 668-8890

MILITARY
GED Administrator
Canadian Forces
234 Laurier Avenue
Export Building, 16th Floor
DPPS/NDHQ
Ottawa, ON K1A OK2
(613) 996-2429 Fax: (613) 995-2701

MILITARY
Training Development/Education
Officer
National Defense Headquarters
Administrative Unit, Berger Building
Ottawa, ON K1A OK2
(613) 995-8334

AMERICAN SAMOA
Director of Education
Government of American Samoa
Pago Pago, AS 96799
011 (684) 633-5237
Fax: 011 (684) 633-4240

GUAM
Guam Community College
P.O. Box 23069
Main Postal Facility
Guam, GU 96921
011 (671) 734-4310 ext. 9
Fax: 011 (671) 734-4311

KWAJALEIN
Attn: Community Education
P.O. Box 54
APO
San Francisco, CA 96555
(805) 238-7994 ext. 1078
Fax: (805) 238-7994

MARSHALL ISLANDS
GED Administrator and President
College of the Marshall Islands
P.O. Box 1258
Republic of Marshall Islands
Majuro, MH 96960
(692) 625-4551
DC (202) 785-5083

MICRONESIA
GED State Administrator
Federated States of Micronesia National
Government
Palikir, Pohnpei, FM 96941
011 (691) 320-2647/2609

NORTHERN MARIANA ISLANDS
GED Administrator
Northern Marianas College
Adult Basic Education Program
P.O. Box 1250
Saipan, MP 96950
011 (670) 235-4940
Fax: 011 (670) 234-0759/1270

PANAMA
GED Administrator
Panama Canal College
DODDS Panama Region
APO
Miami, FL 34002
011 (507) 52-3107/3304

PUERTO RICO
GED Administrator
Educational Extension Area
Department of Education
P.O. Box 190759
San Juan, PR 00919-0759
(809) 753-9211

VIRGIN ISLANDS
Director
Division of Adult Education
Department of Education
St. Thomas, VI 00802
(809) 774-5394 Fax: (809) 774-4679

# About This Book

This book serves two purposes. First, to prepare you for the GED (General Educational Development) examination in mathematics. Second, to help you learn mathematics. Toward that end, the book is divided into three broad sections: arithmetic, algebra, and geometry. Arithmetic is not really mathematics, but rather a tool that permits you to solve problems in mathematics. When you know all about arithmetic, you will **not** know mathematics, and without arithmetic, you could not do mathematics. That is probably why the single largest portion of the GED mathematics examination is concerned with arithmetic.

The portion of this book that deals with arithmetic is divided into several sections: The first deals with the arithmetic of whole numbers. Lewis Carroll, who was a mathematician when he wasn't leading Alice through Wonderland, described the four branches of arithmetic as Ambition, Distraction, Uglification, and Derision. We know them better as addition, subtraction, multiplication, and division. The second section deals with fractions — that terrible monster that makes educated children call their mothers liars. I refer, of course, to the mother who fixes a sandwich for lunch and offers to share it with her child. Unselfishly, she says: "You take the bigger half." Alas, by the time the child has reached the third grade, he or she is aware that there is no such thing as a bigger half, and is not shy about saying so. Finally, our study of arithmetic will take us through the mysterious worlds of decimals and percentages. Neither of those topics need be so mysterious if you realize that they are just different ways of writing fractions.

Mathematics is very different from most other branches of human studies. It is, to quote Mr. Spock, "logical." Indeed, it is very logical. If anything is sound mathematically, then it must work. More than that, it is capable of being analyzed to find out **why** it works. For that reason, I suggest that you memorize nothing in this book. Rather, each time a new concept is introduced to you, study it. Analyze it. Ask yourself: "Does this make sense?" If it does, that is terrific. If it does not, mull it over. See if you can make sense out of it. If it still does not make sense, then the failing is that of the author; not of you.

Algebra is a mathematical discipline. It is a structured means for translating word-problems into mathematical shorthand, and then solving them. The rules of algebra are reasonable, and can be applied to many different situations. Once you have mastered algebraic thinking, you may well wonder how you were ever able to get along without it.

Geometry, too, is a way of reasoning. It differs from algebra, in that it is reasoning as applied to certain figures. The rules of geometry apply primarily to angles and line segments, and to the closed figures that can be made (triangles, rectangles, and so on) by combining those forms. Geometry is much older than algebra, having been formalized nearly 2500 years ago by a Greek named Euclid. It was his gift to the centuries that followed. Now you might well think as the Trojans did, "Beware of Greeks bearing gifts." Still, is there not something appealing about the notion that two things equal to the same thing are equal to each other? Or what about a straight line as being the shortest distance between two points? Logical, isn't it?

Each section of the instructional portion of this book is preceded by a pre-test. That is a short test to help you determine how well you know the subject matter that will be covered in that section. If you do well on the pre-test, then there is no point to your studying that section. Concentrate on only those areas where you need help.

The answer key which immediately follows each pre-test will serve to guide your course of study. Each section is also followed by a post-test. By comparing the results on your post-test with those on the pre-test, you will be able to determine how much studying the section has helped you. The post-test should help you to isolate those topics which may need some more intensive work.

Finally, at the end of the entire instruction section, you will find a set of additional practice exercises keyed to each of the topics that you have studied. You may wish to use the additional practice at a later time, just to refresh your memory and your skills. If, however, you have found it necessary to review a section following the post-test on that section, the additional practice exercises may serve as new reinforcement materials, or as a new post-test.

**You will, incidentally, find that the entire instructional portion of the book is preceded by a large pre-test. That pre-test is, in fact, a simulated half-length GED mathematics examination. It should help you to locate the areas with which you need the most help. Following the instructional portion, and concluding this volume, you will find two full-length simulated GED practice examinations. They will serve to help you finely tune your skills under simulated testing conditions.**

Now, as you press onward with your studies, keep in mind what was said earlier in this introduction. Mathematics is logical, and the more you work at it, the more fully you will develop your skills. We hope that you will enjoy the book, and find that it helps you on your way to success.

# *Acknowledgments*

For a book like this, there are always many people who contribute to making it what it is — some of whom had a direct hand in its making, and some of whom contributed unknowingly just by being there. I wish to express extreme personal thanks to Karen Dale Foster who gave unstintingly of her time to contribute many ideas, suggestions, problems, and good humor to this volume. I must also thank Linda Bernbach for her patience and encouragement. Special thanks as well to Henry Smolinski, Margaret Smolinski, Mema Koenig, James and Melissa Foster, and Thomas Eisenberg. Last, but not least, I wish to thank Geoffrey, Alessandra, Dylan, Jason, and Carol. Midnight will have to wait for the next book.

# 1. PRE-TEST OF GED MATHEMATICS SKILLS

Following is a half-length simulated GED mathematics examination. It contains 13 problems in arithmetic, 6 in algebra, and 6 from geometry. After taking it, use the answer key immediately following the test to score yourself. The answer key will help you to identify those areas in mathematics where you most need work.

Before taking this pre-test, provide yourself with a quiet place where you will not be interrupted. You should have several sheets of blank paper and three or four sharpened pencils. Since the actual GED examination must be answered in pencil, it is a good idea to accustom yourself to working in pencil rather than pen.

You may wish to have a clock with a second hand nearby. If you were taking this examination under actual test conditions, you would be allowed 45 minutes to complete the 25 questions. For that reason, you may wish to time yourself just to get an idea of how many questions you can complete in 45 minutes. Continue working, however, until you have completed the pre-test. Work quickly, carefully, and do not spend a great length of time on any single question. If a certain question gives you difficulty, skip it, making a mark next to it in the margin. You can come back to that question later, if you wish. When taking the actual examination, you would come back to skipped questions, if time permitted. It is good practice, then, to learn when a question has been worked on for too much time.

All of the problems are followed by a choice of five possible answers. Work out the answer for yourself before looking at the choices. Otherwise, you may be tricked by answers that appear to be reasonable, but which are actually incorrect.

On an actual GED examination, answers will be marked on a separate machine-scored answer sheet. You will find answer spaces on this pre-test to the right of each question. Blacken the number of the answer which you believe to be correct.

*Example*

What is the cost of 6 pounds of tomatoes at 79¢ per pound?

(1) $3.85
(2) $4.34                                     ① ② ③ ● ⑤
(3) $4.54
(4) $4.74
(5) $4.94

The cost is $4.74. That is why answer 4 is marked.

# PRE-TEST

**Directions:** Choose the best answer for each problem.

1) A plane ticket from New York to Chicago costs $89.24. A ticket from Chicago to Austin costs $134.39. What is the cost of flying from New York to Austin by way of Chicago?

   (1) $223.63
   (2) $45.15              ① ② ③ ④ ⑤
   (3) $134.39
   (4) $224.00
   (5) $316.00

2) A leather briefcase cost $145.37. A second one cost $128.58. What was the difference in their prices?

   (1) $237.95
   (2) $273.95            ① ② ③ ④ ⑤
   (3) $16.79
   (4) $61.79
   (5) $26.79

3) 865 persons paid $4.75 each for tickets to a basketball game. 479 persons bought $6.25 tickets. How much money was paid for tickets in all?

   (1) $7681.50
   (2) $6718.50           ① ② ③ ④ ⑤
   (3) $7102.50
   (4) $4108.75
   (5) $1115.00

4) 5745 meters of electrical cable are to be used for the electrical wiring of 15 new houses. Each house will use the same amount of cable. How much cable will each house use?

   (1) 5760 meters
   (2) 86,175 meters        ① ② ③ ④ ⑤
   (3) 5730 meters
   (4) 383 meters
   (5) 403 meters

5) Helen Hardy usually pays $3.95 for a bottle of 250 lecithin capsules at the natural foods store. This week the store ran a sale on lecithin capsules, charging only $5.95 for a bottle of 500. Helen takes one capsule daily. How much money would Helen save in the course of a year if she purchases the sale bottle?

   (1) $5.77
   (2) $4.34             ① ② ③ ④ ⑤
   (3) $1.19
   (4) $1.43
   (5) $1.58

6) Heloise Aylor usually blinks her eyes every 12 seconds but when a man in uniform enters the room, she bats her eyelashes at the incredible speed of 72 blinks per minute. What is the percent of increase in Heloise's blinking rate?

(1) 13.40%
(2) 72%
(3) 720%
(4) 144%
(5) 1340%

① ② ③ ④ ⑤

7) Rosemarie decided to do some spring cleaning. She figured it would take her 2 hours 15 minutes to scrub the floors, 25 minutes to dust and polish, 45 minutes to vacuum, 1 hour 45 minutes to clean the windows, and 1 hour 30 minutes to wash, press, and re-hang her curtains. How much time will her spring cleaning chores require?

(1) 4 hours, 40 minutes
(2) 5 hours, 45 minutes
(3) 6 hours, 20 minutes
(4) 6 hours, 40 minutes
(5) 7 hours, 10 minutes

① ② ③ ④ ⑤

8) Mrs. Winfield bought 8 dozen apples for her children's snacks. Mrs. Winfield has 4 children and each receives an apple a day. How many days will her supply of apples last?

(1) 16
(2) 24
(3) 32
(4) 68
(5) 96

① ② ③ ④ ⑤

9) An auctioneer is given an 8% commission on sales plus $60 a week. Last week, the auctioneer sold $794.25 worth of items. How much money did he make that week?

(1) $63.54
(2) $72.90
(3) $163.54
(4) $172.90
(5) $123.54

① ② ③ ④ ⑤

10) 20% of the students in Mr. Mendoza's English class failed his final exam. Two-thirds of those who failed were girls. If a total of 120 students took the exam, how many girls failed?

(1) 16
(2) 20
(3) 24
(4) 28
(5) 32

① ② ③ ④ ⑤

11) If it takes a truck driving over a bridge $\frac{1}{20}$ of an hour to cross the bridge and the truck is traveling at a speed of 12 mph, how long is the bridge?

(1) $\frac{1}{3}$ miles
(2) $\frac{1}{2}$ miles
(3) $\frac{3}{5}$ miles
(4) $\frac{3}{4}$ miles
(5) $\frac{2}{3}$ miles

① ② ③ ④ ⑤

12) 50 micrograms of a particular multiple vitamin contain 833% of the U.S. Recommended Daily Allowance. How many micrograms would satisfy the requirement for 100%?

(1) 5
(2) 6
(3) 7
(4) 8
(5) 9

① ② ③ ④ ⑤

13) What number is .459 less than 3.30?

(1) 2.841
(2) 2.859
(3) 3.759
(4) 2.849
(5) 2.749

① ② ③ ④ ⑤

14) On a 345 mile trip to Hoboken, N.J., the Winkleman family averaged 48.6 mph. Approximately how long did it take them to reach their destination?

(1) $5\frac{1}{2}$ hours
(2) 6 hours
(3) $6\frac{1}{2}$ hours
(4) 7 hours
(5) $7\frac{1}{2}$ hours

① ② ③ ④ ⑤

15) Mrs. Manzini's hair is beginning to turn white. She claims she gets a new white hair every time her son Salvatore goes out at night with his friends. Of the 160,000 hairs on her head, 20% have already turned white. If Sal averages 2 nights out a week and assuming Mrs. Manzini's theory is correct, about how long will it be before Mrs. Manzini's head is 50% white?

(1) 5 years
(2) 45 years
(3) 105 years
(4) 405 years
(5) 450 years

① ② ③ ④ ⑤

16) A butcher has a smoked ham weighing $17\frac{3}{4}$ pounds. If he cuts it into 3 equal pieces, how much will each of the smaller hams weigh?

(1) $5\frac{1}{4}$ pounds
(2) $5\frac{5}{12}$ pounds
(3) $5\frac{7}{12}$ pounds
(4) $5\frac{11}{12}$ pounds
(5) $5\frac{15}{16}$ pounds

① ② ③ ④ ⑤

17) If $x^2 - 5x + 4 = 0$, then $x =$

(1) 1 and 5
(2) ⁻1 and ⁻5
(3) ⁻1 and ⁻4
(4) 1 and 4
(5) 4 only

18) Two sides of a rectangular park are 50 meters and 120 meters long. A path runs diagonally from one corner of the park to the opposite corner. The length of the path must be

(1) 100 meters
(2) 110 meters
(3) 120 meters
(4) 130 meters
(5) 140 meters

① ② ③ ④ ⑤

19) A wheel with a diameter of 3 feet rolls along the ground. How far does it travel in 7 revolutions? (Use ²²⁄₇ for pi.)

(1) 33 feet
(2) 44 feet
(3) 55 feet
(4) 66 feet
(5) 77 feet

① ② ③ ④ ⑤

20) A square has an area of 36 cm². What is the area of the largest circle that could be drawn inside that square?

(1) $9\pi$ cm²
(2) $6\pi$ cm²
(3) $3\pi$ cm²
(4) $8\pi$ cm²
(5) $5\pi$ cm²

① ② ③ ④ ⑤

21) Two points on a graph are at coordinates (⁻2,5) and (4,6). What is the distance between the two points?

(1) 3
(2) $\sqrt{7}$
(3) $\sqrt{37}$
(4) $\sqrt{3}$
(5) 17

① ② ③ ④ ⑤

22) Two trains leave the same station at the same time and travel in opposite directions, one averaging 45 mph and the other averaging 60 mph. In how long will the trains be 630 miles apart?

(1) 5 hours
(2) 6 hours
(3) 7.25 hours
(4) 7.50 hours
(5) 7.75 hours

① ② ③ ④ ⑤

23) Karen bought a dinette set that listed for $575. She paid only $310 for it. What percent of the list price did Karen save?

   (1) 23%
   (2) 46%
   (3) 35%
   (4) 52%
   (5) 44%

① ② ③ ④ ⑤

24) Ms. McIntosh invested $18,000 in two different types of investments. Some of the money was invested in certificates of deposit that pay 10% interest, while the rest was invested in 20% corporate bonds. Her income for the year from both investments was $2400. How much of Ms. McIntosh's money was invested in the bonds?

   (1) $12,000
   (2) $10,000
   (3) $8000
   (4) $6000
   (5) $4000

① ② ③ ④ ⑤

25) The local movie theatre charges $3 per adult and $1.90 per child for admission. On a certain day, 405 tickets were sold and $934.50 was collected. How many children's tickets were sold on that day?

   (1) 150
   (2) 255
   (3) 225
   (4) 200
   (5) 193

① ② ③ ④ ⑤

# Answers

**1.** (1) Add the costs of the two tickets and get $223.63.

**2.** (3) Difference means subtraction. $145.37 − 128.58 = $16.79.

**3.** (3) First multiply 865 × $4.75 to get the total amount taken in from $4.75 tickets. That comes to $4108.75. Next multiply $6.25 by 479 to get the total receipts at that price, $2993.75. Then add the two totals: $7102.50.

**4.** (4) Divide 5745 into 15 equal parts. Each part is 383 meters.

**5.** (4) At $3.95 for a bottle of 250, each capsule costs $\frac{395}{250}$ pennies, or 1.58¢. A year's supply will cost 365 (days/year) times that, or $5.77 (rounded to the nearest penny). The sale bottle costs $\frac{595}{500}$ pennies, or 1.19¢ per capsule. That makes a year's supply cost 365 × 1.19, or $4.34. Subtracting 4.34 from 5.77, we find that Helen would have saved $1.43.

**6.** (5) A blink every 12 seconds is 5 blinks per minute (60 seconds/12 seconds). The amount of increase is $72 - 5 = 67$. To find the percent increase, set up a proportion:

$$\frac{67}{5} = \frac{x}{100}$$
$$6700 = 5x$$
$$x = 1340\%$$

**7.** (4) First add all the minutes together and get 160 minutes. That translates to 2 hours and 40 minutes (since 60 minutes make an hour). Next add all the hours together and get 4. To those 4 hours add 2 hours and 40 minutes for a grand total of 6 hours 40 minutes.

**8.** (2) 8 dozen is a total of $8 \times 12 = 96$ apples. Since 4 apples are eaten per day, the supply will last $\frac{96}{4}$, or 24 days.

**9.** (5) 8% of $794.25 is found by multiplying that figure by .08. The result is $63.54, to which $60 must be added to get a total of $123.54.

**10.** (1) 20% of 120 is 24 ($.20 \times 120 = 24$). $\frac{2}{3} \times 24 = 16$.

**11.** (3) If a truck is travelling at 12 mph, it is travelling 1 mile every 5 minutes (60 minutes divided by $12 = 5$). $\frac{1}{20}$ of an hour is $\frac{60}{20} = 3$ minutes. If the truck travels 1 mile in 5 minutes, it travels $\frac{3}{5}$ that distance in 3 minutes. Hence, the bridge is $\frac{3}{5}$ of a mile long.

Alternate solution: $D = rt$
$$D = 12 \cdot \frac{1}{20}$$
$$D = \frac{12}{20} = \frac{3}{5} \text{ mile.}$$

**12.** (2) Write a proportion:

$$\frac{50}{833} = \frac{x}{100}$$
$$833x = 5000$$
$$x = 6 \text{ micrograms}$$

**13.** (1)
$$\begin{array}{r} 3.30 \\ - .459 \end{array} = \begin{array}{r} 3.300 \\ - .459 \\ \hline 2.841 \end{array}$$

**14.** (4) $D = rt$
$$345 = 48.6t$$
$$t = \frac{345}{48.6} = 7.098 = 7.1 \text{ hours}$$

That's about 7 hours.

**15.** (5) 10% of 160,000 is 16,000. She needs $3 \times 16,000$ white hairs to make up the difference between the 20% white on her head, and the 50% that it will be. That's 48,000 white hairs to go. If Sal goes out twice a week, it will take half as many weeks as hairs needed, or 24,000 weeks. Since that's more than 450 years, Mrs. Manzini shouldn't worry.

**16.** (4) $17\frac{3}{4}$ divided by $3 = \frac{71}{4} \times \frac{1}{3} = \frac{71}{12} = 5\frac{11}{12}$ pounds

**17.** (4) $x^2 - 5x + 4 = 0$
$(x - 4)(x - 1) = 0$
$x - 4 = 0 \qquad x - 1 = 0$
$x = 4 \qquad\qquad x = 1$

**18.** (4) The diagonal path cuts the park into two right triangles, each of which has sides of 50 and 120. The path then, is the hypotenuse of either of those right triangles, and its length may be found from the Pythagorean theorem:

$c^2 = a^2 + b^2$
$c^2 = 50^2 + 120^2$
$c^2 = 2500 + 14,400 = 16,900$
$c = 130$ meters

**19.** (4) Each revolution of the wheel covers a distance of one circumference of the wheel, or $\pi d$. In 7 turns it will go $7\pi d$, or $7(\frac{22}{7})(3) = 66$ feet

**20.** (1) If a square has an area of 36 cm², its side must be 6 cm, since $s^2 = $ area for a square. 6, then, is also the diameter of the circle that fits inside it. Half of 6, or 3, is the radius of that circle. Since the area of a circle is $\pi r^2$, the area of this circle is $\pi 3^2 = 9\pi$ cm².

**21.** (3) The horizontal distance between the two points is $^-2 - 4$, or $^-6$, which is equivalent as a distance to 6. The vertical distance is $6 - 5$, or 1. (The distance vertically is determined by the difference of the $y$-coordinates while the difference of the $x$-coordinates gives the horizontal distance.) It is then left to find the hypotenuse of the right triangle with legs 1 and 6:

$c^2 = a^2 + b^2$
$c^2 = 6^2 + 1^2$
$c^2 = 36 + 1$
$c^2 = 37$
$c = \sqrt{37}$

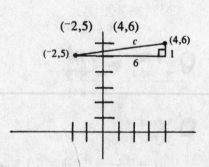

**22.** (2) Assume that one train is standing still while the other is moving away at their combined speed of 105 mph.

Then, since $D = rt$,
$630 = 105t$
$t = 6$ hours

**23.** (2) She saved $575 − $310 = $265.

As a percent, $\dfrac{265}{575} = \dfrac{x}{100}$

$575x = 26500$

$x = 46\%$ (about)

**24.** (4) Let $x =$ the amount invested in bonds. Then $18,000 − x$ is invested in certificates. The equation for determining her income is:

$.20x + .10(18,000 − x) = 2400$

$.20x + 1800 − .10x = 2400$

$.10x = 600$

$x = \$6000$

**25.** (2)

| | Quantity | Unit price | Total value |
|---|---|---|---|
| Adult | $x$ | 300 | $300x$ |
| Child | $405 − x$ | 190 | $190(405 − x)$ |

$300x + 190(405 − x) = 93,450$

$300x + 76,950 − 190x = 93,450$

$110x = 16,500$

$x = 150$

$405 − x = 255$ children's tickets

# 2. WHOLE NUMBERS

## WHOLE NUMBERS PRE-TEST

Complete.

1) In the numeral 8,461,027,953,/6 is in the _____ place.

Solve.

2) 1524 + 397 + 8140 + 6

| 3) | 542<br>−321 | 4) | 1634<br>−857 | 5) | 2001<br>−1836 | 6) | 497<br>×8 |

| 7) | 67<br>×34 | 8) | 564<br>×278 | 9) 7 ) 5705 | 10) 43 ) 7582 |

### Answers

| **1.** | 10 millions | **2.** | 10,067 | **3.** | 221 | **4.** | 777 | **5.** | 165 |
|---|---|---|---|---|---|---|---|---|---|
| **6.** | 3976 | **7.** | 2278 | **8.** | 156,792 | **9.** | 815 | **10.** | 176 R 14 |

## ANALYSIS OF PRE-TEST ITEMS

Guide your studies in this chapter by the items that you answered incorrectly, or that gave you difficulty even though you got them correct. The topics covered by each question and the page numbers on which additional information about each question can be found are listed below:

1. Reading place-value numerals      Pages 13–19
2. Adding in columns      Pages 19–29
3. Subtracting without renaming      Pages 29–32
4. Subtracting with renaming      Pages 33–39
5. Subtracting with zeros on top      Pages 39–40
6. Multiplying by one digit      Pages 40–47
7. Multiplying by two digits      Pages 47–51
8. Multiplying larger numbers      Pages 51–52
9. Dividing by one digit      Pages 53–61
10. Two-digit divisors      Pages 61–64

# PLACE-VALUE NUMERATION

The system that we use for representing numbers is known as the decimal system of numeration. Decimal means tens, so indeed our system of writing numerals — the symbols that represent numbers — is based on groupings of tens. A number is an idea of quantity. A numeral is the symbol that we use to represent that idea.

Look at the fingers on both your hands. Get an idea of how many fingers there are. You are now aware of a number. If you are like most people, the number that is in your head is the same as the number that is in mine. If you were a Roman, you would represent that number by the symbol, *X*. That would be your numeral for the number of fingers that you have. If you were a caveperson, you might lay out ten stones, and that would be your numeral for naming the number of fingers that you have. Most of us would write the symbol, 10. That is the decimal numeral for the number of fingers that each of us has. You might think that 10 is a very natural way to represent the number ten. In fact, however, it took thousands of years to develop such a symbol. That symbol was worked on by the Hindus and then by the Arabs, until it came to be what we now recognize as standing for ten objects.

Decimal numeration has several aspects to it. Let us consider them one at a time.

## DIGITS

There are ten digits available to us in the decimal system. Those digits are: 0, 1, 2, 3, 4, 5, 6, 7, 8, 9. A digit is the name given to a single-place numeral. It is not a coincidence that digit is also the name given to a finger or toe. Using the ten digits listed above, it is possible to write any numeral. That is, we may represent any number, no matter how small or how large, by using some combination of those ten digits.

## PLACES

When we write a numeral in the decimal system, we consider more than just the face value of any digit. We must also consider what place the digit holds within the numeral. Look at the chart below, and examine numerals *A*, *B*, *C*, and *D*.

| | | | | |
|---|---|---|---|---|
| *A* | | | | 3 |
| *B* | | 3 | | |
| *C* | | | 3 | |
| *D* | 3 | | | |

You will notice that *A*, *B*, *C*, and *D* are each represented by a single digit 3. They represent four quite different numbers. Were they to be removed from the columns that they are in, zeroes would have to be added to *B, C,* and *D* to indicate the place in each numeral where the digit 3 actually belongs. They would be written:

|   |      |
|---|------|
| *A* | 3    |
| *B* | 300  |
| *C* | 30   |
| *D* | 3000 |

There is quite a range between three and three thousand, yet if we do not consider the place in which each digit is written, they are each represented by the same digit, as are thirty and three hundred.

Once more, we turn to the fact that the decimal system is based upon the number ten. That fact tells the relationship of one place to another within any decimal numeral.

|     | ... | 10 × 100 | 10 × 10 | 10 × 1 | 1 | ... |
|-----|-----|----------|---------|--------|---|-----|
| *A* |     |          |         |        | 3 |     |
| *B* |     |          | 3       |        |   |     |
| *C* |     |          |         | 3      |   |     |
| *D* |     | 3        |         |        |   |     |

Notice that in the chart, the column on the right has a 1 as its name. That means that any digit written in that column must be multiplied by one to find its true value. All right, there's a three in that column. How much is $3 \times 1$? Then numeral *A* is worth 3!

Now, move left one column heading. You will see that the next place is worth ten times as much as the column to its right. Since $10 \times 1 = 10$, any digit written in that place is worth 10 times its face value. What is numeral *C*'s real value?

Move left again. The third column from the right is worth ten times as much as the place to its right. $10 \times 10 = 100$, so numeral *B*, which is written in that place, actually is worth 3 times 100. You can figure out the value of numeral *D* for yourself. The three dots to the left of the thousands place are there to indicate that as you continue to move to the left one place at a time, each place will be worth ten times as much as the place to its right. The three dots on the extreme right are there as a teaser. This system does not end at the ones place, but we are not going to worry about decimal fractions for a while.

## ZERO AS A PLACE-HOLDER

We do not normally go around writing numerals on charts that look like the one above. That is why we need to have some way of indicating what place a digit is in, even though it is not written in a column. That is where the idea of a place-holder comes in. A place-holder is a digit which does not have any value of its own, but will fill up the holes left in a numeral when that numeral is written without column headings. Zero does just that. If you look back at numeral *B*, you will notice that there are two empty places to the right of the digit, 3. When we write numeral *B* without the columns, we use zeroes to fill in, or hold the place of, those empty columns. That is why numeral *B* is written as 300. Two empty places; two place-holders!

Look at the chart below. To the right of each numeral, write the numeral in place-value form (with the appropriate place-holders).

| | 1,000,000 | 100,000 | 10,000 | 1000 | 100 | 10 | 1 | | |
|---|---|---|---|---|---|---|---|---|---|
| A | | | | | | 5 | | A | _____ |
| B | | | | 4 | | | | B | _____ |
| C | | | 7 | | | | | C | _____ |
| D | | 6 | | | | | | D | _____ |
| E | | | | | 2 | | | E | _____ |
| F | | | 3 | | 5 | | | F | _____ |
| G | 1 | | 5 | | | 2 | | G | _____ |
| H | | 4 | | 8 | | | 1 | H | _____ |
| I | 7 | | | | | 3 | | I | _____ |

## Answers

**A.** 50    **B.** 4000    **C.** 70,000    **D.** 600,000    **E.** 200

**F.** 30,500    **G.** 1,050,020    **H.** 408,001    **I.** 7,000,030

If you need additional practice using zero as a place-holder, see page 259.

# USE OF COMMAS

You may have noticed the commas that were used in the last section in the numerals which were greater than a thousand. The purpose of placing commas in large numerals is to make them easier to read. The traditional rule for placement of commas was really quite simple: if a numeral contains four digits or more, start at the right, and for each group of three digits that you count, place a comma, like so:

42369178

42369178
3 2 1 3 2 1

42,369,178

"Oh, that's all very nice," you say, "but I notice that you did not write 4000 (above) as 4,000. It has four digits."

I'm glad you noticed that. I did say that the traditional method was quite simple. Unfortunately, there have been some changes lately, both in textbook writing and in thinking on the subject. Some educators are now saying that commas should only be included if the numeral contains five digits or more, although the rule of counting by threes from the right still applies. They would write 4000, but would still write 70,000. Then there is the system of international units (SI, for short) which prefers that no commas be used at all. Instead, they would group numerals with four or more digits into threes, like so: 4 000 or 70 000 or, for the big one on page 15, 42 369 178.

What to do; what to do?! Do not get upset. As noted before, the whole idea of grouping with commas is to make it easier to read the numeral. Be aware of the fact that there are three different ways in which commas may be used. All of them group the digits into threes starting at the right side, and all of them look similar. In this book we'll follow the second method, but you should feel free to follow either the first or the second. The third method is not widely used in this country at present.

| First method | Second method | Third method |
|---|---|---|
| 5,000 | 5000 | 5 000 |
| 23,000 | 23,000 | 23 000 |
| 786 | 786 | 786 |
| 24,172,000 | 24,172,000 | 24 172 000 |

## READING LARGE NUMERALS

If you sometimes find it difficult to read numerals which contain many digits, you are not alone. Many people find large numerals confusing, and difficult to read. You may, however, find it interesting to learn that, as is true in so much of mathematics, there is a pattern to the way in which numerals are written in the decimal system. That pattern is formed by the constant repetition of the first three place names: hundreds, tens, and units.

Look at the numeral 432. Read 432 aloud. It is read four hundred thirty-two. Don't stick an "and" in there. We're saving the "and" for fractions. 432 is four hundred thirty-two. Try 687. Did you read it six hundred eighty-seven? Now, notice how the places are arranged:

Hundreds     Tens     Units

We will abbreviate the headings as H, T, and U. (Units is just another way of saying "ones"). The places occupied by the 4, 3, and 2 in 432, and by the 6, 8, and 7 in 687 would look like this:

H     T     U

4     3     2

6     8     7

Now, stay with us for one more round, and you'll see the pattern. Remember, we said that there was going to be a pattern formed by repeating hundreds, tens, and units, or, simply, H's, T's, and U's. Now, look at the numeral 531,789. Let's see how it fits under the repeating place-headings:

H     T     U     H     T     U

5     3     1     7     8     9

If it follows the pattern of reading each digit from left to right and saying the name of the column head after it, we should read this numeral five hundred thirty-one, seven hundred eighty-nine. What's that? You say "that can't be right?" Well, not exactly, but it's very close. There is just one thing missing. Those H's, T's, and U's repeat and repeat periodically. All that we need to do is to tell one period from another. Now the rightmost period is called the ones period. We never bother to say its name. Every other period beside the ones, however, must be named. Now the next period after the ones is the thousands. If we put those period names into place, the numeral will look like this:

| Periods: | Thousands | | | Ones | | |
|---|---|---|---|---|---|---|
| | H | T | U | H | T | U |
| | 5 | 3 | 1 , | 7 | 8 | 9 |

Now try reading it from left to right, but after each period — except the ones — say the period's name. You should have read five hundred thirty-one **thousand**, seven hundred eighty-nine. Did you get that? If you did not, try it again. (Psst! Just between us, did you notice how the comma separates the two periods?) Now try these three:

| Thousands | | | Ones | | | Write the numeral's name: |
|---|---|---|---|---|---|---|
| H | T | U | H | T | U | |
| | | 7 , | 8 | 4 | 3 | _____ |
| | 3 | 5 , | 6 | 5 | 7 | _____ |
| 4 | 5 | 9 , | 6 | 8 | 2 | _____ |

The first was seven thousand, eight hundred forty-three. The second was thirty-five thousand, six hundred fifty-seven. And the last was four hundred fifty-nine thousand, six hundred eighty-two. If you had trouble with any of those, look them over again. Read the numerals in the leftmost period as if you were reading a three digit numeral; say the name of the period. Then read the next three digits as if it were a three digit numeral, and since it is the ones period, do not say the period name. Get it?

## STILL BIGGER NUMERALS

Now that you're becoming such an expert at reading those big numerals, we're going to expand your horizon by two more period names. The next period to the left of the thousands is the millions. (You might notice that each period name is a thousand times the previous period's name. A thousand ones make a thousand, a thousand thousands make a million. Do you know what a thousand millions are?) To the left of the millions comes the billions:

| Billions | | | Millions | | | Thousands | | | Ones | | |
|---|---|---|---|---|---|---|---|---|---|---|---|
| H | T | U | H | T | U | H | T | U | H | T | U |
| | 4 | 0 , | 0 | 0 | 0 , | 0 | 0 | 0 , | 0 | 0 | 0 |

Can you read that number? You might read it as forty billion, no million, no thousand, no ones. The numeral is forty billion. See whether you can identify the numerals on the next page.

| Billions | | | Millions | | | Thousands | | | Ones | | |
|---|---|---|---|---|---|---|---|---|---|---|---|
| H | T | U | H | T | U | H | T | U | H | T | U |
| | | | | | 6 | , 4 | 3 | 0 | , 0 | 0 | 0 | *A* _____ |
| | | | 2 | 0 | 3 | , 0 | 0 | 0 | , 0 | 0 | 0 | *B* _____ |
| | 2 | 3 | , 1 | 7 | 5 | , 0 | 0 | 0 | , 0 | 0 | 6 | *C* _____ |
| 3 | 5 | 7 | , 0 | 0 | 0 | , 2 | 3 | 0 | , 0 | 1 | 7 | *D* _____ |
| 4 | 0 | 0 | , 0 | 5 | 0 | , 0 | 2 | 0 | , 9 | 0 | 0 | *E* _____ |

## Answers

**A.**  6 million, 430 thousand

**B.**  203 million

**C.**  23 billion, 175 million, 6

**D.**  357 billion, 230 thousand, 17

**E.**  400 billion, 50 million, 20 thousand, 9 hundred

Now, for the ultimate test of reading large numerals. Below are several large numerals written in decimal form. There is no chart of periods or places. See whether you can name these numerals without referring back to the chart. If you have difficulty, then you may refer back to the chart, but first try them on your own.

A.  247,000   _____

B.  5,617,000   _____

C.  25,419,002   _____

D.  138,000,045   _____

E.  7,632,491,228   _____

F.  84,000,720,000   _____

G.  367,591   _____

H.  2,516,794   _____

I.  83,704,003   _____

J.  563,807,004,010   _____

**Answers**

**A.** 247 thousand

**B.** 5 million, 617 thousand

**C.** 25 million, 419 thousand, 2

**D.** 138 million, 45

**E.** 7 billion, 632 million, 491 thousand, 228

**F.** 84 billion, 720 thousand

**G.** 367 thousand, 591

**H.** 2 million, 516 thousand, 794

**I.** 83 million, 704 thousand, 3

**J.** 563 billion, 807 million, 4 thousand, 10

For additional practice, see page 259.

# ADDITION OF WHOLE NUMBERS

Addition is a combining operation. When you add, you are putting together certain quantities to get a larger quantity. There are key phrases and words to look for that let you know when a problem or a situation requires addition. Examine the following problem:

Arthur brought eight guests to the party, Joan brought seven guests, and Michael brought four. Altogether, how many guests were brought to the party?

Reading the problem through once, it is apparent that you are being asked to find a total: the total number of guests brought to the party. That fact is underscored by the problem's use of the word "altogether." Ask yourself whether the total will be more or less than the number of guests any one person brings. It should be apparent from the fact that the number of guests that any one person brings is just a part of those that are brought **altogether**, that the total will be **more**. That calls for a combining operation.

The next step is to recognize which combining operation is needed. Are the numbers to be combined the same? If they **are** all the same, then addition **may** be used, but there might also be an alternative.* **If the numbers to be combined are not all the same, then you must add.** Adding 8 + 7 + 4, you will find that 19 guests were brought to the party.

Now examine the problem below and see whether you can find the key word(s) that tell you what to do:

What is the sum of 9, 15, and 23?

There is really only one key word, sum. In case you do not know it, sum is the name given to the solution of an addition. To find the solution to the problem, therefore, you must add. What if you did not know the meaning of sum? Would you be stuck, or is there another way that you could figure out what was required?

*The alternative is multiplication.

Even if you are not familiar with subtraction, division, or multiplication at this point, and do not feel confident with any of them, you have experienced all of them before. How many numbers can you multiply together? Subtract? Divide?

The answer to all three of those questions is two. You multiply or divide one number by another number. You subtract one number from another number. Since this problem required an operation to be done on three numbers, it is a pretty safe bet that the operation required is addition. See, mathematics really is logical. Do not ever be hesitant about thinking a problem through. You just might find exactly what you were looking for.

We will deal at much greater length with analyzing word problems later in this volume. Now, let us turn our attention to the actual operation of addition.

## FINDING SUMS LESS THAN TWENTY

If you can add up to 18, you can add any two numbers in the decimal system. That is because the largest unique addition that is possible to write in the decimal system is $9 + 9$. Are you skeptical? Then consider the following addition:

$$\begin{array}{r} 342 \\ +527 \\ \hline \end{array}$$

At first glance, it appears that you are being asked to add two numbers in the hundreds. However, if you add in columns, not one of the columns in that addition sums to more than 9:

$$\begin{array}{r} 342 \\ +527 \\ \hline 9 \end{array} \qquad \begin{array}{r} 342 \\ +527 \\ \hline 69 \end{array} \qquad \begin{array}{r} 342 \\ +527 \\ \hline 869 \end{array}$$

So, you think that was pretty sneaky, don't you? "What about 'carrying'?" you ask. Well, I never said that there would never be a time when you had to find a sum greater than 9. I said that the sum would never be greater than 18. That allows for "carrying." (Notice that I keep putting quotation marks around "carrying." That is because it is a very non-mathematical word, and will not be used again in this book. It is being used here only because it probably has some meaning to you from the past.)

There are lots of clever shortcuts available in mathematics as well as alternative ways to do certain operations if you are having difficulty doing it the "standard" way — whatever that means. This book is full of such shortcuts and alternatives. However, there is no shortcut or alternative for learning the addition-facts through 10. If you do not know every combination that adds up to 10 or less well enough to do the exercises that follow without having to count on your fingers or think about them, you are in trouble. Try these. Time yourself. They should not take you more than one minute.

1) $2 + 3 =$      2) $4 + 3 =$      3) $5 + 2 =$      4) $4 + 6 =$

5) $3 + 5 =$      6) $6 + 4 =$      7) $8 + 2 =$      8) $2 + 7 =$

9) $2 + 5 =$      10) $5 + 5 =$      11) $3 + 4 =$      12) $1 + 9 =$

13) 2 + 2 =          14) 4 + 4 =          15) 5 + 3 =          16) 4 + 2 =

17) 3 + 3 =          18) 2 + 8 =          19) 3 + 6 =          20) 3 + 2 =

21) 2 + 4 =          22) 3 + 7 =          23) 2 + 6 =          24) 6 + 3 =

25) 4 + 5 =          26) 6 + 2 =          27) 5 + 4 =          28) 9 + 1 =

## Answers

| | | | | | | | | | | | |
|---|---|---|---|---|---|---|---|---|---|---|---|
| **1.** | 5 | **2.** | 7 | **3.** | 7 | **4.** | 10 | **5.** | 8 | **6.** | 10 |
| **7.** | 10 | **8.** | 9 | **9.** | 7 | **10.** | 10 | **11.** | 7 | **12.** | 10 |
| **13.** | 4 | **14.** | 8 | **15.** | 8 | **16.** | 6 | **17.** | 6 | **18.** | 10 |
| **19.** | 9 | **20.** | 5 | **21.** | 6 | **22.** | 10 | **23.** | 8 | **24.** | 9 |
| **25.** | 9 | **26.** | 8 | **27.** | 9 | **28.** | 10 | | | | |

If you are thoroughly conversant with addition facts through 10, the exercise above should have taken less than 30 seconds. If you took more than a minute, or got any of the answers incorrect, do not go any farther in this book until you make yourself a set of flash-cards with the exercises above on them, and learn them so that you can recite the answers in your sleep without hesitation. There are very few things in mathematics that need to be absolutely perfectly committed to memory, but this is one of them.

Once you are thoroughly versed with all the addition facts that sum to 10 or less, it is a relatively simple matter to deal with facts in the teens. Mainly, it is a matter of applying the facts that you already know to derive those that you do not. This is a theme that is repeated over and over again in mathematics. Consider the following sum:

$$8 + 9 = \underline{\hspace{2cm}}$$

Now, even if you already know what the sum is, follow along with the logic that is involved:

a) I am familiar with all sums to 10, and this is not one of them. It therefore follows that this sum is more than 10.

b) If the sum is more than 10, then it must be 10 and something.

c) Looking at 8 + 9, I know that I must add 2 to the 8 to make 10. The 2 I add to the 8 must come from the 9.

d) I can rewrite 8 + 9 as 10 + 7. 10 + 7 is 17:

$$\begin{array}{r} 10 \\ +7 \\ \hline 17 \end{array}$$

Therefore, 8 + 9 = 17.

The only tricky part was in step "c." One of the numbers must be changed to a 10. It is changed to a 10 by adding whatever must be added to it to make it into a 10. In the case of 8, it required 2 more for it to become 10. Of course, the 2 to be added to the 8 must come from somewhere, and the only place for it to come from is the other number:

$$8 + 9 = (8 + 2) + 7 = 10 + 7 = 17$$

When the 2 is taken from the 9 to add to the 8, then only 7 of the 9 remains. 10 + 7 then makes a total of 17.

This form of addition is known as grouping to ten. Below, you will find several exercises in grouping to 10. Try them.

1) 7 + 6 = 10 + _____      2) 6 + 9 = 10 + _____

3) 5 + 8 = 10 + _____      4) 8 + 4 = 10 + _____

5) 9 + 6 = 10 + _____      6) 7 + 4 = 10 + _____

7) 3 + 8 = 10 + _____      8) 9 + 4 = 10 + _____

9) 5 + 7 = 10 + _____      10) 4 + 7 = 10 + _____

11) 7 + 9 = 10 + _____     12) 8 + 6 = 10 + _____

13) 6 + 6 = 10 + _____     14) 8 + 8 = 10 + _____

15) 9 + 9 = 10 + _____     16) 4 + 9 = 10 + _____

17) 7 + 8 = 10 + _____     18) 6 + 7 = 10 + _____

## Answers

| | | | | | | | | | | | |
|---|---|---|---|---|---|---|---|---|---|---|---|
| **1.** | 3 | **2.** | 5 | **3.** | 3 | **4.** | 2 | **5.** | 5 | **6.** | 1 |
| **7.** | 1 | **8.** | 3 | **9.** | 2 | **10.** | 1 | **11.** | 6 | **12.** | 4 |
| **13.** | 2 | **14.** | 6 | **15.** | 8 | **16.** | 3 | **17.** | 5 | **18.** | 3 |

For additional practice, see page 260.

## LARGER SUMS

Have you ever stopped to consider what makes 20 different from 2, or 70 different from 7? For that matter, what makes 5 different from 50, different from 500, or different from 5000? It is only the place that the digit other than zero is in. There are additional place-holders in all these other numerals, but the computational part of all are the same. Here's an example:

| | | | |
|---|---|---|---|
| 5 | 50 | 500 | 5000 |
| +4 | +40 | +400 | +4000 |
| 9 | 90 | 900 | 9000 |

Notice that other than those extra place-holders, the additions, and the sums, are in all cases identical. But what happens when the sum is greater than ten? Do you think that the same idea will still apply?

| 9 | 90 | 900 | 9000 |
|---|---|---|---|
| +8 | +80 | +800 | +8000 |
| 17 | 170 | 1700 | 17000 |

Does that answer the question?

All right, that's all very interesting, but what does it have to do with practical addition? That is a question that will have to be answered in two parts. First, let us consider what is known as expanded notation. Expanded notation is simply a way of writing numerals that spell out the value of the digit in each place.

98 written in expanded form would be 90 + 8.
76 in expanded form would be written 70 + 6.
235 would be written in expanded form as 200 + 30 + 5.

In other words, each digit is multiplied by the value of the place that it is in, and then the result is written down. (If you just got lost, look back at the section on place-value on page 13.)

Try writing the following place-value numerals in expanded form.

1) 38 _____   2) 59 _____

3) 135 _____   4) 246 _____

5) 1784 _____   6) 2497 _____

## Answers

**1.** 30 + 8     **2.** 50 + 9     **3.** 100 + 30 + 5

**4.** 200 + 40 + 6     **5.** 1000 + 700 + 80 + 4     **6.** 2000 + 400 + 90 + 7

Now let us take a look at an addition involving two larger numbers. Suppose we wish to add 346 + 232. First, let us expand the two numerals:

| 346 | ⟶ | 300 + 40 + 6 |
|---|---|---|
| +232 | | +200 + 30 + 2 |

Next we add the ones together, the tens together, and the hundreds together:

$$
\begin{array}{r}
300 + 40 + 6 \\
+200 + 30 + 2 \\
\hline
500 + 70 + 8
\end{array}
$$

Finally, to get the answer back into place-value form (instead of expanded form), we stack up the numerals from the sum in column form and add them together. Since no digit gets added to anything but zeroes, the solution is rather straightforward:

$$
\begin{array}{r}
500 \\
70 \\
8 \\
\hline
578
\end{array}
$$

Try these.

1)   526          $500 + 20 + 6$
    +473          $+ 400 + 70 + 3$
    ———————————→  ___ + ___ + ___ = _____

2)   435          $400 + 30 + 5$
    +264          $+$___ $+$ ___ $+$ ___
    ———————————→  ___ + ___ + ___ = _____

3)   173          ___ + ___ + ___
    +514          $+$___ $+$ ___ $+$ ___
    ———————————→  ___ + ___ + ___ = _____

## Answers

**1.**   $900 + 90 + 9 = 999$                 **2.**   $600 + 90 + 9 = 699$

**3.**   $600 + 80 + 7 = 687$

You will find additional practice on pages 260–261.

Now let us try to handle a somewhat more complex addition in expanded form. How about the sum of 584 and 249?

584          $500 + 80 + 4$
+249         $+200 + 40 + 9$
————————————→

First, we'll get those zeroes into place, since they are only place-holders and are not involved in the actual addition:

$$500 + 80 + 4$$
$$+200 + 40 + 9$$
$$\overline{\phantom{0}00 + \phantom{00}0 +}$$

Next, we'll perform the actual addition of ones, tens, and hundreds:

$$500 + 80 + 4$$
$$+200 + 40 + 9$$
$$\overline{700 + 120 + 13}$$

Well now, that 700 looks fine, but the 120 and the 13. . . . 120 is a mixture of hundreds and tens. We only want tens in that position. The problem in the right hand column is similar. We want only ones in that position, but we have 13 — a mixture of tens and ones. Do you see a solution?

Let's take the sum as it is currently written, and then expand the parts of it that are causing the difficulty:

$$700 + 120 + 13$$
$$700 + (100 + 20) + (10 + 3)$$

The parentheses above are used to indicate the numerals that were expanded. $120 = 100 + 20$, while $13 = 10 + 3$. Next we will regroup those numerals so that the hundreds can be combined and the tens can be combined. This time parentheses are used to show the numbers that will be added together:

$$700 + 100 + 20 + 10 + 3$$
$$(700 + 100) + (20 + 10) + 3$$

Adding them, we get:

$$800 + 30 + 3 \text{ which equals } 833.$$

Does this seem to you to be a long and involved process for adding two numbers? It is. Furthermore, it is not a method that is recommended for everyday use. The primary purpose of this technique is, in fact, to give you a better understanding of how numbers can be grouped and regrouped in order to make them more convenient to work with. In other words, if you are not familiar with a particular way of solving a certain problem or doing a particular computation, you may be able to rework the problem to make it "friendlier." With that in mind, try solving these in expanded form.

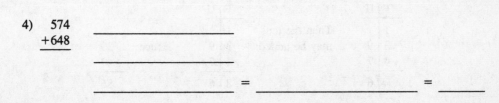

1) 365
   +473
   _____ + _____ + _____
   + 400 + 70 + 3
   _____
   _____ + ___ + ___ = (700 + 100) + ___ + ___ = _____

2) 486
   +395
   _____ + _____ + _____
   ___ + ___
   _____
   _____ + ___ + ___ = _____ = _____

3) 139
   +386

4) 574
   +648

## Answers

1. $700 + 130 + 8 = (700 + 100) + 30 + 8 = 838$
2. $700 + 170 + 11 = (700 + 100) + (70 + 10) + 1 = 881$
3. $400 + 110 + 15 = (400 + 100) + (10 + 10) + 5 = 525$
4. $1100 + 110 + 12 = 1000 + (100 + 100) + (10 + 10) + 2 = 1222$

## COLUMN ADDITION

No matter how many numbers you may wish to add, it is impossible to add more than two at a time. Try it. Add $4 + 7 + 5$. Did you do it? Did you add all three at the same time? Think about it. If you added the numbers in the order that their numerals are written, then you first added $4 + 7$ and got 11. Then you added 11 and 5 to get 16. You might have added them in a different order, but you definitely added only two at a time. If you do not feel confident about your ability to add long columns of numerals, then you can take advantage of the binary (two at a time) nature of addition. Here is an example:

| | | | | | | |
|---|---|---|---|---|---|---|
| 45 | | 45 | | | | 45 |
| | | +57 | | | | |
| 57 | First: | 102 | Then: | 102 | | 57 |
| | | | | +68 | | |
| 68 | | | | 170 | Finally: | 170 | 68 |
| | | | | | | +34 |
| 34 | | | | 204 | Hence: | 34 |
| | | | | | | 204 |

That's right, it really works! Unfortunately, we are getting a little ahead of ourselves. We still have to look at the idea of renaming, or regrouping. Consider the following addition:

| 39 | First we will | T | U | Then add up | T | U |
|---|---|---|---|---|---|---|
| +47 | mark the places: | 3 | 9 | the units: | 3 | 9 |
| | | +4 | 7 | | +4 | 7 |
| | | | | | | 16 |

Now, as you may notice, 16 is too large a number to be in the units place. In fact, 16 is a ten and 6 units. The solution is to **rename** the ten extra units as one ten:

| T | U | | T | U | | |
|---|---|---|---|---|---|---|
| 1 | | Then the tens | 1 | | | |
| 3 | 9 | may be added: | 3 | 9 | Hence: | 39 |
| +4 | 7 | | +4 | 7 | | +47 |
| | 6 | | 8 | 6 | | 86 |

Notice that we use the word **rename**; not **carry**. That is because renaming is exactly what we are doing. One ten is another name for ten ones. Either way, they are worth the same amount — ten.

Follow the next example through step by step:

| H | T | U |
|---|---|---|
|  | 5 | 6 | 4 |
| +2 | 8 | 9 |
|  |  |  |

First add the units:

| H | T | U |
|---|---|---|
| 5 | 6 | 4 |
| +2 | 8 | 9 |
|  |  | 13 |

10 of the 13 units must be renamed as 1 ten:

| H | T | U |
|---|---|---|
|  |  | 1 |
| 5 | 6 | 4 |
| +2 | 8 | 9 |
|  |  | 3 |

Next the tens are added together:

| H | T | U |
|---|---|---|
|  |  | 1 |
| 5 | 6 | 4 |
| +2 | 8 | 9 |
|  | 15 | 3 |

Now there are 10 extra tens. They must be renamed as 1 hundred:

| H | T | U |
|---|---|---|
| 1 | 1 |  |
| 5 | 6 | 4 |
| +2 | 8 | 9 |
|  | 5 | 3 |

Did you understand that last step? If not, look at it again. Any time there are 10 or more in a single column, 10 must be renamed into the next column to the left. There it becomes one of whatever that new column is. For example, 10 ones become 1 ten; 10 tens become 1 hundred; 10 hundreds become 1 thousand. . . .

The addition is completed by adding up the digits in the hundreds column:

| H | T | U |
|---|---|---|
| 1 | 1 |  |
| 5 | 6 | 4 |
| +2 | 8 | 9 |
| 8 | 5 | 3 |

Now try these.

1)

| H | T | U |
|---|---|---|
| 4 | 7 | 5 |
| +4 | 9 | 7 |

2)

| H | T | U |
|---|---|---|
| 3 | 8 | 9 |
| +5 | 7 | 6 |

3)

| H | T | U |
|---|---|---|
| 6 | 7 | 4 |
| +2 | 9 | 7 |

4)

| H | T | U |
|---|---|---|
| 5 | 2 | 8 |
| +1 | 8 | 5 |

5)

| H | T | U |
|---|---|---|
| 3 | 4 | 7 |
| +2 | 7 | 4 |

6)

| H | T | U |
|---|---|---|
| 2 | 8 | 5 |
| +5 | 5 | 8 |

7)

| H | T | U |
|---|---|---|
| 1 | 6 | 7 |
| +7 | 7 | 4 |

8)

| H | T | U |
|---|---|---|
| 4 | 7 | 3 |
| +2 | 2 | 7 |

## Answers

**1.** 972 **2.** 965 **3.** 971 **4.** 713

**5.** 621 **6.** 843 **7.** 941 **8.** 700

Now you know almost everything there is to know about addition. There is one remaining situation that we have not yet dealt with. It should not cause you any difficulty, but it is essential that we get it out into the open. Consider this:

|     |                | T | U |
|-----|----------------|---|---|
| 57  | Let us first   | 5 | 7 |
| 99  | add the units: | 9 | 9 |
| 86  |                | 8 | 6 |
| 49  |                | 4 | 9 |
|     |                |   | 31 |

Thirty-one?! Do you know how to deal with that many ones?

You may recall that we just finished dealing with the matter of renaming ten of anything as one in the next column to the left (ten ones = one ten, etc.). The same applies to multiples of ten. Thirty-one is one more than thirty, and thirty is a multiple of ten. Other multiples of ten are twenty, forty, fifty, and so forth. Actually, any numeral ending in a zero represents a multiple of ten. There may never be a multiple of ten written in any single place. If a sum contains a ten in a single place, you know to rename it as 1 in the next column to the left. Well, following the same principle, 20 ones would become 2 tens; 30 ones would be 3 tens; 40 ones, 4 tens, etc. With that in mind:

| H | T | U |
|---|---|---|
|   | 3 |   |
|   | 5 | 7 |
|   | 9 | 9 |
|   | 8 | 6 |
|   | 4 | 9 |
|   | 29 | 1 |

| H | T | U |
|---|---|---|
| 2 | 3 |   |
|   | 5 | 7 |
|   | 9 | 9 |
|   | 8 | 6 |
|   | 4 | 9 |
|   | 9 | 1 |

| H | T | U |
|---|---|---|
| 2 | 3 |   |
|   | 5 | 7 |
|   | 9 | 9 |
|   | 8 | 6 |
|   | 4 | 9 |
| 2 | 9 | 1 |

And that is the complete story of renaming. Now it's time for you to try some.

1)

| H | T | U |
|---|---|---|
|   | 3 | 4 | 6 |
| + | 4 | 9 | 6 |

2)

| H | T | U |
|---|---|---|
|   | 5 | 4 | 3 |
| + | 3 | 8 | 6 |

3)

| H | T | U |
|---|---|---|
|   | 2 | 5 | 9 |
| + | 9 | 7 | 7 |

4)

| H | T | U |
|---|---|---|
|   | 1 | 8 | 7 |
| + | 4 | 6 | 6 |

5)

| H | T | U |
|---|---|---|
|   | 7 | 8 |
|   | 8 | 7 |
|   | 6 | 5 |
|   | 8 | 8 |

6)

| H | T | U |
|---|---|---|
|   | 6 | 9 |
|   | 5 | 6 |
|   | 8 | 5 |
|   | 7 | 4 |

7)

| H | T | U |
|---|---|---|
| 3 | 4 | 7 |
|   | 5 | 8 |
|   | 9 | 7 |
|   | 5 | 3 |

8)

| H | T | U |
|---|---|---|
|   | 9 | 6 |
| 4 | 7 | 7 |
| 2 | 8 | 5 |
|   | 9 | 8 |

9)

| H | T | U |
|---|---|---|
| 3 | 5 | 6 |
| 9 | 6 | 7 |
| 8 | 9 | 4 |
| 1 |   | 5 |

10)

| H | T | U |
|---|---|---|
| 7 | 4 | 2 |
| 8 | 3 | 0 |
| 2 | 0 | 5 |
| 6 | 8 | 4 |

11)

| H | T | U |
|---|---|---|
| 4 | 8 | 0 |
| 6 | 4 | 8 |
| 2 | 9 | 2 |
| 1 | 7 | 0 |

12)

| H | T | U |
|---|---|---|
| 7 | 5 | 8 |
| 5 | 9 | 6 |
|   | 8 | 7 |
| 8 | 6 | 3 |

You may add place-value headings to the following if you wish.

13)  3 6 5
    +2 3 8

14)  4 1 7
    +3 8 5

15)  5 3 6
    +3 7 5

16)  2 9 8
    +1 6 3

17)  4 1 5
    +5 9 4

18)  7 3
     8 2
     7 7
     4 6

19)  6 8
     4 7
     9 4
     3 5

20)  9 2
     8 7
     7 5
     6 7
     5 7

21)  7 4
     6 5
     8 3
     8 6
     8 8

22)  5 8
     7 3
     6 4 7
     4 0 5

23)  3 6 4
     5 9
     5 7 3
     7 6 4

24)  5 9 3
     6 8
     6 4 0
     8 3 4
     5 5 9

## Answers

| 1. | 842 | 2. | 929 | 3. | 1236 | 4. | 653 | 5. | 318 |
|---|---|---|---|---|---|---|---|---|---|
| 6. | 284 | 7. | 555 | 8. | 956 | 9. | 2232 | 10. | 9961 |
| 11. | 1590 | 12. | 2304 | 13. | 603 | 14. | 802 | 15. | 911 |
| 16. | 461 | 17. | 1009 | 18. | 278 | 19. | 244 | 20. | 378 |
| 21. | 396 | 22. | 1183 | 23. | 1760 | 24. | 2694 | | |

You will find additional practice on page 261.

If you still feel shaky in your ability to do addition, refer back to whichever sections cover the area(s) of which you are unsure. You may also wish to use the Additional Practice section for further reinforcement of your addition skills. It is one thing to understand how something works, and quite another to be proficient at exercising skill in applying it. If addition was an area with which you needed to work, we suggest that you not put the subject aside just because you have finished this section. Make up additional exercises for yourself from time to time, and check your work using a calculator or a computer.

# DIFFERENCES BETWEEN WHOLE NUMBERS

The key word to recognizing subtraction lies in the title of this section. Subtracting is used to find the **difference** between two quantities. Observe:

Bill is 19 years old, and Susan is 14. What is the difference in their ages?

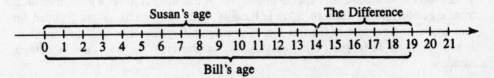

Susan's age

The Difference

0 1 2 3 4 5 6 7 8 9 10 11 12 13 14 15 16 17 18 19 20 21

Bill's age

The first brace on the top of the number line shows Susan's age. The brace on the bottom shows Bill's. The second brace on the top indicates the difference in their ages. By counting the **spaces** between their ages, you will find that the difference is 5. Another way to find the difference in their ages is to subtract 14 from 19: $19 - 14 = 5$.

Another key subtraction word is **remainder**:

> Alessandra received a check for $80. She paid a bill for $30. How much of her check remained?

This problem could be solved on the number line, just as the one about Bill's and Susan's ages was, but we would need a very long number line to do it. Since, however, we recognize remainder as a word indicating that subtraction is called for, we simply subtract: $80 - 30 = 50$. Alessandra had $50 left.

## SUBTRACTION FACTS

We must assume that you already know your addition facts backward and forward, or you would not yet be in this section of the book. Your knowing them backward and forward is a good thing, because addition facts backward are subtraction facts. In fact, subtraction is addition backwards. Consider the following "family of facts:"

$$4 + 5 = 9 \qquad 5 + 4 = 9$$
$$9 - 5 = 4 \qquad 9 - 4 = 5$$

If that set of relationships is not quite graphic enough, solve the following "missing addend" relationships:

$$3 + \underline{\hspace{1cm}} = 8 \qquad 5 + \underline{\hspace{1cm}} = 8 \qquad 9 + \underline{\hspace{1cm}} = 17 \qquad 8 + \underline{\hspace{1cm}} = 17$$

The answers are, respectively, 5, 3, 8, and 9. How did you find them? For the first one, did you ask yourself "three plus what equals eight?" Or did you ask yourself "Eight take away three equals what?" Whichever way you did it, you were adding backward. In other words, **you were subtracting**.

## SUBTRACTING BY GROUPING TO TEN

Since you are fully conversant with your addition facts through ten, there is no need to go into subtraction facts through ten in any greater detail than has already been done. What makes subtraction even easier than addition, is that there is **never** a need to subtract from a number greater than 18. That is because of the way numerals are grouped for subtraction, and because of the fact that subtraction always involves only two numbers at a time. There is no such thing as "column subtraction" the way there is column addition.

Subtraction will always consist of subtracting a single digit number from another, or subtracting a single digit number from a number in the teens so as to give a single digit remainder. Here are some examples:

| 9 | 7 | 8 | 12 | 15 | 17 | 14 |
|---|---|---|----|----|----|----|
| −6 | −4 | −5 | −7 | −8 | −9 | −6 |
| 3 | 3 | 3 | 5 | 7 | 8 | 8 |

If you are not terribly sure of subtractions from the teens, there is a little trick that you can use. Consider in each case what you would need to take away in order to get to ten. Here is an example:

| 17 | 17 | 2 of the 9 remains | 10 | | 17 |
|----|----|---------------------|-----|------------|-----|
| −9 | −7 | to be subtracted: | −2 | Therefore: | −9 |
| | 10 | | 8 | | 8 |

Here is another example:

| 15 | To get the 15 down | 15 | 3 of the 8 remains | 10 | | 15 |
|----|---------------------|-----|---------------------|-----|-----------|-----|
| −8 | to 10, take away 5: | −5 | to be subtracted: | −3 | Therefore: | −8 |
| | | 10 | | 7 | | 7 |

If you have difficulty with teen subtractions, try the exercises below. Bear in mind that you must practice this technique until it becomes second nature to you. Remember, when you take your GED examination, speed will count. That is why all the basic techniques must be practiced repeatedly for speed, accuracy, and appropriateness.

Complete the following.

1)
$$\begin{array}{c} 1\ 4 \\ -\ 6 \\ \hline \end{array} \rightarrow \begin{array}{c} 1\ 4 \\ -\underline{\phantom{0}} \\ \hline 1\ 0 \end{array} \rightarrow \begin{array}{c} 1\ 0 \\ -\underline{\phantom{0}} \\ \hline 8 \end{array} \rightarrow \begin{array}{c} 1\ 4 \\ -\ 6 \\ \hline \end{array}$$

2)
$$\begin{array}{c} 1\ 3 \\ -\ 7 \\ \hline \end{array} \rightarrow \begin{array}{c} 1\ 3 \\ -\underline{\phantom{0}} \\ \hline \end{array} \rightarrow \begin{array}{c} 1\ 0 \\ -\underline{\phantom{0}} \\ \hline \end{array} \rightarrow \begin{array}{c} 1\ 3 \\ -\ 7 \\ \hline \end{array}$$

3)
$$\begin{array}{c} 1\ 5 \\ -\ 9 \\ \hline \end{array} \rightarrow \begin{array}{c} 1\ 5 \\ -\underline{\phantom{0}} \\ \hline \end{array} \rightarrow \begin{array}{c} 1\ 0 \\ -\underline{\phantom{0}} \\ \hline \end{array} \rightarrow \begin{array}{c} 1\ 5 \\ -\ 9 \\ \hline \end{array}$$

4)
$$\begin{array}{c} 1\ 2 \\ -\ 6 \\ \hline \end{array} \rightarrow \begin{array}{c} 1\ 2 \\ -\underline{\phantom{0}} \\ \hline \end{array} \rightarrow \begin{array}{c} 1\ 0 \\ -\underline{\phantom{0}} \\ \hline \end{array} \rightarrow \begin{array}{c} 1\ 2 \\ -\ 6 \\ \hline \end{array}$$

5)
$$\begin{array}{c} 1\ 6 \\ -\ 9 \\ \hline \end{array} \rightarrow \qquad \rightarrow \qquad \rightarrow \begin{array}{c} 1\ 6 \\ -\ 9 \\ \hline \end{array}$$

6)
$$\begin{array}{c} 1\ 8 \\ -\ 9 \\ \hline \end{array} \rightarrow \qquad \rightarrow \qquad \rightarrow \begin{array}{c} 1\ 8 \\ -\ 9 \\ \hline \end{array}$$

## Answers

1.
$$\begin{array}{ccc} 14 & 10 & 14 \\ -4 & -2 & -6 \\ \hline 10 & 8 & 8 \end{array}$$

2.
$$\begin{array}{ccc} 13 & 10 & 13 \\ -3 & -4 & -7 \\ \hline 10 & 6 & 6 \end{array}$$

3.
$$\begin{array}{ccc} 15 & 10 & 15 \\ -5 & -4 & -9 \\ \hline 10 & 6 & 6 \end{array}$$

4.
$$\begin{array}{ccc} 12 & 10 & 12 \\ -2 & -4 & -6 \\ \hline 10 & 6 & 6 \end{array}$$

5.
$$\begin{array}{ccc} 16 & 10 & 16 \\ -6 & -3 & -9 \\ \hline 10 & 7 & 7 \end{array}$$

6.
$$\begin{array}{ccc} 18 & 10 & 18 \\ -8 & -1 & -9 \\ \hline 10 & 9 & 9 \end{array}$$

If you still need more practice, make up your own exercises.

# SUBTRACTION WITHOUT RENAMING

The simplest form of subtraction involves no renaming. It is done by moving from the ones place to the left, one place at a time. Here are three examples:

| *Example 1* | 345 | 345 | 345 | 345 |
|---|---|---|---|---|
| | −134 | −134 | −134 | −134 |
| | | 1 | 11 | 211 |

| *Example 2* | 435 | 435 | 435 | 435 |
|---|---|---|---|---|
| | −103 | −103 | −103 | −103 |
| | | 2 | 32 | 332 |

| *Example 3* | 678 | 678 | 678 | 678 |
|---|---|---|---|---|
| | − 34 | − 34 | − 34 | − 34 |
| | | 4 | 44 | 644 |

You may have noticed that the main feature of this type of subtraction is that the digit being "taken away" is always smaller than the digit it is being taken away from. That is to say, the top digit in any place is never smaller than the digit below it. Try the subtractions below, just for practice.

1)
$$\begin{array}{r} 489 \\ -254 \\ \hline \end{array}$$

2)
$$\begin{array}{r} 567 \\ -165 \\ \hline \end{array}$$

3)
$$\begin{array}{r} 794 \\ -434 \\ \hline \end{array}$$

4)
$$\begin{array}{r} 835 \\ -232 \\ \hline \end{array}$$

5)
$$\begin{array}{r} 372 \\ -140 \\ \hline \end{array}$$

6)
$$\begin{array}{r} 758 \\ -741 \\ \hline \end{array}$$

7)
$$\begin{array}{r} 843 \\ -841 \\ \hline \end{array}$$

8)
$$\begin{array}{r} 947 \\ - 36 \\ \hline \end{array}$$

9)
$$\begin{array}{r} 651 \\ -551 \\ \hline \end{array}$$

10)
$$\begin{array}{r} 138 \\ - 37 \\ \hline \end{array}$$

## Answers

| | | | | | | | | | |
|---|---|---|---|---|---|---|---|---|---|
| **1.** 235 | **2.** 402 | **3.** 360 | **4.** 603 | **5.** 232 |
| **6.** 17 | **7.** 2 | **8.** 911 | **9.** 100 | **10.** 101 |

# SUBTRACTION WITH RENAMING

Look at the following subtraction:

$$43$$
$$-28$$

Try taking the bottom digit in the units column away from the top digit in the same column, and you will discover that you have a problem. In the realm of natural numbers, there is no way that 8 can be taken away from 3.*

As the first step in making some sense out of what the solution to this subtraction will be, let us consider the numerals in expanded form:

$$43 = \quad 40 + 3$$
$$-28 = -(20 + 8)$$

(The minus sign outside the parentheses is there to indicate that both the 20 and the 8 are being subtracted from the 43, even though the 20 and the 8 are related to each other by the plus sign.)

Notice that in the expanded form, the top numerals represent a total value of 43 — exactly with what we started. The 43, however, is obtained in a configuration that is somewhat different from the original one. In fact, we could configure those numerals in any way that we wished, so long as the total value of the top row remained 43. Let us choose a new configuration that will help us to accomplish what we initially set out to do — subtracting 28 from 43. We will rewrite the expanded numerals as follows:

$$40 + 3 = \quad 30 + 13$$
$$-(20 + 8) = -(20 + \ 8)$$

Notice that the 40 + 3 has been **renamed** as 30 + 13. To do so, we simply took one full group of 10 from the 40 and moved it over, combining it with the 3. Notice also that the value of the top row is still 43. Now the subtraction can be accomplished easily:

$$30 + 13$$
$$-(20 + \ 8)$$
$$\overline{10 + \ 5 \ = 15}$$

That means that 43 − 28 = 15.

Did you follow that? If not, look it over again. Now look at the problem that follows:

$$67 = \quad 60 + 7 = \quad 50 + 17 = \quad 50 + 17 = \quad 67$$
$$-38 = -(30 + 8) = -(30 + \ 8) = -(30 + \ 8) = -38$$
$$\overline{\qquad\qquad\qquad\qquad\qquad\qquad\qquad 20 + 9 \qquad 29}$$

In keeping with our running commentary, you will notice that the 8 of 38 cannot be subtracted from the 7 of 67. We therefore expanded both the 67 and the 38. Next, the 60 + 7 is renamed by moving a 10 from the 60 over to the 7 and adding. We have actually subtracted 10 from the 60 and added 10 to the 7. By adding and subtracting 10 to the same number, 67, there has been no net change in the value of that number. It still totals 67. Yet, it now has been renamed as 50 + 17. Following that renaming, it is

---

*In point of fact, 3 − 8 = ⁻5, but we are not yet ready to deal with the realm of negative numbers.

possible to subtract, and we get a difference of 20 + 9, which, when added together makes 29. Hence, 67 − 38 = 29.

Here are some subtractions for you to complete.

1)  81 =  (80 + 1) =  (70 + __)
    −57 = −(50 + 7) = −(50 +  7)
                         __ + __ = __

2)  53 =  (50 + 3) =  (40 + __)
    −26 = −(20 + 6) = −(20 +  6)
                         __ + __ = __

3)  74 =  (70 + 4) =  (__ + __)
    −49 = −(40 + 9) = −(__ + __)
                         __ + __ = __

4)  65 =  (60 + 5) =  (__ + __)
    −27 = −(20 + 7) = −(__ + __)
                         __ + __ = __

5)  62 =  (__ + __) =  (__ + __)
    −33 = −(__ + __) = −(__ + __)
                         __ + __ = __

6)  98 =  (__ + __) =  (__ + __)
    −59 = −(__ + __) = −(__ + __)
                         __ + __ = __

7)  31 =  (__ + __) =  (__ + __)
    −24 = −(__ + __) = −(__ + __)
                         __ + __ = __

8)  50 =  (__ + __) =  (__ + __)
    −26 = −(__ + __) = −(__ + __)
                         __ + __ = __

## Answers

**1.**    70 + 11
       −(50 +  7)
          20 +  4  = 24

**2.**    40 + 13
       −(20 +  6)
          20 +  7  = 27

**3.**    60 + 14
       −(40 +  9)
          20 +  5  = 25

**4.**    50 + 15
       −(20 +  7)
          30 +  8  = 38

**5.**    50 + 12
       −(30 +  3)
          20 +  9  = 29

**6.**    80 + 18
       −(50 +  9)
          30 +  9  = 39

**7.**    20 + 11
       −(20 +  4)
           0 +  7  = 7

**8.**    40 + 10
       −(20 +  6)
          20 +  4  = 24

You will find additional practice on page 262.

# SUBTRACTION WITH TWO RENAMINGS

Now that you have mastered the technique of renaming to subtract, you should be able to handle any two digit subtraction that may arise. As you may have surmised, however, not all subtractions are two digit ones. Consider the following example:

          523
        −289

If you examine this subtraction, you will notice that as it is now written, both the units and the tens places have situations in which the bottom digit is larger than the top one. Let us expand this subtraction, and see what it looks like:

$$523 = 500 + 20 + 3$$
$$-289 = -(200 + 80 + 9)$$

(Note once more that the minus sign and parentheses around the bottom expanded numeral indicate that each part of that numeral is to be subtracted from the quantity above it. The plus signs relate each part of the numeral to the other parts of the same numeral, that is $200 + 80 + 9$ equals 289.)

Now, if we apply the same technique that we used when dealing with two digit numerals, the tens and ones places would be changed as follows:

$$500 + 20 + 3 = 500 + 10 + 13$$
$$-(200 + 80 + 9) = -(200 + 80 + 9)$$

It is now possible to subtract in the ones place, however the tens place still presents a problem. What should we do about that problem? How about this:

$$500 + 10 + 13 = 400 + 110 + 13$$
$$-(200 + 80 + 9) = -(200 + 80 + 9)$$

Is that the solution that you thought of? Mind you, it is not the only solution possible, but it is in keeping with the one that we used for two digit numerals. We have done a second renaming, subtracting one of the hundreds from the 500 and adding it back on to the 10, so that the top row now has the same value as it did before. $400 + 110 + 13$ still equals 523. Now it is possible to subtract in all three sections of the expanded notation:

$$400 + 110 + 13$$
$$-(200 + 80 + 9)$$
$$\overline{\phantom{00}200 + 30 + 4} = 234$$

Hence:

$$523$$
$$-289$$
$$\overline{234}$$

Try this one on your own. Fill in the blanks and then subtract. A detailed solution follows the exercise:

$$647 = \underline{\phantom{0}} + \underline{\phantom{0}} + 7 = \underline{\phantom{0}} + \underline{\phantom{0}} + 17) = 500 + \underline{\phantom{0}} + 17 = 647$$
$$-459 = -(400 + 50 + 9) = -(400 + 50 + 9) = -(400 + 50 + 9) = -459$$
$$\underline{\phantom{0}} + \underline{\phantom{0}} + \underline{\phantom{0}} = \underline{\phantom{0}}$$

Solution: 647 was first expanded to be $600 + 40 + 7$. 459 was expanded to $400 + 50 + 9$. In the next step, 10 was subtracted from the 40 and added to the 7 to make $600 + 30 + 17$. That took care of the problem in the rightmost grouping. Next 100 was subtracted from the 600 and added to the 30 to make $500 + 130 + 17$. Check to see that that still adds up to 647. Next, you should have subtracted to get $100 + 80 + 8$. Adding that together so as to put it back into standard (place-value) form, you should have found that $647 - 459 = 188$.

Here are some exercises to try on your own.

1)  $345 = \quad 300 + 40 + 5) = \quad 300 + \underline{\ } + \underline{\ }) = \quad \underline{\ } + \underline{\ } + 15$
$-187 = -(\underline{\ } + \underline{\ } + \underline{\ }) = -(100 + 80 + 7) = -(100 \quad 80 + 7)$
$\underline{\ } + \underline{\ } + \underline{\ } = \underline{\ }$

2)  $764 = \quad \underline{\ } + \underline{\ } + \underline{\ }) = \quad \underline{\ } + \underline{\ } + \underline{\ }) = \quad \underline{\ } + \underline{\ } + \underline{\ }$
$-379 = -(\underline{\ } + \underline{\ } + \underline{\ }) = -(\underline{\ } + \underline{\ } + \underline{\ }) = -(\underline{\ } + \underline{\ } + \underline{\ })$
$\underline{\ } + \underline{\ } + \underline{\ } = \underline{\ }$

3)  $851 = \quad \underline{\ } + \underline{\ } + \underline{\ }) = \quad \underline{\ } + \underline{\ } + \underline{\ }) = \quad \underline{\ } + \underline{\ } + \underline{\ }$
$-263 = -(\underline{\ } + \underline{\ } + \underline{\ }) = -(\underline{\ } + \underline{\ } + \underline{\ }) = -(\underline{\ } + \underline{\ } + \underline{\ })$
$\underline{\ } + \underline{\ } + \underline{\ } = \underline{\ }$

4)  $435 = \quad \underline{\ } + \underline{\ } + \underline{\ }) = \quad \underline{\ } + \underline{\ } + \underline{\ }) = \quad \underline{\ } + \underline{\ } + \underline{\ }$
$-296 = -(\underline{\ } + \underline{\ } + \underline{\ }) = -(\underline{\ } + \underline{\ } + \underline{\ }) = -(\underline{\ } + \underline{\ } + \underline{\ })$
$\underline{\ } + \underline{\ } + \underline{\ } = \underline{\ }$

5)  $154 = \quad \underline{\ } + \underline{\ } + \underline{\ }) = \quad \underline{\ } + \underline{\ } + \underline{\ }) = \quad \underline{\ } + \underline{\ } + \underline{\ }$
$- 75 = -(\underline{\ } + \underline{\ } + \underline{\ }) = -(\underline{\ } + \underline{\ } + \underline{\ }) = -(\underline{\ } + \underline{\ } + \underline{\ })$
$\underline{\ } + \underline{\ } + \underline{\ } = \underline{\ }$

6)  $523 = \quad \underline{\ } + \underline{\ } + \underline{\ }) = \quad \underline{\ } + \underline{\ } + \underline{\ }) = \quad \underline{\ } + \underline{\ } + \underline{\ }$
$-267 = -(\underline{\ } + \underline{\ } + \underline{\ }) = -(\underline{\ } + \underline{\ } + \underline{\ }) = -(\underline{\ } + \underline{\ } + \underline{\ })$
$\underline{\ } + \underline{\ } + \underline{\ } = \underline{\ }$

## Answers

1.
$$\begin{array}{r} 200 + 130 + 15 \\ -(100 + \ 80 + \ 7) \\ \hline 100 + \ 50 + \ 8 = 158 \end{array}$$

2.
$$\begin{array}{r} 600 + 150 + 14 \\ -(300 + \ 70 + \ 9) \\ \hline 300 + \ 80 + \ 5 = 385 \end{array}$$

3.
$$\begin{array}{r} 700 + 140 + 11 \\ -(200 + \ 60 + \ 3) \\ \hline 500 + \ 80 + \ 8 = 588 \end{array}$$

4.
$$\begin{array}{r} 300 + 120 + 15 \\ -(200 + \ 90 + \ 6) \\ \hline 100 + \ 30 + \ 9 = 139 \end{array}$$

5.
$$\begin{array}{r} 0 + 140 + 14 \\ -(0 + \ 70 + \ 5) \\ \hline 0 + \ 70 + \ 9 = 79 \end{array}$$

6.
$$\begin{array}{r} 400 + 110 + 13 \\ -(200 + \ 60 + \ 7) \\ \hline 200 + \ 50 + \ 6 = 256 \end{array}$$

You will find additional practice on page 263.

## SUBTRACTION IN PLACE-VALUE FORM

Everything that you have read and practiced in subtraction up to this point has been preparing you for this section. Expanded form is an excellent way to learn how something works and to gain experience with applying the concept of renaming. Practically speaking, it is too time consuming a process to use for subtraction on a GED examination. You will now see how the technique of renaming can be applied in place-value form, while saving you considerable time and ink (or graphite). Look at the following subtraction:

$$\begin{array}{r} 53 \\ -26 \\ \hline \end{array}$$

Remember, when we rename in addition we often have to exchange ten ones for one ten. When subtracting, the exchange goes the other way. We exchange one ten for ten ones:

| | T | U | | T | U | | T | U |
|---|---|---|---|---|---|---|---|---|
| (a) | 5 | 3 | (b) | ⁴$\not5$ | 13 | (c) | ⁴$\not5$ | 13 |
| | −2 | 6 | | −2 | 6 | | −2 | 6 |
| | | | | | | | 2 | 7 |

In step (a), Tens and Units headings are placed over each place (as a reminder of the value of the digit beneath). In step (b), one of the 5 tens has been renamed as ten units, and added to the 3 units. That leaves 4 tens in the tens place. Finally, in step (c), we subtract and get a difference of 27.

Try this one.

| | T | U |
|---|---|---|
| 75 | ⁶$\not7$ | _5 |
| −36 | −3 | 6 |

One ten from the 70 should have been renamed as 10 units and added to the five units that are already there. That makes a 15 in the units column. $15 - 6 = 9$. Then, subtracting 3 tens from 6 tens, you should have gotten a remainder of 3 in the tens column. That makes a total remainder of 39.

Try these. (You may add frames and column headings if you wish.)

| 1) | 46 | 2) | 67 | 3) | 84 | 4) | 61 | 5) | 93 |
|---|---|---|---|---|---|---|---|---|---|
| | −27 | | −38 | | −49 | | −26 | | −58 |

| 6) | 23 | 7) | 54 | 8) | 45 | 9) | 72 | 10) | 88 |
|---|---|---|---|---|---|---|---|---|---|
| | −18 | | −16 | | −37 | | −27 | | −49 |

## Answers

| **1.** | 19 | **2.** | 29 | **3.** | 35 | **4.** | 35 | **5.** | 35 |
|---|---|---|---|---|---|---|---|---|---|
| **6.** | 5 | **7.** | 38 | **8.** | 8 | **9.** | 45 | **10.** | 39 |

If you had much difficulty with the exercises above, review the model examples and explanation. Then try the additional practice exercises on page 264.

## THREE PLACES IN PLACE-VALUE FORM

Three-digit numerals in subtraction are handled in place-value form about the same way as two-digit ones. The one difference, of course, is that an extra renaming may be needed. In that case, remember that 10 tens and 1 hundred are interchangeable expressions. Here's an example:

|     |     | H | T | U |
|-----|-----|---|---|---|
| (a) |     | 9 | 5 | 4 |
|     |  −  | 6 | 8 | 5 |

|     |     | H | T | U |
|-----|-----|---|---|---|
| (b) |     | 9 | $\cancel{5}^4$ | 14 |
|     |  −  | 6 | 8 | 5 |

|     |     | H | T | U |
|-----|-----|---|---|---|
| (c) |     | $\cancel{9}^8$ | $\cancel{5}^{14}$ | 14 |
|     |  −  | 6 | 8 | 5 |
|     |     | 2 | 6 | 9 |

Step (a), above, names the subtraction that is to be performed. You will notice the place names (H, T, and U) over each column for reference purposes. Notice that in both the tens and the units places, the top digit is less than the bottom digit.

In step (b), one 10 from the five 10's has been renamed as 10 ones. That leaves a 4 in the top line of the "T" column, and a 14 in the top line of the "U" column. So far, you will notice that we have done exactly the same thing as when we had only two-digit numerals.

For step (c), we ignore the units column completely (at least until our renaming is done). To all intents and purposes, we have a two-digit subtraction, but the two digits that we deal with are in the "H" and "T" places. One of the 9 hundreds is renamed as 10 tens. It is then added to the 4 tens that are already there, to make a total of 14 tens. Of course, only 8 hundreds will remain in the "H" place. Finally, we subtract, to get a difference of 269.

Here is a second example:

| H | T | U |     |     | H | T | U |     |     | H | T | U |
|---|---|---|-----|-----|---|---|---|-----|-----|---|---|---|
| 7 | 3 | 6 | First we must |   | 7 | $\cancel{3}^2$ | 16 | Next we must re- |   | $\cancel{7}^6$ | $\cancel{3}^{12}$ | 16 |
| −2 | 8 | 9 | rename one ten |   | −2 | 8 | 9 | name one hundred |   | −2 | 8 | 9 |
|   |   |   | as ten ones: |   |   |   |   | as ten tens: |   |   |   |   |
|   |   |   |   |   |   |   |   | Then subtract: |   | 4 | 4 | 7 |

You try these:

|     |     | H | T | U |
|-----|-----|---|---|---|
| 1)  |     | 8 | 4 | 6 |
|     |  −  | 4 | 7 | 8 |

|     |     | H | T | U |
|-----|-----|---|---|---|
| 2)  |     | 5 | 8 | 2 |
|     |  −  | 2 | 9 | 9 |

|     |     | H | T | U |
|-----|-----|---|---|---|
| 3)  |     | 6 | 1 | 3 |
|     |  −  | 5 | 6 | 4 |

Solutions:

|     |     |   |   |   |
|-----|-----|---|---|---|
| 1)  |     | $\cancel{8}^7$ | $\cancel{4}^{13}$ | 16 |
|     |  −  | 4 | 7 | 8 |
|     |     | 3 | 6 | 8 |

|     |     |   |   |   |
|-----|-----|---|---|---|
| 2)  |     | $\cancel{5}^4$ | $\cancel{8}^{17}$ | 12 |
|     |  −  | 2 | 9 | 9 |
|     |     | 2 | 8 | 3 |

|     |     |   |   |   |
|-----|-----|---|---|---|
| 3)  |     | $\cancel{6}^5$ | $\cancel{1}^{10}$ | 13 |
|     |  −  | 5 | 6 | 4 |
|     |     |   | 4 | 9 |

The following exercises are provided for your practice. If you wish to add frames and place names, you may. Remember, as you solve each one, not all places need renaming.

Rename only when the lower digit in any place is larger than the top digit in the same place.

Solve.

| 1) | 5 6 4 <br> − 2 8 5 | 2) | 3 2 8 <br> − 1 5 7 | 3) | 7 2 9 <br> − 3 8 9 | 4) | 6 5 3 <br> − 2 8 8 | 5) | 8 6 7 <br> − 1 5 9 |
|---|---|---|---|---|---|---|---|---|---|
| 6) | 4 5 9 <br> − 1 8 9 | 7) | 8 2 7 <br> − 3 8 9 | 8) | 6 2 5 <br> − 4 6 7 | 9) | 5 3 2 <br> − 1 2 2 | 10) | 2 1 4 <br> − 1 1 7 |

## Answers

| **1.** 279 | **2.** 171 | **3.** 340 | **4.** 365 | **5.** 708 |
|---|---|---|---|---|
| **6.** 270 | **7.** 438 | **8.** 158 | **9.** 410 | **10.** 97 |

## ZERO IN THE TOP NUMERAL

One situation which may arise in subtraction remains to be dealt with. That is the situation in which a zero appears in the top numeral. Consider the following three examples:

*Example 1*      650
                −286

There is no difference in the way you would approach this solution from the way you would solve any place-value subtraction. First, a ten must be renamed as ten ones:

$$\begin{array}{cc} {\scriptstyle 4} & \\ 6 \ \cancel{5}\,10 \\ -\ 2 \ 8 \ 6 \end{array}$$   Then a hundred must be renamed as ten tens:   $$\begin{array}{cc} {\scriptstyle 5 \ \ 14} \\ \cancel{6} \ \cancel{5}\,10 \\ -\ 2 \ 8 \ 6 \end{array}$$   And, finally, we subtract:   $$\begin{array}{cc} {\scriptstyle 5 \ \ 14} \\ \cancel{6} \ \cancel{5}\,10 \\ -\ 2 \ 8 \ 6 \\ \hline 3 \ 6 \ 4 \end{array}$$

*Example 2*      504
                −368

Here, there is a difference from what we have been doing. That is because, while we need ten ones to add to the 4, there are no tens in the tens place. In order to get some tens in the tens place, we must first rename one hundred as ten tens:

$$\begin{array}{cc} {\scriptstyle 4} \\ \cancel{5}\,10 \ 4 \\ -\ 3 \ 6 \ 8 \end{array}$$   Now we have ten tens from which to rename one and add it to 4:   $$\begin{array}{cc} {\scriptstyle 4 \ \ 9} \\ \cancel{5} \ \cancel{10}\,14 \\ -\ 3 \ 6 \ 8 \end{array}$$   Finally, we can subtract:   $$\begin{array}{cc} {\scriptstyle 4 \ \ 9} \\ \cancel{5} \ \cancel{10}\,14 \\ -\ 3 \ 6 \ 8 \\ \hline 1 \ 3 \ 6 \end{array}$$

*Example 3*      700
                −312

The solution to this subtraction is close to the one used for example 2. Again, since there are no tens to rename as ones, we must first go to the hundreds and rename a hundred as ten tens:

| | | | |
|---|---|---|---|
| ⁶$\phantom{}$ $\not{7}$ 10 0 $-$ 3 1 2 | Now there are ten tens from which to rename ones as ten ones: | ⁶ ⁹ $\not{7}$ $\not{10}$ 10 $-$ 3 1 2 | Finally, subtract: |

$$
\begin{array}{r}
^6\,^9 \\
\not{7}\ \not{10}\ 10 \\
-\ 3\ \ 1\ \ 2 \\
\hline
3\ \ 8\ \ 8
\end{array}
$$

Try these for practice.

1)  607
    −319

2)  580
    −437

3)  900
    −546

4)  570
    −167

5)  704
    −588

6)  800
    −763

7)  800
    −508

8)  603
    −361

9)  5002
    −496

10)  4050
    −1284

11)  7000
    −4173

## Answers

**1.** 288    **2.** 143    **3.** 354    **4.** 403    **5.** 116    **6.** 37

**7.** 292    **8.** 242    **9.** 4506    **10.** 2766    **11.** 2827

You will find additional practice on all forms of three digit subtraction in place–value notation on page 264.

# MULTIPLICATION OF WHOLE NUMBERS

Multiplication is a combining operation, and as such is very close to the other combining operation, addition. In fact, multiplication is a shorthand for **repeated addition of the same number**.

$$7 + 7 + 7 + 7 + 7 + 7 = 6 \times 7 = 42$$

Six times seven is another way of writing $7 + 7 + 7 + 7 + 7 + 7$. The first numeral names the number of times the number represented by the second numeral is being added to itself. In this case, 7 is being added to itself six different **times**.

Any problem that can be solved by multiplication can also be solved by addition. Do you think the reverse is true?

*Example 1*   Martha, Alice, David, Geoffrey, and Erica each have 6 headaches per week. How many headaches do they have altogether in a week?

Multiplication solution:

$$
\begin{array}{r}
6 \\
\times 5 \\
\hline
30
\end{array}
$$

Addition solution:

$$
\begin{array}{r}
6 \\
6 \\
6 \\
6 \\
6 \\
\hline
30
\end{array}
$$

*Example 2*   Stephanie has $150, Marjorie has $230, Jonah has $112. How much money do they have altogether?

|  Multiplication solution: | Addition solution: |
|---|---|
|  ? | $150 |
|   | 230 |
|   | 112 |
|   | $492 |

In example 1, the same number was being added repeatedly. That is why the solution can be obtained by multiplication or addition. In example 2, different numbers are being combined. Multiplication cannot do that.

## MULTIPLICATION FACTS

Those multiplications between $0 \times 0$ and $10 \times 10$ are known as the multiplication facts. You may have learned them as "times tables." In either case, they are the bases upon which all multiplications are built. You are the judge of how well you know your multiplication facts. To help you to decide how well you know them, the inventory below is provided. Consider it a pre-test on multiplication facts. Time yourself while you take it. You should not need more than three minutes to complete the inventory.

1) $1 \times 1 =$ _____    $2 \times 5 =$ _____    $3 \times 3 =$ _____    $4 \times 2 =$ _____    $5 \times 7 =$ _____

2) $5 \times 10 =$ _____    $1 \times 2 =$ _____    $2 \times 6 =$ _____    $3 \times 4 =$ _____    $4 \times 3 =$ _____

3) $4 \times 4 =$ _____    $3 \times 2 =$ _____    $1 \times 3 =$ _____    $2 \times 7 =$ _____    $5 \times 9 =$ _____

4) $3 \times 1 =$ _____    $2 \times 10 =$ _____    $4 \times 10 =$ _____    $1 \times 4 =$ _____    $2 \times 8 =$ _____

5) $2 \times 9 =$ _____    $5 \times 8 =$ _____    $3 \times 5 =$ _____    $4 \times 9 =$ _____    $1 \times 5 =$ _____

6) $1 \times 6 =$ _____    $3 \times 6 =$ _____    $4 \times 5 =$ _____    $5 \times 1 =$ _____    $5 \times 6 =$ _____

7) $3 \times 7 =$ _____    $1 \times 7 =$ _____    $4 \times 1 =$ _____    $5 \times 5 =$ _____    $2 \times 4 =$ _____

8) $5 \times 4 =$ _____    $3 \times 8 =$ _____    $1 \times 8 =$ _____    $2 \times 3 =$ _____    $4 \times 6 =$ _____

9) $4 \times 7 =$ _____    $2 \times 2 =$ _____    $3 \times 9 =$ _____    $1 \times 9 =$ _____    $5 \times 2 =$ _____

10) $2 \times 1 =$ _____    $3 \times 10 =$ _____    $4 \times 8 =$ _____    $5 \times 3 =$ _____    $1 \times 10 =$ _____

11) $9 \times 1 =$ _____    $8 \times 10 =$ _____    $10 \times 5 =$ _____    $7 \times 2 =$ _____    $6 \times 10 =$ _____

12) $8 \times 9 =$ _____    $9 \times 2 =$ _____    $10 \times 6 =$ _____    $6 \times 9 =$ _____    $7 \times 1 =$ _____

13) $7 \times 3 =$ _____    $10 \times 7 =$ _____    $6 \times 8 =$ _____    $9 \times 3 =$ _____    $8 \times 8 =$ _____

14) $9 \times 4 =$ _____    $6 \times 7 =$ _____    $7 \times 4 =$ _____    $8 \times 7 =$ _____    $10 \times 8 =$ _____

15) 6 × 6 = \_\_\_\_\_     10 × 9 = \_\_\_\_\_     9 × 5 = \_\_\_\_\_     7 × 5 = \_\_\_\_\_     8 × 6 = \_\_\_\_\_

16) 10 × 10 = \_\_\_\_\_     9 × 6 = \_\_\_\_\_     7 × 6 = \_\_\_\_\_     8 × 5 = \_\_\_\_\_     6 × 5 = \_\_\_\_\_

17) 7 × 7 = \_\_\_\_\_     8 × 4 = \_\_\_\_\_     9 × 7 = \_\_\_\_\_     6 × 4 = \_\_\_\_\_     10 × 4 = \_\_\_\_\_

18) 8 × 3 = \_\_\_\_\_     7 × 8 = \_\_\_\_\_     6 × 3 = \_\_\_\_\_     10 × 3 = \_\_\_\_\_     9 × 8 = \_\_\_\_\_

19) 9 × 9 = \_\_\_\_\_     6 × 2 = \_\_\_\_\_     7 × 9 = \_\_\_\_\_     8 × 2 = \_\_\_\_\_     10 × 2 = \_\_\_\_\_

20) 6 × 1 = \_\_\_\_\_     10 × 1 = \_\_\_\_\_     9 × 10 = \_\_\_\_\_     7 × 10 = \_\_\_\_\_     8 × 1 = \_\_\_\_\_

## Answers

| | | | | | | | | | | | | | | | |
|---|---|---|---|---|---|---|---|---|---|---|---|---|---|---|---|
| **1.** | 1 | 10 | 9 | 8 | 35 | **2.** | 50 | 2 | 12 | 12 | 12 | **3.** | 16 | 6 | 3 | 14 | 45 |
| **4.** | 3 | 20 | 40 | 4 | 16 | **5.** | 18 | 40 | 15 | 36 | 5 | **6.** | 6 | 18 | 20 | 5 | 30 |
| **7.** | 21 | 7 | 4 | 25 | 8 | **8.** | 20 | 24 | 8 | 6 | 24 | **9.** | 28 | 4 | 27 | 9 | 10 |
| **10.** | 2 | 30 | 32 | 15 | 10 | **11.** | 9 | 80 | 50 | 14 | 60 | **12.** | 72 | 18 | 60 | 54 | 7 |
| **13.** | 21 | 70 | 48 | 27 | 64 | **14.** | 36 | 42 | 28 | 56 | 80 | **15.** | 36 | 90 | 45 | 35 | 48 |
| **16.** | 100 | 54 | 42 | 40 | 30 | **17.** | 49 | 32 | 63 | 24 | 40 | **18.** | 24 | 56 | 18 | 30 | 72 |
| **19.** | 81 | 12 | 63 | 16 | 20 | **20.** | 6 | 10 | 90 | 70 | 8 | | | | | | |

Whether you did well on the multiplication fact inventory or not, you may find this section interesting as well as helpful, therefore it is a good idea to continue reading. Traditionalists suggest that it is essential to memorize multiplication facts by rote, so that they are always on the tip of your tongue. While it is not a bad idea to know the tables well, there are alternative methods of learning them — one of which is also quite helpful anytime you happen to forget a multiplication fact, and may also prove of assistance in learning to compute more efficiently mentally. We call it two-step multiplication.

## TWO-STEP MULTIPLICATION

Remember, multiplication and addition are related. Often, we forget that relationship and fail to take advantage of it. If we know certain multiplication facts, we can put them together to find the ones we do not know. For openers, let us consider the basic — easiest — multiplication tables. From those, we will build the others, using two steps at a time.

The easiest of all multiplication tables is the ones table. It is a re-statement of what mathematicians call the "identity property." Simply stated, the principle says that one times any number is that number. In other words, $1 \times 1 = 1$, $1 \times 2 = 2$, $1 \times 3 = 3$, etc.

Next easiest is multiplying by ten. To multiply any number by ten, annex a zero to the end of the numeral: $10 \times 3 = 30$, $10 \times 12 = 120$, $10 \times 36 = 360$, for example.

The two times table is commonly known as doubling. If you are not sure of your two table, you still probably know how to double already. Simply think of 2× anything as adding the number to itself. $1 + 1, 2 + 2, 3 + 3, 4 + 4, \ldots$ are all examples of doubling, i.e. of the 2 times table. To find any member of the two table, the alternative method is counting by twos, and keeping track of how many twos you have counted. For example, count 2, 4, 6, 8. You've counted by 2 four times, so 8 is $4 \times 2$, or $2 \times 4$.

The last table you absolutely must know is the fives table. Once more, counting by fives is as good a way as any to learn and use the fives table.

## DO NOT READ BEYOND THIS POINT IF YOU DO NOT KNOW THE $1\times$, $2\times$, $5\times$, AND $10\times$ TABLES!!!

Once you know the $1\times$, $2\times$, $5\times$, and $10\times$ tables, you can develop any other multiplication fact in two steps:

| | | | | |
|---|---|---|---|---|
| Desired fact: | $3 \times 8$ | | Desired fact: | $4 \times 8$ |
| Rationale: | $3 = 2 + 1$ | | Rationale: | $4 = 2 + 2$ |
| Technique: | $2 \times 8 = 16$ | | Technique: | $2 \times 8 = 16$ |
| | $+(1 \times 8) = 8$ | | | $+(2 \times 8) = 16$ |
| Therefore: | $3 \times 8 = 24$ | | Therefore: | $4 \times 8 = 32$ |
| Desired fact: | $6 \times 8$ | | Desired fact: | $7 \times 8$ |
| Rationale: | $6 = 5 + 1$ | | Rationale: | $7 = 5 + 2$ |
| Technique: | $5 \times 8 = 40$ | | Technique: | $5 \times 8 = 40$ |
| | $+(1 \times 8) = 8$ | | | $+(2 \times 8) = 16$ |
| Therefore: | $5 \times 8 = 48$ | | Therefore: | $7 \times 8 = 56$ |

Hopefully, you can see from the above that all multiplication facts between $1 \times 1$ and $7 \times 10$ can be developed in either a single step or a simple addition of two numbers. The eight and nine times tables could be developed in the same way — that is, by adding 3 multiplications together; for example, $5\times + 2\times + 1\times$ makes $8\times$, or $5\times + 2\times + 2\times$ makes $9\times$, however, at the beginning of this section we said you could do any multiplication in two steps; not in two or three steps. Well, why not throw in a little subtraction — which, as we have already seen, is backward addition? Then, we might find that:

| | | | | |
|---|---|---|---|---|
| Desired fact: | $8 \times 8$ | | Desired fact: | $9 \times 8$ |
| Rationale: | $8 = 10 - 2$ | | Rationale: | $9 = 10 - 1$ |
| Technique: | $10 \times 8 = 80$ | | Technique: | $10 \times 8 = 80$ |
| | $-(2 \times 8) = 16$ | | | $-(1 \times 8) = 8$ |
| Therefore: | $8 \times 8 = 64$ | | Therefore: | $9 \times 8 = 72$ |

Two-step multiplication is a means to two ends. It is not an end in itself. The first end that it is a path to is the eventual committing to memory of the multiplication facts. In order for you to succeed with more complex multiplications, and with division, it is really essential that you commit the multiplication facts to memory. Otherwise, you will find that the amount of time that you consume in working out each problem requiring multiplication will prevent you from completing the number of problems needed to succeed on the GED examination. This method will permit you to work with multiplication even before you have learned all of your tables. Hopefully, by working with multiplication instead of trying to learn the tables by rote, you will eventually memorize them. The second purpose of two-step multiplication is to better enable you to compute mentally. We will have more to say about that later in this book. The following two-step multiplications are provided for you to practice the skill.

Complete the following, using only $1\times$, $2\times$, $5\times$, and $10\times$ tables, or combinations thereof.

1) $4 \times 6$:   $\underline{\quad} \times 6 = \underline{\quad}$
    $+(\underline{\quad} \times 6) = \underline{\quad}$
    $\quad 4 \times 6 = \underline{\quad}$

2) $7 \times 7$:   $\underline{\quad} \times 7 = \underline{\quad}$
    $+(\underline{\quad} \times 7) = \underline{\quad}$
    $\quad 7 \times 7 = \underline{\quad}$

3) $3 \times 9$:   $\underline{\quad} \times 9 = \underline{\quad}$
    $+(\underline{\quad} \times 9) = \underline{\quad}$
    $\quad 3 \times 9 = \underline{\quad}$

4) $8 \times 6$:   $\underline{\quad} \times 6 = \underline{\quad}$
    $-(\underline{\quad} \times 6) = \underline{\quad}$
    $\quad 8 \times 6 = \underline{\quad}$

5) $6 \times 9$:   $\underline{\quad} \times 9 = \underline{\quad}$
    $+(\underline{\quad} \times 9) = \underline{\quad}$
    $\quad 6 \times 9 = \underline{\quad}$

6) $9 \times 7$:   $\underline{\quad} \times 7 = \underline{\quad}$
    $-(\underline{\quad} \times 7) = \underline{\quad}$
    $\quad 9 \times 7 = \underline{\quad}$

7) $6 \times 8$:

8) $4 \times 7$:

9) $9 \times 9$:

10) $4 \times 9$:

11) $8 \times 7$:

12) $7 \times 9$:

## Answers

**1.**
$\quad 2 \times 6 = 12$
$+(2 \times 6) = 12$
$\quad 4 \times 6 = 24$

**2.**
$\quad 5 \times 7 = 35$
$+(2 \times 7) = 14$
$\quad 7 \times 7 = 49$

**3.**
$\quad 2 \times 9 = 18$
$+(1 \times 9) = \phantom{0}9$
$\quad 3 \times 9 = 27$

**4.**
$\quad 10 \times 6 = 60$
$-(2 \times 6) = 12$
$\quad 8 \times 6 = 48$

**5.**
$\quad 5 \times 9 = 45$
$+(1 \times 9) = \phantom{0}9$
$\quad 6 \times 9 = 54$

**6.**
$\quad 10 \times 7 = 70$
$-(1 \times 7) = \phantom{0}7$
$\quad 9 \times 7 = 63$

**7.**
$\quad 5 \times 8 = 40$
$+(1 \times 8) = \phantom{0}8$
$\quad 6 \times 8 = 48$

**8.**
$\quad 2 \times 7 = 14$
$+(2 \times 7) = 14$
$\quad 4 \times 7 = 28$

**9.**
$\quad 10 \times 9 = 90$
$-(1 \times 9) = \phantom{0}9$
$\quad 9 \times 9 = 81$

**10.**
$\quad 2 \times 9 = 18$
$+(2 \times 9) = 18$
$\quad 4 \times 9 = 36$

**11.**
$\quad 10 \times 7 = 70$
$-(2 \times 7) = 14$
$\quad 8 \times 7 = 56$

**12.**
$\quad 5 \times 9 = 45$
$+(2 \times 9) = 18$
$\quad 7 \times 9 = 63$

## MULTIPLYING DECADES, ETC.

Multiples of ten are called decades. 10, 20, 30, are examples of decades. You may recall that any number may be multiplied by ten simply by annexing a zero to the end of it, for example, $10 \times 4 = 40$, and $10 \times 23 = 230$. Now consider the case of multiplying any decade by a single digit number:

*Example 1*  7 × 30 = ?

We know that 30 = 3 × 10. Therefore, we may rewrite this multiplication to look like this:

7 × (3 × 10)

Now, when two or more numbers are being multiplied together, the way they are grouped for multiplication does not affect the result.* We may, therefore, regroup the numerals as follows:

(7 × 3) × 10

Since 7 × 3 = 21, we now have:

21 × 10

By annexing a zero to the 21, we complete the multiplication:

21 × 10 = 210

Therefore, 7 × 30 = 210.

Do you see a shortcut that could have been used to solve example 1? Look at the two numerals, 7 and 30. To multiply them, all that had to be done was to multiply the tens digit, 3, by 7, and then annex a zero. 7 × 3 = 21. Annex a zero to 21 and you have 210.

*Example 2*  6 × 40 = ?

Multiply 6 × 4:

6 × 4 = 24

Then annex a zero:

6 × 40 = 240

Try these.

1) 5 × 80 = _____   2) 4 × 70 = _____   3) 9 × 50 = _____

4)  60      5)  40      6)  20      7)  30      8)  70      9)  90     10)  60
    ×3          ×4          ×5          ×6          ×7          ×8          ×9

Multiplying by hundreds works the same, but you annex **two** zeroes. 7 × 300 = 2100. How do you think you multiply thousands?

Complete.

11)  300    12)  400    13)  500    14)  600    15)  700    16)  800    17)  900
     ×6          ×8          ×4          ×7          ×3          ×5          ×6

18)  3000   19)  4000   20)  7000   21)  8000   22)  6000   23)  5000
     ×  4        ×  9        ×  6        ×  3        ×  7        ×  8

*This is known technically as the Associative Property for Multiplication. As in addition, or any other arithmetic operation, only two numbers at a time can actually be multiplied. Try multiplying 2 × 3 × 2 in your head, and you will discover that you actually perform two separate multiplications. You will also see that it makes no difference which two of the three numbers you multiply together first.

## Answers

| | | | | | | | | | | | |
|---|---|---|---|---|---|---|---|---|---|---|---|
| **1.** 400 | **2.** 280 | **3.** 450 | **4.** 180 | **5.** 160 | **6.** 100 |
| **7.** 180 | **8.** 490 | **9.** 720 | **10.** 540 | **11.** 1800 | **12.** 3200 |
| **13.** 2000 | **14.** 4200 | **15.** 2100 | **16.** 4000 | **17.** 5400 | **19.** 36,000 |
| **20.** 42,000 | **21.** 24,000 | **22.** 42,000 | **23.** 40,000 | | |

# *MULTIPLYING TWO DIGITS BY ONE*

There are several alternative methods of multiplication which will lead to the desired product (answer). If you now are able to multiply two or more digits by two or more digits, stick with the method that works for you. If your current method of multiplication is not working well for you, then perhaps one of the alternatives examined below will work better.

Follow the model multiplication below:

36    This multiplication means that you
×7    must find the total of 7 36's.

Begin by finding seven sixes (i.e., multiply 7 × 6).

36
×7
—
42    42 is the result of multiplying 7 × 6. There is still a thirty (from the 36) to be multiplied.

Remember, multiplying a decade requires multiplying the tens digit and then annexing a zero. (See Multiplying Decades on page 44.)

| | | |
|---|---|---|
| 36 | This time we will place the zero first, as you see has been done | 36 |
| ×7 | on the left. Then we multiply 7 × 3 and get 21 (on the right). | ×7 |
| 42 | | 42 |
| 0 | | 210 |

Finally, we add the two partial products together:

$$\begin{array}{r} 36 \\ \times 7 \\ \hline \end{array}$$

Partial products:  42
210

Final product:  252

Now try these.

1)
```
    5 8
  ×   6
  _____
    4 8
  3⟨2⟩0
  _____
  3 4 8
```

2)
```
    3 9
  ×   4
  _____
  _   6
  2 _
  _____
  5 _
```

3)
```
    6 4
  ×   9
  _____
  3 _
  _____
  5 _ _
```

4)
```
    8 7
  ×   3
  _____
  _ _
  ======
  _ 6 _
```

5)
```
    7 6
  ×   5
  _____
  _ _
  ======
  _ _ _
```

6)
```
    8 3
  ×   7
  _____
  _ _
  ======
  _ _ _
```

7)
```
    5 9
  ×   8
  _____
  _ _
  ======
  _ _ _
```

8)
```
    2 5
  ×   4
  _____
  _ _
  ======
  _ _ _
```

9)
```
    4 4
  ×   6
  _____
  _ _
  ======
  _ _ _
```

10)
```
    6 8
  ×   3
  _____
  _ _
  ======
  _ _ _
```

11)
```
    9 5
  ×   8
  _____
  _ _
  ======
  _ _ _
```

12)
```
    4 8
  ×   7
  _____
  _ _
  ======
  _ _ _
```

## Answers

| | | | | | | | | | | | |
|---|---|---|---|---|---|---|---|---|---|---|---|
| **1.** | 48 | **2.** | 36 | **3.** | 36 | **4.** | 21 | **5.** | 30 | **6.** | 21 |
| | 300 | | 120 | | 540 | | 240 | | 350 | | 560 |
| | 348 | | 156 | | 576 | | 261 | | 380 | | 581 |
| **7.** | 72 | **8.** | 20 | **9.** | 24 | **10.** | 24 | **11.** | 40 | **12.** | 56 |
| | 400 | | 80 | | 240 | | 180 | | 720 | | 280 |
| | 472 | | 100 | | 264 | | 204 | | 760 | | 336 |

You will find additional practice in multiplying two digits by one digit on page 265.

## TWO DIGITS TIMES TWO DIGITS

Multiplying by a two-digit numeral requires one step more than multiplying by a one-digit numeral. The same scheme followed when multiplying two digits by one may be followed. Additionally, however, multiplication by the tens digit must be done. Observe the model below:

```
   35
  ×28
```
1. First do 8 × 5:
```
   35
  ×28
  ___
   40
```
2. Then 8 × 30:
```
   35
  ×28
  ___
   40
  240
```

3.  Next comes 20 × 5:

$$
\begin{array}{r}
35 \\
\times 28 \\
\hline
40 \\
240 \\
100 \\
\end{array}
$$

4.  Last, 20 × 30:

$$
\begin{array}{r}
35 \\
\times 28 \\
\hline
40 \\
240 \\
100 \\
600 \\
\end{array}
$$

5.  Finally, add:

$$
\begin{array}{r}
35 \\
\times 28 \\
\hline
40 \\
240 \\
100 \\
600 \\
\hline
980 \\
\end{array}
$$

When you feel comfortable with the model, try the following exercises. The notes on the side are there for your convenience.

Complete.

1)
```
        4 6
    ×   3 4
    _____
        2 4    = 4 × 6
    _ _ 0      = 4 × 40
    _ _ _      = 30 × 6
  _ _ 0 0      = 30 × 40
  _____
  _ _ _ _
```

2)
```
        5 9
    ×   2 5
    _____
      _ _      = 5 × 9
    _ _ 0      = 5 × 50
    _ _ _      = 20 × 9
  _ _ 0 0      = 20 × 50
  _____
  _ _ _ _
```

3)
```
        6 3
    ×   2 9
    _____
      _ _      = 9 × 3
    _ _ 0      = 9 × 60
    _ _ 0      = 20 × 3
  _ _ 0 0      = 20 × 60
  _____
  _ _ _ _
```

4)
```
        7 4
    ×   3 7
    _____
      _ _      = 7 × 4
    _ _ _      = 7 × 70
    _ _ _      = 30 × 4
  _ _ _ _      = 30 × 70
  _____
  _ _ _ _
```

5)
```
        8 5
    ×   1 9
    _____
      _ _      = 9 × 5
    _ _ _      = 9 × 80
    _ _ _      = 10 × 5
  _ _ _ _      = 10 × 80
  _____
  _ _ _ _
```

6)
```
        9 7
    ×   6 3
    _____
      _ _      = 3 × 7
    _ _ _      = 3 × 90
    _ _ _      = 60 × 7
  _ _ _ _      = 60 × 90
  _____
  _ _ _ _
```

7)
```
        3 9
    ×   2 6
    _____
      _ _      = 6 × __
    _ _ _      = 6 × __
    _ _ _      = __ × __
  _ _ _ _      = __ × __
  _____
  _ _ _ _
```

8)
```
        5 4
    ×   3 7
    _____
      _ _      = 7 × __
    _ _ _      = 7 × __
    _ _ _      = __ × __
  _ _ _ _      = __ × __
  _____
  _ _ _ _
```

9)
```
        8 2
    ×   5 8
    _____
      _ _      = 8 × __
    _ _ _      = 8 × __
    _ _ _      = __ × __
  _ _ _ _      = __ × __
  _____
  _ _ _ _
```

## Answers

| 1. | | 2. | | 3. | | 4. | | 5. | |
|---|---|---|---|---|---|---|---|---|---|
| | 24 | | 45 | | 27 | | 28 | | 45 |
| | 160 | | 250 | | 540 | | 490 | | 720 |
| | 180 | | 180 | | 60 | | 120 | | 50 |
| | 1200 | | 1000 | | 1200 | | 2100 | | 800 |
| | 1564 | | 1475 | | 1827 | | 2738 | | 1615 |

| 6. | | 7. | | 8. | | 9. | |
|---|---|---|---|---|---|---|---|
| | 21 | | 54 | | 28 | | 16 |
| | 270 | | 180 | | 350 | | 640 |
| | 420 | | 180 | | 120 | | 100 |
| | 5400 | | 600 | | 1500 | | 4000 |
| | 6111 | | 1014 | | 1998 | | 4756 |

# STREAMLINING TWO-DIGIT MULTIPLICATION

The exercises just done were provided to help you to get a better understanding of how two-digit multiplication works. In practice, shortcuts are available and can be easily adjusted to. The main shortcut favored in two-digit multiplication consists of performing multiplication by each digit in a single line. Observe:

35
×28

1. Multiply 8 × 5, but do not write the 10's digit in the answer:

```
  4
 35
×28
  0
```

Note where the 10's digit from 8 × 5 = 40 is placed.

2. Multiply 8 × 3, and add the regrouped 4 to the product:

```
  4
 35
×28
280
```

Note, 8 × 3 = 24. Add 4, and get 28.

3. Place a zero in the ones place before multiplying by 2 (tens):

```
 35
×28
280
  0
```

Since we next multiply by 2 tens, there will be no ones in the answer.

4. Multiply 2 × 5: Notice where the ones and tens digits are placed.

```
  1
 35
×28
280
 00
```

5. Multiply 2 × 3, and add the regrouped 1:

```
  1
 35
×28
280
700
```

2 × 3 = 6; 6 + 1 = 7

6. Add the partial
   products:

$$
\begin{array}{r}
35 \\
\times 28 \\
\hline
280 \\
700 \\
\hline
980
\end{array}
\left.\vphantom{\begin{array}{c}280\\700\end{array}}\right\} \text{Add}
$$

See whether you can follow this one.

$$
\begin{array}{r}
5\ 8 \\
\times 4\ 6 \\
\hline
\end{array}
\qquad
\overset{4}{\phantom{0}}
\begin{array}{r}
5\ 8 \\
\times 4\ 6 \\
\hline
8
\end{array}
\qquad
\overset{4}{\phantom{0}}
\begin{array}{r}
5\ 8 \\
\times 4\ 6 \\
\hline
3\ 4\ 8
\end{array}
$$

Note that the 4 "carried" from 6 × 8
is added to the product of 6 × 5 (30).

Before multiplying by 4 tens, place the "0."

$$
\begin{array}{r}
5\ 8 \\
\times 4\ 6 \\
\hline
3\ 4\ 8 \\
0
\end{array}
\qquad
\overset{3}{\phantom{0}}
\begin{array}{r}
5\ 8 \\
\times 4\ 6 \\
\hline
3\ 4\ 8 \\
2\ 0
\end{array}
\qquad
\overset{3}{\phantom{0}}
\begin{array}{r}
5\ 8 \\
\times 4\ 6 \\
\hline
3\ 4\ 8 \\
2\ 3\ 2\ 0
\end{array}
\qquad
\begin{array}{r}
5\ 8 \\
\times 4\ 6 \\
\hline
3\ 4\ 8 \\
2\ 3\ 2\ 0 \\
\hline
2\ 6\ 6\ 8
\end{array}
\left.\vphantom{\begin{array}{c}348\\2320\end{array}}\right\} \text{Add}
$$

Notice that each time you multiply (be it by the ones or the tens digit) the top numeral is being treated as a whole entity. Try completing the multiplications below.

1)
$$
\begin{array}{r}
5\ 7 \\
\times\ 3\ 4 \\
\hline
2\ 2\ 8 \\
\_\ \_\ \_\ 0 \\
\hline
1\ \_\ 3\ 8
\end{array}
$$

2)
$$
\begin{array}{r}
6\ 4 \\
\times\ 4\ 6 \\
\hline
3\ \_\ 4 \\
\_\ 5\ \_\ 0 \\
\hline
2\ 9\ \_\ 4
\end{array}
$$

3)
$$
\begin{array}{r}
9\ 8 \\
\times\ 2\ 7 \\
\hline
\_\ 8\ \_ \\
\_\ 9\ \_\ 0 \\
\hline
\_\ 6\ \_\ \_
\end{array}
$$

4)
$$
\begin{array}{r}
8\ 3 \\
\times\ 4\ 9 \\
\hline
7\ \_\ 7 \\
\_\ \_\ 2\ \_ \\
\hline
4\ \_\ \_\ \_
\end{array}
$$

## Answers

1.
$$
\begin{array}{r}
57 \\
\times 34 \\
\hline
228 \\
1710 \\
\hline
1938
\end{array}
$$

2.
$$
\begin{array}{r}
64 \\
\times 46 \\
\hline
384 \\
2560 \\
\hline
2944
\end{array}
$$

3.
$$
\begin{array}{r}
98 \\
\times 27 \\
\hline
686 \\
1960 \\
\hline
2646
\end{array}
$$

4.
$$
\begin{array}{r}
83 \\
\times 49 \\
\hline
747 \\
3320 \\
\hline
4067
\end{array}
$$

The following are multiplication exercises to permit you to practice the skills just introduced. Try to complete them in the manner just described.

| 1) 86 ×18 | 2) 69 ×18 | 3) 65 ×53 | 4) 97 ×90 | 5) 86 ×27 |
|---|---|---|---|---|
| 6) 25 ×67 | 7) 90 ×37 | 8) 72 ×15 | 9) 91 ×26 | 10) 33 ×70 |
| 11) 82 ×73 | 12) 86 ×69 | 13) 32 ×23 | 14) 40 ×29 | 15) 84 ×66 |
| 16) 75 ×24 | 17) 44 ×26 | 18) 94 ×74 | 19) 91 ×41 | 20) 40 ×10 |
| 21) 70 ×41 | 22) 31 ×19 | 23) 99 ×39 | 24) 73 ×17 | 25) 83 ×48 |
| 26) 48 ×33 | 27) 59 ×98 | 28) 94 ×81 | 29) 61 ×34 | 30) 66 ×23 |
| 31) 53 ×14 | 32) 50 ×97 | 33) 62 ×34 | 34) 85 ×50 | 35) 41 ×23 |

## Answers

| | | | | | |
|---|---|---|---|---|---|
| **1.** 1548 | **2.** 1242 | **3.** 3445 | **4.** 8730 | **5.** 2322 | **6.** 1675 |
| **7.** 3330 | **8.** 1080 | **9.** 2366 | **10.** 2310 | **11.** 5986 | **12.** 5934 |
| **13.** 736 | **14.** 1160 | **15.** 5544 | **16.** 1800 | **17.** 1144 | **18.** 6956 |
| **19.** 3731 | **20.** 400 | **21.** 2870 | **22.** 589 | **23.** 3861 | **24.** 1241 |
| **25.** 3984 | **26.** 1583 | **27.** 5782 | **28.** 7614 | **29.** 2074 | **30.** 1518 |
| **31.** 742 | **32.** 4850 | **33.** 2108 | **34.** 4250 | **35.** 943 | |

For additional practice, see page 265.

## MULTIPLYING LARGER NUMBERS

Three-digit multiplication works in almost exactly the same way as two-digit. Since there are three digits in the multiplier (the bottom numeral), there will be three lines of partial products before the final addition. Also, as the second line in a two-digit multiplication begins with the placing of the zero in the ones place, the third line begins with the placing of two zeroes. Since the third line is multiplication by hundreds, there will be zero ones, and zero tens:

*Model Example*

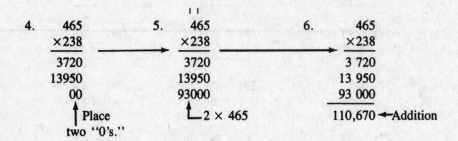

Try these. Refer to the model example if necessary.

| | | | | | | | |
|---|---|---|---|---|---|---|---|
| 1) | 447<br>×265 | 2) | 970<br>×206 | 3) | 834<br>×294 | 4) | 207<br>×118 |
| 5) | 317<br>×186 | 6) | 785<br>×583 | 7) | 380<br>×286 | 8) | 855<br>×703 |
| 9) | 822<br>×480 | 10) | 757<br>×485 | 11) | 576<br>×167 | 12) | 610<br>×112 |
| 13) | 438<br>×254 | 14) | 485<br>×159 | 15) | 279<br>×265 | 16) | 489<br>×296 |

## Answers

| | | | | | | | |
|---|---|---|---|---|---|---|---|
| 1. | 118,455 | 2. | 199,820 | 3. | 245,196 | 4. | 24,426 |
| 5. | 58,962 | 6. | 457,655 | 7. | 108,680 | 8. | 601,065 |
| 9. | 394,560 | 10. | 367,145 | 11. | 96,192 | 12. | 68,320 |
| 13. | 111,252 | 14. | 77,115 | 15. | 73,935 | 16. | 144,744 |

Additional practice will be found on page 266.

# DIVIDING WHOLE NUMBERS

Addition and multiplication taken together are combining operations. Both put smaller quantities together to make larger quantities. Add two dollars to five dollars, and you get seven dollars, a quantity larger than either two or five. If you have four seven dollar checks, to find out the total amount of money that you have, you may multiply four by seven. Four times seven is twenty-eight, so you have a total of twenty-eight dollars — an amount larger than either the four or the seven that you began with.

Since mathematics is nothing if it is not logical, it makes sense that there should be two operations to undo the combining made possible by addition and multiplication. Those taking apart operations are subtraction and division. With both subtraction and division, you start out with a quantity, and you end up with a smaller one. The operation of subtraction was already explored, beginning on page 29. Let us now take a look at division.

Division is the single operation with which most students of whole number arithmetic have difficulty. That difficulty occurs most often from a lack of understanding of division. In fact, division is related to two other operations, subtraction and multiplication. Division may be defined as the undoing of multiplication. For example, if 3 times 5 makes 15, then 15 divided by 5 equals 3. The sign, $\div$, is mathematical shorthand for "divided by."

Below you will find a series of exercises designed to emphasize and demonstrate the relationship between multiplication and division. Study the model example first, to make sure that you understand what to do. They try the exercises.

*Model Example*

$$3 \times 4 = 12 \qquad 4 \times 3 = 12$$
$$12 \div 4 = 3 \qquad 12 \div 3 = 4$$

Complete the following.

1) $5 \times 6 = 30$     $6 \times 5 = 30$     2) $7 \times 9 = 63$     $9 \times 7 = 63$
   $30 \div 6 = \underline{\hphantom{00}}$     $30 \div 5 = \underline{\hphantom{00}}$     $63 \div 9 = \underline{\hphantom{00}}$     $63 \div 7 = \underline{\hphantom{00}}$

3) $8 \times 7 = 56$     $7 \times 8 = 56$     4) $4 \times 6 = 24$     $6 \times 4 = 24$
   $56 \div 7 = \underline{\hphantom{00}}$     $56 \div 8 = \underline{\hphantom{00}}$     $24 \div 4 = \underline{\hphantom{00}}$     $24 \div 6 = \underline{\hphantom{00}}$

5) $3 \times 9 = \underline{\hphantom{00}}$     $9 \times 3 = \underline{\hphantom{00}}$     6) $2 \times 8 = \underline{\hphantom{00}}$     $8 \times 2 = \underline{\hphantom{00}}$
   $27 \div 9 = \underline{\hphantom{00}}$     $27 \div 3 = \underline{\hphantom{00}}$     $16 \div 8 = \underline{\hphantom{00}}$     $16 \div 2 = \underline{\hphantom{00}}$

7) $6 \times 7 = \underline{\hphantom{00}}$     $7 \times 6 = \underline{\hphantom{00}}$     8) $5 \times 9 = \underline{\hphantom{00}}$     $9 \times 5 = \underline{\hphantom{00}}$
   $42 \div 7 = \underline{\hphantom{00}}$     $42 \div 6 = \underline{\hphantom{00}}$     $45 \div 9 = \underline{\hphantom{00}}$     $45 \div 5 = \underline{\hphantom{00}}$

9) $3 \times 7 = \underline{\hphantom{00}}$     $7 \times 3 = \underline{\hphantom{00}}$     10) $6 \times 8 = \underline{\hphantom{00}}$     $8 \times 6 = \underline{\hphantom{00}}$
   $21 \div 7 = \underline{\hphantom{00}}$     $21 \div 3 = \underline{\hphantom{00}}$     $48 \div 8 = \underline{\hphantom{00}}$     $48 \div 6 = \underline{\hphantom{00}}$

## Answers

**1.** 5, 6     **2.** 7, 9     **3.** 8, 7     **4.** 6, 4     **5.** 27, 27, 3, 9

**6.** 16, 16, 2, 8     **7.** 42, 42, 6, 7     **8.** 45, 45, 5, 9     **9.** 21, 21, 3, 7     **10.** 48, 48, 6, 8

Division also bears the same relationship to subtraction as multiplication does to addition. Multiplication, you may recall, is an operation for performing repeated addition of the same number. Division is an operation for accomplishing repeated subtraction of the same number. 42 ÷ 6 may be thought of as asking "How many times can 6 be subtracted from 42?"

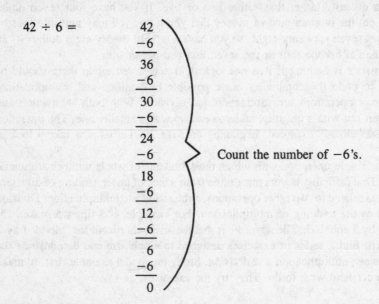

$$42 \div 6 =$$

Count the number of −6's.

Count the number of 6's that were subtracted, and you will find that there are seven of them. Therefore, 42 ÷ 6 = 7.

Division may be thought of as separating an amount of things into one or more equal groups. So, for example, suppose a woman has 45 poker chips, and she wishes to place five equal bets. To find out how many chips must be bet each time, we would divide 45 by 5. Since 5 × 9 = 45, 45 ÷ 5 = 9.

There are many different forms for accomplishing division. If you are already familiar with one that works for you, continue to use it. The exercises will give you the chance to polish your skills with the operation. If, however, you are not comfortable with division of larger numbers, you may find a method here that will work better for you than the method you once learned.

Before launching into the different forms of division, we should say a word or two about remainders. A remainder is what you get when one number does not divide into another an exact number of times. For example, when 7 is divided by 2, one rapidly discovers that three 2's fit into 7, and 1 will be left over. That 1 is called the remainder. Now once, representing a remainder as a fraction was taught as the "grown-up way" to treat remainders, and from about 4th grade on, remainders were always expressed as fractions. A fractional remainder may be formed by placing the remainder above the number being divided by (otherwise known as the divisor). Observe:

$$\begin{array}{r} 3 \text{ R1*} \\ 2\overline{)7} \end{array} \qquad \text{or} \qquad \begin{array}{r} 3\frac{1}{2} \\ 2\overline{)7} \end{array}$$

The so-called "grown-up" notion of expressing remainders exclusively as fractions, is no longer favored. Rather, the decision to represent a remainder as a fraction or to leave

*The word "remainder" is usually abbreviated by an R, hence this answer would be read: "Three, remainder 1."

it in the "R" form must depend upon the wording of the problem that is being solved. Here are two problems with identical numbers. Read and solve each:

1) An electrician wishes to cut a 38 foot length of wire into four equal parts. How long must each part be?

2) 38 pupils are to be seated equally at 4 tables. How many pupils will sit at each table?

In problem 1, it is stated that the wire must be cut into four equal lengths. Now 38 divided by 4 gives a result of 9, Remainder 2. We cannot, however, have four 9 foot lengths of wire and a 2 foot length and still satisfy the conditions of the problem. It is therefore necessary to express the remainder as a fraction, so that each length will be $9\frac{2}{4}$, or $9\frac{1}{2}$ feet long:

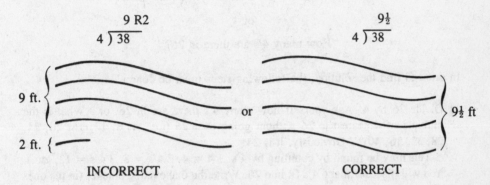

INCORRECT          or          CORRECT

The figures in problem 2, as previously stated, are identical to those in problem 1. But, there is a difference. One cannot cut pupils in half in order to get an equal number at each table. 9, R2 is then the required solution, meaning that 9 students will sit at each table, and 2 will remain standing.

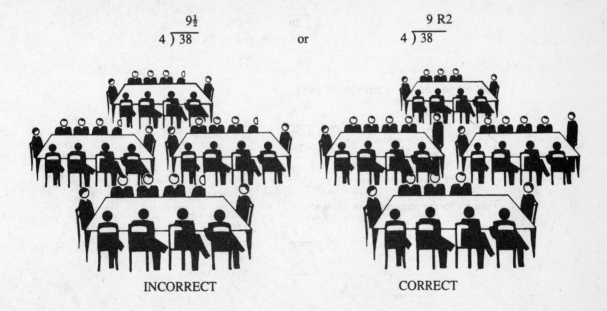

INCORRECT          CORRECT

## DIVIDING TWO DIGITS BY ONE

Any form of division, except for the basic division facts (which are, of course, the multiplication facts backward) consists of repeating three steps. Those steps are:

Divide
Multiply
Subtract

Sometimes, the division and multiplication steps are so closely combined that it is difficult to recognize that two separate steps have taken place, but they always do. Consider the following division:

$4\overline{)26}$     Which may be read "26 divided by 4 equals what?"

or

"How many 4's are there in 26?"

In order to find the solution, the following steps must be done:

1) Divide 26 by 4: Ask yourself how many 4's there are in 26, or "What is the multiple of 4 nearest to 26 without going over 26 (i.e., 4, 8, 12, 16, 20, 24, 28, 32, 36, 40)?" Obviously, it is 24.
   This may be found by counting by 4's. 1 4 = 4, 2 4's = 8, 3 4's = 12, etc.). You will discover that 6 4's fit into 26. Write the 6 above the bracket (in the ones place):

$$\begin{array}{r} 6 \\ 4\overline{)26} \end{array}$$

2) Multiply the number in the quotient (the 6) times the divisor

$$\begin{array}{r} 6 \\ 4\overline{)26} \\ \underline{24} \leftarrow 6 \times 4 = 24 \end{array}$$

3) Subtract to find the remainder (if any).

$$\begin{array}{r} 6 \\ 4\overline{)26} \\ \underline{-24} \\ 2 \end{array}$$

Then write the remainder as shown:

$$\begin{array}{r} 6\ R2 \\ 4\overline{)26} \\ \underline{24} \\ 2 \end{array}$$

The multiplication and division that took place in steps 1 and 2 are actually so inter-mingled that it is at times difficult to separate one from the other. Nevertheless, both are occurring. The subtraction, on the other hand, is easy to see.

Follow the steps in the model below:

$$
8\overline{)35} \longrightarrow 8\overline{)35} \longrightarrow 8\overline{)35} \longrightarrow 8\overline{)35} \longrightarrow \overset{4}{8\overline{)35}} \longrightarrow \overset{\times\ 4}{8\overline{)35}} \longrightarrow \overset{4}{8\overline{)35}} \longrightarrow \overset{4\ R3}{8\overline{)35}}
$$

$$
8 \times \underline{\ \ } = 35? \qquad 3 \times 4 = 32! \qquad\qquad =32 \qquad \dfrac{-32}{3}
$$

Again, notice the steps: Divide, multiply, subtract. Try the following. Refer to the model if needed.

Divide.

1) $2\overline{)11}$  2) $3\overline{)14}$  3) $5\overline{)29}$  4) $4\overline{)27}$  5) $7\overline{)56}$

6) $6\overline{)51}$  7) $9\overline{)43}$  8) $5\overline{)38}$  9) $6\overline{)54}$  10) $8\overline{)71}$

11) $6\overline{)49}$  12) $5\overline{)46}$  13) $4\overline{)35}$  14) $7\overline{)53}$  15) $6\overline{)19}$

16) $8\overline{)45}$  17) $3\overline{)22}$  18) $9\overline{)84}$  19) $4\overline{)39}$  20) $8\overline{)74}$

## Answers

| | | | | | | | | | |
|---|---|---|---|---|---|---|---|---|---|
| **1.** | 5, R1 | **2.** | 4, R2 | **3.** | 5, R4 | **4.** | 6, R3 | **5.** | 8 |
| **6.** | 8, R3 | **7.** | 4, R7 | **8.** | 7, R3 | **9.** | 9 | **10.** | 8, R7 |
| **11.** | 8, R1 | **12.** | 9, R1 | **13.** | 8, R3 | **14.** | 7, R4 | **15.** | 3, R1 |
| **16.** | 5, R5 | **17.** | 7, R1 | **18.** | 9, R3 | **19.** | 9, R3 | **20.** | 9, R2 |

You will find additional practice on page 266.

## ADDING A FOURTH STEP TO THE DIVISION PROCESS

As you have probably suspected, not all divisions are going to work out quite so con-veniently as the ones above. No matter what the division, the three steps of divide, mul-tiply, and subtract will apply. However, it will often be necessary to add a fourth step. That fourth step is known as "bringing down the next digit." Bringing down is neces-sitated in divisions such as in the model example that follows:

*Model Example*

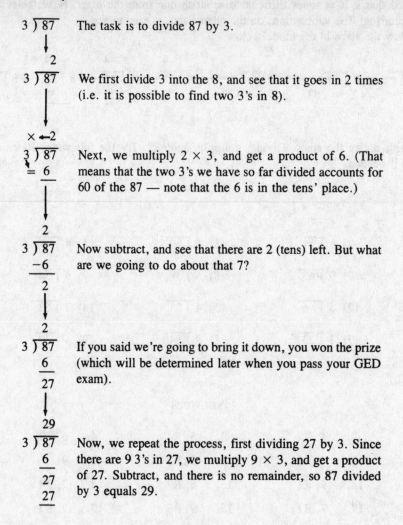

3 ⟌ 87     The task is to divide 87 by 3.

3 ⟌ 87     We first divide 3 into the 8, and see that it goes in 2 times
(i.e. it is possible to find two 3's in 8).

3 ⟌ 87     Next, we multiply 2 × 3, and get a product of 6. (That
= 6        means that the two 3's we have so far divided accounts for
60 of the 87 — note that the 6 is in the tens' place.)

3 ⟌ 87     Now subtract, and see that there are 2 (tens) left. But what
−6         are we going to do about that 7?

3 ⟌ 87     If you said we're going to bring it down, you won the prize
6          (which will be determined later when you pass your GED
27         exam).

3 ⟌ 87     Now, we repeat the process, first dividing 27 by 3. Since
6          there are 9 3's in 27, we multiply 9 × 3, and get a product
27         of 27. Subtract, and there is no remainder, so 87 divided
27         by 3 equals 29.

Note that when we first divided by 3, and said that there are two 3's in eight, we were perpetrating a fiction. It was not really 8, but, rather, 80 that we were dividing by 3. When we multiplied, we placed the 6 beneath the 8, in the tens column, so that 6 was really worth 6 tens, or 60. This particular form of division uses many fictions, but has been popular for a number of years. If it has given you difficulty before, or if you never really knew how to divide before, we recommend that you skip this form completely and go directly to the "Ladder Division" section on page 67. Ladder division plays fewer games with place-value concepts, and is, in the author's opinion, easier to learn, while every bit as efficient as the form being dealt with in this section.

If you are still with us at this point, and have not yet turned to "Ladder Division," try the exercises below.

1) 3 ⟌ 72        2) 5 ⟌ 85        3) 6 ⟌ 96        4) 4 ⟌ 96

5) 7 ⟌ 98        6) 9 ⟌ 99        7) 6 ⟌ 83        8) 5 ⟌ 72

**Answers**

$$\begin{array}{r} 24 \\ 3\overline{)72} \\ 6\downarrow \\ \hline 12 \\ 12 \\ \hline \end{array}$$

1.

$$\begin{array}{r} 17 \\ 5\overline{)85} \\ 5\downarrow \\ \hline 35 \\ 35 \\ \hline \end{array}$$

2.

$$\begin{array}{r} 16 \\ 6\overline{)96} \\ 6\downarrow \\ \hline 36 \\ 36 \\ \hline \end{array}$$

3.

$$\begin{array}{r} 24 \\ 4\overline{)96} \\ 8\downarrow \\ \hline 16 \\ 16 \\ \hline \end{array}$$

4.

$$\begin{array}{r} 14 \\ 7\overline{)98} \\ 7\downarrow \\ \hline 28 \\ 28 \\ \hline \end{array}$$

5.

$$\begin{array}{r} 11 \\ 9\overline{)99} \\ 9\downarrow \\ \hline 9 \\ 9 \\ \hline \end{array}$$

6.

$$\begin{array}{r} 13 \text{ R5} \\ 6\overline{)83} \\ 6\downarrow \\ \hline 23 \\ 18 \\ \hline 5 \end{array}$$

7.

$$\begin{array}{r} 14 \text{ R2} \\ 5\overline{)72} \\ 5\downarrow \\ \hline 22 \\ 20 \\ \hline 2 \end{array}$$

8.

# ADDING ANOTHER DIGIT TO THE DIVIDEND

We have tried to avoid technical terminology in this volume. When it becomes clear that it is necessary to use fifteen words just to avoid defining one single term, then it is obvious that a few definitions would be to everyone's advantage. With that in mind, consider the following diagram:

$$\text{Divisor} \overline{)\text{Dividend}}^{\text{Quotient}}$$

As an example of the above in the division,

$$5\overline{)35}^{7}$$

The divisor is 5.

The dividend is 35.

The quotient is 7.

We have been working until now with two-digit dividends and one-digit divisors. There are two possibilities that arise when a third digit is added to the dividend. The following model examples explore both of those possibilities.

*Model Example 1*

$5\overline{)723}$  Since 7 is divisible by 5
(can be divided by 5)
everything proceeds as
it did before, . . .

$5\overline{)723}$
$\underline{-5}$
$22$

$5\overline{)723}$
$5$
$\underline{22}$
$-20$
$2$

$144$

$5\overline{)723}$  . . . except that after the
$5$        second subtraction, a
$22$       second "bringing
$20$       down" is needed.
$\underline{23}$
$-20$
$3$

$144$ R3

*Model Example 2*

$9\overline{)345}$  Since 3 is **not** divisible
by 9, the 3 is put
together with the digit
to its right, and 34 is
divided by 9. Note that
the 3 in the quotient is
written over the 4 —
not over the 3 — in the
dividend.

$9\overline{)345}$
$27$
$7$

$3$

$9\overline{)345}$
$27$
$75$

$38$

$9\overline{)345}$  Everything else then
$27$       proceeds as before.
$75$
$\underline{-72}$
$3$

$38$ R3

**Divide.**

1) $4\overline{)273}$     2) $6\overline{)985}$     3) $7\overline{)346}$     4) $8\overline{)957}$

5) $5\overline{)738}$     6) $9\overline{)217}$     7) $3\overline{)849}$     8) $8\overline{)361}$

9) $6\overline{)954}$     10) $5\overline{)875}$     11) $9\overline{)311}$     12) $7\overline{)862}$

13) $4\overline{)935}$     14) $3\overline{)972}$     15) $7\overline{)581}$     16) $9\overline{)634}$

## Answers

**1.**  $68\frac{1}{4}$
$4\overline{)273}$
$24$
$33$
$32$
$1$

**2.**  $164\frac{1}{6}$
$6\overline{)985}$
$6$
$38$
$36$
$25$
$24$
$1$

**3.**  $49\frac{3}{7}$
$7\overline{)346}$
$28$
$66$
$63$
$3$

**4.**  $119\frac{5}{8}$
$8\overline{)957}$
$8$
$15$
$8$
$77$
$72$
$5$

**5.** $147\frac{3}{5}$
$$5 \overline{)738}$$
5↓
23
20↓
38
35
3

**6.** $24\frac{1}{9}$
$$9 \overline{)217}$$
18↓
37
36
1

**7.** 283
$$3 \overline{)849}$$
6↓
24
24↓
9
9

**8.** $45\frac{1}{8}$
$$8 \overline{)361}$$
32↓
41
40
1

**9.** 159
$$6 \overline{)954}$$
6↓
35
30↓
54
54

**10.** 175
$$5 \overline{)875}$$
5↓
37
35↓
25
25

**11.** $34\frac{5}{9}$
$$9 \overline{)311}$$
27↓
41
36
5

**12.** $123\frac{1}{7}$
$$7 \overline{)862}$$
7↓
16
14↓
22
21
1

**13.** $233\frac{3}{4}$
$$4 \overline{)935}$$
8↓
13
12↓
15
12
3

**14.** 324
$$3 \overline{)972}$$
9↓
7
6↓
12
12

**15.** 83
$$7 \overline{)581}$$
56↓
21
21

**16.** $70\frac{4}{9}$
$$9 \overline{)634}$$
63↓
4
0
4

You may have noticed that the answers to all the previous problems were expressed with fractional remainders. That was done as a reminder that there is, indeed, more than one way in which to express the remainder. Your answer to problem 1, for example, would be correct whether you wrote it as $68\frac{1}{4}$ or 68 R1.

Did problem 16 throw you, or did you figure it out for yourself? If you had trouble with 16, take a look at it now. After dividing 9 into 63, and multiplying 7 times 9, you subtract to get a remainder (difference) of 0. Bringing down a 4 (from the 634), it becomes necessary to divide 4 by 9. Thinking about that momentarily, it should become evident that there are no 9's in 4. That means that a 0 must be placed in the quotient, above the 4. Multiplying, we find that 0 times 9 equals 0. Subtract, and you get a remainder of 4.

You will find additional practice on page 267.

## TWO-DIGIT DIVISORS

Up to this point, our study of division has dealt exclusively with single-digit divisors. In the real world, and in the GED examination, single-digit divisors do not appear nearly as frequently as two-digit ones. The most important thing to remember when approaching division by two digits is that the four steps that were used with one-digit divisors remain the same: divide, multiply, subtract, bring down. Those four steps are repeated as many times as necessary until all the digits of the dividend have been brought down and divided.

Follow the solution of the model example, and you will see that there is nothing really new in the process:

*Model Example*

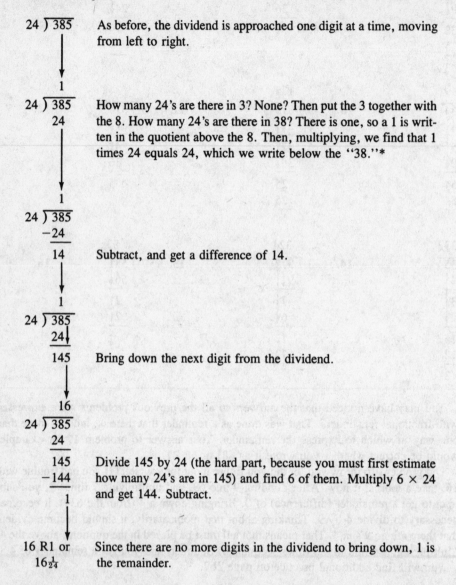

24 ) 385    As before, the dividend is approached one digit at a time, moving from left to right.

1
24 ) 385    How many 24's are there in 3? None? Then put the 3 together with
24          the 8. How many 24's are there in 38? There is one, so a 1 is writ-
            ten in the quotient above the 8. Then, multiplying, we find that 1
            times 24 equals 24, which we write below the "38."*

1
24 ) 385
−24
14          Subtract, and get a difference of 14.

1
24 ) 385
24↓
145         Bring down the next digit from the dividend.

16
24 ) 385
24
145         Divide 145 by 24 (the hard part, because you must first estimate
−144        how many 24's are in 145) and find 6 of them. Multiply 6 × 24
1           and get 144. Subtract.

16 R1 or    Since there are no more digits in the dividend to bring down, 1 is
$16\frac{1}{24}$    the remainder.

The major difference between single-digit division and dividing by two-digit divisors is that a familiarity with the multiplication tables makes dividing by one-digit relatively simple. It is not too difficult, for example, to recognize that 4 divides into 25 6 times. How many 24's there are in 145, however, is a somewhat more difficult question. After all, who is familiar with the 24 table? The solution lies in estimating what the quotient will be (that is, approximating how many 24's there are in 145).

*Since the 1 in the quotient is in the tens place, we are really multiplying 10 times 24 and getting 240, which we subtract from 385 to get 145. In practice, you need not worry about that, but that is why it works.

To estimate a quotient, first look at the numbers with which the division is to be performed:

$$24 \qquad\qquad\qquad 145$$

Then remove the last digit of each:

$$2\cancel{4} \qquad\qquad\qquad 14\cancel{5}$$

That leaves us with:

$$2 \qquad\qquad\qquad 14$$

How many 2's are there in 14?

Since there are 7 2's in 14, we can estimate that there will be 7 24's in 145. Now remember, the answer that we get from estimating is not necessarily accurate, but it is a ballpark figure. That is to say, it will be in the neighborhood of the number we are looking for. To find out how close we are, let's take our estimated 7 and multiply it by 24, the actual divisor, to see how close we come to the actual dividend, 145:

$$\begin{array}{r} 24 \\ \times\, 7 \\ \hline 168 \end{array}$$

168 is larger than the 145 that we are looking for. That tells us that our estimated quotient, 7, is too big. Since 7 24's is too big, try 6 24's:

$$\begin{array}{r} 24 \\ \times\, 6 \\ \hline 144 \end{array}$$

There we have it. 6 24's is just the number we were looking for. It is almost 145, and does not exceed 145.

In the model examples below, you will see two estimated quotients, and then the way in which those estimations are refined:

*Model Example 1*

1. ②3)⑱7
       ↓
2. 2 ) 18
        9

3. Estimate: 9 23's in 187.

4. Check:  $\begin{array}{r} 23 \\ \times\, 9 \\ \hline 201 \end{array}$ ← Too big.

5. Try 8 23's.

6. Check:  $\begin{array}{r} 23 \\ \times\, 8 \\ \hline 184 \end{array}$ ← Perfect.

7.  $\begin{array}{r} 8\text{ R}3 \\ 23\,\overline{)\,187} \\ \underline{184} \\ 3 \end{array}$

*Model Example 2*

1. ②9)⑯

2. 2)16
   8

3. Estimate: 8 29's in 165.

4. Check:   29
           × 8
           232 ← Way too big.

5. Try 6 29's.

6. Check:   29
           × 6
           174 ← Slightly too
                 big. 5 29's
                 should do it.

7. 29)165     5 R20
       145
        20

---

Once more, note that the estimate does not give an exact answer each time, but it can speed the process of finding the correct quotient by leading you to it. Solve the following divisions. First estimate the quotients, then divide.

1) 19)178    2) 23)217    3) 35)295    4) 46)398

5) 52)417    6) 61)579    7) 37)231    8) 84)719

9) 34)458    10) 43)692    11) 28)736    12) 31)945

## Answers

1. 19)178    9 R7       2. 23)217    $9\frac{10}{23}$    3. 35)295    8 R15     4. 46)398    8 R30
      171                     207                     280                    368
        7                      10                      15                     30

5. 52)417    $8\frac{1}{52}$    6. 61)579    $9\frac{30}{61}$    7. 37)231    6 R9      8. 84)719    $8\frac{47}{84}$
      416                     549                     222                    672
        1                      30                       9                     47

9. 34)458    13 R16    10. 43)692    $16\frac{4}{43}$    11. 28)736    26 R8    12. 31)945    30 R15
      34                      43                      56                     93
      118                     262                     176                     15
      102                     258                     168
       16                       4                       8

You will find additional practice on pages 267–268.

# MORE ON ESTIMATING QUOTIENTS

You may have noticed that some of the quotients that you estimated in the last set of exercises were a bit far away from the actual quotient you were looking for. That was especially true in model example 2 on page 64. The reason for that is in the nature of the form of estimating that you were doing. If the divisor in a given division example were 20, you would estimate by using the 2. If the divisor in another division were 29, you would still estimate by using the 2. Now there is a considerable gap between 20 and 29 — large enough, in fact, to make using the 2 to estimate with each time somewhat less than wholly satisfactory.

The form of estimating that you have been doing is known as "estimating by rounding down." That is because the digit that you used to make the estimation was always the name of the ten lower than the two-digit number you were dealing with. In other words, if you were dealing with 37, you rounded down to 30, and used the 3. If the divisor were 43, you rounded down to 40, and used the 4, and so on. Now it should be clear that while 43 is certainly closer to 40 than it is to any other ten, 37 is closer to 40 than it is to 30. We would, therefore, be much more likely to get an accurate estimate of the quotient if we used 4 rather than 3 as our estimating divisor. Look at the two models below.

| *Estimating by Rounding Down* | *Estimating by Rounding Up* |
|---|---|
| 1. ⑧7)㉔ | 1. 87)㉔3 |
| ↓ | 2. Close to |
| 3  Estimate 3 87's in 243. | 90 |
| 2. 8)24 | ↓ |
|  | 2  Estimate 2 87's in 243. |
| 3. Check:  87 | 3. ⑨)24 |
|  × 3 |  |
|  261 ← Too big! | 4. Check:  87 |
|  |  × 2 |
| 4. Try 2 87's. |  174 |
|  |  |
| 5. Check:  87 |  2 R69 |
|  × 2 | 5. 87)243 |
|  174 |  174 |
|  |  69 |
|  2 R69 |  |
| 6. 87)243 |  |
|  174 |  |
|  69 |  |

Clearly, in this particular case, estimating by rounding up to the next decade (90) was a more efficient method than rounding down. Does that mean that you should always estimate by rounding up? Hopefully, you have hit upon the answer for yourself. Sometimes it is better to round down, and sometimes it is better to round up. When the one's digit of the divisor is less than 5 (i.e., 0, 1, 2, 3, 4), round down as we did in the last section. When the one's digit of the divisor is 5 or greater, round up.

The rounded tens digit that we use in order to estimate the quotient is known as a **trial divisor**. Tell what the trial divisor would be for each of the following divisors. The first two have been done for you.

Name the trial divisor.

1) 32 is closer to 30, so the trial divisor would be 3.

2) 46 is closer to 50, so the trial divisor would be 5.

3) 29 is closer to _____ , so the trial divisor would be _____ .

4) 82 is closer to _____ , so the trial divisor would be _____ .

5) 73 is closer to _____ , so the trial divisor would be _____ .

6) 54 is closer to _____ , so the trial divisor would be _____ .

7) 68 is closer to _____ , so the trial divisor would be _____ .

8) 25 is closer to _____ , so the trial divisor would be _____ .

9) 66 is closer to _____ , so the trial divisor would be _____ .

10) 15 is closer to _____ , so the trial divisor would be _____ .

## Answers

| | | | | | | | |
|---|---|---|---|---|---|---|---|
| **3.** | 30, 3 | **4.** | 80, 8 | **5.** | 70, 7 | **6.** | 50, 5 |
| **7.** | 70, 7 | **8.** | 30, 3 | **9.** | 70, 7 | **10.** | 20, 2 |

Now, try applying the two different forms of estimating to some slightly more complex division exercises. Remember, once you have determined your trial divisor for an exercise, that trial divisor will remain the same, no matter how many times you need to divide to complete that division.

Estimate by rounding up or rounding down. Record your trial divisor, then divide.

1) 38 $\overline{)\,5943}$

T.D. = _____

2) 51 $\overline{)\,6782}$

T.D. = _____

3) 47 $\overline{)\,3895}$

T.D. = _____

4) 62 $\overline{)\,9437}$

T.D. = _____

5) 55 $\overline{)\,7482}$

T.D. = _____

6) 38 $\overline{)\,4729}$

T.D. = _____

7) 42 $\overline{)\,3816}$

T.D. = _____

8) 66 $\overline{)\,9583}$

T.D. = _____

9) 79 $\overline{)\,8243}$

T.D. = _____

10) 24 $\overline{)\,6357}$

T.D. = _____

11) 35 $\overline{)\,8124}$

T.D. = _____

12) 56 $\overline{)\,4982}$

T.D. = _____

## Answers

| | | | | | | | |
|---|---|---|---|---|---|---|---|
| **1.** 4; 156 R15 | **2.** 5; 132 R50 | **3.** 5; 82 R41 | **4.** 6; 152 R13 |
| **5.** 6; 136 R2 | **6.** 4; 124 R17 | **7.** 4; 90 R36 | **8.** 7; 145 R13 |
| **9.** 8; 104 R27 | **10.** 2; 264 R21 | **11.** 4; 232 R4 | **12.** 6; 88 R54 |

## *LADDER DIVISION*

Ladder division is an alternate method of dividing, based upon the relationship between division and subtraction, and taking advantage of the students's knowledge of place-value. Many people find it far more logical than the traditional approach to division — especially when dealing with larger numbers. Ladder division may be done with much less mastery of multiplication than may the traditional form discussed in the preceding pages. If you are shaky in traditional division, and/or traditional multiplication, then this may be just what you have been looking for. If division is not a serious problem for you, skip this section. Nobody needs to know how to divide two different ways.

Ladder division is built upon the type of division with which we opened the discussion of division, namely that the operation can be thought of as repeated subtraction of the same number. Below, it is stated that 42 divided by 6 could be thought of as asking: How many 6's can be subtracted from 42? That question can be answered by subtracting 6 from 42 over and over again, until there are none left:

$$6 \overline{)42}$$

```
6 ) 42
   -6
   36
   -6
   30
   -6
   24
   -6
   18
   -6
   12
   -6
    6
   -6
    0
```

By counting the number of times 6 has been subtracted from 42, you may conclude that there are seven 6's in 42, or, put another way, 42 divided by 6 is 7.

Ladder division takes this very simple concept and from it builds a completely different method of division — one which is really not difficult to master (with practice).

While the illustration on page 67 shows single 6's being subtracted from the 42, there is no reason why larger groupings of 6 could not have been subtracted. In the examples below, the same division is worked in different ways. The number to the right of each vertical line keeps track of how many 6's were removed:

| 1. | $6\overline{)42}$ | | 2. | $6\overline{)42}$ | | 3. | $6\overline{)42}$ | |
|---|---|---|---|---|---|---|---|---|
| | $-30$ | 5 | | $-18$ | 3 | | $-12$ | 2 |
| | $12$ | | | $24$ | | | $30$ | |
| | $-12$ | 2 | | $-18$ | 3 | | $-24$ | 4 |
| | $0$ | 7 | | $6$ | | | $6$ | |
| | | | | $-6$ | 1 | | $-6$ | 1 |
| | | | | $0$ | 7 | | $0$ | 7 |

When all the 6's that can be removed have been removed, the numbers to the right of the vertical line are added up and the quotient is found, 7. Notice how the number of 6's removed are tracked on the right side of the vertical line, while the total that has been removed from the dividend (e.g. 5 — 6's = 30) are tracked on the left. This gives the impression of rungs on a ladder, hence the name, ladder division. The beauty of ladder division is that there is no prescription as to how many divisors you must remove from the dividend at each step. Take out as many as you can find, or as many as you feel comfortable with. That is why in examples 1, 2, and 3, above, there were a different number of 6's removed at each step in each division, yet the quotient still ended up as 7 each time.

When solving a division by the ladder method, it is helpful to estimate the total quotient before beginning. Consider, for instance:

$8\overline{)322}$    It is essential to know about how large the quotient is going to be. Estimating takes place in multiples of 10. So, for example, we begin by asking ourselves whether there are 10 groups of 8 in 322. Since 10 8's make 80, and 80 is less than 322, we can conclude that there are. Next, ask whether there are 100 groups of 8 in 322. Since 100 8's make 800, and 800 is larger than 322, there are not. We have now estimated that our quotient will be greater than 10, but less than 100. We are now ready to attack the problem's solution. Here, first, is a solution that requires the least amount of thinking, but which is somewhat lengthy:

| $8\overline{)322}$ | | |
|---|---|---|
| 80 | 10 | Since we already know that there are 10 groups of 8, let's remove 10 8's from 322, and see what's left. Then let's do it again . . . |
| 242 | | |
| 80 | 10 | |
| 162 | | |
| 80 | 10 | . . . and again . . . |
| 82 | | |
| 80 | 10 | . . . and again. |
| 2 | 40 R2 | Since there is not another 8 remaining, we cannot divide again. Add up the column to the right of the line and get 40 R2. |

Now, if you would rather get to the quotient more quickly, we can sophisticate our approach:

$$8\ )\overline{\ 322}$$

If 10 8's = 80, then twice 10 8's, or 20 8's =
$$
\begin{array}{r}
80 \\
+80 \\
\hline
160\ (20\ 8\text{'s})
\end{array}
$$

But 20 8's and another 20 8's =
$$
\begin{array}{r}
160 \\
+160 \\
\hline
320\ (40\ 8\text{'s})
\end{array}
$$

$$
8\ )\overline{\ 322}
$$

That's pretty close. Let's write it.

$$
\begin{array}{r|l}
8\ )\overline{\ 322} & \\
320 & 40 \\
\hline
2 & 40\ \text{R2}
\end{array}
$$

And that's that!

If you understand the principle involved, removing as much at one time from the dividend as you are comfortable removing, then you have the whole story. Just remember to keep track (on the right of the line) of the number of divisors that you have removed at each step. Try these.

1) $7\ )\overline{\ 532}$

2) $5\ )\overline{\ 168}$

3) $4\ )\overline{\ 234}$

4) $8\ )\overline{\ 567}$

5) $7\ )\overline{\ 384}$

6) $9\ )\overline{\ 638}$

7) $7\ )\overline{\ 461}$

8) $5\ )\overline{\ 316}$

9) $6\ )\overline{\ 225}$

## Answers

In the solutions that follow, your solution might well be quite different from the one shown. Your answer, however, should not be.

**1.**
$$
\begin{array}{r|l}
7\ )\overline{\ 532} & \\
490 & 70 \\
\hline
42 & \\
42 & 6 \\
\hline
 & 76
\end{array}
$$

**2.**
$$
\begin{array}{r|l}
5\ )\overline{\ 168} & \\
150 & 30 \\
\hline
18 & \\
15 & 3 \\
\hline
3 & 33\ \text{R3}
\end{array}
$$

**3.**
$$
\begin{array}{r|l}
4\ )\overline{\ 234} & \\
200 & 50 \\
\hline
34 & \\
32 & 8 \\
\hline
2 & 58\ \text{R2}
\end{array}
$$

**4.**
```
8 ) 567
    560 | 70
      7 | 70 R7
```

**5.**
```
7 ) 384
    350 | 50
     34 |
     28 | 4
      6 | 54 R6
```

**6.**
```
9 ) 638
    630 | 70
      8 | 70 R8
```

**7.**
```
7 ) 461
    420 | 60
     41 |
     35 | 5
      6 | 65 R6
```

**8.**
```
5 ) 316
    300 | 60
     16 |
     15 | 3
      1 | 63 R1
```

**9.**
```
6 ) 225
    180 | 30
     45 |
     42 | 7
      3 | 37 R3
```

# LADDER DIVISION WITH TWO-DIGIT DIVISORS

There is essentially no difference between ladder division with single-digit divisors, and ladder division with multiple-digit divisors. Exactly the same rules apply. Indeed, the only significant change is in the magnitude of the numbers being worked with. Examine the model example below.

*Model Example*

```
32 ) 6843
     6400 | 200
     ─────
      443
      320 | 10
     ─────
      123
       96 | 3
     ─────
       27 | 213 R27
```

First, the quotient must be estimated. Since 100 32's make 3200, and 1000 make 32,000, it is obvious that the answer must be in the hundreds.

200 32's make 6400. That fact is taken care of on the first step of the ladder. 10 more 32's are removed on the second step, and finally the last 3 are taken care of.

As before, there is no one correct way to solve a ladder division, and so the model example shows just one possible solution, but there are many others just as possible — most a bit longer than the one shown. Try your hand at the divisions below.

Divide using the ladder method.

1) 34 ) 688

2) 53 ) 792

3) 46 ) 983

4) 22 ) 517

5) 18 ) 376

6) 57 ) 697

7) 38 ) 6431

8) 29 ) 8537

9) 53 ) 6947

10) 82 ) 7386

11) 47 ) 8526

12) 34 ) 5264

13) 23 ) 9537

14) 38 ) 9438

15) 42 ) 7159

16) 63 ) 27,584

17) 48 ) 35,829

18) 26 ) 86,635

## Answers

**1.**  34 ) 688

| 680 | 20 |
|-----|-----|
| 8 | 20 R8 |

**2.**  53 ) 792

| 530 | 10 |
|-----|-----|
| 262 | |
| 212 | 4 |
| 50 | 14 R50 |

**3.**  46 ) 983

| 920 | 20 |
|-----|-----|
| 63 | |
| 46 | 1 |
| 17 | 21 R17 |

**4.**  22 ) 517

| 440 | 20 |
|-----|-----|
| 77 | |
| 66 | 3 |
| 11 | 23 R11 |

**5.**  18 ) 376

| 360 | 20 |
|-----|-----|
| 16 | 20 R16 |

**6.**  57 ) 697

| 570 | 10 |
|-----|-----|
| 127 | |
| 114 | 2 |
| 13 | 12 R13 |

**7.**  38 ) 6431

| 3800 | 100 |
|------|------|
| 2631 | |
| 1900 | 50 |
| 731 | |
| 380 | 10 |
| 351 | |
| 342 | 9 |
| 9 | 169 R9 |

**8.**  29 ) 8537

| 5800 | 200 |
|------|------|
| 2737 | |
| 2610 | 90 |
| 127 | |
| 116 | 4 |
| 11 | 294 R11 |

**9.**  53 ) 6947

| 5300 | 100 |
|------|------|
| 1647 | |
| 1590 | 30 |
| 57 | |
| 53 | 1 |
| 4 | 131 R4 |

**10.**  82 ) 7386
  7380 | 90
  ___
  6 | 90 R6

**11.**  47 ) 8526
  4700 | 100
  ___
  3826
  3760 | 80
  ___
  66
  47 | 1
  ___
  19 | 181 R19

**12.**  34 ) 5264
  3400 | 100
  ___
  1864
  1700 | 50
  ___
  164
  136 | 4
  ___
  28 | 154 R28

**13.**  23 ) 9537
  9200 | 400
  ___
  337
  230 | 10
  ___
  107
  92 | 4
  ___
  15 | 414 R15

**14.**  38 ) 9438
  7600 | 200
  ___
  1838
  1520 | 40
  ___
  318
  304 | 8
  ___
  14 | 248 R14

**15.**  42 ) 7159
  4200 | 100
  ___
  2959
  2940 | 70
  ___
  19 | 170 R19

**16.**  63 ) 27,584
  25,200 | 400
  ___
  2384
  1890 | 30
  ___
  494
  441 | 7
  ___
  53 | 437 R53

**17.**  48 ) 35,829
  33,600 | 700
  ___
  2229
  1920 | 40
  ___
  309
  288 | 6
  ___
  21 | 746 R21

**18.**  26 ) 86,635
  78,000 | 3000
  ___
  8635
  7800 | 300
  ___
  835
  780 | 30
  ___
  55
  52 | 2
  ___
  3 | 3332 R3

You will find additional practice in ladder division with larger numbers on page 268

# WHOLE NUMBERS POST-TEST

Complete.

1) In the numeral 4,682,159,370, 8 is in the _____ place and

   1 is in the _____ place.

Solve.

2) 4718 + 65 + 1835 + 427          3) 4684 − 2998

4)   6007
   −3948

5) 534
   ×6

6)   85
   ×47

7) 843
   ×69

8)   674
   ×538

9) 8 ) 4765

10) 37 ) 8493

## Answers

| | | | | | |
|---|---|---|---|---|---|
| **1.** | 10 millions; 100 thousands | **2.** | 7045 | **3.** | 1686 |
| **4.** | 2059 | **5.** 3204 | **6.** | 3995 | **7.** | 58,167 |
| **8.** | 362,612 | **9.** 595 R5 | **10.** | 229 R20 | | |

# ANALYSIS OF ANSWERS TO POST-TEST

Following are the skills which were tested by the various items in the post-test. Should the results indicate that you need additional practice with any one or more skills, refer to the appropriate pages in the chapter, and to the Additional Practice section that goes with the type of skill in question.

| | | |
|---|---|---|
| 1. | Reading place value numerals | Pages 13–19 |
| 2. | Adding in columns | Pages 19–29; 261 |
| 3. | Subtracting with renaming | Pages 33–39; 262–264 |
| 4. | Subtracting with zeros on top | Pages 39–40; 264 |
| 5. | Multiplying by one digit | Pages 40–47; 265 |
| 6. | Multiplying by two digits | Pages 47–51; 265 |
| 7, 8. | Multiplying larger numbers | Pages 51–52; 266 |
| 9. | Dividing by one digit | Pages 53–61; 266–267 |
| 10. | Two-digit divisors | Pages 61–64; 267–268 |

# 3. FRACTIONAL NUMBERS

## FRACTION PRE-TEST

Solve. Express all answers in lowest terms.

1) $\frac{3}{5} + \frac{1}{5} =$ _____

2) $\frac{3}{4} + \frac{1}{8} =$ _____

3) $\frac{3}{8} + \frac{2}{3} =$ _____

4) $\frac{5}{6} - \frac{1}{2} =$ _____

5) $\frac{9}{11} - \frac{2}{3} =$ _____

6) $\frac{4}{5} \times \frac{3}{4} =$ _____

7) $\frac{25}{36} \times \frac{12}{20} =$ _____

8) $\frac{5}{8} \div \frac{1}{4} =$ _____

9) $\quad 5\frac{1}{2}$
   $\quad +3\frac{1}{4}$
   $\quad \overline{\phantom{xxx}}$

10) $\quad 6\frac{2}{3}$
    $\quad -4\frac{3}{5}$
    $\quad \overline{\phantom{xxx}}$

11) $\quad 7\frac{1}{4}$
    $\quad -5\frac{7}{8}$
    $\quad \overline{\phantom{xxx}}$

12) $3\frac{3}{4} \times 4\frac{2}{3} =$ _____

13) $5\frac{2}{5} \div 2\frac{3}{8} =$ _____

### Answers

1. $\frac{4}{5}$  2. $\frac{7}{8}$  3. $1\frac{1}{24}$  4. $\frac{1}{3}$  5. $\frac{5}{33}$  6. $\frac{3}{5}$  7. $\frac{5}{12}$

8. $2\frac{1}{2}$  9. $8\frac{3}{4}$  10. $2\frac{1}{15}$  11. $1\frac{3}{8}$  12. $17\frac{1}{2}$  13. $2\frac{26}{95}$

Guide your studies in this chapter by the items that you got incorrect, or that gave you difficulty even though you got them correct. If your computation was correct, and you had trouble expressing your answer in lowest terms, see Equivalent Fractions on page 78. The other topics covered in this chapter are listed below, with page numbers:

## WHAT IS A FRACTION?

The concept of fraction, and operating with fractions, is one that has caused difficulty to students of mathematics for many years. Indeed, fraction is probably one of the most poorly taught of all the ideas in elementary mathematics. A major cause of the difficulty in teaching fractional concepts is the fact that there is no single definition for fraction. Indeed, fractions are used to represent many things, including a part of a whole, a part of a group of things, a comparison (or ratio), a way to represent division, and as a whole to be further operated upon. Let us examine those definitions one at a time:

A fraction as a part of a whole assumes that there is one whole object, such as a cake or a paycheck, and when you speak of a fraction, you are referring to less than the entire object. In order to name the fraction that is being considered, one must look at two components. The first is the number of equal parts that the whole is separated into. The second is the number of those parts being considered. Look at the following:

one of four equal parts:
one-fourth ($\frac{1}{4}$)

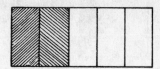

two of five equal parts:
two-fifths ($\frac{2}{5}$)

four of seven equal parts:
four-sevenths ($\frac{4}{7}$)

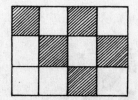

five of twelve equal parts:
five-twelfths ($\frac{5}{12}$)

Notice that the part of a fraction that tells the number of parts into which the whole has been separated is at the bottom (known technically as the denominator). The top of the fraction (the numerator) names the number of parts that are being considered (in these cases the number of parts that are shaded).

The illustrations below serve to demonstrate the meaning of fraction as a part of a group:

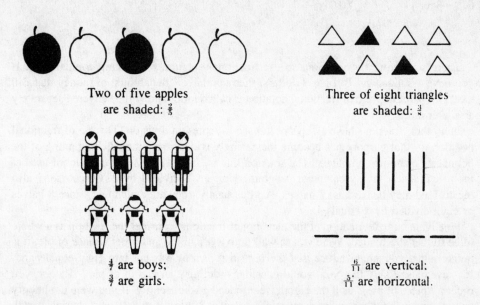

Two of five apples
are shaded: $\frac{2}{5}$

Three of eight triangles
are shaded: $\frac{3}{8}$

$\frac{4}{7}$ are boys;
$\frac{3}{7}$ are girls.

$\frac{6}{11}$ are vertical;
$\frac{5}{11}$ are horizontal.

There is considerable difference between $\frac{1}{2}$ apple and $\frac{1}{2}$ a group of people. The latter contains only whole people. The former contains no whole apples.

Name the fraction indicated by the shaded portion in each diagram.

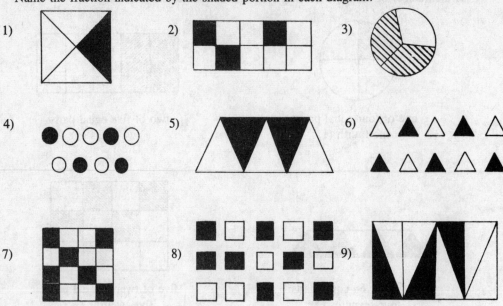

**Answers**

1.  $\frac{1}{4}$        2.  $\frac{3}{10}$        3.  $\frac{2}{3}$        4.  $\frac{4}{9}$        5.  $\frac{2}{5}$

6.  $\frac{5}{10}$ or $\frac{1}{2}$        7.  $\frac{7}{16}$        8.  $\frac{8}{15}$        9.  $\frac{3}{8}$

There are frequently occasions to use fractional notation for making comparisons. If you have 4 dollars and Bill has 7 dollars, then you have $\frac{4}{7}$ the amount of money that Bill has. This particular use of fractional notation is called ratio, and will be covered separately at a later time.

In algebra, fractions have always been used to represent division. The use of fractional notation for that purpose has become increasingly widespread since the beginning of the popularity of home computers. The fraction line is, in fact, the standard symbol used to indicate division in any computer program. $\frac{8}{2}$ means 8 divided by 2. Of course, $\frac{8}{2}$ also means (and may be read as) 8 halves. Arithmetically, they are equivalent, since 8 halves or eight divided by 2 equals 4.

Finally, in our examination of the meaning of fractions, consider the fraction as a whole to be further subdivided. Were you to walk into a restaurant and order a piece of pie, it is unlikely that you might notice that the pie (in the case) was cut into eight equal parts. It is even less likely that you would consider ordering "an eighth of pie." Rather, you order a "piece of pie," as if the eighth were indeed a whole entity. If you were not hungry enough to eat the whole piece, you might consider cutting it in half, and sharing it with your dinner companion. Would it ever occur to you that you were eating a sixteenth of the original pie? Most likely, you would be content just to eat "a half a piece of pie."

# ADDING AND SUBTRACTING FRACTIONS

## *ADDING AND SUBTRACTING FRACTIONS WITH LIKE DENOMINATORS*

Fractional numbers, like any numbers, are capable of being added, subtracted, multiplied, and divided. Addition and subtraction of fractional numbers are approached together here, since the rules that govern those operations are essentially similar. In fact, there is really only one rule that governs the ability for fractions to be added or subtracted:

**Fractions may be added or subtracted if they have like denominators.**

You may recall, the denominator of a fraction is the numeral on the bottom, and it names the number of parts into which the whole object or group has been separated. It is critical to remember that the denominator names the size of the parts that are being dealt with. So, for example, if an object is divided into eighths, there will be twice as many parts as there would be if the same object were divided into fourths. Each eighth, however, would be half the size of each fourth.

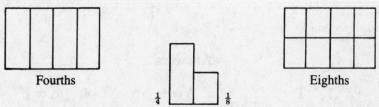

For the same or for equal objects, the more parts there are, the smaller each part is!

The diagram below shows the addition of $\frac{1}{5}$ and $\frac{2}{5}$:

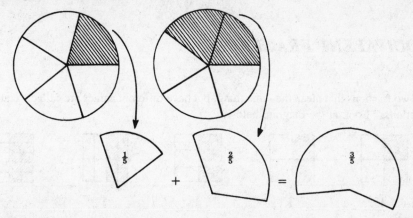

Notice that the numerators (top numerals in the fractions) tell the number of parts being considered. That is, 1 names the first amount of fifths, and 2 names the second amount of fifths. Adding one and two gives three, hence adding $\frac{1}{5}$ and $\frac{2}{5}$ gives $\frac{3}{5}$. Notice that since you started with fifths, and ended with fifths, the denominators do not change. **Only the numerators are added.**

Here is another one:

$$\frac{1}{4} \quad + \quad \frac{2}{4} \quad = \quad \frac{3}{4}$$

Subtracting fractional numbers works in exactly the same way as addition, except that the numerators are subtracted rather than added:

$$\frac{4}{4} \quad - \quad \frac{1}{4} \quad = \quad \frac{3}{4}$$

Try your hand at the fractional additions and subtractions below. Pay attention to the signs, so that you know whether to add or subtract.

1) $\frac{2}{5} + \frac{2}{5} =$ _____    2) $\frac{3}{8} + \frac{4}{8} =$ _____    3) $\frac{5}{12} - \frac{2}{12} =$ _____    4) $\frac{9}{15} - \frac{6}{15} =$ _____

5) $\frac{5}{21} + \frac{6}{21} =$ _____    6) $\frac{8}{19} + \frac{5}{19} =$ _____    7) $\frac{4}{9} + \frac{3}{9} =$ _____    8) $\frac{11}{12} - \frac{6}{12} =$ _____

9) $\frac{3}{14} + \frac{8}{14} =$ _____    10) $\frac{15}{16} - \frac{4}{16} =$ _____    11) $\frac{1}{2} + \frac{2}{2} =$ _____    12) $\frac{2}{3} - \frac{1}{3} =$ _____

13) $\frac{9}{18} + \frac{5}{18} =$ _____    14) $\frac{4}{7} - \frac{3}{7} =$ _____    15) $\frac{21}{30} - \frac{11}{30} =$ _____

## Answers

1. $\frac{4}{5}$          2. $\frac{7}{8}$          3. $\frac{3}{12}$ or $\frac{1}{4}$          4. $\frac{3}{15}$ or $\frac{1}{5}$          5. $\frac{11}{21}$

6. $\frac{13}{19}$          7. $\frac{7}{9}$          8. $\frac{5}{12}$          9. $\frac{11}{14}$          10. $\frac{11}{16}$

11. $\frac{3}{2}$ or $1\frac{1}{2}$          12. $\frac{1}{3}$          13. $\frac{14}{18}$ or $\frac{7}{9}$          14. $\frac{1}{7}$          15. $\frac{10}{30}$ or $\frac{1}{3}$

## EQUIVALENT FRACTIONS

Two fractions that mean the same thing, but have different names are called "equivalent fractions." Look at the diagram below:

$$\frac{1}{2} \qquad \frac{2}{4} \qquad \frac{3}{6} \qquad \frac{4}{8} \qquad \frac{5}{10}$$

Each fraction shaded in has a different name, as you can see from the numerals beneath each picture. Yet, upon close inspection you should notice that the size of the piece shaded in each of the pictures is the same as the size piece shaded in every other picture. These fractions are equivalent. It can be stated, therefore, that $\frac{1}{2}$, $\frac{2}{4}$, $\frac{3}{6}$, $\frac{4}{8}$, and $\frac{5}{10}$ are all equivalent fractions.

Name these equivalent fractions:

1)

_____ _____ _____ _____

2)

_____ _____ _____ _____

3)

_____ _____ _____ _____

## Answers

**1.** $\frac{1}{3}, \frac{2}{6}, \frac{3}{9}, \frac{4}{12}$  **2.** $\frac{1}{4}, \frac{2}{8}, \frac{4}{16}, \frac{3}{12}$  **3.** $\frac{2}{5}, \frac{4}{10}, \frac{6}{15}, \frac{8}{20}$

Now you are probably saying to yourself, "There must be an easier way to tell whether fractions are equivalent than by drawing boxes." You are right. You can tell equivalent fractions by finding common factors in the numerator **and** denominator of each. Consider the halves in the model problem on the previous page:

$$\frac{2}{4} = \frac{2 \times 1}{2 \times 2} = \frac{2}{2} \times \frac{1}{2} \text{ (but } \frac{2}{2} = 1, \text{ so)} = 1 \times \frac{1}{2} = \frac{1}{2}$$

$$\frac{3}{6} = \frac{3 \times 1}{3 \times 2} = \frac{3}{3} \times \frac{1}{2} \text{ (but } \frac{3}{3} = 1, \text{ so)} = 1 \times \frac{1}{2} = \frac{1}{2}$$

$$\frac{4}{8} = \frac{4 \times 1}{4 \times 2} = \frac{4}{4} \times \frac{1}{2} \text{ (but } \frac{4}{4} = 1, \text{ so)} = 1 \times \frac{1}{2} = \frac{1}{2}$$

$$\frac{5}{10} = \frac{5 \times 1}{5 \times 2} = \frac{5}{5} \times \frac{1}{2} \text{ (but } \frac{5}{5} = 1, \text{ so)} = 1 \times \frac{1}{2} = \frac{1}{2}$$

By finding the common factor that is contained in both the numerator and denominator of each fraction, we are able to write each fraction in lowest possible terms. The lowest possible terms for each of the fractions turns out to be $\frac{1}{2}$.

In case you had not figured it out for yourself, based upon what you just read, any fraction that is written as a number in the numerator over the same number in the denominator (e.g. $\frac{2}{2}$, $\frac{3}{3}$, $\frac{4}{4}$, $\frac{5}{5}$) has a value of 1. If you are not sure why, think about it. Two halves make one whole, three thirds make one whole, and so forth. If that is still not clear, remember that any fraction can also be thought of as a division exercise. Hence, $\frac{2}{2}$ means 2 divided by 2, which is 1; and $\frac{3}{3}$ means 3 divided by 3, which is 1. . . .

There is yet one more key to writing equivalent fractions. Look at the following question:

$$\frac{2}{3} = \frac{?}{9}$$

Ask yourself what the 3 in the first denominator was multiplied by in order to get the 9 of the second denominator. Then multiply the first numerator by the same amount:

$$\frac{2}{3} \times 3 = \frac{?}{9} \qquad \therefore^* \qquad \frac{2}{3} \times \frac{3}{3} = \frac{6}{9}$$

Notice once again, that the first fraction has been multiplied by another name for one ($\frac{3}{3}$). Examine the two model problems.

*Model Problem 1*

$$\frac{3}{5} \diagup \frac{?}{15}$$

$$\frac{3}{5} \times \frac{?}{3} = \frac{?}{15}$$

$$\frac{3}{5} \times \frac{3}{3} = \frac{9}{15}$$

$$\frac{3}{5} = \frac{9}{15}$$

*Model Problem 2*

$$\frac{4}{9} = \frac{24}{?}$$

$$\frac{4}{9} \times \frac{6}{?} = \frac{24}{?}$$

$$\frac{4}{9} \times \frac{6}{6} = \frac{24}{54}$$

$$\frac{4}{9} = \frac{24}{54}$$

Complete the following to form equivalent fractions.

1) $\dfrac{1}{4} = \dfrac{}{8} = \dfrac{}{12} = \dfrac{}{16} = \dfrac{}{20} = \dfrac{}{24} = \dfrac{}{28} = \dfrac{}{32} = \dfrac{}{36}$

2) $\dfrac{2}{6} = \dfrac{}{12} = \dfrac{}{18} = \dfrac{}{24} = \dfrac{}{30} = \dfrac{}{36} = \dfrac{}{42} = \dfrac{}{48} = \dfrac{}{54}$

3) $\dfrac{5}{8} = \dfrac{10}{} = \dfrac{15}{} = \dfrac{20}{} = \dfrac{25}{} = \dfrac{30}{} = \dfrac{35}{} = \dfrac{40}{} = \dfrac{45}{}$

4) $\dfrac{7}{12} = \dfrac{}{36}$    5) $\dfrac{9}{11} = \dfrac{36}{}$    6) $\dfrac{12}{15} = \dfrac{}{60}$    7) $\dfrac{5}{18} = \dfrac{}{54}$

8) $\dfrac{8}{9} = \dfrac{72}{}$    9) $\dfrac{5}{7} = \dfrac{30}{}$    10) $\dfrac{8}{13} = \dfrac{}{117}$

---

*$\therefore$ is mathematical shorthand for "therefore."

## Answers

**1.** 2, 3, 4, 5, 6, 7, 8, 9     **2.** 4, 6, 8, 10, 12, 14, 16     **3.** 16, 24, 32, 40, 48, 56, 64, 72

**4.** 21     **5.** 44     **6.** 48     **7.** 15     **8.** 81     **9.** 42     **10.** 72

You will find additional practice on page 269.

## *GREATEST COMMON FACTOR AND LEAST COMMON MULTIPLE*

Look at the following group of numbers: {9, 12, 18, 24}. All of the numbers in the group (or set) are divisible by 1. (Since all whole numbers are divisible by 1 — that is 1 goes into each number a whole number of times — that should hardly be surprising.) All of the numbers in the set are also divisible by 3. Can you find another number that is a factor of **all** the numbers in that set? Since there is none, we may safely say that 3 is the greatest number by which 9, 12, 18, and 24 are divisible. Said differently, 3 is the **Greatest Common Factor** (GCF) of 9, 12, 18, and 24.

Find the greatest common factor of {10, 20, 30, 45}. One, of course, is a factor of each number in the set. So is five. Ten divides perfectly into each number in the set except the last. That means the greatest common factor of the four numbers is 5.

Find the greatest common factor of each of the following sets.

1) 14, 21, 28 _____     2) 6, 12, 15 _____     3) 8, 12, 20 _____

4) 25, 40 _____     5) 18, 30 _____     6) 24, 36 _____     7) 45, 60 _____

8) 12, 17, 30 _____     9) 12, 16, 36 _____     10) 16, 24, 32 _____

## Answers

**1.** 7     **2.** 3     **3.** 4     **4.** 5     **5.** 6

**6.** 12     **7.** 15     **8.** 1     **9.** 4     **10.** 8

Another extremely useful concept, when dealing with fractional computations, is the Least Common Multiple. You will see how it is used in the next section. The notion of LCM (Least Common Multiple) is not a complex one. Consider two numbers, say 2 and 4. Now look at some of the multiples of 2 and 4:

Multiples of 2:   2, 4, 6, 8, 10, 12, 14, 16, 20 . . .

Multiples of 4:   4, 8, 12, 16, 20 . . .

Now, circle the common multiples of 2 and 4 — that is the numbers that appear in both sets of multiples. Don't read on, until you've done it.* You should have circled 4, 8, 12, 16, and 20. Those are all common multiples of 2 and 4. Now, remember, the LCM is the common multiple with the lowest value (**Least Common Multiple**). Therefore, the LCM for 2 and 4 is 4.

List the first 10 multiples for each of the following pairs of numbers.

1) 3 _____      2) 5 _____

   4 _____         3 _____

3) 6 _____      4) 8 _____

   8 _____         4 _____

5) 7 _____      6) 9 _____

   12 _____        8 _____

Now name the LCM for each of the above.

1) _____   2) _____   3) _____   4) _____   5) _____   6) _____

## Answers

1.  3, 6, 9, 12, 15, 18, 21, 24, 27, 30       2.  5, 10, 15, 20, 25, 30, 35, 40, 45, 50
    4, 8, 12, 16, 20, 24, 28, 32, 36, 40          3, 6, 9, 12, 15, 18, 21, 24, 27, 30

3.  6, 12, 18, 24, 30, 36, 42, 48, 54, 60     4.  8, 16, 24, 32, 40, 48, 56, 64, 72, 80
    8, 16, 24, 32, 40, 48, 56, 64, 72, 80         4, 8, 12, 16, 20, 24, 28, 32, 36, 40

5.  7, 14, 21, 28, 35, 42, 49, 56, 63, 70     6.  9, 18, 27, 36, 45, 54, 63, 72, 81, 90
    12, 24, 36, 48, 60, 72, 84, 96, 108, 120      8, 16, 24, 32, 40, 48, 56, 64, 72, 80

**LCM's**

1.  12      2.  15      3.  24      4.  8      5.  84      6.  72

Find the LCM's for the following pairs of numbers.

1) 7, 11      2) 8, 3      3) 5, 4      4) 4, 6      5) 9, 12

6) 8, 2      7) 5, 17      8) 2, 18      9) 3, 20      10) 18, 4

*For the technical reader, zero is also considered to be a multiple of all numbers. It has been omitted from the listings of multiples here, however, because its inclusion would have served no purpose. When seeking to find an LCM, we always want the LCM other than zero.

11) 6, 11     12) 9, 17     13) 4, 10     14) 10, 14     15) 6, 15

16) 6, 14     17) 2, 9     18) 15, 3     19) 4, 14     20) 8, 20

## Answers

| | | | | | | | | | |
|---|---|---|---|---|---|---|---|---|---|
| **1.** | 77 | **2.** | 24 | **3.** | 20 | **4.** | 12 | **5.** | 36 |
| **6.** | 8 | **7.** | 85 | **8.** | 18 | **9.** | 60 | **10.** | 36 |
| **11.** | 66 | **12.** | 153 | **13.** | 20 | **14.** | 70 | **15.** | 30 |
| **16.** | 42 | **17.** | 18 | **18.** | 15 | **19.** | 28 | **20.** | 40 |

## USING EQUIVALENT FRACTIONS TO ADD AND SUBTRACT

When we first looked at addition and subtraction of fractional numbers, it was emphatically stated that addition and subtraction cannot take place unless the denominators are the same. Unfortunately, the likelihood of all fractions that one wishes to add having identical denominators is slim. Fractions just are not generally that obliging. That fact, in case you were wondering, is responsible for the three sections that came between our first look at addition and subtraction of fractional numbers and this one. Consider the following problem.

*Model Problem*

Mr. Anderson painted $\frac{3}{8}$ of his garage. Mrs. Anderson then painted another $\frac{1}{6}$. How much of the garage was painted?

Since one painted a part of the garage, and then the other did another part of the same job, to find out how much of the job was done altogether, addition is called for:

$$\frac{3}{8} + \frac{1}{6} = ?$$

You will recall that this addition, as it stands, is impossible to do. The denominators are not the same.

Now, however, you know that for any fraction, equivalent fractions can be written. Look, then, at the denominators of the two fractions in question. They are 8 and 6. We find that the least common multiple of 8

$$\frac{}{8} + \frac{}{6}$$

$$LCM = 24$$

and 6 is 24. Having found that, we proceed to write equivalent fractions for $\frac{3}{8}$ and $\frac{1}{6}$, using 24 as the **Least Common Denominator** (abbreviated LCD).

$$\frac{3}{8} = \frac{?}{24}$$

$$\frac{1}{6} = \frac{?}{24}$$

Once the equivalent fractions are written, they may be added to find the sum.

$$\frac{3}{8} = \frac{9}{24}$$
$$+\frac{1}{6} = \frac{4}{24}$$
$$\overline{\phantom{+} \frac{13}{24}}$$

Now let's review the steps for adding fractions with unlike denominators:

1. Find the LCM of the denominators.

2. Make the LCM the denominator (LCD) to use for writing equivalent fractions.

3. Write equivalent fractions.

4. Add the equivalent fractions to find the sum.

The two model examples below are done for you to show two different styles of notation. Decide on the style that will work best for you, and then stick with it.

*Model Example 1*

$$\frac{1}{3} + \frac{2}{5} + ?$$

LCM for 3 and 5 = 15

LCD = 15ths

Write equivalent fractions:

$$\frac{1}{3} = \frac{5}{15}$$
$$+\frac{2}{5} = \frac{6}{15}$$
$$\overline{\phantom{+} \frac{11}{15}}$$

*Model Example 2*

$$\frac{4}{7} + \frac{1}{5} = ?$$

LCM for 7 and 5 = 35

LCD = 35ths

$$\frac{\phantom{20}}{35} + \frac{\phantom{7}}{35} = \frac{\phantom{27}}{35}$$

$$\frac{20}{35} + \frac{7}{35} = \frac{27}{35}$$

Subtraction of fractional numbers is, once again, identical to addition, so that once the denominators are the same (by using equivalent fractions if necessary) you simply subtract the numerators.

Add or subtract.

1) $\frac{2}{3} + \frac{1}{4} = ?$     2) $\frac{1}{3} + \frac{1}{5} = ?$     3) $\frac{7}{8} - \frac{3}{5} = ?$     4) $\frac{9}{10} - \frac{5}{6} = ?$

5) $\frac{3}{8} + \frac{5}{12} = ?$     6) $\frac{3}{7} + \frac{5}{14} = ?$     7) $\frac{1}{2} + \frac{1}{9} = ?$     8) $\frac{3}{4} - \frac{7}{12} = ?$

9) $\frac{9}{13} - \frac{1}{2} = ?$     10) $\frac{3}{11} + \frac{5}{44} = ?$     11) $\frac{2}{5} + \frac{1}{9} = ?$     12) $\frac{17}{18} - \frac{11}{12} = ?$

## Answers

1. $\frac{11}{12}$     2. $\frac{8}{15}$     3. $\frac{11}{40}$     4. $\frac{2}{30}$ or $\frac{1}{15}$     5. $\frac{19}{24}$     6. $\frac{11}{14}$

7. $\frac{11}{18}$     8. $\frac{2}{12}$ or $\frac{1}{6}$     9. $\frac{5}{26}$     10. $\frac{17}{44}$     11. $\frac{38}{45}$     12. $\frac{1}{36}$

## EXPRESSING FRACTIONS IN LOWEST TERMS

We have already discussed that the same fractional number can be written in many different ways (equivalent fractions). In many applications — and especially on the GED test — it is often necessary to express a fraction in its lowest terms. Lowest terms means the smallest numerator and denominator with which it is possible to write a fraction equivalent to the one in question. Here is an example:

$\frac{24}{32}$     can be written as an equivalent fraction by dividing the numerator and the denominator by 2. Doing so, we get

$\frac{12}{16}$     But this fraction can have its numerator and denominator divided by 2, in which case we get

$\frac{6}{8}$     You will note that 2 is a factor of both 6 and 8. Dividing both by 2, we get a result of

$\frac{3}{4}$     There is no number, save 1, that can be divided exactly into 3 and into 4. That means that $\frac{3}{4}$ is the lowest terms in which $\frac{24}{32}$ can be expressed.

The method described above required finding a common factor in the numerator and denominator, and then dividing both by that amount. The process was repeated and repeated until no common factor of both the numerator and denominator remained. This method works fine, but may be unnecessarily time consuming. Do you remember what is meant by greatest common factor? (See page 81.) Let's go back to the original fraction, $\frac{24}{32}$. What is the GCF for 24 and 32? If you calculated it to be 8, you are correct. 8 is the largest number by which both 24 and 32 can be divided exactly.

Having found the greatest common factor, divide both numerator and denominator by it:

$$\frac{24 \div 8}{32 \div 8} = \frac{3}{4}$$

Remember, when a number is divided by 1 (expressed as $\frac{8}{8}$ in this case), its value does not change. That means that $\frac{3}{4}$ is equivalent to $\frac{24}{32}$, and is, in fact, that fraction expressed in lowest (or simplest) terms.

Express the following fractions in lowest terms.

1) $\frac{8}{10} =$ _____     2) $\frac{16}{32} =$ _____     3) $\frac{15}{20} =$ _____     4) $\frac{18}{24} =$ _____

5) $\frac{6}{15} =$ _____     6) $\frac{12}{18} =$ _____     7) $\frac{24}{30} =$ _____     8) $\frac{25}{45} =$ _____

9) $\frac{40}{50} =$ _____     10) $\frac{32}{36} =$ _____     11) $\frac{54}{63} =$ _____     12) $\frac{21}{28} =$ _____

13) $\frac{56}{80} =$ _____     14) $\frac{45}{75} =$ _____     15) $\frac{25}{50} =$ _____     16) $\frac{75}{100} =$ _____

### Answers

**1.** $\frac{4}{5}$    **2.** $\frac{1}{2}$    **3.** $\frac{3}{4}$    **4.** $\frac{3}{4}$    **5.** $\frac{2}{5}$    **6.** $\frac{2}{3}$    **7.** $\frac{4}{5}$    **8.** $\frac{5}{9}$

**9.** $\frac{4}{5}$    **10.** $\frac{8}{9}$    **11.** $\frac{6}{7}$    **12.** $\frac{3}{4}$    **13.** $\frac{7}{10}$    **14.** $\frac{3}{5}$    **15.** $\frac{1}{2}$    **16.** $\frac{3}{4}$

It is customary for solutions to fractional arithmetic to be expressed in lowest terms. Some books refer to expressing fractions in lowest terms as "reducing." Even though that term was widely used not so long ago, be wary. When fractions are expressed in lowest terms, they are not reduced (made smaller). Rather, the sizes of the numerator and denominator are reduced. The fractional part represented, however, stays the same size.

Fractional arithmetic answers on the GED examination are usually expressed in lowest terms. It is therefore a good idea to get into the habit of always expressing the answers to any computations that you do in that form.

Solve and express your answers in lowest terms.

1) $\frac{2}{4} + \frac{1}{3} =$ _____

2) $\frac{6}{8} + \frac{1}{4} =$ _____

3) $\frac{1}{3} + \frac{2}{8} =$ _____

4) $\frac{2}{6} + \frac{1}{9} =$ _____

5) $\frac{5}{12} + \frac{3}{12} =$ _____

6) $\frac{3}{15} + \frac{6}{15} =$ _____

7) $\frac{11}{12} - \frac{1}{4} =$ _____

8) $\frac{17}{20} - \frac{1}{4} =$ _____

9) $\frac{7}{18} - \frac{1}{6} =$ _____

10) $\frac{1}{3} + \frac{2}{7} =$ _____

11) $\frac{19}{20} - \frac{3}{4} =$ _____

12) $\frac{1}{6} + \frac{1}{2} =$ _____

13) $\frac{3}{5} - \frac{4}{15} =$ _____

14) $\frac{23}{24} - \frac{1}{8} =$ _____

15) $\frac{17}{18} - \frac{1}{2} =$ _____

## Answers

1. $\frac{5}{6}$   2. $1$   3. $\frac{2}{3}$   4. $\frac{4}{9}$   5. $\frac{2}{3}$   6. $\frac{3}{5}$   7. $\frac{2}{3}$   8. $\frac{3}{5}$

9. $\frac{2}{9}$   10. $\frac{13}{21}$   11. $\frac{1}{5}$   12. $\frac{2}{3}$   13. $\frac{1}{3}$   14. $\frac{5}{6}$   15. $\frac{4}{9}$

You will find additional practice on page 269.

# MULTIPLYING FRACTIONS

Multiplication of fractional numbers does not at first appear to be analogous to multiplication of whole numbers, even though it is performed in almost the same manner. That is because when whole numbers are multiplied together, the product (answer) is greater than those numbers. When fractional numbers are multiplied together, however, the product is smaller. To understand this fact, substitute the word "of" for the times sign in a whole number multiplication and then in a fractional one:

$3 \times 4$  Look at the four. Change the $\times$ to *of*.

$3$ of $4$  Here are three of them.

$3$ 4's $= 12$  Three fours make twelve.

Now see what happens with fractional numbers:

$\frac{1}{2} \times \frac{1}{2}$  Look at the second one-half. Change the $\times$ to *of*.

$\frac{1}{2}$ of $\frac{1}{2}$  Here is one-half of one-half.

$\frac{1}{2}$ of $\frac{1}{2} = \frac{1}{4}$  Half of one-half is one-fourth.

As you can see from the illustration on the previous page, fractional multiplication may be thought of as taking a part of a part of something. When taking a part of a part of something, it is only to be expected that that part will be smaller than the original part.

Multiplication of fractional numbers is accomplished by multiplying numerator by numerator and denominator by denominator. Examine the model problem below.

*Model Problem*

$$\frac{2}{3} \times \frac{5}{7} = \frac{2 \times 5}{3 \times 7} = \frac{10}{21}$$

Multiply the following, and express the products in lowest terms.

1) $\frac{2}{3} \times \frac{3}{4} =$ _____

2) $\frac{5}{8} \times \frac{4}{5} =$ _____

3) $\frac{3}{7} \times \frac{4}{9} =$ _____

4) $\frac{5}{8} \times \frac{4}{7} =$ _____

5) $\frac{3}{8} \times \frac{1}{3} =$ _____

6) $\frac{3}{4} \times \frac{5}{8} =$ _____

7) $\frac{2}{11} \times \frac{6}{7} =$ _____

8) $\frac{1}{7} \times \frac{1}{9} =$ _____

9) $\frac{3}{10} \times \frac{5}{6} =$ _____

10) $\frac{2}{13} \times \frac{5}{11} =$ _____

11) $\frac{4}{5} \times \frac{3}{8} =$ _____

12) $\frac{1}{2} \times \frac{3}{4} =$ _____

13) $\frac{5}{6} \times \frac{1}{3} =$ _____

14) $\frac{2}{7} \times \frac{4}{11} =$ _____

15) $\frac{5}{8} \times \frac{1}{6} =$ _____

## Answers

1. $\frac{1}{2}$  2. $\frac{1}{2}$  3. $\frac{4}{21}$  4. $\frac{5}{14}$  5. $\frac{1}{8}$  6. $\frac{15}{32}$  7. $\frac{12}{77}$  8. $\frac{1}{63}$

9. $\frac{1}{4}$  10. $\frac{10}{143}$  11. $\frac{3}{10}$  12. $\frac{3}{8}$  13. $\frac{5}{18}$  14. $\frac{8}{77}$  15. $\frac{5}{48}$

# CANCELLING

A technique which makes it somewhat easier to multiply two fractions and express the results in lowest terms is known as **cancelling**. Cancelling is really a device which permits you to assure the product of two fractions will be in lowest terms before even multiplying them. Here is how it works:

*Model Example 1*

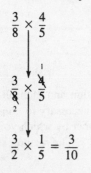

Pretend that you are attempting to express a fraction in lowest terms. You would then seek to find the greatest common factor in the numerator and the denominator. Having found it, you would divide numerator and denominator by that number. When fractions are being multiplied together, you may seek to divide common factors out of either or all numerators and denominators, whether or not they are parts of the same fraction.

*Model Example 2*

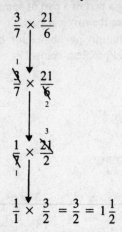

3 is the GCF for 3 and 6 . . .

7 is GCF for 7 and 21.

$$\frac{1}{1} \times \frac{3}{2} = \frac{3}{2} = 1\frac{1}{2}$$

Cancel before multiplying, if possible. If your product is not in lowest terms, check back to see what else you could have cancelled.

1) $\frac{3}{4} \times \frac{5}{9} =$ _____

2) $\frac{4}{7} \times \frac{3}{8} =$ _____

3) $\frac{5}{11} \times \frac{3}{10} =$ _____

4) $\frac{7}{12} \times \frac{6}{11} =$ _____

5) $\frac{1}{9} \times \frac{3}{8} =$ _____

6) $\frac{8}{15} \times \frac{5}{12} =$ _____

7) $\frac{8}{14} \times \frac{7}{10} =$ _____

8) $\frac{9}{16} \times \frac{4}{6} =$ _____

9) $\frac{12}{24} \times \frac{3}{10} =$ _____

10) $\frac{3}{7} \times \frac{14}{21} =$ _____

11) $\frac{9}{32} \times \frac{16}{12} =$ _____

12) $\frac{7}{18} \times \frac{9}{21} =$ _____

13) $\frac{18}{25} \times \frac{5}{9} \times \frac{5}{2} =$ _____

14) $\frac{1}{9} \times \frac{3}{8} \times \frac{3}{2} =$ _____

15) $\frac{12}{24} \times \frac{8}{26} \times \frac{3}{5} =$ _____

## Answers

1. $\frac{5}{12}$   2. $\frac{3}{14}$   3. $\frac{3}{22}$   4. $\frac{7}{22}$   5. $\frac{1}{6}$   6. $\frac{2}{9}$   7. $\frac{2}{5}$   8. $\frac{3}{8}$

9. $\frac{3}{16}$   10. $\frac{2}{7}$   11. $\frac{3}{8}$   12. $\frac{1}{6}$   13. 1   14. $\frac{1}{3}$   15. $\frac{1}{10}$

You will find additional practice on page 269.

# DIVISION OF FRACTIONS

Division of fractional numbers takes advantage of the fact that division and multiplication are reciprocal operations. To understand what that means, it is necessary to consider the meaning of reciprocals. The reciprocal of a number is the number by which you must multiply to get a product of one. The reciprocal of 2 is $\frac{1}{2}$: $2 \times \frac{1}{2} = 1$. The reciprocal of $\frac{1}{4}$ is 4. $\frac{1}{4} \times 4 = 1$.

Name the reciprocal.

1) 7      2) 9      3) 23      4) 67      5) $\frac{1}{8}$      6) $\frac{1}{7}$      7) $\frac{1}{25}$

8) $\frac{1}{235}$      9) $\frac{2}{3}$      10) $\frac{3}{4}$      11) $\frac{5}{17}$      12) $\frac{7}{36}$      13) $\frac{6}{93}$

## Answers

**1.** $\frac{1}{7}$    **2.** $\frac{1}{9}$    **3.** $\frac{1}{23}$    **4.** $\frac{1}{67}$    **5.** 8    **6.** 7    **7.** 25

**8.** 235    **9.** $\frac{3}{2}$    **10.** $\frac{4}{3}$    **11.** $\frac{17}{5}$    **12.** $\frac{36}{7}$    **13.** $\frac{93}{6}$

Any division example is capable of being solved as a multiplication, where the reciprocal of the divisor is used to multiply the dividend. Consider the two division examples below. Each has been rewritten as a multiplication by the reciprocal of the divisor.

*Model Example 1*          *Model Example 2*

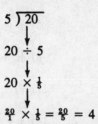

$$8 \div 2$$
$$\downarrow$$
$$8 \times \tfrac{1}{2}$$
$$\downarrow$$
$$\tfrac{8}{1} \times \tfrac{1}{2} = \tfrac{8}{2} = 4$$

$$5 \,\overline{)\,20}$$
$$\downarrow$$
$$20 \div 5$$
$$\downarrow$$
$$20 \times \tfrac{1}{5}$$
$$\downarrow$$
$$\tfrac{20}{1} \times \tfrac{1}{5} = \tfrac{20}{5} = 4$$

Note in the model examples that it is always the number being **divided by** whose reciprocal is used. Look at the divisions below. Change each to a reciprocal multiplication, and solve. The numbers are familiar ones, so that you should have no difficulty in determining whether your answers are correct. It is the method that is of concern here.

1) $12 \div 3 = \frac{12}{1} \times \underline{\quad} = \underline{\quad}$

2) $6 \,\overline{)\,30} = 30 \div \underline{\quad} = \frac{30}{1} \times \underline{\quad} = \underline{\quad}$

3) $15 \div 5 = \frac{15}{1} \times \underline{\quad} = \underline{\quad}$

4) $18 \div 9 = \frac{18}{1} \times \underline{\quad} = \underline{\quad}$

5) $32 \div 4 = \underline{\quad} \times \underline{\quad} = \underline{\quad}$

6) $21 \div 3 = \underline{\quad} \times \underline{\quad} = \underline{\quad}$

7) $63 \div 7 = \underline{\quad} \times \underline{\quad} = \underline{\quad}$

## Answers

**1.** $\frac{1}{3}$, 4      **2.** $\frac{1}{6}$, 5      **3.** $\frac{1}{5}$, 3      **4.** $\frac{1}{9}$, 2

**5.** $\frac{32}{1}$, $\frac{1}{4}$, 8      **6.** $\frac{21}{1}$, $\frac{1}{3}$, 7      **7.** $\frac{63}{1}$, $\frac{1}{7}$, 9

Fractional division is identical to the reciprocal multiplication form shown on page 89. In order to divide one fraction by another, we multiply by the reciprocal of the divisor. Note that in the standard form in which fractional multiplications are written, the divisor is always the second numeral. That means that it is always the second numeral whose reciprocal you must use to multiply by. Look at the model examples.

*Model Example 1*

$$\frac{3}{4} \div \frac{2}{3}$$

$$\frac{3}{4} \times \frac{3}{2}$$

$$\frac{3}{4} \times \frac{3}{2} = \frac{9}{8} = 1\frac{1}{8}$$

*Model Example 2*

$$\frac{5}{14} \div \frac{1}{2}$$

$$\frac{5}{14} \times \frac{2}{1}$$

$$\frac{5}{\underset{7}{14}} \times \frac{\overset{1}{2}}{1} = \frac{5}{7}$$

Divide. Express the quotients in lowest terms.

1) $\frac{1}{2} \div \frac{1}{4} =$ _____

2) $\frac{3}{5} \div \frac{2}{7} =$ _____

3) $\frac{6}{11} \div \frac{4}{5} =$ _____

4) $\frac{3}{8} \div \frac{3}{4} =$ _____

5) $\frac{6}{7} \div \frac{12}{14} =$ _____

6) $\frac{5}{9} \div \frac{4}{5} =$ _____

7) $\frac{7}{12} \div \frac{3}{4} =$ _____

8) $\frac{11}{16} \div \frac{22}{32} =$ _____

9) $\frac{5}{8} \div \frac{10}{11} =$ _____

10) $\frac{9}{16} \div \frac{2}{3} =$ _____

11) $\frac{7}{13} \div \frac{5}{6} =$ _____

12) $\frac{2}{3} \div \frac{1}{4} =$ _____

13) $\frac{4}{5} \div \frac{1}{3} =$ _____

14) $\frac{2}{3} \div \frac{3}{4} =$ _____

15) $\frac{1}{5} \div \frac{3}{8} =$ _____

16) $\frac{9}{10} \div \frac{11}{12} =$ _____

17) $\frac{5}{9} \div \frac{6}{7} =$ _____

18) $\frac{1}{2} \div \frac{5}{7} =$ _____

19) $\frac{2}{7} \div \frac{5}{8} =$ _____

20) $\frac{1}{4} \div \frac{3}{8} =$ _____

21) $\frac{4}{9} \div \frac{3}{5} =$ _____

## Answers

1. 2
2. $2\frac{1}{10}$
3. $\frac{15}{22}$
4. $\frac{1}{2}$
5. 1
6. $\frac{25}{36}$
7. $\frac{7}{9}$
8. 1
9. $\frac{11}{12}$
10. $\frac{27}{32}$
11. $\frac{42}{65}$
12. $2\frac{2}{3}$
13. $2\frac{2}{5}$
14. $\frac{8}{9}$
15. $\frac{8}{15}$
16. $\frac{54}{55}$
17. $\frac{35}{54}$
18. $\frac{7}{10}$
19. $\frac{12}{35}$
20. $\frac{2}{3}$
21. $\frac{20}{27}$

You will find additional practice on page 270.

# MIXED NUMERALS

A numeral consisting of a digit (or several digits) and a fraction, is known as a mixed numeral. 2 is a digit. $\frac{1}{2}$ is a fraction. $2\frac{1}{2}$ (read two and one-half) is a mixed numeral. Any fraction whose denominator is smaller than its numerator may be written as a whole or mixed numeral. The transformation is accomplished by dividing the numerator by the denominator. Look at the model examples on the next page.

*Model Example 1*

$$\frac{23}{2}$$
$$\downarrow$$
$$2\,\overline{)\,23}$$
$$\downarrow$$
$$11\tfrac{1}{2}$$

*Model Example 2*

$$\frac{32}{4}$$
$$\downarrow$$
$$4\,\overline{)\,32}$$
$$\downarrow$$
$$8$$

# ADDING WITH MIXED NUMERALS

Since mixed numerals contain both a whole number portion and a fractional number portion, the technique used in adding them consists of treating each component separately. First the fractions are combined in the usual manner. Then the whole numbers are added. It is important that the addition take place in that order: **fractions first; then whole numbers.** That is so since, if the fractional addition yields a mixed numeral, the whole number portion of it may be incorporated in the addition of the whole numbers. Examine the model examples.

*Model Example 1*

$$3\tfrac{1}{8} + 4\tfrac{3}{8}$$
$$\downarrow$$
$$3\tfrac{1}{8}$$
$$+4\tfrac{3}{8}$$
$$\overline{\phantom{0}}$$
$$\tfrac{4}{8}$$
$$\downarrow$$
$$3\tfrac{1}{8}$$
$$+4\tfrac{3}{8}$$
$$\overline{7\tfrac{4}{8}} \to 7\tfrac{1}{2}$$

*Model Example 2*

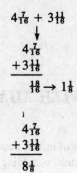

$$4\tfrac{7}{16} + 3\tfrac{11}{16}$$
$$\downarrow$$
$$4\tfrac{7}{16}$$
$$+3\tfrac{11}{16}$$
$$\overline{\phantom{0}}$$
$$\tfrac{18}{16} \to 1\tfrac{1}{8}$$

$$4\tfrac{7}{16}$$
$$+3\tfrac{11}{16}$$
$$\overline{8\tfrac{1}{8}}$$

*Model Example 3*

$$5\tfrac{1}{8} \;\to\; 5\tfrac{2}{16} \;\to\; 5\tfrac{2}{16}$$
$$+3\tfrac{7}{16} \;\to\; 3\tfrac{7}{16} \;\to\; 3\tfrac{7}{16}$$
$$\overline{\phantom{0}} \qquad \overline{\tfrac{9}{16}} \qquad \overline{8\tfrac{9}{16}}$$

Note that the fractions must have like denominators to be added.

*Model Example 4*

$$3\tfrac{9}{10} \to 3\tfrac{18}{20} \to 3\tfrac{18}{20} \qquad \to 3\tfrac{18}{20} \to 3\tfrac{18}{20}$$
$$+4\tfrac{17}{20} \to 4\tfrac{17}{20} \to 4\tfrac{17}{20} \qquad \to 4\tfrac{17}{20} \to 4\tfrac{17}{20}$$
$$\overline{\phantom{0}} \qquad \overline{\tfrac{35}{20} = 1\tfrac{3}{4}} \quad \overline{\tfrac{3}{4}} \quad \overline{8\tfrac{3}{4}}$$

Add. Express the sum as a mixed numeral in lowest terms.

| 1) $4\frac{1}{3}$ $+2\frac{1}{3}$ | 2) $5\frac{2}{8}$ $+2\frac{3}{8}$ | 3) $3\frac{2}{7}$ $+4\frac{3}{7}$ | 4) $1\frac{5}{8}$ $+6\frac{1}{8}$ | 5) $3\frac{1}{8}$ $+2\frac{2}{8}$ |
|---|---|---|---|---|
| 6) $4\frac{1}{5}$ $+3\frac{3}{10}$ | 7) $6\frac{1}{7}$ $+4\frac{5}{21}$ | 8) $3\frac{1}{8}$ $+4\frac{5}{16}$ | 9) $2\frac{1}{4}$ $+3\frac{1}{6}$ | 10) $4\frac{5}{9}$ $+3\frac{1}{4}$ |
| 11) $6\frac{1}{3}$ $+5\frac{1}{4}$ | 12) $4\frac{2}{7}$ $+3\frac{1}{5}$ | 13) $3\frac{5}{8}$ $+2\frac{1}{2}$ | 14) $2\frac{7}{9}$ $+6\frac{5}{8}$ | 15) $7\frac{3}{4}$ $+5\frac{5}{8}$ |
| 16) $4\frac{7}{8}$ $+3\frac{5}{8}$ | 17) $3\frac{8}{11}$ $+2\frac{3}{4}$ | 18) $5\frac{5}{8}$ $+6\frac{7}{8}$ | 19) $2\frac{5}{8}$ $+3\frac{3}{4}$ | 20) $4\frac{9}{10}$ $+2\frac{7}{8}$ |

## Answers

| 1. $6\frac{2}{3}$ | 2. $7\frac{5}{8}$ | 3. $7\frac{5}{7}$ | 4. $7\frac{3}{4}$ | 5. $5\frac{3}{8}$ |
|---|---|---|---|---|
| 6. $7\frac{1}{2}$ | 7. $10\frac{8}{21}$ | 8. $7\frac{7}{16}$ | 9. $5\frac{5}{12}$ | 10. $7\frac{29}{36}$ |
| 11. $11\frac{7}{12}$ | 12. $7\frac{17}{35}$ | 13. $6\frac{1}{8}$ | 14. $9\frac{11}{18}$ | 15. $13\frac{3}{12}$ |
| 16. $8\frac{17}{24}$ | 17. $6\frac{21}{44}$ | 18. $12\frac{55}{72}$ | 19. $6\frac{7}{12}$ | 20. $7\frac{31}{40}$ |

## *SUBTRACTING WITH MIXED NUMERALS*

Up to a point, subtraction of mixed numerals is the same as addition of mixed numerals, except that you subtract instead of adding. Try the following subtractions, subtracting the fractions first, and then the whole numbers.

| 1) $5\frac{7}{8}$ $-3\frac{1}{8}$ | 2) $9\frac{4}{5}$ $-3\frac{1}{6}$ | 3) $8\frac{3}{4}$ $-5\frac{2}{3}$ | 4) $6\frac{11}{16}$ $-2\frac{3}{8}$ |
|---|---|---|---|
| 5) $8\frac{3}{5}$ $-4\frac{1}{7}$ | 6) $10\frac{9}{10}$ $-4\frac{3}{8}$ | 7) $6\frac{11}{12}$ $-2\frac{1}{2}$ | 8) $9\frac{5}{8}$ $-4\frac{1}{3}$ |

## Answers

| 1. $2\frac{3}{4}$ | 2. $6\frac{19}{30}$ | 3. $3\frac{1}{12}$ | 4. $4\frac{5}{16}$ |
|---|---|---|---|
| 5. $4\frac{16}{35}$ | 6. $6\frac{21}{40}$ | 7. $4\frac{5}{12}$ | 8. $5\frac{1}{2}$ |

Not all fractional subtractions, however, are quite that straightforward. Consider, for example, the following model example.

*Model Example*

$5\frac{1}{4}$      You should notice that since $\frac{3}{4}$ is larger than $\frac{1}{4}$, it cannot be subtracted
$-2\frac{3}{4}$      from it.*

In order to be able to subtract one fraction from the other, it is necessary to rename one from the five as a fraction, $\frac{4}{4}$.

$$
\begin{array}{c}
5\frac{1}{4} \\
-2\frac{3}{4}
\end{array}
\longrightarrow \quad 4 + \frac{4}{4} + \frac{1}{4} \quad \longrightarrow
\begin{array}{c}
4\frac{5}{4} \\
-2\frac{3}{4}
\end{array}
$$

Now, of course, since there is a larger fraction on top than on the bottom, it is possible to subtract:

$$
\begin{array}{c}
4\frac{5}{4} \\
-2\frac{3}{4} \\
\hline
2\frac{2}{4} = 2\frac{1}{2}
\end{array}
$$

Using the model problem above as your guide, subtract the following.

1)  $\begin{array}{c} 6\frac{3}{8} \\ -2\frac{5}{8} \end{array}$   $\left|\begin{array}{c} 5 + \frac{8}{8} + \frac{3}{8} \\ -2\frac{5}{8} \end{array}\right.$   $\left|\begin{array}{c} 5\frac{11}{8} \\ -2\frac{5}{8} \\ \hline 3\frac{6}{8} = \underline{\hspace{1cm}} \end{array}\right.$

2)  $\begin{array}{c} 7\frac{2}{5} \\ -1\frac{4}{5} \end{array}$

3)  $\begin{array}{c} 6\frac{7}{16} \\ -3\frac{11}{16} \end{array}$

4)  $\begin{array}{c} 9\frac{1}{3} \\ -5\frac{2}{3} \end{array}$

5)  $\begin{array}{c} 6\frac{3}{7} \\ -3\frac{6}{7} \end{array}$

6)  $\begin{array}{c} 8\frac{1}{4} \\ -5\frac{3}{4} \end{array}$

7)  $\begin{array}{c} 7\frac{1}{8} \\ -2\frac{5}{8} \end{array}$

8)  $\begin{array}{c} 6\frac{1}{9} \\ -4\frac{8}{9} \end{array}$

9)  $\begin{array}{c} 9\frac{2}{3} \\ -8\frac{3}{4} \end{array}$

## Answers

| | | | | |
|---|---|---|---|---|
| **1.** $3\frac{3}{4}$ | **2.** $5\frac{3}{5}$ | **3.** $2\frac{3}{4}$ | **4.** $3\frac{2}{3}$ | **5.** $2\frac{4}{7}$ |
| **6.** $2\frac{1}{2}$ | **7.** $4\frac{1}{2}$ | **8.** $1\frac{2}{9}$ | **9.** $\frac{5}{6}$ | |

*At least, it cannot be subtracted from it and yield a positive value, which at this point is what we are interested in maintaining. We will consider negative numbers later in this book.

Of course, unlike the subtractions shown on page 93, there is also no guarantee that the denominators of the fractional parts of the mixed numerals are going to be identical. The next model problems put together all of the steps that may be encountered in a mixed numeral subtraction.

*Model Problem 1*

$$7\frac{2}{5} \longrightarrow 7\frac{16}{40} \longrightarrow 6\frac{40}{40} + \frac{16}{40} \longrightarrow 6\frac{56}{40}$$
$$-3\frac{5}{8} \longrightarrow -3\frac{25}{40} \longrightarrow\ \ \ \ \ \ \ \ \ \ \ \ \ \ \ \ \ \ \ \ \ -3\frac{25}{40}$$
$$3\frac{31}{40}$$

*Model Problem 2*

$$8\frac{2}{3} \longrightarrow 8\frac{8}{12} \longrightarrow 7\frac{12}{12} + \frac{8}{12} \longrightarrow 7\frac{20}{12}$$
$$-5\frac{3}{4} \longrightarrow -5\frac{9}{12} \longrightarrow\ \ \ \ \ \ \ \ \ \ \ \ \ \ \ \ \ \ \ \ \ -5\frac{9}{12}$$
$$2\frac{11}{12}$$

Solve the following mixed numeral subtractions.

| 1) $4\frac{7}{8}$ | 2) $6\frac{3}{8}$ | 3) $8\frac{2}{3}$ | 4) $5\frac{3}{8}$ | 5) $6\frac{1}{4}$ |
|---|---|---|---|---|
| $-2\frac{3}{8}$ | $-2\frac{3}{4}$ | $-5\frac{1}{4}$ | $-2\frac{2}{3}$ | $-4\frac{1}{2}$ |

| 6) $7\frac{1}{5}$ | 7) $6\frac{3}{8}$ | 8) $11\frac{2}{7}$ | 9) $12\frac{1}{3}$ | 10) $5\frac{1}{8}$ |
|---|---|---|---|---|
| $-3\frac{1}{2}$ | $-2\frac{3}{4}$ | $-8\frac{4}{5}$ | $-5\frac{7}{12}$ | $-3\frac{7}{8}$ |

| 11) $6\frac{1}{8}$ | 12) $12\frac{1}{2}$ | 13) $8\frac{3}{10}$ | 14) $9\frac{5}{13}$ | 15) $7\frac{1}{3}$ |
|---|---|---|---|---|
| $-4\frac{9}{16}$ | $-11\frac{7}{12}$ | $-4\frac{5}{8}$ | $-8\frac{3}{4}$ | $-6\frac{5}{7}$ |

**Answers**

| 1. $2\frac{1}{2}$ | 2. $4\frac{1}{12}$ | 3. $3\frac{5}{12}$ | 4. $2\frac{17}{24}$ | 5. $1\frac{3}{4}$ |
|---|---|---|---|---|
| 6. $3\frac{7}{10}$ | 7. $3\frac{5}{8}$ | 8. $2\frac{17}{35}$ | 9. $6\frac{3}{4}$ | 10. $1\frac{1}{4}$ |
| 11. $1\frac{29}{48}$ | 12. $\frac{11}{12}$ | 13. $3\frac{27}{40}$ | 14. $\frac{33}{52}$ | 15. $\frac{13}{21}$ |

You will find additional practice on page 270.

# MULTIPLICATION AND DIVISION WITH MIXED NUMERALS

Unlike addition and subtraction, multiplication and division of mixed numerals is not readily carried out by working first with the fractions and then with the integers. Rather, it is necessary to first convert the entire mixed numeral to a fraction. Then, the fractions are multiplied or divided in the normal fashion.

To change a mixed numeral to a fraction, follow the formula below:

**Denominator × Integer + Numerator**

Change $3\frac{5}{8}$ to a fraction:

$3\frac{5}{8}$ ← start        $8 \times 3 = 24$        $\therefore\ 3\frac{5}{8} = \frac{29}{8}$

$24 + 5 = 29$

Note:   The denominator is unchanged.

First the denominator (8) is multiplied by the integer (3). Then the numerator (5) is added to the product (24). That determines the new numerator (29). The denominator for the new fraction is the same as the old denominator.

Here is another example:

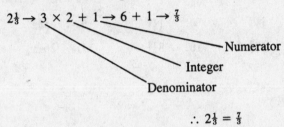

$2\frac{1}{3} \rightarrow 3 \times 2 + 1 \rightarrow 6 + 1 \rightarrow \frac{7}{3}$

Numerator

Integer

Denominator

$\therefore\ 2\frac{1}{3} = \frac{7}{3}$

Express the following mixed numerals as fractions. Refer to the examples above for guidance, if needed.

1) $2\frac{1}{2}$ = _____

2) $3\frac{1}{4}$ = _____

3) $4\frac{1}{5}$ = _____

4) $5\frac{2}{3}$ = _____

5) $6\frac{3}{8}$ = _____

6) $7\frac{1}{5}$ = _____

7) $8\frac{3}{4}$ = _____

8) $9\frac{2}{7}$ = _____

9) $6\frac{7}{8}$ = _____

10) $3\frac{4}{5}$ = _____

11) $5\frac{6}{7}$ = _____

12) $4\frac{7}{12}$ = _____

13) $5\frac{8}{9}$ = _____

14) $2\frac{3}{16}$ = _____

15) $3\frac{5}{9}$ = _____

16) $4\frac{5}{24}$ = _____

17) $4\frac{7}{11}$ = _____

18) $3\frac{7}{18}$ = _____

19) $2\frac{5}{23}$ = _____

20) $6\frac{7}{20}$ = _____

## Answers

1. $\frac{5}{2}$

2. $\frac{13}{4}$

3. $\frac{21}{5}$

4. $\frac{17}{3}$

5. $\frac{51}{8}$

6. $\frac{39}{5}$

7. $\frac{35}{4}$

8. $\frac{65}{7}$

9. $\frac{55}{8}$

10. $\frac{19}{5}$

11. $\frac{41}{7}$

12. $\frac{55}{12}$

13. $\frac{53}{9}$

14. $\frac{35}{16}$

15. $\frac{32}{9}$

16. $\frac{101}{24}$

17. $\frac{51}{11}$

18. $\frac{61}{18}$

19. $\frac{51}{23}$

20. $\frac{127}{20}$

When multiplying or dividing mixed numerals, as previously noted, you must first change those mixed numerals to fractions. Since the fractions' terms will often be large, always try to cancel (if possible) before multiplying.

Change to fractions, then multiply or divide (as indicated).

1) $2\frac{1}{2} \times 3\frac{1}{2} =$ _____  2) $3\frac{1}{4} \times 2\frac{2}{3} =$ _____  3) $4\frac{1}{3} \div 5\frac{1}{2} =$ _____

4) $3\frac{2}{3} \div 2\frac{1}{4} =$ _____  5) $5\frac{5}{8} \times 4\frac{3}{8} =$ _____  6) $2\frac{3}{16} \div 1\frac{5}{8} =$ _____

7) $3\frac{5}{7} \div 2\frac{8}{21} =$ _____  8) $4\frac{5}{8} \times 3\frac{4}{7} =$ _____  9) $4\frac{3}{8} \div 3\frac{7}{12} =$ _____

10) $2\frac{5}{8} \times 3\frac{4}{7} =$ _____  11) $5\frac{3}{4} \times 4\frac{5}{8} =$ _____  12) $3\frac{5}{16} \div 4\frac{13}{15} =$ _____

## Answers

1. $8\frac{3}{4}$  2. $8\frac{2}{3}$  3. $\frac{26}{33}$  4. $1\frac{17}{27}$  5. $25\frac{23}{48}$  6. $1\frac{9}{26}$

7. $1\frac{14}{25}$  8. $17\frac{11}{12}$  9. $1\frac{18}{86}$  10. $8\frac{16}{21}$  11. $26\frac{7}{36}$  12. $\frac{159}{222}$

# FRACTION POST-TEST

Solve the following. Express answers in lowest terms (where appropriate).

1) $\frac{3}{8} + \frac{5}{8} =$ _____  2) $\frac{14}{15} - \frac{4}{15} =$ _____  3) $\frac{7}{8} \times \frac{4}{21} =$ _____

4) $\frac{2}{3} + \frac{3}{8} =$ _____  5) $\frac{3}{4} - \frac{5}{12} =$ _____  6) $\frac{4}{15} \div \frac{2}{3} =$ _____

7) $\frac{8}{13} \div \frac{9}{26} =$ _____  8) $\frac{56}{81} \times \frac{54}{42} =$ _____  9) $\frac{15}{20} = \frac{}{4}$

10) $\frac{6}{7} = \frac{}{42}$  11) $\frac{5}{8} = \frac{25}{\ \ }$  12) $3\frac{5}{8} = \frac{}{8}$

13) $4\frac{6}{7} = \frac{}{7}$  14) $6\frac{1}{4} + 5\frac{3}{8} =$ _____  15) $7\frac{2}{3} - 3\frac{1}{4} =$ _____

16) $4\frac{1}{2} \times 3\frac{1}{3} =$ _____  17) $5\frac{5}{8} \times 2\frac{4}{7} =$ _____  18) $8\frac{3}{4} \div 5\frac{1}{2} =$ _____

19) $6\frac{5}{8} \div 3\frac{7}{12} =$ _____  20) $5\frac{3}{7}$  21) $6\frac{5}{8}$  22) $3\frac{5}{8}$
$\phantom{19)}$  $\quad -2\frac{9}{10}$  $\quad -4\frac{17}{24}$  $\quad +2\frac{5}{8}$

## Answers and Key to Post-test

Following are the answers to the items on the post-test on fractional numbers. They are arranged by the skills which were tested by the various items. Should the results indicate that you need additional practice with any one or more skills, refer to the appropriate page(s) in the chapter, and to the Additional Practice section that goes with the type of skill in question.

| | | | | | | | | | | | |
|---|---|---|---|---|---|---|---|---|---|---|---|
| **1.** | $1\frac{2}{5}$ | **2.** | $\frac{2}{3}$ | **3.** | $\frac{1}{6}$ | **4.** | $1\frac{7}{24}$ | **5.** | $\frac{1}{3}$ | **6.** | $\frac{2}{3}$ |
| **7.** | $1\frac{1}{3}$ | **8.** | $\frac{1}{9}$ | **9.** | $3$ | **10.** | $36$ | **11.** | $45$ | **12.** | $29$ |
| **13.** | $34$ | **14.** | $11\frac{3}{8}$ | **15.** | $4\frac{5}{12}$ | **16.** | $15$ | **17.** | $14\frac{13}{14}$ | **18.** | $1\frac{13}{22}$ |
| **19.** | $1\frac{10}{43}$ | **20.** | $2\frac{37}{70}$ | **21.** | $1\frac{11}{12}$ | **22.** | $6\frac{7}{18}$ | | | | |

| | | |
|---|---|---|
| 1, 4. | Addition | Pages 77–86; 269 |
| 2, 5. | Subtraction | Pages 77–86; 269 |
| 3, 8. | Multiplication | Pages 86–88; 269 |
| 6, 7. | Division | Pages 88–90; 270 |
| 9–11. | Writing equivalent fractions | Pages 78–81; 269 |
| 12, 13. | Mixed numerals as fractions | Pages 90–91 |
| 14, 22. | Mixed numeral addition | Pages 91–92 |
| 15, 20, 21. | Mixed numeral subtraction | Pages 92–94; 270 |
| 16, 17. | Mixed numeral multiplication | Pages 94–96 |
| 18, 19. | Mixed numeral division | Pages 94–96 |

# 4. DECIMAL FRACTIONS

## DECIMAL FRACTION PRE-TEST

Express as a decimal fraction.

1) $\frac{3}{100}$　　　　　2) $\frac{17}{1000}$　　　　　3) $\frac{5}{8}$　　　　　4) $4\frac{4}{5}$

Express as a common fraction in lowest terms, or as a mixed numeral.

5) 2.7　　　　　6) .008　　　　　7) 31.204

Solve the following.

8) $8.3 + .008 + .67 =$ _____　　　9) $56 + .09 + .334 + 6.1 =$ _____

10) $52.36 - 23.89 =$ _____　　　11) $42.3 - 13.7 =$ _____

12) $.07 \times 34 =$ _____　　　13) $.67 \times .89 =$ _____

14) $2.31 \times .0006 =$ _____　　　15) $.07 \overline{)6.986}$　　16) $2.4 \overline{)3801}$

### Answers

| | | | | | | | |
|---|---|---|---|---|---|---|---|
| **1.** | .03 | **2.** | .017 | **3.** | .625 | **4.** | 4.8 |
| **5.** | $2\frac{7}{10}$ | **6.** | $\frac{1}{125}$ | **7.** | $31\frac{51}{250}$ | **8.** | 8.978 |
| **9.** | 62.524 | **10.** | 28.47 | **11.** | 28.6 | **12.** | 2.38 |
| **13.** | .5963 | **14.** | .001386 | **15.** | 99.8 | **16.** | 1583.75 |

Guide your study of this chapter by the skills on this pre-test with which you encountered difficulty. Use the following as your guide:

## WHAT IS A DECIMAL FRACTION?

Having completed our study of common fractions, perhaps you thought that you were through seeing the word fraction for awhile. In fact, even more important to the mathematics of today, is a different kind of fraction — the decimal fraction. What makes decimal fractions so important is that they are a logical rightward extension of the decimal system in which we reckon all whole numbers. Decimal fractions follow all the rules of place value numeration, and can be easily fit together with whole number operations. Two rather recent innovations make decimal fractions particularly significant in our day-to-day lives. One is the fact that pocket calculators, as well as computers, are capable of readily handling fractions when they are in decimal form, but not when they are in common (numerator and denominator) form. Second is that the universal adoption of the metric system for calculating weights and measures may soon make common fractions all but obsolete, with computations taking place with decimals exclusively. Finally, as an additional sidelight, it should be noted that our monetary system is based upon decimal notation, with $0.25 being a quarter of a dollar, $.50 being a half dollar, and so forth.

The word **decimal** means tenth. As you move from left to right across a place-value chart, each place is worth one-tenth as much as the one to its immediate left:

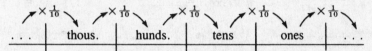

| . . . | thous. | hunds. | tens | ones | . . . |

You will notice in the chart above, that there is no beginning and there is no end. As you move along the chart, each place is multiplied by one-tenth to find the value of the place to the right. After the ones' place, a decimal point is placed. That decimal point is used to separate the whole numbers from the fractions:

| . . . | hundreds | tens | ones | . | tenths | . . . |

All digits to the left of the decimal point are whole numbers. All digits to the right of the decimal point are fractional numbers. Consider the value of each 3 in the place value chart below.

| Write | . . . | 100's | 10's | 1's | .10ths | 100ths | 1000ths | . . . | Value |
|-------|-------|-------|------|-----|--------|--------|---------|-------|-------|
| 300 | | 3 | | | | | | | 300 |
| 30 | | | 3 | | | | | | 30 |
| 3 | | | | 3 | | | | | 3 |
| .3 | | | | | 3 | | | | $\frac{3}{10}$ |
| .03 | | | | | | 3 | | | $\frac{3}{100}$ |
| .003 | | | | | | | 3 | | $\frac{3}{1000}$ |

Examine the model examples below. Then try the exercises that follow.

*Model Examples*

1. $0.5 = \frac{5}{10}$

2. $0.05 = \frac{5}{100}$     **Notice that each denominator is a multiple of ten. Note**
   **that the number of zeroes in the denominator corresponds**
3. $0.005 = \frac{5}{1000}$     **to the number of places to the left of the decimal point.**

4. $0.0005 = \frac{5}{10,000}$

Write the fraction or mixed numeral that means the same thing.

1) .4 = _____     2) .8 = _____     3) .02 = _____

4) .05 = _____     5) .006 = _____     6) .009 = _____

7) .00001 = _____     8) .00004 = _____

Write the decimal fraction that means the same thing.

9) $\frac{5}{10}$ = _____     10) $\frac{7}{10}$ = _____     11) $\frac{3}{100}$ = _____

12) $\frac{1}{1000}$ = _____     13) $\frac{9}{100}$ = _____     14) $\frac{5}{1000}$ = _____

15) $\frac{9}{10}$ = _____     16) $\frac{6}{10,000}$ = _____     17) $\frac{9}{1000}$ = _____

18) $\frac{7}{10,000}$ = _____     19) $\frac{4}{100,000}$ = _____     20) $\frac{8}{1,000,000}$ = _____

## Answers

| | | | | |
|---|---|---|---|---|
| **1.** $\frac{4}{10}$ | **2.** $\frac{8}{10}$ | **3.** $\frac{2}{100}$ | **4.** $\frac{5}{100}$ | **5.** $\frac{6}{1000}$ |
| **6.** $\frac{9}{1000}$ | **7.** $\frac{1}{100,000}$ | **8.** $\frac{4}{100,000}$ | **9.** .5 | **10.** .7 |
| **11.** .03 | **12.** .001 | **13.** .09 | **14.** .005 | **15.** .9 |
| **16.** .0006 | **17.** .009 | **18.** .0007 | **19.** .00004 | **20.** .000008 |

When a decimal fraction contains more than a single digit, it is named by the place occupied by the digit farthest to the right. So, for example, .17 would be read as 17 hundredths, .23 is 23 hundredths, and .024 is 24 thousandths. .345 is read as three hundred forty-five thousandths, and .00216 is two hundred sixteen hundred-thousandths.

Name these decimal fractions.

1) .24 _____     2) .68 _____

3) .069 _____     4) .053 _____

5) .437 _____     6) .619 _____

7) .0085 _____     8) .0136 _____

9) .00148 _____     10) 7.00045 _____

## Answers

| | | |
|---|---|---|
| **1.** | 24 hundredths | **2.** 68 hundredths |
| **3.** | 69 thousandths | **4.** 53 thousandths |
| **5.** | 437 thousandths | **6.** 619 thousandths |

7.   85 ten-thousandths                    8.   136 ten-thousandths

9.   148 hundred-thousandths               10.  7 and 45 hundred-thousandths

# EXPRESSING COMMON FRACTIONS AS DECIMAL FRACTIONS

Certain common fractions are easily expressed as decimal fractions. That is particularly true of common fractions whose denominators are multiples of ten, such as tenths, hundredths, thousandths. Other common fractions can be changed to decimal fractions by first writing equivalent fractions whose denominators are multiples of ten. See the model examples below.

*Model Examples*

1. $\frac{1}{4} = \frac{}{100} \rightarrow \frac{1}{4} = \frac{25}{100} = .25$

   4 does not divide perfectly into 10, but it goes into 100 25 times.

2. $\frac{3}{5} = \frac{}{10} \rightarrow \frac{3}{5} = \frac{6}{10} = .6$

   5 divides perfectly into 10.

3. $\frac{3}{8} = \frac{}{1000} \rightarrow \frac{3}{8} = \frac{375}{1000} = .375$

   8 divides perfectly into neither 10 nor 100. It does fit into 1000 125 times.

Express the following common fractions as decimal fractions.

1) $\frac{3}{4} = \frac{}{100} = $ _____     2) $\frac{1}{2} = \frac{}{10} = $ _____     3) $\frac{2}{5} = \frac{}{10} = $ _____

4) $\frac{5}{8} = \frac{}{1000} = $ _____     5) $\frac{7}{20} = \frac{}{100} = $ _____     6) $\frac{7}{8} = \frac{}{1000} = $ _____

## Answers

1.   .75     2.   .5     3.   .4     4.   .625     5.   .35     6.   .875

As you may have guessed, not all fractions are as obliging as the ones listed above. That is, not all of them will convert quite so readily to equivalent fractions with denominators that are multiples of ten. Fortunately, however, there is a technique that can be employed that will allow any common fraction to be expressed as a decimal. That technique requires dividing the numerator of any fraction by its denominator. Consider the following models.

*Model Examples*

1. $\frac{1}{4} \rightarrow 4\overline{)1} \rightarrow 4\overline{)1.00} \rightarrow 4\overline{)1.00}^{.25}$

To find the decimal equivalent of $\frac{1}{4}$, 1 must be divided by 4. To do so, a decimal point is placed after the 1, and two zeroes are added. (1.00 = 1) Place a decimal point in the quotient over the decimal point in the dividend, and get the decimal .25.

2. $\frac{3}{5} \rightarrow 5\overline{)3} \rightarrow 5\overline{)3.0} \rightarrow 5\overline{)3.0}^{.6}$

To divide 3 by 5, one zero after the decimal point is enough, although adding a second zero after the decimal point will yield the same answer (since .60 = .6). Proceed as in model example 1.

3. $\frac{1}{3} \rightarrow 3\overline{)1} \rightarrow 3\overline{)1.00} \rightarrow 3\overline{)1.00}^{.3\overline{3}}$

No matter how many zeroes are added after the decimal point, 3's will keep appearing in the quotient. The fraction $\frac{1}{3}$ translates to what is known as a "repeating decimal." The bar over the second 3 in the quotient indicates that the 3 keeps repeating.

# ROUNDING DECIMALS

It is often either inconvenient or unnecessary to express a scrupulously accurate quantity. When, for example, estimating the crowd at a baseball game, the fact that 48,143 persons attended is generally an excessively accurate piece of information. It is usually sufficient to say that there were about 48,000 in attendance. 48,000 is the attendance figure rounded to the nearest thousand.

In order to round a number, there are two things that must be considered. First is the place to which the number is to be rounded. Second is the figure in the place immediately to the right of the place to which you wish to round the number. Look at the model examples below.

*Model Examples*

1. Round 34,567 to the nearest hundred.

$$34,567 \longrightarrow 34,567 \longrightarrow 34,600$$

| Place to be rounded to. | Five or larger. | Rounded up to 6. |

2. Round 34,567 to the nearest 10,000.

$$34,567 \longrightarrow 34,567 \longrightarrow 30,000$$

| Place to be rounded to. | Less than five. | Stays a 3. |

3. Round 27.635 to the nearest tenth.

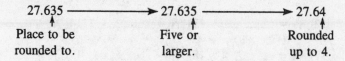

$$27.635 \longrightarrow 27.635 \longrightarrow 27.6$$

| Place to be rounded to. | Less than five. | Stays a 6. |

4. Round 27.635 to the nearest hundredth.

$$27.635 \longrightarrow 27.635 \longrightarrow 27.64$$

| Place to be rounded to. | Five or larger. | Rounded up to 4. |

You may have noticed that when rounding to a whole number, the place rounded to is the last one in which a significant digit appears. Each place to the right contains a zero (note that 34,567 to the nearest 10,000 became 30,000). When rounding a fraction, however, the place to which you rounded is the last digit that will appear in the rounded numeral. No zeroes are inserted to follow it (see model examples 3 and 4).

Try the following exercises in rounding off. If needed, use the model examples (above) as your guide.

Round to the nearest     hundred,          ten,          tenth,          hundredth:

1) 4562.738    _____    _____    _____    _____

2) 328.4929    _____    _____    _____    _____

3) 255.555    _____    _____    _____    _____

4) 8134.8134    _____    _____    _____    _____

5) 2121.9192    _____    _____    _____    _____

## Answers

**1.**  4600, 4560, 4562.7, 4562.74        **2.**  300, 330, 328.5, 328.49

**3.**  300, 260, 255.6, 255.56        **4.**  8100, 8130, 8134.8, 8134.81

**5.**  2100, 2120, 2121.9, 2121.92

Now, in case you have been wondering what a discussion of rounding off was doing in the middle of a discussion of changing common fractions to decimals, here is the answer. Since many fractions do not translate evenly into decimal fractions, it is often necessary to round them off. You already saw that ⅓ translates to .333333 when expressed as a decimal. It is far from being a unique case. It is a good rule of thumb, therefore, to round off decimal fractions that do not work out evenly to the nearest hundredth. In order to round off to the nearest hundredth, however, you must work a decimal out to the thousandths place. It is, after all, the digit in the thousandths place that will tell you whether to leave the digit in the hundredths place as it is, or to round it up to the next higher digit. Bear this in mind when working the exercises on page 104.

Express each common fraction as a decimal fraction. Where necessary, round to the nearest hundredth.

1) $\frac{5}{16}$ = _____  2) $\frac{5}{9}$ = _____  3) $\frac{2}{3}$ = _____  4) $\frac{4}{5}$ = _____  5) $\frac{8}{11}$ = _____

6) $\frac{7}{12}$ = _____  7) $\frac{4}{7}$ = _____  8) $\frac{5}{8}$ = _____  9) $\frac{11}{20}$ = _____  10) $\frac{17}{35}$ = _____

11) $\frac{15}{40}$ = _____  12) $\frac{9}{17}$ = _____  13) $\frac{9}{14}$ = _____  14) $\frac{3}{4}$ = _____  15) $\frac{5}{12}$ = _____

16) $\frac{1}{2}$ = _____  17) $\frac{9}{15}$ = _____  18) $\frac{1}{11}$ = _____  19) $\frac{2}{13}$ = _____  20) $\frac{1}{6}$ = _____

## Answers

| **1.** | .31 | **2.** | .56 | **3.** | .67 | **4.** | .80 | **5.** | .73 | **6.** | .58 | **7.** | .57 |
|---|---|---|---|---|---|---|---|---|---|---|---|---|---|
| **8.** | .625 | **9.** | .55 | **10.** | .49 | **11.** | .375 | **12.** | .53 | **13.** | .64 | **14.** | .75 |
| **15.** | .42 | **16.** | .50 | **17.** | .60 | **18.** | .09 | **19.** | .15 | **20.** | .17 | | |

# ADDITION OF DECIMAL FRACTIONS

There is one and only one key to the addition of decimal fractions and mixed numerals — the decimal points must be lined up one beneath another. The decimal point in the sum is placed beneath the decimal points in the addition, and then the numbers are added in the usual manner. If no decimal point is shown in a numeral, then it is understood that the decimal point appears to the right of the last digit in the numeral. Study the model examples below.

*Model Examples*

1. $2.4 + 1.8 + 3.72 \rightarrow$

| 2.4 | | 2.4 |
|---|---|---|
| 1.8 | $\rightarrow$ | 1.8 |
| 3.72 | | 3.72 |
| . | | 7.92 |

(First place decimal point)   (Then add)

2. $3.6 + .074 + 59 + 16.08 \rightarrow$

| 3.6 | | 3.6 |
|---|---|---|
| .074 | $\rightarrow$ | .074 |
| 59. | | 59. |
| 16.08 | | 16.08 |
| . | | 78.754 |

Now try solving the additions below. Bear in mind that the decimal points must be aligned one beneath the other.

1)   3.4
     2.86
   12.5

2)   5.61
     .007
   21.0

3)   6.81
     .009
   5.73
   24.0

4) 6.2 + 7.5 + 3.82

5) 9.4 + 3.56 + 21.5

6) 18.7 + 17.39 + 6.25

7) 25 + .08 + 3.5

8) 342 + .007

9) 46 + .38 + 2.592

10) 17.2 + 8.09 + 4.6

11) 61.9 + 3.85 + 596 + .35

12) 63 + .34 + 5.21 + .098 + 351.7 + 84.2

13) 19.6 + .342 + 8.29 + .074 + 39

14) .159 + 28.6 + 3.14 + 9 + .8 + .216

15) 4.72 + 15.3 + 69.25 + 47 + .356 + 9 + .05

## Answers

| 1. | 18.76 | 2. | 26.617 | 3. | 36.549 | 4. | 17.52 | 5. | 34.46 |
|---|---|---|---|---|---|---|---|---|---|
| 6. | 42.34 | 7. | 28.58 | 8. | 342.007 | 9. | 48.972 | 10. | 29.89 |
| 11. | 662.1 | 12. | 504.548 | 13. | 67.306 | 14. | 41.915 | 15. | 145.676 |

You will find additional practice on page 270.

# SUBTRACTION OF DECIMAL FRACTIONS

As with addition of decimals, subtraction is accomplished by lining the decimal points up, one beneath the other. With one exception, subtraction would then take place in the usual manner. The exception is illustrated in the model example below.

*Model Example*

8.6 − 3.425      The subtraction is first rewritten in column form, lining up
$\downarrow$      the decimal points one below the other.

  8.6
−3.425      . . . but what are the 2 and the 5 to be subtracted from?

$\downarrow$

  8.600      Zeroes are annexed to the top numeral in order to fill the
−3.425      empty places. The values of 8.6 and 8.600 are identical.

$\downarrow$

  8.600      Now subtraction can take place. Note the decimal point's
−3.425      placement in the difference.

  5.175

Remember: Adding zeroes after the last significant figure to the right of the decimal point does not change the number's value. Consider that .6, .60, and .600 are equivalent to $\frac{6}{10}$, $\frac{60}{100}$, and $\frac{600}{1000}$ respectively. All three of those fractions expressed in lowest terms are equal to $\frac{3}{5}$.

Subtract.

| | | | |
|---|---|---|---|
| 1) 8.69<br>−3.54 | 2) 15.7<br>−5.9 | 3) 36.4<br>−7.8 | 4) 57.9<br>−24.6 |
| 5) 11.35<br>−8.59 | 6) 24.21<br>−19.8 | 7) 81.6<br>−49.83 | 8) 64.2<br>−38.97 |

9) 29.8 − 15.6

10) 34.7 − 8.9

11) 19.5 − 12.71

12) 59.2 − 23.84

13) 125 − .02

14) 67.1 − .875

15) 143.5 − 68.9

16) 234.2 − 7.895

17) 4.60 − .349

18) 7 − .23

19) 14 − 1.761

20) 11 − .2487

## Answers

| | | | | | | | | | |
|---|---|---|---|---|---|---|---|---|---|
| **1.** | 5.15 | **2.** | 9.8 | **3.** | 28.6 | **4.** | 33.3 | **5.** | 2.76 |
| **6.** | 4.41 | **7.** | 31.77 | **8.** | 25.23 | **9.** | 14.2 | **10.** | 25.8 |
| **11.** | 6.79 | **12.** | 35.36 | **13.** | 124.98 | **14.** | 66.225 | **15.** | 74.6 |
| **16.** | 226.305 | **17.** | 4.251 | **18.** | 6.77 | **19.** | 12.239 | **20.** | 10.7513 |

You will find additional practice on page 271.

# MULTIPLICATION OF DECIMALS

The rationale for multiplication of decimal fractions can be found in an examination of the multiplication of common fractions whose denominators are multiples of ten. That rationale can be seen by examining the table on page 107. Note that each line contains a single multiplication, first expressed in common fractions and then in decimal fractions.

| Multiplication | Product | Multiplication | Product |
|---|---|---|---|
| $\frac{1}{10} \times \frac{1}{10}$ | $\frac{1}{100}$ | .1 × .1 | .01 |
| $\frac{1}{10} \times \frac{1}{100}$ | $\frac{1}{1000}$ | .1 × .01 | .001 |
| $\frac{1}{100} \times \frac{1}{100}$ | $\frac{1}{10,000}$ | .01 × .01 | .0001 |
| $\frac{1}{10} \times \frac{1}{1000}$ | $\frac{1}{10,000}$ | .1 × .001 | .0001 |
| $\frac{1}{100} \times \frac{1}{1000}$ | $\frac{1}{100,000}$ | .01 × .001 | .00001 |
| $\frac{1}{1000} \times \frac{1}{1000}$ | $\frac{1}{1,000,000}$ | .001 × .001 | .000001 |
| $\frac{1}{10} \times \frac{1}{10,000}$ | $\frac{1}{100,000}$ | .1 × .0001 | .00001 |

Count up the number of figures to the right of the decimal point in each of the multiplications above. Then count up the number of digits to the right of the decimal point in each product. Do you see a pattern? When multiplying decimals, the number of digits to the right of the decimal point in the product will equal the number of digits to the right of the point in the multiplication.

In order to see how the procedure of counting digits to the right of the decimal point works in actual usage, examine the model problems below. Notice that no attention whatsoever is paid to the decimal points while the multiplication is taking place. **It is only after the product is computed that the decimal point is placed.**

*Model Examples*

1.
```
    2.5 ◄── 1 digit  to the right
  × 1.2 ◄── 1 digit  to the right
─────────
     50     2 digits to the right in all.
    250
─────────              ↓
    300               3.00
                    └──── Two digits to the right.
```

2.
```
    7.9 ◄── 1 digit  to the right
  × .002 ◄── 3 digits to the right
─────────
    158     4 digits to the right in all.

                       ↓
                     .0158
                    └──── 4 digits to the right.
```

3.
```
    .006 ◄╲
  × .002 ◄─╲ ➤ 6 digits to the right in all.
─────────
      12                ↓
                     .000012
                    └──── 6 digits to the right.
```

The following multiplications have been computed for you, but the decimal point has not been placed in the product. Place the decimal point in the correct place in each product.

1) 12.4
   × .01
   ─────
   1 2 4

2) 3.56
   × .12
   ─────
   4 2 7 2

3) 4.7
   ×1.6
   ─────
   7 5 2

4) 28
   ×.3
   ───
   8 4

5) 1.56
   ×.04
   ─────
   6 2 4

6) 124.3
   × 1.5
   ─────
   1 8 6 4 5

7) 697
   × 0.3
   ─────
   2 0 9 1

8) 7.55
   × .13
   ─────
   9 8 1 5

9) .214
   × .001
   ─────
   2 1 4

10) .715
    × .008
    ─────
    5 7 2 0

11) .3641
    × .0003
    ─────
    1 0 9 2 3

12) .00005
    ×.0002
    ─────
    1 0

## Answers

1. .124   2. .4272   3. 7.52   4. 8.4   5. .0624   6. 186.45

7. 209.1   8. .9815   9. .000214   10. .005720   11. .00010923   12. .00000001

If the answer to number 12 (above) confused you, remember that a zero after the last significant figure to the right of the decimal point has no meaning, just as a zero to the left of the first significant figure to the left of a decimal point has no meaning. (.6 = .60; 025.3 = 25.3) It could have been written .000000010.

Now that you have had practice placing the decimal point, it is time to try doing the entire multiplication from scratch. Once more, remember that the multiplication proceeds as any whole number multiplication would. It is only after the computation has been completed that the decimal point is placed.

Multiply. Then place the decimal point correctly.

1) 2.6
   × 4

2) 3.7
   ×.5

3) 4.9
   ×.6

4) 5.8
   ×.7

5) .35
   × 2

6) .48
   × 5

7) .45
   ×.7

8) .63
   ×.6

9) .73
   ×.04

10) .89
    ×.62

11) .96
    ×2.7

12) .085
    ×.31

13) .058
    ×.012

14) 1.79
    ×1.3

15) 38.4
    ×.05

16) 67.3
    ×1.7

17) 4.9
    ×5.6

18) 7.4
    ×.58

19) 9.20
    ×.35

20) .0064
    ×.037

**Answers**

| | | | | | | | | | |
|---|---|---|---|---|---|---|---|---|---|
| **1.** | 10.4 | **2.** | 1.85 | **3.** | 2.94 | **4.** | 4.06 | **5.** | .7 |
| **6.** | 2.4 | **7.** | .315 | **8.** | .378 | **9.** | .0292 | **10.** | .5518 |
| **11.** | 2.592 | **12.** | .02635 | **13.** | .000696 | **14.** | 2.327 | **15.** | 1.92 |
| **16.** | 114.41 | **17.** | 27.44 | **18.** | 4.292 | **19.** | 3.22 | **20.** | .0002368 |

You will find additional practice on page 271.

# MULTIPLICATION AND DIVISION BY POWERS OF 10

Any whole number may be multiplied by 10 simply by annexing a zero to the end of it. For example, 10 × 2 is 20, 10 × 8 = 80, 10 × 35 = 350, and 10 × 237 = 2370. How do you think you might multiply a number by 100? By 1000? By 10,000?

Just in case you hadn't guessed, to multiply a whole number by 100, annex two zeroes (3 × 100 = 300; 46 × 100 = 4600; 342 × 100 = 34,200). To multiply a whole number by 1000, annex three zeroes (6 × 1000 = 6000; 57 × 1000 = 57,000; 416 × 1000 = 416,000). To multiply by 10,000, annex four zeroes; to multiply by 100,000 annex five zeroes, etc.

This formula (annexing the same number of zeroes as there are in the multiple of ten you are multiplying by) is a convenient, if not quite accurate, mechanism for dealing with multiplying whole numbers by powers of ten. Now that you are familiar with the meaning of a decimal point in a numeral, consider the following alternative explanation for multiplying by powers of ten:

To multiply by 10, move the decimal point 1 place to the right.

To multiply by 100, move the decimal point 2 places to the right.

To multiply by 1000, move the decimal point 3 places to the right.

To multiply a number by any power of ten, move the point a number of spaces to the right equal to the number of zeroes in the power of ten being multiplied by.

This explanation helps to account for the actual process that occurs when zeroes are annexed, and also is applicable to numbers containing decimal fractions. Study the table below.

| Number | × 10 | × 100 | × 1000 | × 10,000 | × 100,000 |
|---|---|---|---|---|---|
| 23 | 230 | 2300 | 23,000 | 230,000 | 2,300,000 |
| 3.4 | 34 | 340 | 3400 | 34,000 | 340,000 |
| .59 | 5.9 | 59 | 590 | 5900 | 5,900 |
| .028 | .28 | 2.8 | 28 | 280 | 2800 |
| .0046 | .046 | .46 | 4.6 | 46 | 460 |
| .00081 | .0081 | .081 | .81 | 8.1 | 81 |

Now, the beauty of this approach to multiplying by powers of 10 becomes even more evident when we consider division by powers of 10. Since division is the undoing of multiplication, then it is to be expected that when dividing by powers of ten, we do the opposite from what we do when multiplying. That is, the decimal point must be moved to the left the same number of places as there are zeroes in the multiple of ten being divided by. Look at the table below.

| Number | ÷ 10 | ÷ 100 | ÷ 1000 | ÷ 10,000 | ÷ 100,000 |
|--------|------|-------|--------|----------|-----------|
| 23 | 2.3 | .23 | .023 | .0023 | .00023 |
| 3.4 | .34 | .034 | .0034 | .00034 | .000034 |
| 567 | 56.7 | 5.67 | .567 | .0567 | .00567 |
| 8936 | 893.6 | 89.36 | 8.936 | .8936 | .08936 |
| 45,382 | 4538.2 | 453.82 | 45.382 | 4.5382 | .45382 |
| 732,971 | 73,297.1 | 7329.71 | 732.971 | 73.2971 | 7.32971 |

Multiply each number in your head by the multiplier specified.

10 ×

1) 3.4     2) .62     3) 41.7     4) .018     5) 6.91     6) 34

100 ×

7) 5.9     8) .82     9) 63.4     10) .052     11) 3.97     12) 78

1000 ×

13) 9.3     14) .93     15) 82.7     16) .095     17) 9.36     18) 5.1

Divide each number in your head by the divisor specified.

10 )‾‾‾‾

19) 3.4     20) .62     21) 41.7     22) .018     23) 6.91     24) 34

100 )‾‾‾‾

25) 5.9     26) .82     27) 63.4     28) .052     29) 3.97     30) 78

1000 )‾‾‾‾

31) 9.3     32) .93     33) 82.7     34) .095     35) 9.36     36) 5.1

## Answers

| | | | | | | | |
|---|---|---|---|---|---|---|---|
| **1.** | 34 | **2.** | 6.2 | **3.** | 417 | **4.** | .18 |
| **5.** | 69.1 | **6.** | 340 | **7.** | 590 | **8.** | 82 |
| **9.** | 6340 | **10.** | 5.2 | **11.** | 39.7 | **12.** | 7800 |
| **13.** | 9300 | **14.** | 930 | **15.** | 82700 | **16.** | 95 |
| **17.** | 9360 | **18.** | 5100 | **19.** | .34 | **20.** | .062 |
| **21.** | 4.17 | **22.** | .0018 | **23.** | .691 | **24.** | 3.4 |

| 25. | .059 | 26. | .0082 | 27. | .634 | 28. | .00052 |
|---|---|---|---|---|---|---|---|
| 29. | .0397 | 30. | .78 | 31. | .0093 | 32. | .00093 |
| 33. | .0827 | 34. | .000095 | 35. | .00936 | 36. | .0051 |

The ability to rapidly multiply and divide by powers of ten, simply by moving the decimal point the appropriate number of places to the right or the left is a skill which can be learned easily, and which will prove invaluable as a time-saver in later operations. If you feel that you need more practice, make up lists of numerals with their decimal points in various places, and then practice multiplying and dividing them by moving the decimal point. An understanding of this skill is essential to understanding how division of decimals works.

# DIVISION OF DECIMALS

When two numbers are to be divided, multiplying both of those numbers by the same quantity will not affect the quotient. Read that last sentence over again, to be certain that you understand its implications. Then look at the proof of that statement below:

$$3 \overline{) 15} \rightarrow \times 100 \rightarrow 300 \overline{) 1500} \quad (=5)$$

$$\times 10 \downarrow$$

$$30 \overline{) 150} \quad (=5)$$

Across, both divisor and dividend are multiplied by 100. Down, both divisor and dividend are multiplied by 10. Whether the division is done straight (as 15 divided by 3) or multiplied, the quotient is still 5.

You may try this trick with any division you like, multiplying divisor and dividend by any number you like, until you convince yourself that the process is a mathematically sound one — that is, it will always work.

The first thing you need to know in order to divide decimals is that **you never divide by** a decimal. Yes, that last sentence does sound contradictory, but nevertheless, it is true. In order to divide by a decimal, **it is first necessary to change that decimal to an integer** (whole number). Carefully study the model examples below, and you will see that the process is, in reality, much easier to actually do than it is to describe.

*Model Examples*

1. $.6 \overline{) 1.8}$   To change .6 to an integer, the decimal point must be moved to the right one place.

   $.6 \overline{) 1.8}$   Moving that decimal point is the same as multiplying by 10. In order to keep the division meaning the same thing, the decimal in the dividend must also be multiplied by 10.

   $6 \overline{) 18.}$   The decimal point in the quotient is then placed directly above the one in the dividend.

   $\overset{3.}{6 \overline{) 18}}$   Dividing, we get a quotient of 3.

2. .09 ) .081    To change .09 to an integer, multiply by 100. (That means moving the decimal point 2 places to the right.)

.09. ) .08.1    Of course if one decimal point is moved 2 places, so must the other one be moved.

09. ) 08.1 = 9 ) 8.1    The zeroes to the left of the first figures are just excess baggage, and meaningless.

9 ) 8.1    Place the decimal point in the quotient directly above the one in the dividend.

   .9
9 ) 8.1    Divide, and get a quotient of .9.

3. 1.2 ) 144    Change 1.2 to an integer by moving the decimal point 1 place to the right.

1.2. ) 144.0.    In order to move the decimal point in 144 one place right, a 0 must be inserted as a place-holder.

12 ) 1440.    Place decimal point in the quotient above the decimal point in the dividend.

    12.
12 ) 1440.    Divide and get a quotient of 12.

Notice, once the divisor has been made into an integer by moving the decimal point, and the dividend's decimal point has been moved and the point placed in the quotient, the actual division process is identical to division with integers, and you may accomplish it by whatever form of division you happen to normally use.

4. 3.2 ) 7.6    Most divisions do not come out evenly. This one begins as have all the others — by moving decimal points:

3.2. ) 7.6.    Points in the divisor and dividend are moved one place each.

32 ) 76.    The decimal point in the quotient is then placed.

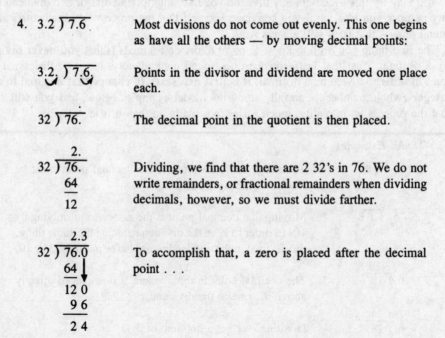

    2.
32 ) 76.    Dividing, we find that there are 2 32's in 76. We do not
   64       write remainders, or fractional remainders when dividing
   ――       decimals, however, so we must divide farther.
   12

    2.3
32 ) 76.0    To accomplish that, a zero is placed after the decimal
   64 ↓      point . . .
   ――
   12 0
    9 6
   ――
    2 4

```
        2.37
  32 ) 76.00          . . . and, when needed, another zero . . .
        64
        12 0
         9 6
         2 40
         2 24
           16
```

```
        2.375
  32 ) 76.000         . . . and when needed, still another zero. If this third zero
        64             had not yielded a precise ending, we would have rounded
        12 0           the answer back to the nearest hundredth.
         9 6
         2 40
         2 24
          160
          160
```

Divide. Where necessary, round the quotients to the nearest hundredth.

1) $.2 \overline{)6.70}$     2) $1.3 \overline{)\,.48}$     3) $2.5 \overline{)64}$     4) $.16 \overline{)35.4}$

5) $8 \overline{)5.72}$     6) $.9 \overline{)56.3}$     7) $4.1 \overline{)57}$     8) $.06 \overline{)3.4}$

9) $.5 \overline{)690}$     10) $.031 \overline{)5.97}$     11) $.42 \overline{)6.82}$     12) $4.7 \overline{)\,.685}$

13) $.64 \overline{)325}$     14) $4.9 \overline{)\,.627}$     15) $8.7 \overline{)43.82}$     16) $2.9 \overline{)72.51}$

17) $6.7 \overline{)\,.3872}$     18) $.53 \overline{)4.691}$     19) $.61 \overline{)5.674}$     20) $.83 \overline{)37.46}$

21) $.009 \overline{)\,.5241}$     22) $.37 \overline{)65.71}$     23) $.48 \overline{)732.8}$     24) $.036 \overline{)4751}$

## Answers

| | | | | | | | | | | | |
|---|---|---|---|---|---|---|---|---|---|---|---|
| **1.** | 33.5 | **2.** | .37 | **3.** | 25.6 | **4.** | 221.25 | **5.** | .715 | **6.** | 62.56 |
| **7.** | 13.90 | **8.** | 56.67 | **9.** | 1380 | **10.** | 192.58 | **11.** | 16.24 | **12.** | .15 |
| **13.** | 507.81 | **14.** | .13 | **15.** | 5.04 | **16.** | 25.00 | **17.** | .06 | **18.** | 8.85 |
| **19.** | 9.30 | **20.** | 45.13 | **21.** | 58.23 | **22.** | 177.59 | **23.** | 1526.67 | **24.** | 131972.22 |

You will find additional practice on page 272.

# DECIMAL FRACTION POST-TEST

Express as a decimal fraction.

1) $\frac{7}{100}$  2) $\frac{183}{1000}$  3) $\frac{2}{3}$  4) $5\frac{3}{4}$

Express as a common fraction in lowest terms or as a mixed numeral.

5) 13.35  6) .015  7) 12.324

Solve the following.

8) $9.5 + 1.27 + 72.6$  9) $84 + 2.13 + .075$

10) $61.27 - 45.88$  11) $15.8 - 2.674$

12) $.81 \times 75$  13) $.067 \times 4.11$

14) $.08 \overline{)36.24}$  15) $.0008 \overline{)76.39}$

## Answers

| | | | | | | | | |
|---|---|---|---|---|---|---|---|---|
| **1.** | .07 | **2.** | .183 | **3.** | .667 | **4.** | 5.75 |
| **5.** | $13\frac{7}{20}$ | **6.** | $\frac{3}{200}$ | **7.** | $12\frac{81}{250}$ | **8.** | 83.37 |
| **9.** | 86.205 | **10.** | 15.39 | **11.** | 13.126 | **12.** | 60.75 |
| **13.** | .27537 | **14.** | 453 | **15.** | 95487.5 | | |

## ANALYSIS OF ANSWERS TO POST-TEST

Following are the skills which were tested by the various items in the post-test. Should the results indicate that you need additional practice with one or more skills, refer to the appropriate pages in the chapter, and to the Additional Practice section, for additional help with the skill in question.

| | | |
|---|---|---|
| 1–4. | Common fractions to decimals | Pages 101–102 |
| 5–7. | Decimal fractions to common fractions | Pages 99–101 |
| 8–9. | Adding decimals | Pages 104–105; 270 |
| 10–11. | Subtracting decimals | Pages 105–106; 271 |
| 12–13. | Multiplying decimals | Pages 106–109; 271 |
| 14–15. | Dividing decimals | Pages 111–114; 272 |

# 5. *INTRODUCTION TO ALGEBRA*

Algebra is a branch of mathematics that was specifically designed to help to solve word-problems, as well as to organize one's thinking in a number of mathematical situations. Many people unfamiliar with the operations of algebra are afraid of it. However, algebra is an extremely useful tool which, once mastered, can be an invaluable aid in many situations that you are likely to encounter in the real world, as well as those which you will find on the GED examination.

## ALGEBRA PRE-TEST

Solve for $x$ or $y$.

1) $x + 7 = 23$

2) $15 - x = 18$

3) $y + 7 = 3y - 9$

4) $\frac{y}{4} = \frac{7}{11}$

5) $\frac{1}{x + 1} = \frac{5}{2}$

6) $x = 36\%$ of 25

7) $x^2 + 2x + 1 = 0$

8) $x^2 - 36 = 0$

9) $3a^4b^5 \cdot 2b^3c^3$

10) $\sqrt{80m^2}$

## Answers

| | | | | |
|---|---|---|---|---|
| **1.** 16 | **2.** $^-3$ | **3.** 8 | **4.** $2\frac{6}{11}$ | **5.** $^-\frac{3}{5}$ |
| **6.** 9 | **7.** $^-1, ^-1$ | **8.** $\pm 6$ | **9.** $6a^4b^8c^3$ | **10.** $4m\sqrt{5}$ |

## Analysis of Pre-test Items

# VARIABLES AND CONSTANTS

In order to understand algebra, we need to first look at the two major elements of algebra — variables and constants. Since constants are by far the easier to understand, let's examine them first.

## *CONSTANTS*

Any real number is a constant. $3 = 3 = 3$. The value of a constant is, for lack of a better word, constant. In case you are unclear on this, examine the number 25. It means 25 now, and will mean 25 later. It is, therefore, a constant.

Which of the following are constants?

1) 36          2) 79          3) 251          4) $y$

5) $4n$          6) $\frac{4}{7}$          7) $2\frac{1}{15}$          8) .0792

Each expression in the exercises above is a constant except $y$ and $4n$. A constant may be a whole number, a fraction, a mixed numeral, a decimal; it may not, however, contain a letter. As soon as you see a letter in an expression, you should recognize that you are not dealing with a constant. Rather, you have a **variable**.

## *VARIABLES*

A variable is a symbol which takes the place of a number. It is usually written as a lower case letter, $a, b, c, \ldots x, y, z,$ although you will occasionally see capital letters, Greek letters, or even geometric symbols used to represent variables. Examine the following expression:

$$n = 4 + 7$$

In this mathematical sentence, the variable, $n$, has been used to represent a number. We can find out what number $n$ is representing by combining the terms on the right hand side of the equal sign. Since $7 + 4 = 11$, the following is true.

$$n = 11$$

If that is clear to you, examine the following statement:

$$n = 19 - 4$$

What number does $n$ represent this time?

By subtracting the 4 from the 19, we arrive at the conclusion that $n$ represents 15. Notice that in two different mathematical sentences $n$ has had two different values. The value of $n$ has varied from expression to expression. $n$ is therefore a variable.

Which of the following are variables?

1) $r$  2) $3a$  3) $\dfrac{m}{7}$  4) 19

5) $\dfrac{9}{h}$  6) 97  7) $\triangle$  8) $\varnothing$

Each of the above is a variable, except for 19 and 97, each of which is a _____.
(If you're not sure look back at the preceding section.)

As already noted, the meaning of a variable (that is, the number it represents) may change from mathematical sentence to mathematical sentence. **Within a single sentence, however, each time the same variable appears it must stand for the same number.** Look at the following sentence.

$$n + 3 = 11 - n$$

If the first $n = 4$, then so must the second. If we substitute 4 for each $n$ in that sentence we get the following:

$$4 + 3 = 11 - 4$$
$$7 = 7$$

This is a true statement. If, however, the second $n$ had stood for anything but 4, the statement would have been false.

## COMBINING VARIABLES

Since variables represent numbers, they can also be treated like numbers. That is to say, variables may be added, subtracted, multiplied, and divided. Let's look at addition first, and see if we can't recognize a pattern.

## ADDITION

Any time you see the term $n$ it means that there is $1n$ present. This seemingly obvious statement is rather critical to an understanding of how variables combine, so let's dwell on it for a moment. If there were 2 or more $n$'s present, you would see them represented as $2n$, $3n$, $28n$, or whatever, meaning $2n$'s, $3n$'s, $28n$'s, etc. If there were no $n$'s being represented ($0n$) you'd see no symbol at all. Zero $n$'s, after all, is the same as just plain 0. Consider:

$$0 \; 2\text{'s} = 0$$
$$0 \; 5\text{'s} = 0$$
$$0 \; 35\text{'s} = 0$$
$$0 \; n\text{'s} = 0$$

Just plain $n$, then, cannot mean 0 $n$'s, does not mean 2 or more $n$'s, and therefore must mean $1n$. The expression "$1n$" is rarely if ever written, however, mathematicians preferring to simply write "$n$".

A numeral written next to a variable is known as that variable's **coefficient**. In the expression $5n$, $n$'s coefficient is 5. In the term $18x$, $x$'s coefficient is 18. In the expression $r$, $r$'s coefficient is . . . . What do you think $r$'s coefficient is? Did you really think about it? It's 1.

Name the coefficient of each variable.

1) $3x$         2) $7n$         3) $s$         4) $19b$

5) $w$         6) $4m$         7) $\frac{2}{3}h$         8) $e$

The coefficients are:

**1.** 3   **2.** 7   **3.** 1   **4.** 19   **5.** 1   **6.** 4   **7.** $\frac{2}{3}$   **8.** 1

Did you get them all? How about the three 1's? Remember, if you do not see a numerical coefficient next to a variable, that variable's coefficient is 1.

It should be pointed out, in the interest of accuracy, that in any algebraic expression, all the members of a single term are, technically speaking, coefficients of each other. That is to say, in the term $5n$, 5 is the coefficient of $n$, but $n$ is also the coefficient of 5. In the term, $a$, 1 is the coefficient of $a$ and $a$ is the coefficient of 1. Try to file this information somewhere in the back of your mind for later use. For the moment, however, we are going to be concerned exclusively with numerical coefficients of variables.

**Only like variables may be combined into a single term by addition.**

When adding like variables, only the numerical coefficients are added. This idea can be illustrated with the following examples:

$$2n + 3n = 5n$$

$$4x + 6x = 10x$$

$$2r + r = 3r \quad \text{(do you know why?)}$$

$$w + w = 2w$$

Adding like variables may be likened to adding like pieces of fruit:

$$2 \text{ apples} + 3 \text{ apples} = 5 \text{ apples}$$

$$4 \text{ oranges} + 6 \text{ oranges} = 10 \text{ oranges}$$

$$2 \text{ peaches} + \text{(a) peach} = 3 \text{ peaches}$$

$$\text{(a) grape} + \text{(a) grape} = 2 \text{ grapes}$$

So far so good? Then try this one.

$$2x + 3y = \underline{\hspace{2cm}}$$

Think of:

$$2 \text{ oranges} + 3 \text{ grapes} = \underline{\hspace{2cm}}$$

Did you really think about that one? You might say that 2 oranges + 3 grapes = 5 pieces of fruit, but frankly, algebra would find that solution far too imprecise. Algebraically speaking:

$$2 \text{ oranges} + 3 \text{ grapes} = 2 \text{ oranges} + 3 \text{ grapes}$$

They cannot be further combined. Now bearing that in mind, you should recognize that:

$$2x + 3y = 2x + 3y$$

If the variables are different, the terms may not be combined into a single new term by adding. Only those terms containing identical variables may be combined into a single new term by addition.

Add these.

1) $4n + 3n$         2) $5x + 2x$         3) $4w + w$

4) $r + r + r$         5) $m + n$         6) $\frac{1}{2}u + u$

7) $3v + 3w$         8) $\frac{1}{4}t + \frac{1}{2}t$         9) $\frac{z}{3} + \frac{z}{3}$

## Answers

**1.** $7n$     **2.** $7x$     **3.** $5w$     **4.** $3r$     **5.** $m + n$

**6.** $1\frac{1}{2}u$     **7.** $3v + 3w$   **8.** $\frac{3}{4}t$     **9.** $^{*}\dfrac{2z}{3}$

## SUBTRACTION

Subtraction of variables works in exactly the same fashion as addition, except, of course, that the numerical coefficient of one is subtracted from (rather than added to) the numerical coefficient of the other. All the other rules governing addition of variables apply.

$$4y - 2y = 2y$$
$$7m - 3m = 4m$$
$$s - s = 0$$

and

$$4p - 3q = 4p - 3q$$

---

*If problem 9 gave you any difficulty, bear in mind that you are combining two fractions with like denominators. The common denominator is 3. Then add the 2 numerators ($z + z$) and get $2z$.

Solve each subtraction.

1) $5z - z$            2) $6r - 2r$            3) $9p - 3p$

4) $6x - 6x$           5) $8m - 4n$          6) $7c - 5c$

7) $u - u$             8) $9w - 4x$           9) $15v - 8v$

### Answers

| **1.** $4z$ | **2.** $4r$ | **3.** $6p$ | **4.** $0$ | **5.** $8m - 4n$ |
|---|---|---|---|---|
| **6.** $2c$ | **7.** $0$ | **8.** $9w - 4x$ | **9.** $7v$ | |

If you are not sure about the reason for the answer to problem 1, remember that there is a 1 in front of the second $z$, even though you cannot see it there. As for problems 5 and 8, since the two variables are different, they cannot be combined by subtraction.

You will find additional practice on page 272.

# A QUESTION OF BALANCE

You have probably, at some time or other, seen a twin pan scale. Such a scale is pictured below. Notice that the scale as shown is in balance.

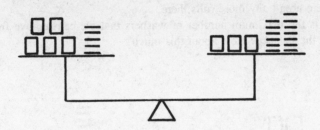

On the left arm of the scale you see 5 rolls of washers, and 5 loose washers. We will assume that there are the same number of washers in each roll, and that the paper in which the washers are rolled is weightless. (While nothing can in fact be completely weightless, this fiction is often used for the sake of simplicity when solving problems in science. The actual weight of the paper would make very little difference anyway, when compared to that of the much heavier washers.) On the right arm, there are three rolls, and 13 loose washers. Since the scale is in balance, the total weight on the left side must equal the total weight on the right.

What we wish to do is to determine how many washers there are in each roll. Do you have any idea of how we might do that? Because the scale is balanced, we may add the same amount of weight to each side or subtract the same amount of weight from each side without destroying that balance. How could we simplify the following picture?

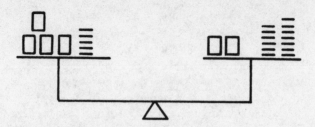

Here we've removed one roll from each side.

Is the scale still in balance?

Let's take the maximum number of rolls possible from each side while keeping them in balance. Then the scale would look like this:

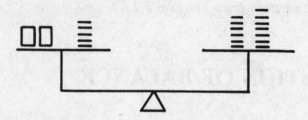

Why could we take no more than two additional rolls from each side? Think about it. If we took another roll from the left side, we would not be able to take another roll from the right side. There aren't any more rolls there.

Now, what is the maximum number of washers that we can remove from each side without losing the balance? How about this much?

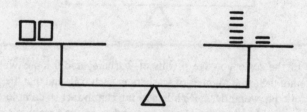

How many washers are in each roll? Can you tell now?

Since we took 5 loose washers from each side of the scale, we are left with 2 rolls on the left and 8 loose washers on the right. If 2 rolls balance 8 washers, then one roll would balance 4 washers, so there must be 4 washers in each roll.

Don't you think that the last balance-picture was much easier to figure out than the first one? And yet, the last balance picture is the result of having simplified the first one, one step at a time.

Now look at the balance-picture below. Simplify it until you can see the solution.

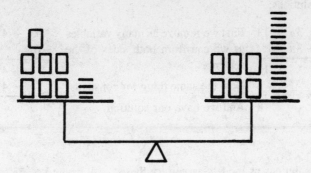

The simplest form for the balance-picture above is obtained when 6 rolls and 4 loose washers are removed from each side. It looks like this:

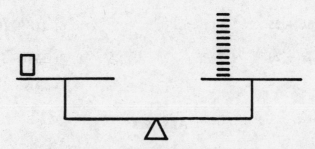

You can now see quite clearly how many washers are in a single roll. Can you see as clearly what this has to do with algebra?

Do you remember the original balance-picture? Here it is again.

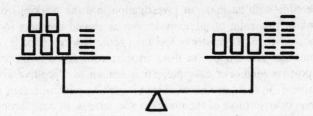

Now, let us translate the rolls and loose washers into a more familiar notation — that of variables and constants. If we use the variable, $n$, to stand for the number of washers in each roll, we can represent the balance-picture with the following sentence:

$$5n + 5 = 3n + 13$$

Can you write the mathematical sentence for the balance picture at the top of this page: The one that had 7 rolls and 4 loose washers on the left?

If we let $x$ be the number of washers in each roll this time, we get:

$$7x + 4 = 6x + 15$$

Mathematical sentences are often solved in the same manner as balance-pictures. Look at these two solutions:

$$5n + 5 = 3n + 13$$
$$-3n \qquad -3n$$
$$\overline{\phantom{aa}2n + 5 = \qquad 13}$$
$$-5 \qquad -5$$
$$\overline{\phantom{aa}2n \quad = \qquad 8}$$
$$n = 4$$

First we remove as many variables as we can from both sides of the sentence.

Now the same thing for constants.

And we have our solution.

$$7x + 4 = 6x + 15$$
$$-6x \qquad -6x$$
$$\overline{\phantom{aa}x + 4 = \qquad 15}$$
$$-4 \qquad -4$$
$$\overline{\phantom{aa}x \quad = \qquad 11}$$

Use the above solutions as models as you try these.

1) $7a + 8 = 6a + 12$

2) $5b + 3 = 4b + 19$

3) $4a + 11 = 3a + 20$

4) $9x + 15 = 7x + 21$

5) $8k + 9 = 6k + 25$

6) $11r + 10 = 9r + 24$

7) $7x + 8 = 4x + 20$

8) $15n + 5 = 11n + 29$

### Answers

**1.** 4   **2.** 16   **3.** 9   **4.** 3   **5.** 8   **6.** 7   **7.** 4   **8.** 6

# SIGNED NUMBERS

Before proceeding with an in-depth investigation into the workings of algebra, it is essential to look at the realm of numbers known as signed numbers (or integers). All numbers except one are either greater or less than zero. The exception is, of course, zero itself. Those numbers that are greater than zero are considered to be positive, and are denoted by a positive sign. For example, $^+6$ is known as "positive six." Six is also known as positive 6. In fact, any numeral that is written without a sign in front of it is considered to be positive. Most of the numbers you have dealt with throughout your life have been positive numbers, as have all of those treated in this book until now.

Those numbers less than zero are called negative numbers. $^-6$ is read "negative 6" and means six away from zero and on the left side of zero, if you are considering position on a number line:

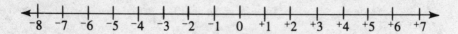

All numbers represented on a number line increase as you move from left to right, and decrease as you move from right to left. So, for example, $^+6$ is greater than $^+4$, but $^-6$ is less than $^-4$. Notice their positions on the number line and you'll readily see why.

## ABSOLUTE VALUE

The absolute value of a number is the distance that that number is from zero. A glance at the number line above will show you that $^-2$ is 2 spaces from 0. That means that the absolute value of negative two is 2. That would be written:

$$|^-2| = 2$$

(The pair of vertical lines are read "the absolute value of.") Now, $^+2$ is also 2 spaces away from zero, so it too has an absolute value of 2, which leads to the following conclusion:

$$|^-2| = |^+2| = 2$$

(Which is read: The absolute value of negative 2 equals the absolute value of positive 2, equals 2.)

Find the absolute values.

1) $|^-7| = $ _____      2) $|^-4| = $ _____      3) $|^+8| = $ _____

4) $|^+9| = $ _____      5) $|^-y| = $ _____      6) $|^+r| = $ _____

7) $|x + 2| = $ _____      8) $|x - 3| = $ _____      9) $|^-m + ^-2| = $ _____

10) $|^+l + ^+3| = $ _____

## Answers

| **1.** | 7 | **2.** | 4 | **3.** | 8 | **4.** | 9 | **5.** | $y$ |
|---|---|---|---|---|---|---|---|---|---|
| **6.** | $r$ | **7.** | $x + 2$ | **8.** | $x - 3$ | **9.** | $m + 2$ | **10.** | $l + 3$ |

The answers to questions 7–10 bear a bit of explaining. Assuming that we knew the value of $x$ in questions 7 and 8, they would have been added or subtracted together with the number inside the absolute value sign to determine a single value before the absolute value of the number was found. In other words, if question 7 had read $|7 + 2|$, you would first have added, and then found the absolute value of 9. If question 8 had read $|7 - 3|$, you would have first subtracted and found the absolute value, 4. By leaving the addition and subtraction signs intact, the expressions $x + 2$ and $x - 3$ mean the same things respectively. In question 9, however, the sum of $^-m + ^-2$ will be the same distance from zero as the sum of $^+m + ^+2$. You can prove this to yourself by selecting any two points on the number line with the same absolute value. Add 2 to the positive number, and subtract 2 from the negative one. You will then end up at two points with the same absolute value:

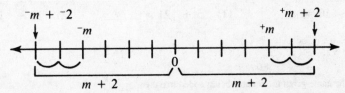

## COMBINING SIGNED NUMBERS

Signed numbers can be combined by addition, subtraction, multiplication, and division, but the rules which govern their combining are somewhat different from those which govern the combining of numbers without signs. For that reason, we will study addition and subtraction separately. Multiplication and division follow the same rules, and so will be considered together.

## ADDING SIGNED NUMBERS

When numbers with like signs are to be added together, their absolute values are added in the usual manner. The sum, however, will have the same sign as the original numbers had:

*Model Example 1*

To add $^+7 + {}^+6$

$|^+7| = 7;\ |^+6| = 6$  Find the absolute values.

$7 + 6 = 13$  Add the absolute values.

$^+7 + {}^+6 = {}^+13$  The sum takes the sign of the addends.*

*Model Example 2*

To add $^-5 + {}^-4$

$|^-5| = 5;\ |^-4| = 4$  Find the absolute values.

$5 + 4 = 9$  Add the absolute values.

$^-5 + {}^-4 = {}^-9$  The sum takes the sign of the addends.

Add.

1) $^+3 + {}^+7 = $ _____

2) $^-4 + {}^-8 = $ _____

3) $^+5 + {}^+8 = $ _____

4) $^-4 + {}^-6 = $ _____

5) $^-3 + {}^-12 = $ _____

6) $^+8 + {}^+9 = $ _____

7) $^-9 + {}^-12 = $ _____

8) $^-13 + {}^-4 = $ _____

9) $^+8 + {}^+12 = $ _____

10) $^-11 + {}^-10 = $ _____

11) $^+5 + {}^+21 = $ _____

12) $^-15 + {}^-13 = $ _____

*Addend is the name given to numbers being added together.

## Answers

| | | | | | | | | | | | |
|---|---|---|---|---|---|---|---|---|---|---|---|
| **1.** $+10$ | **2.** $-12$ | **3.** $+13$ | **4.** $-10$ | **5.** $-15$ | **6.** $+17$ |
| **7.** $-21$ | **8.** $-17$ | **9.** $+20$ | **10.** $-21$ | **11.** $+26$ | **12.** $-28$ |

Adding signed numbers whose signs are different is accomplished by subtracting the absolute value of the two numbers. (That is correct. You have to subtract in order to add.) The sum (even though the operation performed is really subtraction, because it is the answer to an addition, it is still considered a sum) then takes the sign of the larger of the addends (that is the number in the addition with the greater absolute value).

*Model Example 3*

$$+7 + -5$$
$$\downarrow$$
$|+7| = 7; \quad |-5| = 5 \qquad$ Find the absolute values . . .
$$\downarrow$$
$7 - 5 = 2 \qquad$ . . . subtract them . . .
$$\downarrow$$
$+7 + -5 = +2 \qquad$ . . . assign the sum the sign of the addend with the larger absolute value.

*Model Example 4*

$$+6 + -11$$
$$\downarrow$$
$|+6| = 6; \quad |-11| = 11 \qquad$ Find the absolute values . . .
$$\downarrow$$
$11 - 6 = 5 \qquad$ . . . subtract them . . .
$$\downarrow$$
$+6 + -11 = -5 \qquad$ . . . assign the sum the sign of the addend with the larger absolute value.

Add.

1) $+3 + -4 =$ _____

2) $-7 + +5 =$ _____

3) $-8 + +9 =$ _____

4) $-6 + -4 =$ _____

5) $+6 + -14 =$ _____

6) $-8 + -5 =$ _____

7) $+6 + -15 =$ _____

8) $-9 + +12 =$ _____

9) $+4 + +18 =$ _____

10) $-17 + +8 =$ _____

11) $-9 + +15 =$ _____

12) $+15 + -24 =$ _____

13) $-9 + +9 =$ _____

14) $+31 + -27 =$ _____

15) $-23 + +50 =$ _____

## Answers

| | | | | |
|---|---|---|---|---|
| **1.** $-1$ | **2.** $-2$ | **3.** $+1$ | **4.** $-10$ | **5.** $-8$ |
| **6.** $-13$ | **7.** $-9$ | **8.** $+3$ | **9.** $+22$ | **10.** $-9$ |
| **11.** $+6$ | **12.** $-9$ | **13.** $0$ | **14.** $+4$ | **15.** $+27$ |

To add three or more signed numbers, first collect the numbers with like signs. Then add them together. Finally add the numbers with unlike signs together:

*Model Example 5*

$^+3 + {}^-4 + {}^+8 + {}^-7 + {}^-2$

$^+11 + {}^-4 + {}^-7 + {}^-2$         Combine the positive numbers . . .

$^+11 + {}^-11 + {}^-2$         Combine the negative numbers (two at a time) . . .

$^+11 + {}^-13$

$^-2$         Combine the single resultant positive number with the single resultant negative.

---

Add.

1) $^+7 + {}^-5 + {}^+2 =$ _____

2) $^-5 + {}^-9 + {}^+8 =$ _____

3) $^+8 + {}^-4 + {}^+6 + {}^-12 =$ _____

4) $^-7 + {}^+12 + {}^-8 + {}^-5 =$ _____

5) $^-9 + {}^+5 + {}^-7 + {}^+8 =$ _____

6) $^+6 + {}^-8 + {}^-7 + {}^+6 =$ _____

7) $^+10 + {}^+7 + {}^-5 + {}^+8 + {}^-6 + {}^+11 + {}^-8 =$ _____

## Answers

**1.** $^+4$     **2.** $^-6$     **3.** $^-2$     **4.** $^-8$     **5.** $^-3$     **6.** $^-3$     **7.** $^+17$

You will find additional practice with adding signed numbers on page 273.

## *SUBTRACTING SIGNED NUMBERS*

Have you ever considered the meaning of a double negative? Think about this sentence: **I am not not going to the dentist**. What does it mean to you? If you are **not** not going to the dentist, then you must be going to the dentist. The same is true of a double negative when subtracting. Consider the following model example:

*Model Example 1*

$^+12 - {}^-8 =$ _____         $-{}^-8$ is a double negative. It means $^+8$. Therefore we change the example:

$^+12 + 8$         Now we add 12 and 8 to get 20, . . .

$\therefore {}^+12 - {}^-8 = {}^+20$

Notice that the key to effectively subtracting signed numbers is to first deal with the subtraction sign. That is to say, if a double negative is created, exchange both negatives for a plus sign. After that, the subtraction proceeds exactly as a signed number addition would. Study the following models, and you will see how each of the possible signed number subtractions works.

*Model Example 2*

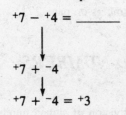

$^-9 - {}^-4 = $ _____ 　　Double negative becomes a plus.

$^-9 + 4 = {}^-5$ 　　Then add.

$$\therefore {}^-9 - {}^-4 = {}^-5$$

*Model Example 3*

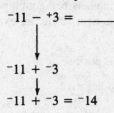

$^+7 - {}^+4 = $ _____ 　　Since not doing something is the same as doing nothing, exchange the $-^+$ signs to make $+^-$.

$^+7 + {}^-4$ 　　Then add.

$^+7 + {}^-4 = {}^+3$

$$\therefore {}^+7 - {}^+4 = {}^+3$$

*Model Example 4*

$^-11 - {}^+3 = $ _____ 　　For the same reason as in example 3, exchange the $-^+$ to make $+^-$.

$^-11 + {}^-3$ 　　Then add.

$^-11 + {}^-3 = {}^-14$

$$\therefore {}^-11 - {}^+3 = {}^-14$$

Notice that in model examples 3 and 4, by exchanging the $+$ and $-$ signs, we were able to create a signed number addition. And, we have already seen from model examples 1 and 2 that a double negative exchanged for a plus also creates an addition. It is therefore safe to conclude that any signed number subtraction can, by a careful manipulation of the two middle signs, be turned into a signed number addition, and then solved in the same way that any signed number addition is solved.

Solve the following subtractions by first turning them into additions.

1) $^-8 - {}^+6 = $ _____　　　2) $^+9 - {}^+4 = $ _____　　　3) $^+12 - {}^+5 = $ _____

4) $^-11 - {}^+8 = $ _____　　　5) $^+7 - {}^-4 = $ _____　　　6) $^-9 - {}^-6 = $ _____

7) $^-13 - {}^+6 = $ _____　　　8) $^+18 - {}^-10 = $ _____　　　9) $^+21 - {}^-8 = $ _____

10) $^+17 - {}^+5 = $ _____　　11) $^-16 - {}^-4 = $ _____　　12) $^-23 - {}^-11 = $ _____

13) $^+15 - {}^-8 =$ _____

14) $^-18 - {}^-6 =$ _____

15) $^-20 - {}^+5 =$ _____

16) $^+19 - {}^+8 =$ _____

17) $^+16 - {}^+7 =$ _____

18) $^-5 - {}^-11 =$ _____

19) $^+4 - {}^-12 =$ _____

20) $^-6 - {}^+15 =$ _____

## Answers

| | | | | | | |
|---|---|---|---|---|---|---|
| **1.** $^-14$ | **2.** $^+5$ | **3.** $^+7$ | **4.** $^-19$ | **5.** $^+11$ | **6.** $^-3$ | **7.** $^-19$ |
| **8.** $^+28$ | **9.** $^+29$ | **10.** $^+12$ | **11.** $^-12$ | **12.** $^-12$ | **13.** $^+23$ | **14.** $^-12$ |
| **15.** $^-25$ | **16.** $^+11$ | **17.** $^+9$ | **18.** $^+6$ | **19.** $^+16$ | **20.** $^-21$ | |

You will find additional practice with subtracting signed numbers on page 273.

## MULTIPLYING AND DIVIDING SIGNED NUMBERS

As noted earlier, the rules governing multiplication and division of signed numbers are identical, and so they will be treated together. Multiplication of signed numbers is the same as any multiplication, as far as the computational part of the exercise is concerned. That is, $3 \times 5$ is 15, regardless of the sign of either of the numbers. It is in the determination of the sign of the product that the signs of the factors (numbers being multiplied) play a role. For determining the sign of the product or the quotient, there are exactly two rules:

If the signs are the same, the sign of the answer is positive.

If the signs are different, the sign of the answer is negative.

The following model examples should serve to illustrate the application of these rules.

*Model Example 1*

$^+3 \times {}^+4$

Signs are the same,

$\therefore {}^+3 \times {}^+4 = {}^+12$

*Model Example 2*

$^+3 \times {}^-4$

Signs are different,

$\therefore {}^+3 \times {}^-4 = {}^-12$

*Model Example 3*

$^-3 \times {}^+4$

Signs are different,

$\therefore {}^-3 \times {}^+4 = {}^-12$

*Model Example 4*

$^-3 \times {}^-4$

Signs are the same,

$\therefore {}^-3 \times {}^-4 = {}^+12$

Since the same rules apply to division, we have not bothered to illustrate any divisions. Nevertheless, you will find both multiplications and divisions in the exercises on the next page.

Solve.

1) $^+5 \times {}^+8 =$ _____

2) $^-6 \times {}^+7 =$ _____

3) $^-7 \times {}^-4 =$ _____

4) $^+6 \times {}^-7 =$ _____

5) $^-12 \div {}^+4 =$ _____

6) $^-6 \div {}^+3 =$ _____

7) $^-24 \div {}^-3 =$ _____

8) $^+7 \times {}^+4 =$ _____

9) $^+9 \div {}^+3 =$ _____

10) $^-3 \times {}^-8 =$ _____

11) $^+30 \div {}^-5 =$ _____

12) $^-5 \times {}^+8 =$ _____

13) $^+5 \times {}^+9 =$ _____

14) $^+16 \div {}^-2 =$ _____

15) $^-15 \div {}^-5 =$ _____

16) $^-10 \div {}^-2 =$ _____

17) $^+6 \times {}^-9 =$ _____

18) $^+8 \times {}^-8 =$ _____

19) $^-9 \times {}^+4 =$ _____

20) $^+18 \div {}^+9 =$ _____

21) $^+14 \div {}^-7 =$ _____

22) $^-20 \div {}^+4 =$ _____

23) $^+18 \div {}^-6 =$ _____

24) $^-5 \times {}^-8 =$ _____

## Answers

| | | | | | | | | | | | |
|---|---|---|---|---|---|---|---|---|---|---|---|
| **1.** | $^+40$ | **2.** | $^-42$ | **3.** | $^+28$ | **4.** | $^-42$ | **5.** | $^-3$ | **6.** | $^-2$ |
| **7.** | $^+8$ | **8.** | $^+28$ | **9.** | $^+3$ | **10.** | $^+24$ | **11.** | $^-6$ | **12.** | $^-40$ |
| **13.** | $^+45$ | **14.** | $^-8$ | **15.** | $^+3$ | **16.** | $^+5$ | **17.** | $^-54$ | **18.** | $^-64$ |
| **19.** | $^-36$ | **20.** | $^+2$ | **21.** | $^-2$ | **22.** | $^-5$ | **23.** | $^-3$ | **24.** | $^+40$ |

You will find additional practice with multiplication and division of signed numbers on pages 273–274.

# SOLVING EQUATIONS BY EQUAL ADDITIONS

As noted earlier, an algebraic equation is like an equal-arm balance. As long as the same quantity is added to or subtracted from both sides of the balance, equilibrium is maintained. The same is true of an equation.

The main strategy employed when solving an algebraic equation is that of collecting like terms. That is to say, try to get all variables together on one side of the equal sign, and all constants together on the other side. The following model examples explore the technique of adding the same quantity to each side of the equation in order to collect like terms.

*Model Example 1*

$$x - 5 = 14$$

$$\begin{aligned} x - 5 &= 14 \\ +5 &\quad +5 \\ \hline x &= 19 \end{aligned}$$

We don't want 5 on the same side of the equation as the $x$, so, since the 5 is combined with the $x$ by subtraction, add 5 (the opposite of subtraction) to each side.

*Model Example 2*

$$^-n - 6 = 14 - 2n$$

$$\begin{aligned} ^-n - 6 &= 14 - 2n \\ +6 &\quad +6 \end{aligned}$$

We add 6 to each side to move it from the left to the right side of the equation.

$$\begin{aligned} ^-n &= 20 - 2n \\ +2n &\qquad +2n \\ \hline n &= 20 \end{aligned}$$

Then we add $2n$ to each side to move all the $n$'s to the left side of the equation.

When deciding the side of the equals sign to move the variables to (assuming that there are initially variables on both sides), ask yourself which side has the greater number of variables on it. $3x$, for example, is a greater number of variables than $2x$, and $2x$ is greater than $^-5x$. $^-3x$ is greater than $^-9x$. Note the following:

*Model Example 3*

$$\begin{aligned} 5 - 3w &= ^-2w \\ +3w &\quad +3w \\ \hline 5 &= w \\ w &= 5 \end{aligned}$$

You will note that $^-2w$ is larger than $^-3w$. Therefore, it is desirable to collect the variables on the right side of the equation. You may then reverse the order of the solution if you like, so that it reads $w = 5$, although there is no mathematical reason to do so.

Solve by equal additions.

1) $r - 7 = 15$       2) $x - 4 = 9$       3) $m - 12 = 81$

4) $^-2x = 7 - 3x$       5) $^-2y = ^-9 - 3y$       6) $^-6 - 2y = ^-3y - 5$

7) $^-4x - 6 = ^-5x + 7$       8) $^-7r - 2 = ^-6r - 5$       9) $^-4x - 9 = ^-3x - 12$

## Answers

| 1. | 22 | 2. | 13 | 3. | 93 | 4. | 7 | 5. | $^-9$ |
|----|----|----|----|----|----|----|----|----|----|
| 6. | 1  | 7. | 13 | 8. | 3  | 9. | 3 |    |    |

# SOLVING EQUATIONS BY EQUAL SUBTRACTIONS

Sometimes, the terms that you wish to move around in an equation will be connected by + signs. That means that those terms are combined by addition. (Remember, if you do not see any sign before a number, that means that there is a + sign there and that it is by convention just not written. To undo an addition, it is necessary to subtract. Study the model examples to see how this works.

*Model Example 1*

$$5x + 11 = 6x + 3$$

$$\begin{array}{r} 5x + 11 = 6x + 3 \\ -5x \qquad -5x \\ \hline 11 = x + 3 \\ -3 \qquad -3 \\ \hline 8 = x \end{array}$$

First the variables are collected on the right side (by subtracting $5x$).

Then the constants are collected on the left (by subtracting 3).

or

$$x = 8$$

This last step is optional.

*Model Example 2*

$$7y + 5 = 6y + 4$$

$$\begin{array}{r} 7y + 5 = 6y + 4 \\ -6y - 5 \quad -6y - 5 \\ \hline y = {}^{-}1 \end{array}$$

Both $6y$ and 5 are subtracted from each side of the equation.

Solve by subtracting the same quantities from both sides.

1) $y + 9 = 15$      2) $x + 8 = 5$      3) $y + 4 = {}^{-}3$      4) $5x + 7 = 6x + 4$

5) $5y + 3 = 4y + 6$      6) $7y - 9 = 8y + 5$      7) $11y + 4 = 10y + 6$      8) $5x + 2 = 4x + 8$

9) $3y + 5 = 2y + 7$      10) $4m + 8 = 3m - 2$      11) $7n - 4 = 8n$      12) $x + 6 = 2x + 6$

## Answers

| | | | | | |
|---|---|---|---|---|---|
| **1.** 6 | **2.** ${}^{-}3$ | **3.** ${}^{-}7$ | **4.** 3 | **5.** 3 | **6.** ${}^{-}14$ |
| **7.** 2 | **8.** 6 | **9.** 2 | **10.** ${}^{-}10$ | **11.** ${}^{-}4$ | **12.** 0 |

# SOLVING EQUATIONS BY DIVISION AND MULTIPLICATION

Multiplication of a variable by a numerical coefficient is quite common in algebraic equations. To undo a multiplication it is, of course, necessary to divide. Other equations indicate division of a variable by a constant, or multiplication of a variable by a fractional coefficient. In either of those cases, the simplest way to get the variable by itself is to multiply by the reciprocal of that coefficient, so as to create for the variable a coefficient of 1. Examine the model examples below.

*Model Example 1*

$3a = 24$        The variable, $a$, is multiplied by 3 . . .

$$\frac{3a}{3} = \frac{24}{3}$$        . . . so divide both sides by 3 . . .

$a = 8$        . . . and find that $a = 8$.

*Model Example 2*

$$\frac{b}{4} = 9$$        The variable, $b$, is divided by 4 . . .

$$4 \cdot \frac{b}{4} = 9 \cdot 4$$        . . . so multiply both sides by 4.

$$\frac{4}{1} \cdot \frac{b}{4} = 36$$        $4 =$ the fraction $\frac{4}{1}$ . . .

$$\frac{4b}{4} = 36$$        . . . and that makes it easier to multiply.

$$\frac{\cancel{4}b}{\cancel{4}} = 36$$        The 4's cancel, since $\frac{4}{4} = 1$ . . .

$b = 36$        . . . and so, $b = 36$.

*Model Example 3*

$$\frac{1}{7}x = 5$$        The variable $x$ is multiplied by $\frac{1}{7}$. You might divide both sides by $\frac{1}{7}$.

$$\frac{7}{1} \cdot \frac{1}{7}x = 5 \cdot \frac{7}{1}$$        That is the same as multiplying both sides by 7. That's $\frac{1}{7}$'s reciprocal.

$$\frac{7}{1} \cdot \frac{1}{7}x = \frac{5}{1} \cdot \frac{7}{1} \qquad \text{Multiply.}$$

$$\frac{7}{7}x = \frac{35}{1} \qquad \text{Then simplify . . .}$$

$$x = 35 \qquad \text{. . . and get } x = 35.$$

### Model Example 4

$$\frac{3}{4}x = 12 \qquad \text{The variable, } x, \text{ is multiplied by } \frac{3}{4}.$$

$$\frac{4}{3} \cdot \frac{3}{4}x = 12 \cdot \frac{4}{3} \qquad \text{To get a coefficient of 1, multiply by } \frac{4}{3} \ (\frac{3}{4}\text{'s reciprocal)}$$

$$\frac{4}{3} \cdot \frac{3}{4}x = \frac{12}{1} \cdot \frac{4}{3}$$

$$\frac{12}{12}x = \frac{48}{3} \qquad \text{Then simplify . . .}$$

$$x = 16 \qquad \text{. . . and find that } x = 16.$$

Actually, whether a variable is combined with a constant by multiplication or by division, you may consider that you are multiplying by that constant's reciprocal in order to get the variable alone (to have a coefficient of 1). In model example 1, you may consider the $3a$ to have been multiplied by $\frac{1}{3}$ as well as to have been divided by 3 (the two operations accomplish the same thing). In model example 2, we multiplied by 4 because 4 is the reciprocal of $\frac{1}{4}$, and $\frac{b}{4}$ means $\frac{1}{4}b$.

Try your hand at the following equations for which a reciprocal multiplication is required.

Solve for the variable.

1) $3x = 18$

2) $5x = 40$

3) $7n = 56$

4) $\frac{1}{2}n = 9$

5) $\frac{1}{3}r = 17$

6) $\frac{1}{8}y = 4$

7) $\frac{2}{3}m = 42$

8) $\frac{3}{4}y = 21$

9) $\frac{5}{8}x = 20$

10) $\frac{4}{5}w = 24$

11) $\frac{1}{3}m = 7$

12) $4v = 7$

13) $9u = 5$

14) $21m = 7$

15) $\frac{2}{3}l = \frac{3}{4}$

16) $\frac{1}{2}x = \frac{3}{4}$

17) $\frac{2}{3}x = \frac{7}{8}$

18) $6p = \frac{1}{7}$

19) $\frac{s}{5} = 9$

20) $\frac{t}{3} = 8$

21) $\frac{r}{5} = \frac{3}{8}$

## Answers

| | | | | | | | | | | | | | |
|---|---|---|---|---|---|---|---|---|---|---|---|---|---|
| **1.** | 6 | **2.** | 8 | **3.** | 8 | **4.** | 18 | **5.** | 51 | **6.** | 32 | **7.** | 63 |
| **8.** | 28 | **9.** | 24 | **10.** | 30 | **11.** | 21 | **12.** | $1\frac{3}{4}$ | **13.** | $\frac{5}{9}$ | **14.** | $\frac{1}{3}$ |
| **15.** | $1\frac{1}{8}$ | **16.** | $1\frac{1}{2}$ | **17.** | $1\frac{5}{16}$ | **18.** | $\frac{1}{42}$ | **19.** | 45 | **20.** | 24 | **21.** | $1\frac{7}{8}$ |

# PUTTING IT ALL TOGETHER

As you may have suspected, it is rather rare to find an algebraic equation that lends itself to being solved by just one operation alone. Most are solved by some combination of two or more operations. Nevertheless, since we have already looked at the procedures involved for undoing all of the ways by which variables and constants can be combined, being able to solve most equations is just a matter of being able to use the procedures we have already studied in the proper sequence. To assure that the proper sequence is followed, it is helpful to bear in mind three steps which, when followed, will lead to the solutions of most linear equations:

1. Combine like terms on the same side of the equation.

2. Collect terms.

3. Multiply by the reciprocal of the variable's coefficient.

The application of these three steps is illustrated in the rather complex model examples below.

*Model Example 1*

$$5x + 3 - 2x = 23 - x + 4$$

Inspecting the equation, we can see that there are two terms containing variables on the left side, and two terms that are constants on the right side. These like terms must be combined:

$$3x + 3 = 27 - x$$

Since the greater number of variables are on the left, we will collect them on that side. Since 3 is added onto the left side, we subtract 3 from both sides:

$$
\begin{array}{rcl}
3x + 3 &=& 27 - x \\
-3 & & -3 \\
\hline
3x &=& 24 - x
\end{array}
$$

To move the variable, $x$, to the left side, we first notice how it is combined with the 24. Since it is combined by subtraction, we add $x$ to both sides:

$$
\begin{array}{rcl}
3x &=& 24 - x \\
-x & & +x \\
\hline
4x &=& 24
\end{array}
$$

What remains to be done is to undo the multiplication of $x$ by 4. This can be done by multiplying by its reciprocal, or by dividing:

$$(\tfrac{1}{4})(4x) = (24)(\tfrac{1}{4}) \quad \text{or} \quad \frac{4x}{4} = \frac{24}{4}$$

Either way, we finally determine that . . .

$$x = 6$$

Notice in the model example on page 136 that the three steps were followed in the order stated before:

1. Combine like terms on the same side.

2. Collect terms.

3. Multiply by the reciprocal or the variable's coefficient (or divide).

Not every one of those steps need always be followed. Sometimes one or more steps cannot be done, simply because there are no terms with which to perform the step. Such a case can be seen in model example 2, below.

*Model Example 2*

$$5x + 7 = 2x - 5$$

There are no like terms to combine, so we move right on to collecting like terms — first constants with constants . . .

$$\begin{array}{r} 5x + 7 = 2x - 5 \\ -7 \qquad\quad -7 \\ \hline 5x \quad\;\; = 2x - 12 \end{array}$$

. . . and then variables with variables (although they did not need to be done in that order).

$$\begin{array}{r} 5x = \quad 2x - 12 \\ -2x \quad -2x \qquad \\ \hline 3x = \qquad\quad -12 \end{array}$$

Finally, we multiply by the variable's coefficient's reciprocal, or we divide . . .

$$\frac{3x}{3} = \frac{^-12}{3} \quad \text{or} \quad \tfrac{1}{3}(3x) = \tfrac{1}{3}(^-12)$$

. . . and discover that:

$$x = {}^-4$$

In model example 3, the need to collect terms does not exist:

*Model Example 3*

$$\tfrac{3}{4}x + \tfrac{7}{4}x = 12 - 9$$

Combine like terms on the same side of the equal sign . . .

$$\tfrac{10}{4}x = 3$$

. . . Notice that there is no need to collect terms, so the next step is to multiply both sides by the reciprocal of $\tfrac{10}{4}$: $\tfrac{4}{10}$.

$$(\tfrac{4}{10})(\tfrac{10}{4}x) = (\tfrac{4}{10})(\tfrac{3}{1})$$

The result is then expressed in lowest terms — in this case as a mixed numeral:

$$x = \tfrac{12}{10} = 1\tfrac{1}{5}$$

The equations below require a mixture of operations to solve. Remember the order in which the operations should be performed, and you will have little difficulty with them. If necessary, refer to the rules and the model examples above.

Solve for the variable.

1) $3x + 5 = 2x + 7$

2) $8y - 3 = 5y + 18$

3) $2x - 4 = 5x + 7$

4) $8y - 8 = 5y + 7$

5) $9z + 5 - 2z = 6 + 3z + 9$

6) $5 - z = 3z - 11$

7) $3 + 2n = 4n - 9$

8) $4 - 5m + 7 = 2m + 4m$

9) $a - 3 + a = 7 - 3a$

10) $9b - 6 = 6b + 9$

11) $\dfrac{b}{3} + 8 = 7$

12) $\dfrac{x}{2} - 5 = 6 - \dfrac{x}{2}$

13) $\tfrac{1}{4}y + \tfrac{1}{2} = \tfrac{2}{3}$

14) $11 - \tfrac{2}{3}x = \tfrac{1}{3}x - 6$

15) $\tfrac{3}{4}x - 12 = 15 - \tfrac{1}{2}x$

16) $\tfrac{5}{7}p - 4 = \tfrac{3}{7}p - 12$

17) $\dfrac{8r}{5} - 2 = \dfrac{3r}{10} + 8$

18) $\tfrac{1}{8}w + 11 = \tfrac{5}{8}w - 7$

19) $\dfrac{9q}{10} - \dfrac{3}{5}q = \dfrac{3}{4} - \dfrac{1}{8}$

20) $3m + 5 = \tfrac{3}{8}m - 6$

## Answers

| | | | | | | | | | |
|---|---|---|---|---|---|---|---|---|---|
| **1.** | 2 | **2.** | 7 | **3.** | $-\tfrac{11}{3}$, or $-3\tfrac{2}{3}$ | **4.** | 5 | **5.** | $\tfrac{5}{2}$ or $2\tfrac{1}{2}$ |
| **6.** | 4 | **7.** | 6 | **8.** | 1 | **9.** | 2 | **10.** | 5 |
| **11.** | $^-3$ | **12.** | 11 | **13.** | $\tfrac{2}{3}$ | **14.** | 17 | **15.** | $\tfrac{108}{5}$ or $21\tfrac{3}{5}$ |
| **16.** | $^-28$ | **17.** | $\tfrac{100}{13}$ or $7\tfrac{9}{13}$ | **18.** | 27 | **19.** | $\tfrac{25}{12}$ or $2\tfrac{1}{12}$ | **20.** | $\tfrac{-22}{3}$ or $-7\tfrac{1}{3}$ |

You will find additional practice in solving for variables on page 274.

# RATIO AND PROPORTION

## *WHAT IS A RATIO?*

When we looked at the many different ways in which fractions are used (in Chapter 3), we noted that one of those uses was to represent a ratio. Ratio is a mathematical word which means comparison.

**A ratio is a comparison.**

There are two different notations commonly used to represent ratios. One of them is 3:4, and the other is ¾. Whether the colon or the fraction line is used, the ratio should read "3 is to 4 . . . ." Did you get the impression that something should have followed the symbols in quotation marks? Well something should have, and usually does, but before getting into that, consider a few common examples of ratios:

*Model Example 1*

There are 23 women and 17 men in an evening class. Find the ratio of men to women, women to men, and women to students in the class.

The ratio of men to women is 17:23 or $\frac{17}{23}$.

The ratio of women to men is 23:17 or $\frac{23}{17}$.

The ratio of women to students is 23:40 or $\frac{23}{40}$.

It is crucial to notice that in any ratio the order in which the terms or conditions are stated will determine what the ratio looks like. In model example 1, three ratios were formed from just two figures. In fact, however, six ratios are possible from any two figures. In all of those ratios, the order of the terms is extremely significant. Examine model example 2, below, and you will see how the six ratios are formed.

*Model Example 2*

An order from a fast-food restaurant contains 5 hamburgers and 7 cheeseburgers. Form all possible ratios from this data.

| | |
|---|---|
| Hamburgers to cheeseburgers: | 5:7 |
| Cheeseburgers to hamburgers: | 7:5 |
| Cheeseburgers to all burgers: | 7:12 |
| Hamburgers to all burgers: | 5:12 |
| All burgers to cheeseburgers: | 12:7 |
| All burgers to hamburgers: | 12:5 |

. . . and hold the French fries.

Now that you have seen how ratios are formed, see how you do at forming all possible ratios from the data given below.

1) 9 history professors and 2 mathematics professors:

a) history to mathematics professors _____

b) mathematics to history professors _____

c) math professors to those of both subjects _____

d) history professors to those of both subjects _____

e) professors of both subjects to history professors _____

f) professors of both subjects to math professors _____

2) 19 regular letters and 2 special delivery letters:

a) regular to special delivery letters _____

b) special delivery to regular letters _____

c) regular to all letters _____

d) special delivery to all letters _____

e) all letters to regular letters _____

f) all letters to special delivery letters _____

3) 7 spaghetti dinners and 3 fish dinners

a) fish dinners to spaghetti dishes _____

b) spaghetti dinners to all dinners _____

c) all dinners to fish dinners _____

d) spaghetti dinners to fish dinners _____

e) all dinners to spaghetti dinners _____

f) fish dinners to all dinners _____

## Answers

**1.**  9:2, 2:9, 2:11, 9:11, 11:9, 11:2

**2.**  19:2, 2:19, 19:21, 2:21, 21:19, 21:2

**3.**  3:7, 7:10, 10:3, 7:3, 10:7, 3:10

Make 6 different ratios from each pair of numbers.

1) 4, 8 _____

2) 11, 5 _____

3) 6, 13 _____

4) 7, 12 _____

5) 9, 1 _____

## Answers

1.  4:8, 8:4, 4:12, 8:12, 12:4, 12:8

2.  11:5, 5:11, 5:16, 11:16, 16:5, 16:11

3.  6:13, 13:6, 6:19, 13:19, 19:6, 19:13

4.  7:12, 12:7, 7:19, 12:19, 19:7, 19:12

5.  9:1, 1:9, 1:10, 9:10, 10:1, 10:9

Express each ratio as a fraction in lowest terms.

1) 5:9 _____   2) 6:11 _____   3) 5:17 _____   4) 7:3 _____   5) 12:4 _____

6) 8:4 _____   7) 9:12 _____   8) 24:36 _____   9) 18:15 _____   10) 6:9 _____

## Answers

1. $\frac{5}{9}$      2. $\frac{6}{11}$      3. $\frac{5}{17}$      4. $\frac{7}{3}$      5. $\frac{3}{1}$

6. $\frac{2}{1}$      7. $\frac{3}{4}$      8. $\frac{2}{3}$      9. $\frac{6}{5}$      10. $\frac{2}{3}$

# WHAT IS A PROPORTION?

Ratios in and of themselves can be handy for expressing a relationship between two quantities, but are of little use in solving mathematical problems. Once ratios are placed into a proportion, however, they become very useful. **A proportion is an equation involving two ratios**.

6:9 = 2:3 is a proportion. It is read: "Six is to nine as two is to three." That means 6 has the same relationship to 9 as the relationship that 2 has to 3. 6 is $\frac{2}{3}$ of 9, and 2 is $\frac{2}{3}$ of 3. In a proportion, the two terms farthest from each other are known as the **extremes**. The two terms nearest each other are known as the **means**:

Can you recognize the means and the extremes in the following proportion?

$$\tfrac{1}{2} = \tfrac{4}{8}$$

The means are 2 and 4, while 1 and 8 are the extremes. If you are not sure of why that is the case, consider that the proportion could have been written as 1:2 = 4:8 (1 is to 2 as 4 is to 8). Then the means and the extremes would be obvious.

One rule governs operations involving proportions. That rule is:

**The product of the means equals the product of the extremes.**

To see how that rule works, consider the two proportions on page 141. In 3:4 = 15:20, multiply the extremes (3 × 20) and get 60. Then multiply the means (4 × 15) and get 60. 60 = 60, so the product of the extremes equals the product of the means (and vice-versa).

In the proportion $\frac{1}{2} = \frac{4}{8}$, the product of the means (1 × 8) equals the product of the extremes (2 × 4).

Since it is not customary to include colons in mathematical equations, but it is perfectly usual to find fractions, proportions are almost always seen in the fractional form. Since the fractional form is so usual, and since mathematicians are always looking for shortcuts to save time, the multiplication of means together and extremes together in fraction form is often thought of as "cross-multiplication," where the denominator of each ratio is multiplied by the numerator of the other:

$$\frac{1}{2} \underset{\times}{\overset{\times}{\bowtie}} \frac{4}{8} \begin{matrix} = 8 \\ = 8 \end{matrix}$$

$$8 = 8$$

Note that cross-multiplication can only occur when there is a single fraction on either side of an equal sign. **That is the only time that it is permissible.**

## SOLVING PROPORTIONS

Now that we have examined what ratios and proportions are, and the rules that govern them, it is time to see how to put them to work. Below are proportions, each of which has one term missing. Find the missing term by cross-multiplying and then solving for the variable.

Solve each proportion for the variable.

1) $\frac{x}{5} = \frac{8}{20}$    2) $\frac{x}{14} = \frac{21}{42}$    3) $\frac{y}{9} = \frac{4}{3}$    4) $\frac{5}{8} = \frac{x}{40}$    5) $\frac{5}{12} = \frac{n}{60}$    6) $\frac{24}{15} = \frac{56}{n}$

7) $\frac{35}{40} = \frac{14}{r}$    8) $\frac{6}{7} = \frac{z}{8}$    9) $\frac{5}{x} = \frac{4}{9}$    10) $\frac{3}{x} = \frac{7}{11}$    11) $\frac{4}{x} = \frac{32}{72}$    12) $\frac{5}{9} = \frac{x}{12}$

13) $\frac{y}{17} = \frac{8}{11}$    14) $\frac{6}{y} = \frac{8}{13}$    15) $\frac{3}{v} = \frac{8}{21}$    16) $\frac{2}{9} = \frac{g}{8}$    17) $\frac{15}{z} = \frac{6}{21}$    18) $\frac{4}{7} = \frac{9}{w}$

19) $\frac{3x}{5} = \frac{7}{9}$    20) $\frac{5}{4y} = \frac{3}{10}$    21) $\frac{7}{15} = \frac{8}{5y}$

## Answers

| | | | | |
|---|---|---|---|---|
| **1.** 2 | **2.** 7 | **3.** 12 | **4.** 25 | **5.** 25 |
| **6.** 35 | **7.** 16 | **8.** $\frac{48}{7}$ or $6\frac{6}{7}$ | **9.** $\frac{45}{4}$ or $11\frac{1}{4}$ | **10.** $\frac{33}{7}$ or $4\frac{5}{7}$ |
| **11.** 9 | **12.** $\frac{60}{9}$ or $6\frac{2}{3}$ | **13.** $\frac{136}{11}$ or $12\frac{4}{11}$ | **14.** $\frac{39}{4}$ or $9\frac{3}{4}$ | **15.** $\frac{63}{8}$ or $7\frac{7}{8}$ |
| **16.** $\frac{16}{9}$ or $1\frac{7}{9}$ | **17.** $\frac{105}{2}$ or $52\frac{1}{2}$ | **18.** $\frac{63}{4}$ or $15\frac{3}{4}$ | **19.** $\frac{35}{27}$ or $1\frac{8}{27}$ | **20.** $\frac{25}{6}$ or $4\frac{1}{8}$ |
| **21.** $\frac{24}{7}$ or $3\frac{3}{7}$ | | | | |

You will find additional practice in solving proportions on pages 274–275.

# PERCENTS

Many people have difficulty understanding percents, and how they work. In fact, percents are ratios, but they can probably best be understood if they are thought of as fractions. Unlike common fractions (the kind with numerators and denominators) and decimal fractions, percents are not based on a unit of 1. That is to say, when dealing with percents, 1 whole is represented not by the numeral 1, but rather by 100. 100% = 1 whole. Any fraction, therefore, may be changed into a percent simply by establishing a proportion:

$$\frac{\text{numerator}}{\text{denominator}} = \frac{x}{100}$$

Solving for $x$ will then give the percent.

*Model Example 1*

Express the fraction $\frac{3}{4}$ as a percent.

$\frac{3}{4} = \frac{x}{100}$  First a proportion is set up . . .

$4x = 300$  . . . next we cross multiply.

$\frac{4x}{4} = \frac{300}{4}$  . . . divide each side by 4 . . .

$x = 75\%$  . . . and find the percent.

To express any decimal as a percent, the task is even simpler. Since decimals are based upon the unit 1, and percents are based upon the unit 100, all that needs to be done is to multiply the decimal fraction by 100. (You may recall that that is accomplished by moving the decimal point two places to the right.)

*Model Example 2*

Express .35 as a percent.

$$.35 \times 100 = x$$
$$35 = x$$
$$x = 35\%$$

Below, you will find a table listing a few equivalent fractions, decimals, and percents. It is meant merely to demonstrate that any fraction can readily be expressed in any or all three forms.

| FRACTION | DECIMAL | PERCENT |
| --- | --- | --- |
| $\frac{10}{14}$ | .71 | 71% |
| $\frac{2}{17}$ | .11 | 11% |
| $\frac{1}{14}$ | .07 | 7% |
| $\frac{4}{15}$ | .26 | 26% |
| $\frac{3}{14}$ | .21 | 21% |
| $\frac{4}{22}$ | .18 | 18% |
| $\frac{6}{21}$ | .28 | 28% |
| $\frac{2}{8}$ | .25 | 25% |
| $\frac{9}{25}$ | .36 | 36% |
| $\frac{8}{12}$ | .66 | 66% |
| $\frac{8}{15}$ | .53 | 53% |
| $\frac{9}{16}$ | .56 | 56% |
| $\frac{4}{19}$ | .21 | 21% |
| $\frac{8}{14}$ | .57 | 57% |
| $\frac{2}{22}$ | .09 | 9% |

Fill in the blank to write an equivalent fraction, decimal or percent.

| | FRACTION | DECIMAL | PERCENT |
| --- | --- | --- | --- |
| 1) | $\frac{4}{7}$ | _____ | 57% |
| 2) | $\frac{5}{16}$ | .31 | _____ |
| 3) | _____ | .83 | 83% |
| 4) | $\frac{2}{10}$ | _____ | 20% |
| 5) | $\frac{4}{17}$ | .23 | _____ |
| 6) | $\frac{8}{16}$ | .5 | _____ |
| 7) | $\frac{4}{23}$ | _____ | 17% |
| 8) | $\frac{9}{17}$ | _____ | 52% |
| 9) | _____ | .25 | 25% |

| | | | |
|---|---|---|---|
| 10) | $\frac{10}{23}$ | _____ | 43% |
| 11) | _____ | .45 | 45% |
| 12) | _____ | .67 | 67% |
| 13) | $\frac{3}{10}$ | .3 | _____ |
| 14) | $\frac{8}{12}$ | _____ | 67% |
| 15) | _____ | .5 | 50% |
| 16) | $\frac{9}{25}$ | _____ | 36% |
| 17) | $\frac{5}{12}$ | _____ | 41% |
| 18) | $\frac{8}{25}$ | _____ | _____ |
| 19) | $\frac{5}{25}$ | _____ | _____ |
| 20) | $\frac{9}{14}$ | _____ | _____ |

## Answers

| | | | |
|---|---|---|---|
| **1.** .57 | **2.** 31% | **3.** $\frac{5}{6}$ | **4.** .2 |
| **5.** 23% | **6.** 50% | **7.** .17 | **8.** .52 |
| **9.** $\frac{1}{4}$ | **10.** .43 | **11.** $\frac{9}{20}$ | **12.** $\frac{2}{3}$ |
| **13.** 30% | **14.** .67 | **15.** $\frac{1}{2}$ | **16.** .36 |
| **17.** .41 | **18.** .32, 32% | **19.** .2, 20% | **20.** .64, 64% |

You will find additional practice with equivalent fractions, decimals and percents on pages 275–276.

Express each decimal as a percent.

| | | | | | |
|---|---|---|---|---|---|
| 1) .31 | 2) .12 | 3) .62 | 4) .71 | 5) .11 | 6) .6 |
| 7) .72 | 8) .2 | 9) .53 | 10) .46 | 11) .08 | 12) .41 |
| 13) .52 | 14) .57 | 15) .22 | 16) .62 | 17) .41 | 18) .25 |
| 19) .47 | 20) .36 | 21) .4 | 22) .77 | 23) .26 | 24) .45 |
| 25) .46 | 26) .72 | 27) .16 | 28) .42 | 29) .38 | 30) .35 |
| 31) .5 | 32) .41 | | | | |

## Answers

| | | | | | |
|---|---|---|---|---|---|
| **1.** 31% | **2.** 12% | **3.** 62% | **4.** 71% | **5.** 11% |
| **6.** 60% | **7.** 72% | **8.** 20% | **9.** 53% | **10.** 46% |
| **11.** 8% | **12.** 41% | **13.** 52% | **14.** 57% | **15.** 22% |
| **16.** 62% | **17.** 41% | **18.** 25% | **19.** 47% | **20.** 36% |
| **21.** 40% | **22.** 77% | **23.** 26% | **24.** 45% | **25.** 46% |
| **26.** 72% | **27.** 16% | **28.** 42% | **29.** 38% | **30.** 35% |
| **31.** 50% | **32.** 41% | | | |

You will find additional practice with expressing decimals as percents on page 276.

Express each fraction as a percent.

1) $\frac{8}{21}$  2) $\frac{9}{18}$  3) $\frac{4}{6}$  4) $\frac{1}{6}$  5) $\frac{5}{8}$  6) $\frac{9}{17}$  7) $\frac{4}{12}$  8) $\frac{8}{12}$

9) $\frac{8}{9}$  10) $\frac{3}{9}$  11) $\frac{4}{14}$  12) $\frac{10}{22}$  13) $\frac{8}{14}$  14) $\frac{1}{6}$  15) $\frac{8}{12}$  16) $\frac{8}{24}$

17) $\frac{10}{11}$  18) $\frac{4}{11}$  19) $\frac{8}{8}$  20) $\frac{2}{25}$  21) $\frac{4}{5}$  22) $\frac{8}{13}$  23) $\frac{9}{9}$  24) $\frac{5}{15}$

25) $\frac{10}{24}$  26) $\frac{9}{9}$  27) $\frac{7}{23}$  28) $\frac{5}{16}$  29) $\frac{4}{6}$  30) $\frac{7}{14}$  31) $\frac{2}{19}$  32) $\frac{1}{13}$

## Answers

| | | | | | |
|---|---|---|---|---|---|
| **1.** 38% | **2.** 50% | **3.** 66% | **4.** 16% | **5.** 62% |
| **6.** 52% | **7.** 33% | **8.** 66% | **9.** 88% | **10.** 33% |
| **11.** 28% | **12.** 45% | **13.** 57% | **14.** 16% | **15.** 66% |
| **16.** 33% | **17.** 90% | **18.** 36% | **19.** 100% | **20.** 8% |
| **21.** 80% | **22.** 61% | **23.** 100% | **24.** 33% | **25.** 41% |
| **26.** 100% | **27.** 30% | **28.** 31% | **29.** 66% | **30.** 50% |
| **31.** 10% | **32.** 7% | | | |

You will find additional practice with expressing fractions as percents on page 276.

# FINDING A PERCENT OF A NUMBER

You may recall that the words "times" and "of" are mathematically identical. Certainly you have heard expressions such as "Your tip should be 15% of the bill." Fifteen percent of the bill is found by multiplying. But how does one go about multiplying percents? Well, to be quite candid, one does not. Percents cannot be multiplied or divided, and it is quite rare to see them added or subtracted. How then, you well might ask, can we figure out 15% of the bill, or is the waiter just not going to receive a tip? The answer lies in the close relationship between decimals and percents. In order to find fifteen percent of the bill, the 15% must first be converted to a decimal: .15. Then the multiplication can take place:

*Model Example 3*

Find 25% of 300.

$25\% = .25$        First, change the percentage to a decimal.

$x = .25 \times 300$     Then multiply . . .

$x = 75$            . . . to get the answer.

Find each amount.

1) 30% of 944 = _____     2) 44% of 5 = _____     3) 77% of 214 = _____

4) 28% of 504 = _____     5) 38% of 925 = _____     6) 20% of 148 = _____

7) 79% of 895 = _____     8) 23% of 993 = _____     9) 57% of 553 = _____

10) 3% of 450 = _____     11) 10% of 115 = _____     12) 17% of 329 = _____

13) 16% of 500 = _____     14) 5% of 641 = _____     15) 31% of 9 = _____

16) 70% of 141 = _____     17) 95% of 738 = _____     18) 21% of 625 = _____

19) 26% of 757 = _____     20) 1% of 981 = _____     21) 71% of 32 = _____

22) 82% of 979 = _____     23) 53% of 89 = _____     24) 41% of 824 = _____

25) 70% of 447 = _____     26) 7% of 450 = _____     27) 93% of 779 = _____

28) 82% of 567 = _____     29) 16% of 844 = _____     30) 47% of 457 = _____

31) 1% of 149 = _____     32) 27% of 525 = _____     33) 81% of 380 = _____

34) 43% of 592 = _____     35) 54% of 567 = _____     36) 38% of 941 = _____

37) 37% of 10 = _____     38) 71% of 117 = _____     39) 5% of 949 = _____

40) 92% of 474 = _____     41) 3% of 986 = _____     42) 91% of 469 = _____

43) 29% of 257 = _____     44) 22% of 709 = _____     45) 97% of 356 = _____

46) 100% of 753 = _____     47) 73% of 1 = _____     48) 76% of 651 = _____

49) 85% of 464 = _____     50) 82% of 249 = _____

## Answers

| | | | | | | | | | |
|---|---|---|---|---|---|---|---|---|---|
| **1.** | 283.2 | **2.** | 2.2 | **3.** | 164.78 | **4.** | 141.12 | **5.** | 351.5 |
| **6.** | 29.6 | **7.** | 707.05 | **8.** | 228.39 | **9.** | 315.21 | **10.** | 13.5 |
| **11.** | 11.5 | **12.** | 55.93 | **13.** | 80 | **14.** | 32.05 | **15.** | 2.79 |
| **16.** | 98.7 | **17.** | 701.1 | **18.** | 131.25 | **19.** | 196.82 | **20.** | 9.81 |
| **21.** | 22.72 | **22.** | 802.78 | **23.** | 47.17 | **24.** | 337.84 | **25.** | 312.9 |
| **26.** | 31.5 | **27.** | 724.47 | **28.** | 464.94 | **29.** | 135.04 | **30.** | 214.79 |
| **31.** | 1.49 | **32.** | 141.75 | **33.** | 307.8 | **34.** | 254.56 | **35.** | 306.18 |
| **36.** | 357.58 | **37.** | 3.7 | **38.** | 83.07 | **39.** | 47.45 | **40.** | 436.08 |
| **41.** | 29.58 | **42.** | 426.79 | **43.** | 74.53 | **44.** | 155.98 | **45.** | 345.32 |
| **46.** | 753 | **47.** | .73 | **48.** | 494.76 | **49.** | 394.4 | **50.** | 204.18 |

You will find additional practice with percents on pages 277–278.

Finding a percent of a number is useful for figuring discounts on items that are on sale, tips paid as a percentage of the bill at a restaurant, sales tax, grades on examinations, and interest paid on loans, or on money in a savings account. Salespeople often earn commissions as a percentage of what they sell, as do travel agents, ticket agents, and insurance agents. In short, there are many situations in which it is necessary to compute a percentage of a certain number — often a number which expresses a quantity of money. We will look further into some of these applications in the section dealing with word-problems involving percents (beginning on page 190).

# SOME USEFUL PROPERTIES

## *THE CLOSURE PROPERTY*

When numbers are combined, they follow certain laws or rules. For example, we know that adding two whole positive numbers will always result in a sum that is a positive whole number. This leads to the somewhat useful, if technical, statement: The set of counting numbers* is **closed** for addition. Stated more simply, the closure property for addition of counting numbers might read: When two counting numbers are added, a counting number will be the result.

Is the set of counting numbers closed for subtraction? Think about it. Select two counting numbers and subtract one from the other; say 8 take away 2. Does a counting number result? Will a counting number always result? How about if we take 8 away from 2? $2 - 8 = {}^-6$. A negative is not a counting number, therefore the set of counting numbers is not closed for subtraction. Note that you might have tried subtracting hundreds of pairs of counting numbers with the first number of each pair being larger than the second,

*Counting numbers are positive whole numbers, i.e., 1, 2, 3, . . .

and always have gotten a counting number as the difference. Just a single case where that does not occur, however, suffices to prove that the set of counting numbers is not closed for subtraction. It is an interesting feature of both mathematics and science that an exceedingly large number of positive results in an experiment never suffices to prove that something will always work. Just a single negative result, however, is adequate to prove that something will not always work.

Is the set of counting numbers closed for multiplication? Try multiplying two counting numbers and getting a product that is anything other than a counting number. No matter how many pairs of numbers you choose, you will get a product that is a counting number. Mathematicians are, therefore, pretty sure that the set of counting numbers is closed for multiplication. If, on the other hand, you multiply two counting numbers sometime and find that you get a negative result, you may have just disproved this hypothesis. (In all candor, though, it is much more likely that you made a mistake.)

Divide one counting number by another, and the odds are very much in favor of the result's being a fraction (otherwise known as a rational number). 4 divided by 2 is a counting number, 2. 2 divided by 4, however, equals $\frac{1}{2}$, and that is not a counting number. What statement may therefore be made about closure with respect to the set of counting numbers for division?

## REALMS OF NUMBERS

It is a useful device to talk about numbers as belonging to certain realms. Each time a new condition is added to a realm of numbers, a new realm is formed which includes all the members of the last realm, and a whole new group in addition. We have just examined one property of the first realm of numbers that is usually considered, counting numbers. **Counting numbers** derive their name from the fact that when you count objects you start with the first object you see, and call it "1." Then you go on from there with 2, 3, and so on forever. Notice that the first counting number is 1.

The next realm of numbers is obtained by adding zero to the realm of counting numbers. This is the realm known as **natural numbers**. It is an infinite realm, as is the set of counting numbers, in that there is no highest number. Natural numbers start at zero and go on forever. Counting numbers also go on forever, but they start at 1.

The next realm of numbers includes an infinite addition to the already infinite set of natural numbers. It includes all whole numbers that are less than zero, that is, negative whole numbers. This new realm is known as the realm of **integers**. Positive integers consist of 1, 2, 3, . . ., whereas negative integers consist of $^-1$, $^-2$, $^-3$, . . . . (The series of three dots is used to indicate that the series of numbers continues in the same fashion forever.)

The next expansion consists of including any number that can be expressed as a fraction. Since any integer can be expressed as a fraction ($2 = \frac{2}{1}$, or $\frac{4}{2}$), all the numbers from previous realms are included in this new one, which is known as **rational numbers**. Often, you will see fractions referred to as rational numbers, but whole numbers (negative as well as positive) are rational numbers also. Rational numbers also include those numbers which can be expressed as repeating decimals. For example, .6666 . . . is a rational number, as is 4.121212 . . . .

**Irrational numbers** are numbers which cannot be expressed as either fractions or repeating decimals. The set of irrational numbers is not a realm, since it does not include any of the numbers already discussed. $\sqrt{2}$ * is an irrational number, as is the number $\pi$ (pi). Mathematicians have calculated the values of these numbers to many decimal places, and have so far been able to discern no repeating pattern, hence they are referred to as irrational.

When the set of irrational numbers is combined with the realm of rational numbers, we get the most important realm — that known as **real numbers**. The realm of real numbers encompasses all fractions, positive numbers, negative numbers, zero, and irrational numbers. To summarize, then, the realms of numbers are:

| | |
|---|---|
| Counting numbers | (1, 2, 3, . . . .) |
| Natural numbers | (Counting numbers + 0) |
| Integers | (Natural numbers + whole negative numbers) |
| Rational numbers | (Integers + fractions and repeating decimals) |
| Real numbers | (Rational numbers + Irrational numbers) |

## THE COMMUTATIVE PROPERTY

Have you ever tried to add 8 + 6 and ended up adding 6 + 8 instead? Did it make a difference? Of course not. That is because **the order in which you add two numbers does not affect the sum**. That fact is referred to by mathematicians as the **Commutative Property of Addition**. The commutative property deals with two numbers, and might be shown symbolically as $a + b = b + a$.

There is also a commutative property for multiplication. It states that **the order in which two numbers are multiplied together does not affect the product**. Stated symbolically, $a \times b = b \times a$. Consider that $9 \times 5 = 45$, and that $5 \times 9 = 45$. That is the commutative property for multiplication in action. Try applying the commutative property to subtraction or to division, and convince yourself that it does not work.

## THE ASSOCIATIVE PROPERTY

All arithmetic operations are **binary**. That is a fancy way of saying that they involve only two numbers at a time. If you are skeptical, try adding 3 + 4 + 5. If you think that you just added 3 + 4 + 5, you are just fooling yourself. Nobody, and for that matter no computer, is capable of adding three numbers together at the same time. Try it again, only this time do it out loud. Did you do it? You probably said 3 + 4 = 7; + 5 = 12. Notice the ";" that separates the two steps. What you actually did was find the 7, and then combine 7 and 5 to get 12. There were two other options, however. Without changing the order of the numbers, you might have added 4 + 5 to get 9, and then combined 9 with 3 to get 12. The other possibility was to combine the 3 and 5 to make 8, and then add 4 to get 12.

*The square root of two: A number which, when multiplied by itself equals 2. $\sqrt{9}$ is a rational number, since $3 \times 3 = 9$.

Whichever way you combined the numbers, what you were doing was selectively grouping the numbers in order to facilitate adding them. Grouping numbers together for addition is called associating them. The fact that **the way in which numbers are grouped for addition does not affect the sum** is known as the **Associative Property for Addition.** Using the addition on page 150 as an illustration, the associative property would look like this:

$$(3 + 4) + 5 = 3 + (4 + 5)*$$

In general terms, the associative property for addition may be illustrated as:

$$(a + b) + c = a + (b + c)$$

If you think about it, you will recognize that the associative property may also be applied to multiplication. In that case, you would discover that $(2 \times 3) \times 4 = 2 \times (3 \times 4)$, or, generally stated, $(a \times b) \times c = a \times (b \times c)$.

## THE DISTRIBUTIVE PROPERTY

While the three properties discussed above are useful in computational work, they are, for the most part, intuitive. The odds are that even if you had not seen it stated here and given a fancy name, you still would have known that $3 \times 4$ gives the same result as $4 \times 3$. The Distributive Property of Multiplication over Addition is a different story. It is a property that is usually seen only in algebraic applications. The **Distributive Property states that if the sum of two numbers is multiplied by a third, the result is the same as if each of the numbers was first multiplied by the third, and their products added together**. It may be illustrated as follows:

$$a(b + c) = ab + ac$$

Consider the meaning if we substitute the numbers 2, 3, and 4 for $a$, $b$, and $c$, respectively. We would then get:

$$2(3 + 4) = 2 \cdot 3 + 2 \cdot 4$$
$$2(7) = 6 + 8$$
$$14 = 14$$

And there you have it!! You will find a need to apply this property repeatedly in algebraic equations, so it is a good idea to get some practice with it. The exercises on the next page should help you to do just that.

*That illustrates the first two cases discussed previously. The third case involves changes in order as well as grouping, and so is not illustrated.

Write an equivalent expression which is the result of applying the distributive property to the expression already written.

1) $5(n + 3) = 5\underline{\hspace{1cm}} + \underline{\hspace{1cm}}$

2) $6(r + 8) = \underline{\hspace{1cm}}r + \underline{\hspace{1cm}}$

3) $4(7 - b) = \underline{\hspace{1cm}} - \underline{\hspace{1cm}}b$

4) $a(7 + c) = \underline{\hspace{3cm}}$

5) $9(r + w) = \underline{\hspace{3cm}}$

6) $a(x + r) = \underline{\hspace{3cm}}$

7) $c(l + m) = \underline{\hspace{3cm}}$

8) $r(v - h) = \underline{\hspace{3cm}}$

9) $w(2p - 8) = \underline{\hspace{3cm}}$

10) $v(3r - 2x) = \underline{\hspace{3cm}}$

## Answers

1. $5n + 15$
2. $6r + 48$
3. $28 - 4b$
4. $7a + ac$

5. $9r + 9w$
6. $ax + rx$
7. $cl + cm$
8. $rv - rh$

9. $2pw - 8w$
10. $3rv - 2vx$

# EXPONENTS

Exponents are little numerals written above and to the right of other numerals. They are read as **powers**. For example, $x^3$ is read "$x$ to the third power," and $5^2$ is read "5 to the second power."

Exponents are used to represent a number being multiplied by itself a certain number of times.

$$x^3 \text{ means } x \cdot x \cdot x$$

$$n^4 \text{ means } n \cdot n \cdot n \cdot n$$

$$2^3 \text{ means } 2 \cdot 2 \cdot 2 = 8$$

$$3^4 \text{ means } 3 \cdot 3 \cdot 3 \cdot 3 = 81$$

When adding or subtracting numbers which have exponents, only variables raised to the identical power may be combined. Examine the examples below, and you will see what is meant by the last statement:

$$x^3 + x^3 = 2x^3 \qquad\qquad 2y^2 + 5y^2 = 7y^2$$

$$9m^4 + 5m^4 = 14m^4 \qquad\qquad 6r^5 - 2r^5 = 4r^5$$

$$8w^3 - 5w^3 = 3w^3 \qquad\qquad 10ab^4 - 5ab^4 = 5ab^4$$

**but . . .**

$$x^3 + x^2 = x^3 + x^2 \qquad \text{and} \qquad 5z^5 - 2z^2 = 5z^5 - 2z^2$$

Since the variables in each of the last two expressions differ with respect to their exponents, they cannot be further combined by addition or subtraction.

## COMBINING VARIABLES WITH EXPONENTS BY MULTIPLICATION AND DIVISION

If two variables have the same base, that is, the same letter, they may be combined by multiplication. To combine variables with exponents it is only necessary to add their exponents together:

$$x^2 \cdot x^3 = x^{2+3} = x^5 \qquad\qquad y^4 \cdot y^3 = y^{4+3} = y^7$$

See if you can figure these two out:

$$x \cdot x = x^2 \qquad\qquad n \cdot n \cdot n = n^3$$

In case you have not guessed, a variable with no exponent showing has, in fact, an exponent of 1. Hence $x \cdot x$ is $x^1 \cdot x^1 = x^{1+1} = x^2$. $n \cdot n \cdot n = n^1 \cdot n^1 \cdot n^1 = n^{1+1+1} = n^3$.

What do you suppose is the way to divide numbers with exponents? Since exponents were added in multiplication, it would seem to be reasonable to suppose that they will be subtracted during division. Not only is that supposition reasonable; it is also accurate:

$$\frac{x^5}{x^2} = x^{5-2} = x^3$$

$$n^8 \div n^5 = n^{8-5} = n^3$$

Now, since we have seen how exponentiated numbers may be combined by multiplication and division, let us take a little space to justify the rules that we have just examined. First of all, consider a multiplication:

$$2^3 \cdot 2^4$$

$$2^3 = 2 \cdot 2 \cdot 2 = 8$$
$$2^4 = 2 \cdot 2 \cdot 2 \cdot 2 = 16$$

Then, $2^3 \cdot 2^4 = 8 \cdot 16$ which $= 128$.

Now, by the rules just discussed,

$$2^3 \cdot 2^4 = 2^{3+4} = 2^7$$

$$2^7 = 2 \cdot 2 \cdot 2 \cdot 2 \cdot 2 \cdot 2 \cdot 2 = 128$$

. . . and there you have your proof for multiplication. The proof for division we will leave you to work out for yourself. As a bit of a helping hand, however, consider $2^{10}$ divided by $2^6$. $2^{10}$ is worth 1024, while $2^6$ is worth 64.

Evaluate each of the following.

1) $3^2$     2) $2^3$     3) $5^2$     4) $2^5$     5) $3^4$     6) $4^3$     7) $2^{11}$

Express each in simplest form.

8) $a^5 + a^4$     9) $2a^3 + a^4$     10) $3a^2 + a^2$     11) $4b^5 - 3b^3$

12) $f^3 \cdot f^2$     13) $m^5 \cdot m^8$     14) $\dfrac{c^5}{c^3}$     15) $r^9 + r^9$

16) $2j^2 \cdot 3j^3$     17) $2s^4 \cdot 3s^5$     18) $5x^9 \cdot 2y^3$     19) $13d^4 - 9d^4$

20) $\dfrac{6w^8}{3w^6}$     21) $\dfrac{12z^9}{4z^8}$     22) $\dfrac{9k^5}{3k^3}$     23) $5t^4g^7 \cdot 6s^3g^2$

## Answers

| | | | |
|---|---|---|---|
| **1.** 9 | **2.** 8 | **3.** 25 | **4.** 32 |
| **5.** 81 | **6.** 64 | **7.** 2048 | **8.** $a^5 + a^4$ |
| **9.** $2a^3 + a^4$ | **10.** $4a^2$ | **11.** $4b^5 - 3b^3$ | **12.** $f^5$ |
| **13.** $m^{13}$ | **14.** $c^2$ | **15.** $2r^9$ | **16.** $6j^5$ |
| **17.** $6s^9$ | **18.** $10x^9y^3$ | **19.** $4d^4$ | **20.** $2w^2$ |
| **21.** $3z$ | **22.** $3k^2$ | **23.** $30g^9s^3t^4$ | |

## THE ZERO POWER

Any number raised to the zero power has a value of 1. That is to say, $3^0 = 1$, $17^0 = 1$, $335^0 = 1$, and $n^0 = 1$. In order to justify this rather unique situation, consider the following:

$$n^x \div n^x = n^{x-x} = n^0 \qquad \text{(since anything minus itself is zero.)}$$

$$\text{But } \frac{n^x}{n^x} = 1 \qquad \text{(since anything divided by itself = 1.)}$$

If any number divided by itself equals that number to the zero power, and any number divided by itself equals 1, then it follows that any number raised to the zero power equals 1.

## SQUARES AND SQUARE ROOTS

Special names are reserved for situations which occur frequently. In mathematics there is a special name for a number raised to the second power and a number raised to the third power. A number raised to the second power is called a **square**. That is because the area of a square is found by multiplying a side of the figure by itself ($s^2$). A cube's volume is found by multiplying one side of the figure by itself and by itself again ($V = s^3$). For that reason a number raised to the third power is known as that number **cubed**. We will not give any special attention to cubes at this time, but squares play a rather important role in GED mathematics.

Consider the first ten squares of positive integers. To find them, all that is necessary is to start with the first natural number, and square (raise to the second power) it and each of its consecutive successors. $1^2 = 1$; $2^2 = 4$; $3^2 = 9$; $4^2 = 16$ . . . $10^2 = 100$. You fill in the blanks represented by the dots. The numbers just considered are known as **perfect squares**. A perfect square is the result of multiplying any whole integer by itself.

It should be pointed out that there are two ways to make any perfect square. A perfect square is 25, being the product of $5 \cdot 5$. But 25 is also the product of $(^-5)(^-5)$. Both 5 and $^-5$ are considered to be **square roots** of 25. A square root is the whole number which, when multiplied by itself, yields a square. Not all numbers have integers as square roots. In fact, as you may have noticed, of the first 100 natural numbers, only 10 of them are perfect squares (1, 4, 9, 16, 25, 36, 49, 64, 81, and 100).

Since the square of 2 is 4, the square root of 4 is 2.

Since the square of 3 is 9, the square root of 9 is 3.

Since the square of 4 is 16, the square root of 16 is 4.

Now let's continue, but using the appropriate symbols. $\sqrt{\phantom{x}}$ is called a radical sign. It means "the square root of" whatever number is under it:

Since $5^2$ is 25, $\sqrt{25} = 5$.

Since $6^2$ is 36, $\sqrt{36} = 6$.

Since $7^2$ is 49, $\sqrt{49} = 7$.

Since $8^2$ is 64, $\sqrt{64} = 8$. . . .

Obviously, most numbers do not have perfect (i.e. whole number) square roots. There is no whole number which, when multiplied by itself will give a product, 3. The same is true for 2, 5, 7, and, in fact, most numbers. It has therefore become customary to express the square root of a number in as simple terms as possible, by removing as great a perfect square from within a radical sign as possible. Consider, for example, the radical $\sqrt{20}$. 20 contains a perfect square, 4, so that $\sqrt{20} = \sqrt{4 \cdot 5}$. But, since the square root of 4 is 2, $\sqrt{20} = 2\sqrt{5}$. The square root of 4, 2, is multiplied by the square root of 5 which remains in radical form.

Examine the following model examples.

| *Model Example 1* | *Model Example 2* | *Model Example 3* |
|---|---|---|
| $\sqrt{160} = \sqrt{16 \cdot 10}$ | $\sqrt{90} = \sqrt{9 \cdot 10}$ | $\sqrt{500} = \sqrt{100 \cdot 5}$ |
| $= 4\sqrt{10}$ | $= 3\sqrt{10}$ | $= 10\sqrt{5}$ |

The trick, as you can see in the models, is to extract a perfect square from the number under the radical sign. It is not essential that you get the largest perfect square each time you simplify a radical, as long as you eventually get the radical down to its simplest (unfactorable) form. Model example 4 illustrates two different approaches to the same factorization.

*Model Example 4*

$$\sqrt{320} = \sqrt{5 \cdot 64} = 8\sqrt{5}$$    (That is the most efficient approach.)

$$\sqrt{320} = \sqrt{4 \cdot 80} = 2\sqrt{80}$$    Here, only a 4 was recognized . . .

$$2\sqrt{80} = 2\sqrt{4 \cdot 20} = 4\sqrt{20}$$    . . . then another 4. The extracted 2 is multiplied by the 2 that was already outside (the radical's coefficient) . . .

$$4\sqrt{20} = 4\sqrt{4 \cdot 5} = 8\sqrt{5}$$    . . . and so one more time. Note that the final answer obtained this way is identical to the one at the top of the problem.

Express the following radicals in simplest form.

1) $\sqrt{36}$    2) $\sqrt{49}$    3) $\sqrt{121}$    4) $\sqrt{25}$    5) $\sqrt{81}$    6) $\sqrt{169}$

7) $\sqrt{144}$    8) $\sqrt{18}$    9) $\sqrt{50}$    10) $\sqrt{27}$    11) $\sqrt{98}$    12) $\sqrt{72}$

13) $\sqrt{75}$    14) $\sqrt{80}$    15) $\sqrt{x^2}$    16) $\sqrt{y^2}$    17) $\sqrt{m^6}$    18) $\sqrt{2x^2}$

19) $\sqrt{3q^2}$    20) $\sqrt{4n^2}$    21) $\sqrt{y^4}$    22) $\sqrt{16p^2}$    23) $\sqrt{81l^2}$    24) $\sqrt{24y}$

25) $\sqrt{81r}$    26) $\sqrt{144c}$    27) $\sqrt{162r^2}$    28) $\sqrt{16m^3}$

**Answers**

| 1. | 6 | 2. | 7 | 3. | 11 | 4. | 5 | 5. | 9 | 6. | 13 |
|----|---|----|---|----|----|----|---|----|---|----|----|
| 7. | 12 | 8. | $3\sqrt{2}$ | 9. | $5\sqrt{2}$ | 10. | $3\sqrt{3}$ | 11. | $7\sqrt{2}$ | 12. | $6\sqrt{2}$ |
| 13. | $5\sqrt{3}$ | 14. | $4\sqrt{5}$ | 15. | $x$ | 16. | $y$ | 17. | $m^3$ | 18. | $x\sqrt{2}$ |
| 19. | $q\sqrt{3}$ | 20. | $2n$ | 21. | $y^2$ | 22. | $4p$ | 23. | $2l\sqrt{2}$ | 24. | $2\sqrt{6y}$ |
| 25. | $9\sqrt{r}$ | 26. | $12\sqrt{c}$ | 27. | $9r\sqrt{2}$ | 28. | $4m\sqrt{m}$ | | | | | | |

# MONOMIALS, BINOMIALS, AND POLYNOMIALS

When two or more numbers are multiplied together in an algebraic expression, they are considered to be a single term. $3x$ is a single term, as is $4y^2$, or $7a^2b$. Single terms are known as **monomials** (from the prefix "mono-" meaning one, and nomial meaning number). That is to say, monomials are considered to be single numbers. As an extreme case, $12a \cdot 6b \cdot 9a \cdot 11c$ is a monomial, and hence a single number. You may evaluate it if you wish, but that is not the point.

When two terms are separated by a plus or minus sign they are considered to be two numbers — hence $4a + b$ is a **binomial**. Any expression with more than two terms, regardless of how many terms there happen to be, is known as a polynomial (the prefix "poly-" meaning many). $4x^2 + 3x + 2$ and $7z^3 + 5r^2 + 6m + 3r + 8$ are both examples of polynomials.

Polynomials, binomials, and monomials may all be added together, but, as is the case with all expressions containing variables, to get any terms to actually combine, the variables in the terms must be identical with regard to variable name **and** power:

$4x^2 + 3x^2$ can be combined to form $7x^2$.

$4x^2 + 3x$ can be combined no further.

$5ax^3 + 5bx^3$ can be combined no further.

$4ax^6 + 8ax^6$ can be combined to form $12ax^6$.

The binomials $3x + 2$ and $5x - 8$ can be combined as follows:

$$\begin{array}{r} 3x + 2 \\ \underline{5x - 8} \\ 8x - 6 \end{array}$$

In the case of binomials where all terms have different variables, a polynomial will result from combining them:

Adding the binomials $3x + 8$ and $4x^2 + y$ results in $4x^2 + 3x + y + 8$.

Adding the binomials $2x^2 + 7x$ and $3x - 5$ results in $2x^2 + 10x - 5$.

## MULTIPLYING BINOMIALS

Binomials are multiplied together in the same way that two digit numbers are multiplied. The problem usually is that most people do not think of them as working that way. Suppose, for example, you wished to multiply $(x + 2)(x - 3)$. You might set it up as follows:

$$\begin{array}{r} x - 3 \\ \underline{(x + 2)} \\ 2x - 6 \\ \underline{x^2 - 3x} \\ x^2 - x - 6 \end{array}$$

First multiply $2(^-3)$ and $2(x)$.

Then multiply $x(^-3)$ and $x(x)$.

Finally add.

Simple as this procedure is, some people delight in doing such a binomial multiplication mentally. They use a method known as **FOIL**, an acronym that stands for First, Outer, Inner, Last. Consider once more the multiplication $(x + 2)(x - 3)$. Multiply together the

| First, | Outer, | Inner, and | Last | terms. |
|---|---|---|---|---|
| $x \cdot x$ | $^-3 \cdot x$ | $2 \cdot x$ | $2 \cdot {}^-3$ | |
| $x^2 \quad +$ | $^-3x$ | $2x$ | $^-6$ | |

Next, combine like terms, which gives

$$x^2 \qquad ^-x \qquad ^-6$$

Combine the following terms as far as possible.

1) $5x + 7x$

2) $3x^2 + 5x$

3) $(2x + 5) + (6x - 3)$

4) $(8y - 6) + (6y + 9)$

5) $(3y - 8) + (3y + 8)$

6) $(5k - 6) + (6 - 5k)$

7) $(4b + 3)(2b + 6)$

8) $(x + 3)(x - 3)$

9) $(x - 3)(x - 3)$

10) $(x + 3)(x + 3)$

11) $(m - 4)(m + 8)$

12) $(r + 7)(r + 5)$

13) $(7r - 3) - (2r + 5)$

14) $(8g + 7) - (5g + 3)$

15) $(9m - 6) - (3m - 8)$

16) $(12q - 5)(m + 3)$

17) $(5b - 9) + (3b - 9)$

18) $(5b - 9) - (3b - 9)$

19) $(6d + 7)(2d + 3)$

20) $(s - 4)(s + 6)$

21) $(b + \frac{1}{2})(b + \frac{1}{4})$

22) $(n + 2)(n - 2)$

23) $(u + \frac{1}{4})(u - \frac{1}{4})$

24) $(w + 11) - (w + z)$

25) $(r - 8) + (7 - z)$

26) $(t + 5)(8 + j)$

27) $(z - 5)(2z + 9)$

28) $(h + 3)(3h + 4)$

29) $(t - 3)(4 + g)$

30) $(x + y)(x - y)$

## Answers

| | | | | | |
|---|---|---|---|---|---|
| **1.** | $12x$ | **2.** | $3x^2 + 5x$ | **3.** | $8x + 2$ |
| **4.** | $14y + 3$ | **5.** | $6y$ | **6.** | $0$ |
| **7.** | $8b^2 + 30b + 18$ | **8.** | $x^2 - 9$ | **9.** | $x^2 - 6x + 9$ |
| **10.** | $x^2 + 6x + 9$ | **11.** | $m^2 + 4m - 32$ | **12.** | $r^2 + 12r + 35$ |
| **13.** | $5r - 8$ | **14.** | $3g + 4$ | **15.** | $6m + 2$ |
| **16.** | $12mq - 5m + 36q - 15$ | **17.** | $8b - 18$ | **18.** | $2b$ |
| **19.** | $12d^2 + 32d + 21$ | **20.** | $s^2 + 2s - 24$ | **21.** | $b^2 + \frac{3}{4}b + \frac{1}{8}$ |

**22.** $n^2 - 4$    **23.** $u^2 - \frac{1}{16}$    **24.** $11 - z$

**25.** $r - z - 1$    **26.** $8t + tj + 5j + 40$    **27.** $2z^2 - z - 45$

**28.** $3h^2 + 13h + 12$    **29.** $4t + gt - 3g - 12$    **30.** $x^2 - y^2$

## FACTORING BINOMIALS

Do you recall the distributive property of multiplication? If you do not, this would be an excellent time to refresh your memory by turning back to page 151. The reason a knowledge of the distributive property is so essential to the factoring of binomials is that the latter may be thought of as applying the distributive property backwards.

**Factors** are numbers which are multiplied together. One way of factoring was discussed in the section dealing with finding least common denominators on page 83. Factoring a binomial consists of finding a number that is a factor of both terms in the binomial (2 and 3 are two of the factors of 6) and removing it. Examine the model examples below.

*Model Example 1*

Factor $2b + 24$.

In order to factor a binomial, first think:

"What factor is common to $2b$ and to $24$?"

Since 2 is, that is what will be "factored out."

$$2b + 24 = 2(b + 12)$$

As a final check, apply the distributive property to the factored form, $2(b + 12)$, and you will see that the result is $2b + 24$.

*Model Example 2*

Factor $x^2 - 5x$.

Both terms contain $x$ as a factor, therefore:

$$x^2 - 5x = x(x - 5)$$

*Model Example 3*

Factor $3w^2 + 9w$

$w$ is a factor of each term. So is 3. You may factor out one at a time, or both simultaneously. Below it is done one at a time, beginning with the $w$.

$$3w^2 + 9w = w(3w + 9)$$
$$= 3w(w + 3)$$

Bear in mind when working the exercises below that it is not essential to factor out all possible factors in a single step. Certainly, there is nothing wrong with doing so, but if you are more comfortable with two or three steps, then do it that way.

Factor completely.

1) $5x + 25$        2) $3y + 18$        3) $4r + 24$        4) $8z + 32$

5) $4x^2 - 12y$    6) $7b^2 - 49a$    7) $t^2 + 6t$        8) $h^2 + 5h$

9) $p^2 + 3p$      10) $k^2 + dk$      11) $v^2 + 2v$      12) $s^2 + s$

13) $5n^2 + n$     14) $6y^2 + y$     15) $vw - 8w$      16) $rb + ab^2$

17) $3d^2 - 6d$    18) $12m^2 - 18m$  19) $11f^3 + 66f$  20) $9t^2 - 6t$

21) $14t^2 + 21t$  22) $15r^3 - 10r^2$ 23) $6m^3 + 6m^2$  24) $8k^4 - 12k^3$

## Answers

**1.** $5(x + 5)$     **2.** $3(y + 6)$     **3.** $4(r + 6)$     **4.** $8(z + 4)$

**5.** $4(x^2 - 3y)$  **6.** $7(b^2 - 7a)$  **7.** $t(t + 6)$     **8.** $h(h + 5)$

**9.** $p(p + 3)$     **10.** $k(k + d)$    **11.** $v(v + 2)$    **12.** $s(s + 1)$

**13.** $n(5n + 1)$   **14.** $y(6y + 1)$   **15.** $w(v - 8)$    **16.** $b(r + ab)$

**17.** $3d(d - 2)$   **18.** $6m(2m - 3)$  **19.** $11f(f^2 + 6)$  **20.** $3t(3t - 2)$

**21.** $7t(2t + 3)$  **22.** $5r^2(3r - 2)$ **23.** $6m^2(m + 1)$  **24.** $4k^3(2k - 3)$

## *FACTORING THE DIFFERENCE OF TWO SQUARES*

Examine the binomial $b^2 - g^2$. Notice that each of the two terms is a perfect square. (Any number raised to the second power is known as a perfect square, as well as numbers such as 1, 4, 9, etc.) Note also that the two terms are separated by a minus sign. Hence, the entire binomial is known as the difference (subtraction) of two squares. The difference of two squares factors by taking the square root of each term and then multiplying both their sum and difference together:

$$b^2 - g^2 = (b + g)(b - g)$$

Study that factorization carefully. To prove that it is valid, FOIL or multiply the two factors $(b + g)(b - g)$ together:

$$
\begin{array}{r}
b + g \\
(b - g) \\
\hline
- bg - g^2 \\
b^2 + bg \\
\hline
b^2 \qquad - g^2 = b^2 - g^2
\end{array}
$$

Take a look at this one:

*Model Example 1*

$x^2 - 4$ — Notice it is a difference of two squares:

$$x^2 = x \cdot x \qquad 4 = 2 \cdot 2$$

$= (x + 2)(x - 2)$ — Multiply the difference of the roots by the sum.

*Model Example 2*

$3x^2 - 27$ — At first, this binomial does not appear to be the difference of two squares. The only hint at that possibility, in fact, is the minus sign.

$3(x^2 - 9)$ — We can, however, factor a 3 out of both terms. Having done so, you might now notice that both $x^2$ and 9 are perfect squares ($x \cdot x$ and $3 \cdot 3$).

$3(x + 3)(x - 3)$ — Factoring further, here is what we find.

Factor completely.

1) $w^2 - 25$ 　　　　2) $x^2 - 16$ 　　　　3) $y^2 - 49$ 　　　　4) $r^2 - 100$

5) $a^2 - b^2$ 　　　　6) $u^2 - m^2$ 　　　　7) $v^2 - 4c^2$ 　　　　8) $q^2 - 9a^2$

9) $k^2 - 36d^2$ 　　　　10) $25b^2 - f^2$ 　　　　11) $100h^2 - t^2$ 　　　　12) $81z^2 - w^2$

13) $64m^2 - n^2$ 　　　　14) $64p^2 - 9q^2$ 　　　　15) $121s^2 - 81t^2$ 　　　　16) $400w^2 - 256x^2$

17) $18x^2 - 2$ 　　　　18) $3x^2 - 75$ 　　　　19) $98x^2 - 72$ 　　　　20) $6x^2 - 24$

21) $7y^2 - 63$ 　　　　22) $200g^2 - 98h^2$ 　　　　23) $72r^2 - 32w^2$ 　　　　24) $32b^2 - 128c^2$

## Answers

| | | |
|---|---|---|
| **1.** $(w + 5)(w - 5)$ | **2.** $(x + 4)(x - 4)$ | **3.** $(y + 7)(y - 7)$ |
| **4.** $(r + 10)(r - 10)$ | **5.** $(a + b)(a - b)$ | **6.** $(u + m)(u - m)$ |
| **7.** $(v + 2c)(v - 2c)$ | **8.** $(q + 3a)(q - 3a)$ | **9.** $(k + 6d)(k - 6d)$ |
| **10.** $(5b + f)(5b - f)$ | **11.** $(10h + t)(10h - t)$ | **12.** $(9z + w)(9z - w)$ |
| **13.** $(8m + n)(8m - n)$ | **14.** $(8p + 3q)(8p - 3q)$ | **15.** $(11s + 9t)(11s - 9t)$ |
| **16.** $(20w + 16x)(20w - 16x)$ | **17.** $2(3x + 1)(3x - 1)$ | **18.** $3(x + 5)(x - 5)$ |
| **19.** $2(7x + 6)(7x - 6)$ | **20.** $6(x + 2)(x - 2)$ | **21.** $7(y + 3)(y - 3)$ |
| **22.** $2(10g + 7h)(10g - 7h)$ | **23.** $2(6r + 4w)(6r - 4w)$ | **24.** $32(b + 2c)(b - 2c)$ |

*Note:* $x^2 + y^2$ or any binomial of that form is not the difference of two squares, and cannot be factored.

# FACTORING QUADRATIC EXPRESSIONS

A three-place polynomial which contains a variable raised to the second power is called a **quadratic expression**. Quadratic expressions take the form:

$$ax^2 + bx + c$$

In the form above, $a$ and $b$ stand for numerical coefficients of the $x^2$ and the $x$ terms respectively, while $c$ is a constant. A factorization of a quadratic expression is always going to take the form seen in the last section (concerning the difference of two squares). That is to say, the form will be two binomials multiplied together. The FOIL form must be used to insure that the factors multiply together to form the three term quadratic polynomial. The form will be as follows:

(variable * constant)(variable * constant)

Each * above represents either a + or a − sign. To determine which signs belong, examine the signs in the polynomial. There are the following possibilities.

1. $ax^2 + bx + c$     Both signs will be +.

2. $ax^2 - bx + c$     Both signs will be −.

3. $ax^2 + bx - c$

4. $ax^2 - bx - c$     One sign will be + and one will be −.

If we follow the First, Outer, Inner, Last scheme of FOIL, then the value of $ax^2$ and of $c$ are determined exclusively by multiplication of the F's and the L's respectively. Since $c$'s sign is determined by multiplication, two signs that are the same will give a + and two signs that are different will give a − as the constant's sign. The sign of the middle term ($bx$) is determined by adding together the O and the I terms. Examine the model examples below, and you will see how this works.

*Model Example 1*

Factor $x^2 + 2x + 1$     Note that both signs are positive.

(  +  )(  +  )     Next look at the first term. What times what makes $x^2$?

$(x + )(x + )$     Obviously $x \cdot x$ does. Now look at the last term of the polynomial. We need two numbers that multiply together to make 1 . . .

    (Look at the middle term of the polynomial.) . . . and add together to make 2. Therefore,

$(x + 1)(x + 1)$     FOIL this solution and see what you get.

*Model Example 2*

Factor $x^2 - 3x + 2$     Note that the sign of the $c$ term is positive. That means that both signs in the factors must be the same; either both positive, or both negative. The

(  −  )(  −  )     sign of the middle term tells which.

What multiplies together to make $x^2$?

$(x - \phantom{0})(x - \phantom{0})$     Now, from the $c$ term, you need two numbers that multiply together to make 2, and the $b$ term tells you that they must also add together to make $^-3$, hence:

$(x - 2)(x - 1)$     FOIL the solution and see what you get.

*Model Example 3*

Factor $x^2 + 2x - 3$     Note that the last sign is negative. That means that the two factors contain different signs. (Presum-

$(x + \phantom{0})(x - \phantom{0})$     ably you can see why the $x$'s are there.)

Two numbers that multiply together to make $^-3$, but add together to make $^+2$ are $^+3$ and $^-1$.

$(x + 3)(x - 1)$     FOIL the solution and see what happens.

*Model Example 4*

Factor $x^2 - 3x - 4$     Last term is negative, so the signs are different:

$(x + \phantom{0})(x - \phantom{0})$     $^-4$ can be made by multiplying $^-2 \cdot 2$, $^-4 \cdot 1$, or $^-1 \cdot 4$. Which of those pairs add together to make $^-3$?

$(x + 1)(x - 4)$     FOIL and see for yourself.

Refer to the model examples as many times as you have to as you proceed through the exercises below.

Factor completely.

1) $x^2 + 7x + 6$     2) $x^2 + 5x + 4$     3) $x^2 + 5x + 6$     4) $x^2 + 7x + 10$

5) $x^2 - 7x + 10$     6) $x^2 - 8x + 15$     7) $x^2 - 8x + 12$     8) $b^2 - 12b + 20$

9) $y^2 - 7y - 8$     10) $m^2 + 9m - 10$     11) $t^2 + 11t - 12$     12) $z^2 - z - 12$

13) $w^2 + 7w - 18$     14) $x^2 - 19x + 18$     15) $s^2 + 10s + 21$     16) $k^2 - 11k + 28$

17) $v^2 - 10v - 24$     18) $q^2 + 8q - 65$

## Answers

**1.**   $(x + 6)(x + 1)$     **2.**   $(x + 4)(x + 1)$     **3.**   $(x + 3)(x + 2)$

**4.**   $(x + 5)(x + 2)$     **5.**   $(x - 5)(x - 2)$     **6.**   $(x - 3)(x - 5)$

**7.**   $(x - 2)(x - 6)$     **8.**   $(b - 2)(b - 10)$     **9.**   $(y - 8)(y + 1)$

**10.**   $(m + 10)(m - 1)$     **11.**   $(t + 12)(t - 1)$     **12.**   $(z - 4)(z + 3)$

**13.**   $(w - 9)(w + 2)$     **14.**   $(x - 18)(x - 1)$     **15.**   $(s + 7)(s + 3)$

**16.**   $(k - 7)(k - 4)$     **17.**   $(v - 12)(v + 2)$     **18.**   $(q + 13)(q - 5)$

# SOLVING QUADRATIC EQUATIONS BY FACTORING

A quadratic equation is any equation that can be expressed in the form $ax^2 + bx + c = 0$. That, in fact, is known as the **standard form** for a quadratic equation. While not all quadratic equations are capable of being solved by factoring, all of those on the GED test are. For that reason, we will concern ourselves here exclusively with factorable quadratics.

The model examples below include all the steps needed for solution of any quadratic equation that is factorable.

*Model Example 1*

Solve for $x$: $x^2 + 7x - 60 = 0$

First, the polynomial must be in standard form. This one is. Next, factor the polynomial:

$$(x + 12)(x - 5) = 0$$

Now, for two terms multiplied together to equal zero, either one or both of those terms must equal zero. That is because multiplication by zero is the only way to get a product of zero. Let us therefore set each factor equal to zero:

$$(x + 12) = 0 \qquad\qquad (x - 5) = 0$$

Then solve each for $x$.

$$\begin{array}{ll} x + 12 = 0 & x - 5 = 0 \\ x = {}^-12 & x = 5 \end{array}$$

The **roots** of the equation are $^-12$ and/or 5.

This may be checked by substituting either $^-12$ or 5 into the original equation:

$$\begin{array}{ll} x^2 + 7x - 60 = 0 & x^2 + 7x - 60 = 0 \\ (^-12)^2 + 7(^-12) - 60 = 0 & (5)^2 + 7 \cdot 5 - 60 = 0 \\ 144 - 84 - 60 = 0 & 25 + 35 - 60 = 0 \\ 60 - 60 = 0 & 60 - 60 = 0 \\ 0 = 0 & 0 = 0 \end{array}$$

*Model Example 2*

Solve for $x$: $x^2 - 7x = {}^-12$

| | |
|---|---|
| $x^2 - 7x + 12 = 0$ | First put into standard form. |
| $(x - 4)(x - 3) = 0$ | Then factor. |
| $x - 4 = 0 \qquad x - 3 = 0$ | Set each factor equal to zero. |
| $x = 4 \qquad\qquad x = 3$ | Find the two roots. |

You may refer to the two models if you need to while solving the equations on the next page.

Solve each equation for both values of $x$.

1) $x^2 + 7x + 6 = 0$     2) $x^2 + 5x = {}^-4$     3) $x^2 + 5x = {}^-6$     4) $7x + 10 = {}^-x^2$

5) $x^2 - 7x + 10 = 0$     6) $x^2 = 8x - 15$     7) $x^2 = 8x - 12$     8) $x^2 - 12x + 20 = 0$

9) $x^2 = 8 + 7x$     10) $x^2 + 9x = 10$     11) $12 = x^2 + 11x$     12) $x^2 = 12 + x$

13) $18 = 7x + x^2$     14) $x^2 - 19x + 18 = 0$     15) $10x = {}^-x^2 - 21$     16) $x^2 + 28 = 11x$

17) $x^2 + 10x + 24 = 0$     18) $x^2 + 8x = 65$

## Answers

**1.** ${}^-6, {}^-1$    **2.** ${}^-4, {}^-1$    **3.** ${}^-3, {}^-2$    **4.** ${}^-5, {}^-2$    **5.** $2, 5$    **6.** $5, 3$

**7.** $2, 6$    **8.** $2, 10$    **9.** $8, {}^-1$    **10.** $1, {}^-10$    **11.** $1, {}^-12$    **12.** $4, {}^-3$

**13.** $2, {}^-9$    **14.** $1, 18$    **15.** ${}^-7, {}^-3$    **16.** $4, 7$    **17.** ${}^-4, {}^-6$    **18.** $5, {}^-13$

# ALGEBRA POST-TEST

Solve for $x$ or $y$.

1) $y + 11 = 39$     2) $21 - y = 41$     3) $y - 14 = 3y + 18$

4) $\dfrac{x}{5} = \dfrac{3}{14}$     5) $\dfrac{1}{x + 2} = \dfrac{3}{7}$     6) $45\%$ of $81 = x$

7) $x^2 - 3x + 2 = 0$     8) $x^2 - 81 = 0$     9) $2x^3y^2z^4 \cdot 4x^7z^3$

10) $\sqrt{45r^4}$

## Answers

**1.** $28$    **2.** ${}^-20$    **3.** ${}^-16$    **4.** $\frac{14}{15}$    **5.** $\frac{1}{3}$    **6.** $36.45$

**7.** ${}^-1, {}^-2$    **8.** $\pm 9$    **9.** $8x^{10}y^2z^7$    **10.** $3r^2\sqrt{5}$

## *ANALYSIS OF POST-TEST ITEMS*

1. Simple addition in algebraic form       Pages 118–120; 273

2. Transforming equations by subtraction       Pages 120–121; 273

3. Transforming equations by multiple operations       Pages 121–138; 274

# WORD-PROBLEMS

## *PREPARING TO SOLVE WORD-PROBLEMS*

Algebra, as a branch of mathematics, is most useful for the solution of word-problems. It is for that reason that we have avoided the introduction of any type of word-problem until we had progressed to the stage where enough algebra had been learned to make it possible to view word-problems from an algebraic viewpoint. A word-problem is a mathematical situation, requiring a mathematical solution, but stated in verbal terms. That is to say, it is a mathematical problem presented in English sentences. The key to solving word-problems successfully is being able to translate the English sentences into a mathematical sentence. A mathematical sentence is another name for an algebraic equation.

Changing English sentences into mathematical sentences can be viewed as similar to changing from one language to another. Some words translate directly from one language to the other, while certain phrases are idiomatic and have to be translated as groups of words. An example of a word that translates directly is "is," or "the result is." "Exceeds" means "+." "Is more than" also means "+." "The sum is" is yet another way of indicating that things must be added together.

Below, you will find a list of English phrases commonly found in word-problems. Translate each into the appropriate mathematical symbol or group of symbols.

1) 5 more than the number $n$ _____

2) $n$ more than the number 7 _____

3) The product of $n$ and 3 _____

4) The difference of $x$ and 5 _____

5) The difference of 5 and $x$ _____

6) 8 increased by $y$ _____

7) Twice $y$ _____

8) Twice $x$ increased by 6 _____

9) Twice 7 decreased by $m$ _____

10) A number, $r$, diminished by 5 _____

11) 3 more than half of $p$ _____

12) Half the sum of $x$ and 7 _____

13) Twice the difference of $y$ and 5 _____

14) The quotient of 23 and $a$ _____

15) The quotient of $m$ and 16 _____

16) The number that exceeds 5 by $k$ _____

17) The number that exceeds the sum of $t$ and 3 by 11 _____

18) 5 less than the product of 9 and $u$ _____

19) The sum of $t$ and 4 diminished by 5 _____

20) One-fourth the difference of $h$ and 9 _____

## Answers

**1.** $n + 5$ or $5 + n$     **2.** $7 + n$     **3.** $3n$

**4.** $x - 5$     **5.** $5 - x$     **6.** $8 + y$

**7.** $2y$     **8.** $2x + 6$     **9.** $2 \cdot 7 - m$ or $14 - m$

**10.** $r - 5$     **11.** $\frac{1}{2}p + 3$ or $\frac{p}{2} + 3$     **12.** $\frac{1}{2}(x + 7)$ or $\frac{x + 7}{2}$

**13.** $2(y - 5)$     **14.** $\frac{23}{a}$     **15.** $\frac{m}{16}$

**16.** $k + 5$     **17.** $(t + 3) + 11$ or $t + 14$     **18.** $9u - 5$

**19.** $(t + 4) - 5$ or $t - 1$     **20.** $\frac{1}{4}(h - 9)$ or $\frac{h - 9}{4}$

## *NUMBER PROBLEMS*

The last section dealt with mathematical phrases. A sentence, however, usually consists of more than one phrase, together with connecting words. So, a mathematical sentence will always consist of more than one phrase and connectives. A mathematical sentence will always express a complete thought, just as an English sentence expresses a complete thought. Mathematical sentences are easier to construct than English sentences, however, because the main verb is always "is," expressed as an equal sign.* Let us examine a few model problems and see how this whole business works.

*Model Problem 1*

A certain number when added to twice itself is 39. Find the number.

First, we make a "let-statement:"

$$\text{Let } x = \text{the number.}$$

Then we start to translate phrase by phrase:

| | |
|---|---|
| *A certain number . . .* | That means $x$. |
| *. . . when added . . .* | That means $+$. |
| *. . . to twice itself . . .* | That means $2x$. |
| *. . . is . . .* | That means $=$. |
| *. . . 39.* | That means 39. |

In other words, the problem translates to the sentence:

$$x + 2x = 39.$$

Solving the equation, we find

$$3x = 39$$
$$x = 13$$

Therefore, the number is 13.

*Model Problem 2*

3 more than half a certain number is 22. Find the number.

First the let statement:

$$\text{Let } x = \text{the number.}$$

Then the translation:

| | |
|---|---|
| *3 more than . . .* | means $+ 3$. Of course, we have yet to get to the spot to where we add the 3. |
| *. . . half a certain number . . .* | means either $\frac{1}{2}x$ or $\frac{x}{2}$. Both mean the same thing. (That is also what we add the 3 onto.) |
| *. . . is 22.* | That means $= 22$. |

The equation, therefore, is:

$$\tfrac{1}{2}x + 3 = 22.$$

*At least this is true of equations. Inequalities are a different story.

Solving that equation we find that:

$$\tfrac{1}{2}x = 19$$
$$x = 38$$

Therefore the number is 38.

### Model Problem 3

When 5 is added to a number, the result is 9 less than twice the number increased by 7. Find the number.

As complicated as this problem may seem, start with the let statement:

Let $x$ = the number.

Then translate the sentence bit by bit:

| | |
|---|---|
| *When 5 is added to a number . . .* | That means $x + 5$. |
| *. . . the result is . . .* | That means =. |
| *. . . 9 less than . . .* | That means 9 is subtracted from something. |
| *. . . twice the number . . .* | $2x$ is twice the number. |
| *. . . increased by 7.* | That means 7 is added to $2x$. That also means that $2x + 7$ is what we must take 9 from. |

The equation, then, is:

$$x + 5 = 2x + 7 - 9.$$

Solving that equation, we find:

$$x + 5 = 2x - 2$$
$$7 = x$$

Therefore, the number is 7.

### Model Problem 4

Twice the sum of 3 and a number is 1 less than three times the number. Find the number.

Solution:   Let $x$ = the number.

| | |
|---|---|
| *Twice the . . .* | We'll have to multiply something by 2. |
| *. . . sum of 3 and a number . . .* | The sum of 3 and $x$ is what we must multiply by 2. That's $2(3 + x)$. |
| *. . . is . . .* | = |
| *. . . 1 less than . . .* | We'll have to $- 1$ from something. |
| *. . . three times the number.* | $3x$ is what we $- 1$ from. |

The equation must be:

$$2(3 + x) = 3x - 1$$

Solving, we find:

$$2(3 + x) = \quad 3x - 1$$

$$
\begin{array}{rcl}
6 + 2x & = & 3x - 1 \\
+1 - 2x & = & -2x + 1 \\
\hline
7 & = & x
\end{array}
$$

The number must be 7.

---

Find the number described in each of the following word-problems.

1) A certain number added to 5 gives a result of 16. What is it?

2) When a certain number is added to 11, the result is 35. Find it.

3) When a certain number is taken from 47, 29 results. Find the number.

4) Forty-three is 7 less than twice a number. What is the number?

5) When three times a number is added to 17, 68 results. What is the number?

6) Three times a number increased by 4 is the same as four times that number decreased by 11. Find the number.

7) When twice a number is added to itself, the result is 7 less than four times the number. What is the number?

8) When 9 is added to a number, the result is the same as when twice the number is diminished by 6. Find the number.

9) When a number is increased by 11, the result is the same as when twice the number is decreased by 4. Find the number.

10) Five more than half a certain number is 32. Find the number.

11) Nine more than $\frac{1}{4}$ a certain number is 14. What is the number?

12) When half a certain number is increased by 18, the result is the same as when the number is increased by 6. Find the number.

13) Twice the sum of 5 and a number is 3 more than three times the number. What is the number?

14) Three times the sum of a number and 8 is 6 more than 5 times the number. Find the number.

15) Half the sum of a number and 32 is 2 less than twice the number. What is the number?

16) When the product of 3 and a number is increased by 7, the result is 5 less than the product of the number and 5. Find the number.

17) Twice the difference of 31 and a number exceeds twice the number by 30. Find the number.

18) The difference between a number and 29 is 14 less than one-fourth the number. Find the number.

19) Half a number increased by 40 is the same as four times the number decreased by 16. Find the number.

20) Twice the product of 3 and a number exceeds the sum of the number and 80 by 10. Find the number.

## Solutions

**1.**
$$x + 5 = 16$$
$$x = 11$$

**2.**
$$11 + x = 35$$
$$x = 24$$

**3.**
$$47 - x = 29$$
$$x = 18$$

**4.**
$$43 = 2x - 7$$
$$50 = 2x$$
$$x = 25$$

**5.**
$$3x + 17 = 68$$
$$3x = 51$$
$$x = 17$$

**6.**
$$3x + 4 = 4x - 11$$
$$15 = x$$

**7.**
$$2x + x = 4x - 7$$
$$3x = 4x - 7$$
$$7 = x$$

**8.**
$$x + 9 = 2x - 6$$
$$15 = x$$

**9.**
$$x + 11 = 2x - 4$$
$$15 = x$$

**10.**
$$\tfrac{1}{2}x + 5 = 32$$
$$\tfrac{1}{2}x = 27$$
$$x = 54$$

**11.**
$$\tfrac{1}{4}x + 9 = 14$$
$$\tfrac{1}{4}x = 5$$
$$x = 20$$

**12.**
$$\tfrac{1}{2}x + 18 = x + 6$$
$$12 = \tfrac{1}{2}x$$
$$24 = x$$

**13.**
$$2(5 + x) = 3x + 3$$
$$10 + 2x = 3x + 3$$
$$7 = x$$

**14.**
$$3(x + 8) = 5x + 6$$
$$3x + 24 = 5x + 6$$
$$18 = 2x$$
$$9 = x$$

**15.**
$$\tfrac{1}{2}(x + 32) = 2x - 2$$
$$1(x + 32) = 4x - 4$$
$$x + 32 = 4x - 4$$
$$36 = 3x$$
$$12 = x$$

**16.**
$$3x + 7 = 5x - 5$$
$$12 = 2x$$
$$6 = x$$

**17.**
$$2(31 - x) = 2x + 30$$
$$62 - 2x = 2x + 30$$
$$32 = 4x$$
$$8 = x$$

**18.**
$$x - 29 = \tfrac{1}{4}x - 14$$
$$\tfrac{3}{4}x = 15$$
$$x = 20$$

**19.**
$$\tfrac{1}{2}x + 40 = 4x - 16$$
$$x + 80 = 8x - 32$$
$$112 = 7x$$
$$16 = x$$

**20.**
$$2(3x) = (x + 80) + 10$$
$$6x = x + 90$$
$$5x = 90$$
$$x = 18$$

# CONSECUTIVE INTEGER PROBLEMS

Consecutive integer problems differ from the number problems of the last section in two ways. First, you are seeking to find more than a single answer. Secondly, it is necessary to make a multiple let-statement. When we talk about consecutive integers, we mean whole numbers that follow one after the other in counting sequence. For example, 3, 4, and 5 are consecutive integers. So are ⁻6, ⁻5, and ⁻4, or ⁻2, ⁻1, 0, and 1.

Examine any of the sets of consecutive integers above, and you will discover a pattern of the way each integer in any set is related to the others. To get from 3 to 4, for example, you must add 1. To get from 4 to 5, you must add another 1. If we wished to write each set of integers in the first set as based upon the first element of that set, we might call them 3, 3 + 1, and 3 + 2. Examine the last sentence carefully, because it forms the basis for all consecutive integer equations. The last set of integers in the first paragraph (above), might be represented as ⁻2, ⁻2 + 1, ⁻2 + 2, and ⁻2 + 3. Check the value of each of these expressions, and you will find that they respectively equal ⁻2, ⁻1, 0, and 1.

Now, consider that we are seeking to find four consecutive integers. We are given some information about them, but we do not know the values of the integers. We only know that they are consecutive. Obviously a variable is called for. The following let-statement takes care of the four consecutive integers that we are looking for:

Let    $x$ = the first    number
"  $x + 1$ = the second    "
"  $x + 2$ = the third    "
"  $x + 3$ = the fourth    "

And so, we have taken care of representing each of the four consecutive integers.

What if what we are seeking is a set of consecutive even integers? How are even integers related to one another? Consider the first 3 consecutive even integers: 2, 4, 6. How does one get from one to another? Hopefully, you recognized the fact that each is two more than the one that came before it. Three consecutive even integers may therefore be represented as $x$, $x + 2$, and $x + 4$. The let-statement should then be obvious:

Let    $x$ = the first    even integer
"  $x + 2$ = the second    "    "
"  $x + 4$ = the third    "    "

Now for an odd question. What if we are looking for a set of consecutive odd integers? How are odd integers related to one another? Consider the first three odd integers, 1, 3, and 5. Are you surprised at your discovery? Odd integers are related to one another in exactly the same way as even ones, that is they are two apart. The let-statement for three consecutive odd integers would look identical to that for three consecutive even integers, above, save that the word "even" would be replaced by the word "odd."

Now, examine the model problems on page 173, and you will get an idea of how to deal with consecutive integer problems.

*Model Problem 1*

Find three consecutive integers whose sum is 72.

$$\text{Let} \quad x = \text{the first}$$
$$" \quad x + 1 = \text{the second}$$
$$" \quad x + 2 = \text{the third}$$

Next, we set up the equation:

| | |
|---|---|
| $x + x + 1 + x + 2 = 72$ | Sum means add them together. |
| $3x + 3 = 72$ | Combine like terms. |
| $3x = 69$ | Collect terms. |
| $x = 23$ | Divide both sides by 3. |
| Answer: 23, 24, 25 | Refer to let-statement. |

*Model Problem 2*

Find 3 consecutive even integers such that the sum of the first and third equals 40.

$$\text{Let} \quad x = \text{the first}$$
$$" \quad x + 2 = \text{the second}$$
$$" \quad x + 4 = \text{the third}$$

| | |
|---|---|
| $x + x + 4 = 40$ | There's the equation. |
| $2x + 4 = 40$ | Combine like terms. |
| $2x = 36$ | Collect terms. |
| $x = 18$ | Divide both sides by 2. |
| Answer: 18, 20, 22 | Refer to let-statement. |

*Model Problem 3*

Find 3 consecutive odd integers such that the sum of the second and third exceeds the first by 35.

$$\text{Let} \quad x = \text{the first}$$
$$" \quad x + 2 = \text{the second}$$
$$" \quad x + 4 = \text{the third}$$

| | |
|---|---|
| $x + 2 + x + 4 = x + 35$ | Set up the equation. |
| $2x + 6 = x + 35$ | Combine like terms. |
| $x = 29$ | Collect terms. |
| Answer: 29, 31, 33 | Refer to let-statement. |

Solve the following.

1) Find three consecutive integers whose sum is 21.

2) Find three consecutive integers whose sum is 57.

3) Find three consecutive integers whose sum is 96.

4) Find four consecutive integers whose sum is 66.

5) Find four consecutive integers whose sum is 106.

6) Find five consecutive integers whose sum is 140.

7) Find three consecutive even integers whose sum is 66.

8) Find three consecutive even integers whose sum is 42.

9) Find three consecutive odd integers whose sum is 51.

10) Find four consecutive odd integers whose sum is 112.

11) Find three consecutive integers such that twice the first exceeds the third by 3.

12) Find three consecutive integers such that twice the sum of the first and third exceeds the second by 18.

13) Find three consecutive integers such that the first increased by twice the second exceeds the third by 24.

14) Find three consecutive even integers such that one-third the sum of the first two is 93.

15) Find three consecutive odd integers such that twice the sum of the first and second is 144.

16) Find four consecutive integers such that three times the sum of the second and fourth is 24.

17) Find three consecutive integers such that the difference between twice the second and the first is 22.

18) Find three consecutive even integers such that $\frac{1}{2}$ the sum of the first and second is 37.

19) Find three consecutive odd integers such that 480 is 4 times the sum of the first two.

20) Find three consecutive odd integers such that four times the sum of the second and third exceed three times the sum of the first and second by twenty-eight.

## Solutions

**1.** Let $x =$ first integer
$x + 1 =$ second
$x + 2 =$ third

$x + x + 1 + x + 2 = 21$
$3x + 3 = 21$
$3x = 18$

$$\boxed{\begin{aligned} x &= 6 \\ x + 1 &= 7 \\ x + 2 &= 8 \end{aligned}}$$

**2.** $x + x + 1 + x + 2 = 57$
$3x + 3 = 57$
$3x = 54$

$$\boxed{\begin{aligned} x &= 18 \\ x + 1 &= 19 \\ x + 2 &= 20 \end{aligned}}$$

**3.** $x + x + 1 + x + 2 = 96$
$3x + 3 = 96$
$3x = 93$

$$\boxed{\begin{aligned} x &= 31 \\ x + 1 &= 32 \\ x + 3 &= 33 \end{aligned}}$$

**4.** Let $x =$ first integer
$x + 1 =$ second
$x + 2 =$ third
$x + 3 =$ fourth

$x + x + 1 + x + 2 + x + 3 = 66$
$4x + 6 = 66$
$4x = 60$

$$\boxed{\begin{aligned} x &= 15 \\ x + 1 &= 16 \\ x + 2 &= 17 \\ x + 3 &= 18 \end{aligned}}$$

**5.** $x + x + 1 + x + 2 + x + 3 = 106$
$4x + 6 = 106$
$4x = 100$

$$\boxed{\begin{aligned} x &= 25 \\ x + 1 &= 26 \\ x + 2 &= 27 \\ x + 3 &= 28 \end{aligned}}$$

**6.** $x + x + 1 + x + 2 + x + 3 + x + 4 = 140$
$5x + 10 = 140$
$5x = 130$

$$\boxed{\begin{aligned} x &= 26 \\ x + 1 &= 27 \\ x + 2 &= 28 \\ x + 3 &= 29 \\ x + 4 &= 30 \end{aligned}}$$

**7.** Let $x =$ first integer
$x + 2 =$ second
$x + 4 =$ third

$x + x + 2 + x + 4 = 66$
$3x + 6 = 66$
$3x = 60$

$$\boxed{\begin{aligned} x &= 20 \\ x + 2 &= 22 \\ x + 4 &= 24 \end{aligned}}$$

**8.** $x + x + 2 + x + 4 = 42$
$3x + 6 = 42$
$3x = 36$

$$\boxed{\begin{aligned} x &= 12 \\ x + 2 &= 14 \\ x + 4 &= 16 \end{aligned}}$$

**9.** Let $x =$ first integer
$x + 2 =$ second
$x + 4 =$ third

$x + x + 2 + x + 4 = 51$
$3x + 6 = 51$
$3x = 45$

$$\boxed{\begin{aligned} x &= 15 \\ x + 2 &= 17 \\ x + 4 &= 19 \end{aligned}}$$

**10.**  Let    $x =$ first
$x + 2 =$ second
$x + 4 =$ third
$x + 6 =$ fourth

$x + x + 2 + x + 4 + x + 6 = 112$
$4x + 12 = 112$
$4x = 100$

$$\boxed{\begin{aligned} x &= 25 \\ x + 2 &= 27 \\ x + 4 &= 29 \\ x + 6 &= 31 \end{aligned}}$$

**11.**  Let    $x =$ first integer
$x + 1 =$ second
$x + 2 =$ third

$2x = x + 2 + 3$
$2x = x + 5$

$$\boxed{\begin{aligned} x &= 5 \\ x + 1 &= 6 \\ x + 2 &= 7 \end{aligned}}$$

**12.**  $2(x + x + 2) = x + 1 + 18$
$2(2x + 2) = x + 19$
$4x + 4 = x + 19$
$3x = 15$

$$\boxed{\begin{aligned} x &= 5 \\ x + 1 &= 6 \\ x + 2 &= 7 \end{aligned}}$$

**13.**  $x + 2(x + 1) = x + 2 + 24$
$x + 2x + 2 = x + 26$
$3x + 2 = x + 26$
$2x = 24$

$$\boxed{\begin{aligned} x &= 12 \\ x + 1 &= 13 \\ x + 2 &= 14 \end{aligned}}$$

**14.**  $\frac{1}{3}(x + x + 1) = 93$
$\frac{1}{3}(2x + 1) = 93$
(Triple both sides)
$2x + 1 = 279$
$2x = 278$

$$\boxed{\begin{aligned} x &= 139 \\ x + 1 &= 140 \\ x + 2 &= 141 \end{aligned}}$$

**15.**  Let    $x =$ first integer
$x + 2 =$ second
$x + 4 =$ third

$2(x + x + 2) = 144$
$2(2x + 2) = 144$
$4x + 4 = 144$
$4x = 140$

$$\boxed{\begin{aligned} x &= 35 \\ x + 2 &= 37 \\ x + 4 &= 39 \end{aligned}}$$

**16.**  Let    $x =$ first integer
$x + 1 =$ second
$x + 2 =$ third
$x + 3 =$ fourth

$3(x + 1 + x + 3) = 24$
$3(2x + 4) = 24$
$6x + 12 = 24$
$6x = 12$

$$\boxed{\begin{aligned} x &= 2 \\ x + 1 &= 3 \\ x + 2 &= 4 \\ x + 3 &= 5 \end{aligned}}$$

**17.**  Let    $x =$ first integer
$x + 1 =$ second
$x + 2 =$ third

$2(x + 1) - x = 22$
$2x + 2 - x = 22$
$x + 2 = 22$

$$\boxed{\begin{aligned} x &= 20 \\ x + 1 &= 21 \\ x + 2 &= 22 \end{aligned}}$$

**18.**  Let    $x =$ first integer
$x + 2 =$ second
$x + 4 =$ third

$\frac{1}{2}(x + x + 2) = 37$
(Double both sides.)
$x + x + 2 = 74$
$2x + 2 = 74$
$2x = 72$

$$\boxed{\begin{aligned} x &= 36 \\ x + 2 &= 38 \\ x + 4 &= 40 \end{aligned}}$$

**19.** Let $x$ = first integer
$x + 2$ = second
$x + 4$ = third

$$4(x + x + 2) = 480$$
$$4(2x + 2) = 480$$
$$8x + 8 = 480$$
$$8x = 472$$

$$\boxed{\begin{aligned} x &= 59 \\ x + 2 &= 61 \\ x + 4 &= 63 \end{aligned}}$$

**20.**
$$4(x + 2 + x + 4) = 3(x + x + 2) + 28$$
$$4(2x + 6) = 3(2x + 2) + 28$$
$$8x + 24 = 6x + 6 + 28$$
$$8x + 24 = 6x + 34$$
$$2x = 10$$

$$\boxed{\begin{aligned} x &= 5 \\ x + 2 &= 7 \\ x + 4 &= 9 \end{aligned}}$$

# PROBLEMS INVOLVING RATIOS AND PROPORTIONS

Ratios can be extremely useful in all sorts of problem-solving situations. In general, it may be said that when there is a correlation between two related items or situations, and two things are known about one of the items, and a single thing is known about the other, the unknown thing about the other may be found by establishing a proportion. Examine the model problems below, and you will see how this works. If you need refreshing on how to set up ratios or how to solve proportions, refer to the section on ratio and proportion on pages 139–143.

*Model Problem 1*

Henry got 12 hits in the first 20 ballgames of the year. If he were to continue hitting at the same pace, how many hits would he get in a 75 game season?

Let $h$ = number of hits in the season.     1. First is the "let" statement.

$$\frac{\text{hits}}{\text{games}} = \frac{\text{hits}}{\text{games}}$$     2. Then describe the proportion.

$$\frac{12}{20} = \frac{h}{75}$$     3. Establish the proportion.

$$20h = 12(75)$$     4. Solve.

$$20h = 900$$

$$h = 45$$     Henry would get 45 hits.

*Model Problem 2*

Karen's stock portfolio cost her $600. It paid her an income of $90 per year. If she had invested a total of $1400 at the same rate, what would her yearly income have been?

Let $i$ = yearly income (from her new investment)
1. Make the let-statement

$\dfrac{\text{old investment}}{\text{old income}} = \dfrac{\text{new investment}}{\text{new income}}$
2. Describe the proportion.

$\dfrac{600}{90} = \dfrac{1400}{i}$
3. Establish the proportion.

$600i = 90(1400)$
4. Solve.

$600i = 126{,}000$

$i = 210$
Her income would have been $210.

*Model Problem 3*

A 6-foot tall person casts a 9-foot long shadow at the same time that a nearby flagpole casts a 75-foot shadow. How tall is the flagpole?

Let $f$ = the height of the flagpole.
1. Make the let-statement.

$\dfrac{\text{person's height}}{\text{person's shadow}} = \dfrac{\text{flagpole's height}}{\text{flagpole's shadow}}$
2. Describe the proportion.

$\dfrac{6}{9} = \dfrac{f}{75}$
3. Establish the proportion.

$9f = 6(75)$
4. Solve.

$9f = 450$

$f = 50$
The flagpole is 50 feet tall.

The following word-problems are all solvable by use of ratio and proportion. Examine each problem carefully before deciding the ratios that you will establish. Always make sure that both ratios are in the same order (that is, if one ratio is height to weight, then the second must also be height to weight — not weight to height).

Solve by using ratios and proportions.

1) Six raffle tickets cost $1.85. How much would 67 raffle tickets cost?

2) Five persons consume 3 pounds of food at a party. How much food should be ordered for a party of 37?

3) Three records cost $12.96. At that price, how much should 7 records cost?

4) It cost the government 8 million dollars to build 5 supersonic fighter planes. At the same unit cost, how much should the bill for 65 such planes come to?

5) A park with a perimeter of 150 meters is adequate for 24 children's recreational needs. Based upon the same perimeter to child ratio, how many children should be serviced by a park of 525 meters perimeter?

6) Twenty five acres of forest land supply a certain paper company with all of its needs for wood pulp for a period of 7 weeks. How many acres are required by the company for a year's supply of pulp?

7) Four washes require 68 gallons of water. How many gallons of water are needed to do 11 washes?

8) At a ballpark, 23,000 people consumed 630 pounds of frankfurters. At that same rate of consumption, how many frankfurters would have been needed for a crowd of 49,000?

9) The fire department raised $518 at a dance that attracted 67 persons. At that same rate, how much money would have been raised if 200 persons had attended?

10) A chicken farmer got 526 eggs per day from 712 chickens. How many chickens would he have needed to get 1000 eggs per day, if the new chickens produced at the same rate as the old ones?

11) A truck travelled 165 miles in 3 hours. Travelling at the same average rate of speed, how long would it take the truck to go 715 miles?

12) If 6 pounds of peanuts sell for $11.45, to the nearest penny, how much should a 19 pound bag of peanuts cost (assuming the same price per pound)?

13) Seven feet of lead pipe weigh 25 pounds. How much will 40 feet of the same pipe weigh?

14) Five cups of flour were required to bake 24 cupcakes. Using the same recipe, how much flour would be needed for 136 cupcakes?

15) A bus travels 39 miles on 8 gallons of diesel fuel. How much fuel would it use to travel from New York City to Miami, Florida — a distance of about 1200 miles?

16) Forty five volts of electricity causes an electric motor to turn at 1100 rpm. If the speed varies directly with the voltage, how fast would the motor turn when 75 volts were applied?

## Solutions

**1.** Let $c$ = cost of 67 tickets

$$\frac{6}{1.85} = \frac{67}{c}$$
$$6c = 123.95$$
$$c = \$20.66$$

**2.** Let $f$ = food for party

$$\frac{5}{3} = \frac{37}{f}$$
$$5f = 111$$
$$f = 22\tfrac{1}{5} \text{ pounds}$$

**3.** Let $r$ = cost of 7 records

$$\frac{3}{12.96} = \frac{7}{r}$$
$$3r = 90.72$$
$$r = \$30.24$$

**4.** Let $b$ = bill for 65 planes

$$\frac{8}{5} = \frac{b}{65}$$
$$5b = 520$$
$$b = \$104 \text{ million}$$

**5.** Let $n$ = number of children

$$\frac{150}{24} = \frac{525}{n}$$
$$150n = 12{,}600$$
$$n = 84 \text{ children}$$

**6.** Let $a$ = acres needed

$$\frac{25}{7} = \frac{a}{52}*$$
$$7a = 1300$$
$$a = 185\tfrac{5}{7} \text{ acres}$$

**7.** Let $g$ = gallons needed

$$\frac{4}{68} = \frac{11}{g}$$
$$4g = 748$$
$$g = 187 \text{ gallons}$$

**8.** Let $f$ = number of pounds of frankfurters

$$\frac{630}{23{,}000} = \frac{f}{49{,}000}**$$
$$2300f = 63(49{,}000)$$
$$2300f = 3{,}087{,}000$$
$$23f = 30{,}870$$
$$f = 1342\tfrac{4}{23} \text{ pounds}$$

**9.** Let $m$ = money

$$\frac{518}{67} = \frac{m}{200}$$
$$67m = 103{,}600$$
$$m = \$1546.27$$

**10.** Let $c$ = number of chickens

$$\frac{526}{712} = \frac{c}{1000}$$
$$\frac{67}{89} = \frac{c}{1000}$$
$$89c = 67000$$
$$c = 753 \text{ chickens}***$$

**11.** Let $t$ = time

$$\frac{165}{3} = \frac{715}{t}$$
$$165t = 2145$$
$$t = 13 \text{ hours}$$

**12.** Let $a$ = amount (or cost)

$$\frac{6}{11.45} = \frac{19}{a}$$
$$6a = 19(11.45)$$
$$6a = 217.55$$
$$a = \$36.26$$

**13.** Let $w$ = weight

$$\frac{7}{25} = \frac{40}{w}$$
$$7w = 1000$$
$$w = 142\tfrac{6}{7} \text{ pounds}$$

**14.** Let $c$ = cups of flour

$$\frac{5}{24} = \frac{c}{136}$$
$$24c = 680$$
$$c = 28\tfrac{1}{3} \text{ cups}$$

**15.** Let $x$ = amount of fuel

$$\frac{39}{8} = \frac{1200}{x}$$
$$39x = 9600$$
$$x = 246\tfrac{2}{13} \text{ gallons}$$

**16.** Let $s$ = speed

$$\frac{45}{1100} = \frac{75}{s}$$
$$45s = 82500$$
$$s = 1833\tfrac{1}{3} \text{ rpm}$$

---

*52 weeks = 1 year.

**Simplifying the fraction lets us work with lower numbers.

***Although the answer is actually $752\tfrac{74}{89}$, $\tfrac{74}{89}$ of a chicken cannot lay that 1000th egg.

It should be pointed out that each ratio in any of the solutions could have been inverted, as long as the other ratio in the same proportion was also inverted. Each answer then would still have been the same. The choices of variable names were, of course, purely arbitrary.

# SOLVING MOTION PROBLEMS

There are many different ways to get from one place to another. It is only natural then, that there should be many different types of problems about getting from one place to another. These problems do not take into account missing the train, or forgetting your passport or traveler's checks.

All motion problems deal with three quantities. The first is distance. Usually, distance is expressed in miles, kilometers, meters, yards, or feet. The second quantity is time, usually expressed in seconds, minutes, or hours. The third and final quantity with which all distance problems are concerned is rate of travel. This is not quite so cut and dried a quantity as the previous two. That is because there is no ruler nor clock with which rate can be measured. Rate, in fact, is a comparison between the distance travelled, and the amount of time that it took to travel that distance.

$$\text{Rate} = \frac{\text{distance travelled}}{\text{travelling time}}$$

The units in which rates are expressed, are derived from the formula above. Here are some, but by no means all, units of rate:

$$\frac{\text{miles}}{\text{hour}} \qquad \frac{\text{miles}}{\text{minute}} \qquad \frac{\text{feet}}{\text{second}} \qquad \frac{\text{meters}}{\text{hour}} \qquad \frac{\text{kilometers}}{\text{hour}}$$

In reading these rates, the fraction-line is usually replaced by the word "per," and so the rates above would read miles per hour, miles per minute, feet per second, meters per hour, and kilometers per hour. As you can see, a rate may be made up of any unit of distance **per** any unit of time.

Learning to solve motion problems is mainly a matter of "getting the hang of it." Any motion problem can be broken down in such a way as to make it fit into the following formula: Distance = rate × time. This formula is usually abbreviated as follows:

$$d = rt$$

That means, to find the actual distance travelled, the average rate at which the travelling was done must be multiplied by the actual time used in making the trip. Any straight forward motion problem can be solved by simply substituting the known quantities into the formula, and then solving the equation that results for the unknown quantity.

Following are three straightforward motion problems, and their solutions. You will notice that a box has been used to organize the data from each problem. Using this box is a good habit. While it is not really necessary for the problems in this section, as you reach more difficult problems, you'll discover it to be essential. It never hurts to form good work habits early.

*Model Problem 1*

Geoffrey drives for 4 hours at 45 mph. How far does he travel?

Remember: $d = rt$

4 hours is time. 45 mph is rate, so:

| $d$ | $r$ | $t$ |
|-----|-----|-----|
| $d$ | 45 | 4 |

$$d = (45)(4) \qquad \text{(substitute)}$$
$$d = 180 \qquad \text{(multiply)}$$

Geoffrey drove 180 miles.

*Model Problem 2*

Carol drove 320 miles in 4 hours. What was her average speed?

320 miles is distance. 4 hours is time. Speed is just another word for rate, so:

| $d$ | $r$ | $t$ |
|-----|-----|-----|
| 320 | $r$ | 4 |

$$d = rt$$
$$320 = (r)(4) \qquad \text{(substitute)}$$
$$320 = 4r \qquad \text{(multiply)}$$
$$80 = r \qquad \text{(divide both sides by 4)}$$

Having found the value of $r$, you must now look back at the problem. Notice that the distance was given in miles and the time in hours. That means that rate must be expressed as a relation of those two units. Carol's speed, therefore, was 80 mph. (Tsk, tsk! Speeding again.)

*Model Problem 3*

David flew from New York to Des Moines (in an airplane). He covered the 1200 miles at an average rate of 400 mph. How long did the trip take?

Notice that this time we have been given distance and rate. It is time that we must find.

| $d$ | $r$ | $t$ |
|-----|-----|-----|
| 1200 | 400 | $t$ |

$$d = rt$$
$$1200 = 400t \qquad \text{(substitute)}$$
$$3 = t \qquad \text{(divide both sides by 400)}$$

Here again, we must look back at the problem to find the unit in which to express time. Since rate was expressed in miles per hour, time must be in hours. The trip, therefore, took 3 hours.

Below are some problems to try on your own. The starred ones (*) are trickier than the rest.

Solve.

1) Erica can run 60 meters in 10 seconds. What is her average rate?

2) How fast must a train go in order to cover 264 kilometers in 3 hours?

3) Jason rows for 3 hours at an average rate of 6 mph. How far does he get?

4) Alessandra drives at 55 mph for 6 hours. How far does she travel?

5) The tooth fairy flies from pillow to pillow covering 3 kilometers per minute. How long does it take her to go 120 kilometers?

6) Dylan runs at an average speed of 12 yards per second. How long will it take him to run 120 yards?

*7) A plane flies 6 miles in 2 minutes. How far will it go in 3 hours?

*8) A snail travels 7 feet in 7 minutes. At that snail's pace, how long will it take for it to travel 1 mile?

# Solutions

Problems 1–6 are straightforward. Each of them may be solved by substituting the appropriate values into the "distance formula."

**1.**

| $d$ | $r$ | $t$ |
|-----|-----|-----|
| 60  | $r$ | 10  |

$d = rt$

$60 = (r)(10)$      (substitution)

$60 = 10r$         (multiply)

$6 = r$            (divide)

$r = 6$ meters per second      (include units)

**2.**

| $d$ | $r$ | $t$ |
|-----|-----|-----|
| 264 | $r$ | 3   |

$d = rt$

$264 = (r)(3)$

$264 = 3r$

$88 = r$

$r = 88$ kilometers per hour

**3.**

| $d$ | $r$ | $t$ |
|-----|-----|-----|
| $d$ | 6   | 3   |

$d = rt$

$d = (6)(3)$      (substitution)

$d = 18$         (multiply)

$d = 18$ miles      (include units)

**4.**

| $d$ | $r$ | $t$ |
|-----|-----|-----|
| $d$ | 55  | 6   |

$d = rt$

$d = (55)(6)$

$d = 330$

$d = 330$ miles

**5.**

| d | r | t |
|---|---|---|
| 120 | 3 | t |

$d = rt$

$120 = 3t$      (substitute)

$40 = t$      (divide)

$t = 40$ minutes      (include units)

**6.**

| d | r | t |
|---|---|---|
| 120 | 12 | t |

$d = rt$

$120 = 12t$

$10 = t$

$t = 10$ seconds

**7.** The time for flying 2 miles was given in minutes. The information asked for, however, is expressed in hours. Now it just is not possible to deal with two different units of time within the same problem. Did you know what to do about that? Well, 3 hours just happens to be 180 minutes. (60 minutes per hour × 3 hours = 180 minutes.)

Six miles in 2 minutes is not a very useful rate. A rate must be per unit of time. If the plane files 6 miles in 2 minutes, how far does it fly in 1 minute?

| d | r | t |
|---|---|---|
| d | 3 | 180 |

$d = rt$

$d = (3)(180)$      (substitute)

$d = 540$      (multiply)

$d = 540$ miles      (include units)

**8.** This time, feet and miles don't mix. Do you know how many feet there are in a mile? There are 5280, and if you did not know that, this is as good a time as any to incorporate that fact into your general knowledge. The rate, 7 feet in 7 minutes, must also be interpreted. If the snail goes at the pace mentioned, how far will it go in 1 minute? Now look at the solution below.

| d | r | t |
|---|---|---|
| 5280 | 1 | t |

$d = rt$

$5280 = 1t$      (substitute)

$5280 = t$      (divide)

$t = 5280$ minutes, or 88 hours, or 3 days, 16 hours.

Often, motion problems are not quite as easy to substitute into the "distance formula" as those above. They take a good deal of wading through in order to figure out just exactly how to hook the equation that will provide the answer you are looking for. Each of the models that follow will show you how to deal with a different type of motion problem. Keep in mind, though, that no matter how mixed up each problem appears to be, the data provided must in some way fit into the formula. Remember, the more experience you get, the easier you'll find it to solve any kind of motion problem.

*Model Problem 4*

Two trains leave the same station at the same time and travel in opposite directions. The first train averages 60 mph, while the second averages 45 mph. How long will it take for them to be 315 miles apart?

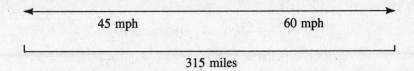

45 mph                60 mph

315 miles

Often a diagram is helpful in visualizing a problem. The one above shows this one. Each arrow represents the direction and rate of a train. The bracket shows the distance being travelled.

Now to organize the data:

|  | $d$ | $r$ | $t$ |
|---|---|---|---|
| Train #1 | $d$ | 60 | $t$ |
| Train #2 | $315 - d$ | 45 | $t$ |

Notice, that we do not know either the distance that each train travelled, or the amount of time that it took. If together the two trains travelled 315 miles, one train travelled part of that distance, and the other travelled the remainder. (Remainder is a key mathematical word, indicating subtraction.) If we call $d$ the distance that the first train travelled, then the second train must have travelled the remainder, or $315 - d$. Since both trains must travel for the same amount of time, we can call each time $t$.

If you are comfortable solving systems of equations in two variables, you need go no further. Two equations can be gotten just from the data in the box:

$$d = 60t$$
$$315 - d = 45t$$

For the rest of us, however, an alternative solution may suggest itself.

Since the times of the two trains are the same, we can make an equation relating the two times:

$$t_1 = t_2$$

All that the above equation says is "the time of train #1 equals the time of train #2." (Mathematicians love symbols.) Now, to make use of this fact, we must rearrange the terms of the "distance formula" by solving it for time.

If $d = rt$, then $t = \dfrac{d}{r}$

If that does not quite make sense to you, then consider this. To solve the equation, $d = rt$ for $t$, each side must be divided by $r$. Now, we can substitute values from the box above.

$$t_1 = t_2$$

$$\frac{d_1}{r_1} = \frac{d_2}{r_2}$$

$$\frac{d}{60} = \frac{315 - d}{45} \qquad \text{(substitute)}$$

$$45d = 18900 - 60d \qquad \text{(cross multiply)}$$

$$105d = 18900 \qquad \text{(add } 60d \text{ to each side)}$$

$$d = 180 \text{ miles} \qquad \text{(divide)}$$

Notice that what has been found is the value of $d$, not the value of $t$. Going back to the box — remember the box? — we can now substitute what we have just found out in the standard formula for train #1. After all, we now know that train #1 travels 180 miles at 60 mph.

$$d = rt$$

$$180 = 60t$$

$$3 = t$$

$$t = 3 \text{ hours}$$

Now let's try a different approach to the same problem:

Two trains leave the same station at the same time and travel in opposite directions. The first train averages 60 mph, while the second averages 45 mph. How long will it take for them to be 315 miles apart?

Since the two trains are travelling in opposite directions, they are moving apart at a speed equal to their combined rates of travel. That is to say, if you imagine yourself to be on one train, the other train is moving away from you at 105 mph (the 60 you're going away from it plus the 45 it's going away from you). It is just as if you were standing still, and the other train is doing all the moving:

60 mph + 45 mph

315 miles

Taking advantage of this fact,

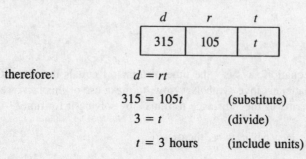

| $d$ | $r$ | $t$ |
|-----|-----|-----|
| 315 | 105 | $t$ |

therefore:

$$d = rt$$

$$315 = 105t \qquad \text{(substitute)}$$

$$3 = t \qquad \text{(divide)}$$

$$t = 3 \text{ hours} \qquad \text{(include units)}$$

So, you see, there is more than one way to approach the same problem.

The problems below are essentially similar to the model that was just worked. You may try to do them in any of the outlined ways, or maybe you'll come up with a method of your own. Before trying to invent your own way, however, see if one of the ways described might not fit your style. It will make things a lot easier if it does.

Solve the following. Check your work against the solutions on pages 188–190.

1) Two ships leave the same harbor at the same time. One steams due south at 35 mph, and the other due north at 30 mph. How far apart will they be after 5 hours?

2) A plane takes off and flies due west at 350 mph. At the same time, a second plane leaves the same airport and flies due east at 400 mph. How long after they take off will the two planes be 1500 miles apart?

3) Two cars start from Chicago at the same time and travel in opposite directions — one averaging 88 km/hr and the other 76 km/hr. How far apart will they be after $4\frac{1}{2}$ hours?

4) An aircraft carrier steams south from Norfolk at 30 km/hr. At the same time a destroyer leaves Norfolk heading north at 50 km/hr. After how many hours will the ships be 360 kilometers apart?

5) Centerville and Middletown are 450 kilometers apart. A car leaves Centerville for Middletown travelling at an average speed of 60 km/hr at the same time that another car, travelling 75 km/hr leaves Middletown for Centerville. How long will the first car have been travelling when the two cars meet?

6) A car leaves South Grapefruit at 9 AM and travels north at 35 mph. An hour later, a second car leaves from the same town and travels in the same direction as the first. It travels at 60 mph. How long will it be until the second car overtakes the first?

7) An airliner leaves Kennedy airport and travels northward at 600 mph. Ninety minutes later, a supersonic plane leaves Kennedy travelling in the same direction as the first airliner. How far will the airliner have travelled before it is overtaken, if the second plane travels at 850 mph?

8) A train leaves Grand Central Station and travels toward Albany at an average speed of 80 km/hr. A second train left Grand Central on the same track two hours later. If the second train overtakes the first in four hours after the second train departed, what was the speed of the second train?

9) A ship leaves Baltimore sailing toward France, travelling at an average speed of 28 mph. Two days later to the minute, an airplane leaves Baltimore travelling in the same direction as the ship, and flying at 630 mph. How far from Baltimore will the plane be over the ship?

10) A crop-dusting plane averaging 130 km/hr leaves an airport and is airborne for 3 hours before returning to the same airport. What is the maximum distance from the airport that the plane might have flown?

11) A car drives from 9 AM until noon at 40 mph. From noon until it stops it goes at 55 mph. Altogether 230 miles were covered. How long did the car drive at each speed?

12) Geoffrey jogged a certain distance at 8 mph. He then walked back at $2\frac{1}{2}$ miles per hour. Altogether he covered 13 miles. He was gone from his home for 3 hours. How long did he jog? How long did he walk?

13) A boat travels downstream at a speed of 24 km/hr. A round trip covers 96 kilometers and requires 5 hours. What is the average speed of the upstream portion of the journey?

*14) A man started walking at 2 mph, while a woman 2 miles behind him began walking at the same time at a rate of 4 mph, and in the same direction. Just then, the man's dog left him and ran toward the woman. Upon reaching her, it instantly turned around and ran back toward the man. And so, the dog continued to run back and forth between them, at a constant rate of 5 mph, until the woman finally overtook the man. How far did the dog run?

## Solutions

1.

S                    0                    N
    35 mph              30 mph

5 hr.

Pretend one ship stays put, and the other travels away from it at 65 mph.

$$d = r \cdot t$$
$$d = 65 \cdot 5$$
$$d = 325 \text{ miles}$$

3.

76 km/hr      0      88 km/hr

$4\frac{1}{2}$ hr.

$$d = r \cdot t$$
$$d = 164 \cdot 4\frac{1}{2}$$
$$d = 164 \cdot 4 + 164 \cdot \frac{1}{2}$$
$$d = 656 + 82$$
$$d = 738 \text{ kilometers}$$

2.

W     350 mph   0   400 mph     E

1500 miles

As in question 1, pretend that only one plane moves. Its speed would be 750 mph.

$$d = r \cdot t$$
$$1500 = 750t$$
$$t = 2 \text{ hours}$$

4.

S   30 km/hr   0   50 km/hr   N

360 km

$$d = r \cdot t$$
$$360 = 80 \cdot t$$
$$t = 4\frac{1}{2} \text{ hours}$$

*This is a classic problem for those who enjoy doing some really heavy thinking.

**5.**

C    60 km/hr    0    75 km/hr    M

450 km

(If both cars leave at the same time, they must both travel for the same time.) They close the gap between them at a speed totalling their combined individual speeds.

$$d = r \cdot t$$
$$450 = 135t$$
$$t = 3\tfrac{1}{3} \text{ hours or}$$
$$\text{3 hours, 20 minutes}$$

**6.**

Car #1  0    35 mph = $r$

$t = t$

Car #2  0    $r$ = 60 mph

$t = (t - 1)$

The second car travels for an hour less than the first. Both cars travel the same distance, hence

$$d_1 = d_2$$
$$\therefore r_1 \cdot t_1 = r_2 \cdot t_2$$
$$35t = 60(t - 1)$$
$$35t = 60t - 60$$
$$25t = 60$$
$$t = 2\tfrac{2}{5} \text{ hours}$$

Second car travels $t - 1$, or $1\tfrac{2}{5}$ hours.

**7.**

#1  0    $r_1$ = 600 mph

$t_1 = t$

#2  0

$r_2$ = 850 mph

$t_2 = t - 1\tfrac{1}{2}$

The distances travelled are identical.

$$d_1 = d_2$$
$$\therefore r_1 t_1 = r_2 t_2$$
$$600t = 850(t - 1\tfrac{1}{2})$$
$$600t = 850t - 1275$$
$$250t = 1275$$
$$t = 5\tfrac{1}{10} \text{ or } 5.1 \text{ hours}$$

Then, to find distance,

$$d = rt$$
$$d = 600 \cdot 51$$
$$d = 3060 \text{ miles}$$

**8.**

#1  0    $r_1$ = 80 km/hr

#2  0    $r_2 = r$

$t_2$ = 4 hours

If the second train overtakes the first in 4 hours, then the first train must have travelled 4 hours + the 2 hour head start, or a total of 6 hours.

$$d_1 = r_1 \cdot t$$
$$d = 80 \cdot 6$$
$$d = 480 \text{ kilometers}$$

Since the second train travelled the same distance as the first, $d_1 = d_2$:

$$d_2 = r \cdot t_2$$
$$480 = r \cdot 4$$
$$r = 120 \text{ km/hr}$$

**9.**

| | $d$ | = $r$ | $\cdot$ $t$ |
|---|---|---|---|
| ship | $28t$ | 28 | $t$ |
| plane | $630(t - 48)$ | 630 | $t - 48$ |

Once more, the distances are the same, $\therefore$,

$$28t = 630(t - 48)$$
$$28t = 630t - 630 \cdot 48$$
$$28t = 630t - 30{,}240$$
$$602t = 30{,}240$$
$$t = 50.23 \text{ hours}$$

Since    $d = 28t$ (see chart),

$$d = 28 \cdot 50.23$$
$$d = 1{,}406.44 \text{ miles}$$

**10.** If the plane is airborne for 3 hours at 130 km/hr, then

$$d = r \cdot t$$
$$d = 130 \cdot 3$$
$$d = 390 \text{ kilometers}$$

. . . but that is total distance. The farthest away the plane could have gone is $\tfrac{1}{2}$ that distance, or 195 kilometers.

**11.** Before noon, the car drove for 3 hours, since it is 3 hours from 9 AM to noon. That means that in the morning the car drove

$$3 \cdot 40 = 120 \text{ miles}$$

That left $230 - 120$, or 110 miles to be covered in the afternoon:

$$d = r \cdot t$$
$$110 = 55 \cdot t$$
$$t = 2 \text{ hours}$$

**12.**

| | $d$ | $=$ | $r$ | $\cdot$ | $t$ |
|---|---|---|---|---|---|
| jog | $8t$ | | $8$ | | $t$ |
| walk | $2\frac{1}{2}(3 - t)$ | | $2\frac{1}{2}$ | | $3 - t$ |

$$8t + 2\frac{1}{2}(3 - t) = 13$$
$$8t + 7\frac{1}{2} - 2\frac{1}{2}t = 13$$
$$5\frac{1}{2}t = 5\frac{1}{2}$$
$$t = 1 \text{ hour jogging}$$
$$3 - t = 2 \text{ hours walking}$$

**13.**

| | $d$ | $=$ | $r$ | $\cdot$ | $t$ |
|---|---|---|---|---|---|
| downstream | $48$ | | $24$ | | $t$ |
| upstream | $48$ | | $\dfrac{48}{5 - t}$ | | $5 - t$ |

If a round trip was 96 kilometers, one way must be $\frac{96}{2}$, or 48 kilometers. Time downstream is found by:

$$48 = 24 \cdot t$$
$$t = 2 \text{ hours}$$

That means it took $5 - 2 = 3$ hours to go upstream.

$$d = r \cdot t$$
$$48 = r \cdot 3$$
$$r = 16 \text{ km/hr}$$

**14.** Start out by ignoring the dog entirely. Considering the man and woman only, it is as if he is standing still, and she is walking toward him at 2 mph. She will then close the two mile gap in one hour.

$$(d = rt; \ 2 = 2t; \ t = 1)$$

Since the dog is running at 5 mph, it will continue to run for the 1 hour necessary for the woman to catch the man.

Dog's $d = 5t$; $d = 5 \cdot 1$; $d = 5$.

The dog will run 5 miles.

## PROBLEMS INVOLVING PERCENTS

Problems involving percents generally fall into one of three categories. The first is the type of problem where it is necessary to take a percent of something in order to find a discounted price or the interest on a loan, the tax on a sale, etc. The second type of problem involving percents will tell you the cost of something both before and after a discount has been taken, and then ask you to determine what the percent discount was. The third and final type of percentage problem will tell you the amount of discount that was taken on an item, as well as the discounted price, and then require that you determine what the original price was before the discount was taken.

Percentage problems have a wide range of applications, most of them being in the world of business and finance. Examine the model problems below carefully. If you are not certain of how to find a percent of a number, you may wish to refer to pages 146–148.

*Model Problem 1*

The list price on a sport jacket is $84. It is being sold at a 23% discount. What is the sale price?

There are two ways in which to solve this problem, as well as this type of problem. Both must take into account the fact that there is an original price, a percent discount, and a reduction of the original price by the amount of the discount. In other words, both multiplication and subtraction are involved. The difference in the two approaches is the order in which those two operations are executed.

Solution 1:

First figure the amount of the discount. In this case, it will be 23% of $84.

$$23\% \text{ of } \$84 = .23 \times 84 = \$19.32$$

Next, the discount must be subtracted from the list price:

$$\$84 - \$19.32 = \$64.68$$

Notice that the multiplication was done first, followed by the subtraction.

Solution 2:

This is a somewhat more interesting solution in that it is useful for different types of problems. It entails doing the subtraction first, but it also develops a formula which may be used in many different discount situations. The formula is as follows:

$$S = L(1.00 - d)$$

In the formula, $S$ stands for the sale price, $L$ stands for the list price, and $d$ stands for the amount of discount. First consider the logic of the solution without the formula:

If the discount is to be 23%, then the amount being paid for the jacket is $100 - 23$, or 77% of the list price. To find 77% of $84, multiply $.77 \times 84$, and get $64.68.

Now, examine the formula, and you'll see that the $1.00 - d$ is responsible for subtracting the percent of the discount from 100%, in order to find the percent actually paid. That percent is then multiplied by the list price to get the sale price. Now see how the formula works for the same problem:

$$S = L(1.00 - d)$$
$$S = 84(1.00 - .23)$$
$$S = 84(.73)$$
$$S = \$64.68$$

*Model Problem 2*

A dress on sale costs $30. Before it was marked down, it sold for $50. Find the percent of the discount.

Remember, a percent is a ratio, or may be expressed as a ratio, with a denominator of 100. We can therefore establish a proportion of the sale price to the original price versus the unknown percent to 100:

$$\frac{30}{50} = \frac{x}{100}$$
$$50x = 3000$$
$$x = 60$$

That means that 60% is the part of the original price that $30 is. If you are paying 60% of the original price, then the discount must have been 100% − 60%, or 40%.

This problem might also be solved by using the formula,

$$S = L(1.00 - d)$$

Substituting the two quantities that we know, we get:

$$30 = 50(1.00 - d)$$
$$30 = 50 - 50d$$
$$50d = 20$$
$$d = \tfrac{20}{50} = .40 = 40\%$$

*Model Problem 3*

After a discount of 35%, a suit was selling for $130. What was its original selling price?

Here, we can once more use the formula that relates sale price, discount, and list price:

$$S = L(100 - d)$$

Since we know two of the three quantities related, we should be able to substitute them into the formula and get the third.

$$130 = L(1.00 - .35)$$
$$130 = L(.65)$$
$$130 = .65L$$
$$L = \$200$$

Solve the following discount problems. Solutions are on page 193.

1) Alessandra wishes to buy a portable tape recorder that lists for $89.00. She sees it advertised as selling for 30% off. How much should she expect to pay for it?

2) Jason saw an ad for a dirt bike on sale. The ad offered a discount of 27% from the $342 price. How much money does he need?

3) A $620 stereo was on sale at Sam Baddy's for 45% off. What was the sale price?

4) Karen saw a $69 dress that had been reduced in price by 29%. Just as she was about to buy it, it was marked for final clearance and its sale price was reduced by 30%. How much did Karen pay for the dress?

5) Dylan's Computer Store deducted an additional 17% off the price of a Peach II Computer bought during the month of May. This was on top of the 26% discount that was already being offered. If a Peach II lists for $1195, how much did it cost to buy one at Dylan's during May?

6) A car that listed for $8000 was selling for $6000. What was the percent of the discount?

7) A dining room set was on sale for $245. It had been reduced from $300. What was the amount of the reduction?

8) A $70,000 house had been reduced for quick sale. The sale price was $53,500. What was the percent of the price reduction?

9) James bought a $575 guitar for $310. What percent did he save?

10) A telephone answering machine was on sale for $204. It had been discounted by 37%. What was the answering machine's list price?

11) Boozer's Liquor Store advertised a bottle of Lafitte Rothschild 1968 vintage wine at $54 instead of the usual $81. By what percent had the bottle been discounted?

12) A rare stamp which normally sells for $240 was being advertised at $210 by Sticky Tongues Inc. What percent had been taken off the stamp's normal price?

13) A set of stainless flatware was on sale at The Knife and Spoon for $36, instead of at its nationally advertised price of $45. By what percent had the set been discounted?

14) After an 18% discount, a sofa sold for $403. What was the sofa's list price?

15) A set of drums sold for $320 after it had been discounted by 20%. What was the list price of the drums?

16) Rosalie got a 33⅓% discount on a set of encyclopedias. She paid $480 for the set. How much would she have had to pay if she had not received the discount?

17) After a 35% discount, a television set sells for $130. What was the set's list price?

18) A $56 radio was on sale for 30% less. After Melissa bought the radio and paid 8% sales tax on it, how much change did she get from a $50 bill?

19) Dale got a 32% discount on a $43 blouse. She paid 7% sale tax. How much money did she have to give the cashier?

## Solutions

**1.**
$S = L(1.00 - d)$
$S = 89(.70)$
$S = \$62.30$

**2.**
$S = 342(.73)$
$S = \$249.66$

**3.**
$S = 620(.55)$
$S = \$341$

**4.**
$S = 69(.71)$
$S = \$48.99 \ldots$

But that is only the initial sale price. To figure the clearance price . . .

$S = 48.99(.70)$
$S = \$34.29$

**5.**
$S = 1195(.74)$
$S = \$884.30 \ldots$

before the special May discount. To figure the final price . . .

$S = 884.30(.83)$
$S = \$733.97$

**6.**
$S = L(1.00 - d)$
$6000 = 8000(1.00 - d)$
$6000 = 8000 - 8000d$
$8000d = 2000$
$d = \frac{2000}{8000} = \frac{1}{4} = .25$
$d = 25\%$

**7.**

$$245 = 300(1.00 - d)$$
$$245 = 300 - 300d$$
$$300d = 55$$
$$d = .1833 = 18\tfrac{1}{3}\%$$

**8.**

$$53,500 = 70,000(1.00 - d)$$
$$53,500 = 70,000 - 70,000d$$
$$70,000d = 16,500$$
$$d = .2357 = 23.6\%$$

**9.**

$$310 = 575(1.00 - d)$$
$$310 = 575 - 575d$$
$$575d = 265$$
$$d = .4608 = 46\%$$

**10.**

$$S = L(1.00 - d)$$
$$204 = L(1.00 - .37)$$
$$204 = L(0.63)$$
$$.63L = 204$$
$$L = \$323.81$$

**11.**

$$54 = 81(1.00 - d)$$
$$54 = 81 - 81d$$
$$81d = 27$$
$$d = \tfrac{1}{3} = .333 = 33\tfrac{1}{3}\%$$

**12.**

$$210 = 240(1.00 - d)$$
$$210 = 240 - 240d$$
$$240d = 30$$
$$d = \tfrac{30}{240} = \tfrac{1}{8} = .125 = 12\tfrac{1}{2}\%$$

**13.**

$$36 = 45(1.00 - d)$$
$$36 = 45 - 45d$$
$$45d = 9$$
$$d = \tfrac{1}{5} = .20 = 20\%$$

**14.**

$$S = L(1.00 - d)$$
$$403 = L(1.00 - .18)$$
$$403 = L(.82)$$
$$.82L = 403$$
$$L = \$491.46$$

**15.**

$$320 = L(1.00 - .20)$$
$$320 = L(.80)$$
$$.80L = 320$$
$$L = \$400$$

**16.**

$$480 = L(1.00 - .333)$$
$$480 = L(.667)$$
$$.667L = 480$$
$$L = \$719.64$$

**17.**

$$130 = L(1.00 - .35)$$
$$130 = L(.65)$$
$$.65L = 130$$
$$L = \$200$$

**18.** First figure the sale price:

$$S = 56(1.00 - .30)$$
$$S = 56(.70)$$
$$S = \$39.20$$

Then take 8% of the sale price . . .

$$.08(39.20) = t$$
$$t = 3.136 = \$3.14$$

. . . and add it to the sale price:

$$\$39.20 + 3.14 = \$42.34$$

Her change is:

$$\$50 - 42.34 = \$7.66$$

**19.**

$$S = L(1.00 - d)$$
$$S = 43(1.00 - .32)$$
$$S = 43(.68)$$
$$S = \$29.24$$

$$t = (29.24)(.07)$$
$$t = \$2.05$$
$$\text{Total} = 29.24 + 2.05 = \$31.29$$

## INTEREST PROBLEMS

Another type of percent problem deals with simple interest. Interest may be figured on money in a savings account, on stocks and bonds, on a mortgage, or on a loan. Remember, though, simple interest assumes that interest is being paid on the amount that was originally in the account (the principal). It does not take into account paying interest on interest.

The standard formula for figuring interest is:

$I = prt$   $I$ stands for interest
   $p$ stands for principal (upon which the interest is paid)
   $r$ is the rate at which the interest is paid (a percent)
   $t$ is time (usually in years)

### Model Problem 1

Andrew put $5000 into a savings certificate at 15% annual interest. What was the total amount of money in his account at the end of a year?

$I = prt$

$I = 5000 \times .15 \times 1$

$I = 750$   We have found that Andrew will receive $750 interest.

$5000 + 750 = \$5750$   Add the interest to the principal to find the total amount in his account.

### Model Problem 2

Mr. Appleby invested part of $18,000 at 10%, and the rest at 20%. His total income was $2400. How much did he invest at each rate?

Let $p$ = the amount invested at 10%.
$18000 - p$ = the amount invested at 20%.

Since no time period was stated, we may assume that one year is the time involved.

The interest earned by the amount at 10% will be $.10(p)$.
The interest earned at 20% will be $.20(18,000 - p)$.

Since we know that the total interest earned was $2400, we write an equation that adds the interest earned at each rate together to get the total interest:

$.10p + .20(18,000 - p) = 2400$

$.10p + 3600 - .20p = 2400$

$^-.10p = {}^-1200$

$.10p = 1200$

$p = 12,000$   That means $12,000 was invested at 10%.

$18,000 - p = 6,000$   So $6,000 was invested at 20%.

Solve the following interest problems. Check your work against the solutions on page 196.

1) What is the annual interest on $5000 if the rate of interest is:

a) 5%      b) $12\frac{1}{2}$%      c) 13%      d) $7\frac{1}{2}$%      e) 19%

2) Ms. Bernbach invested $12,000. Part of it was invested at 12% and part at $15\frac{1}{2}$%. Suppose that $p$ represents the amount invested at 12%. Represent:

   a) the amount invested at $15\frac{1}{2}$%

   b) the interest on the amount invested at $15\frac{1}{2}$%

   c) the interest on the amount invested at 12%

3) Sue Tree invested $x$ at 9%, and $900 more than that at 12%. The total interest from both investments was $1200. How much did she invest at each rate?

4) F. Rugal placed $10,000 into two accounts. The first paid 14% interest, and the second, 16%. After a year, Mr. Rugal collected $1520 interest. How much money was invested in each account?

5) Scott invested a sum of money at 9% and a second sum at 18%. The second amount was $450 less than the first. He received $162 annually from the investments. How much was placed at each rate?

6) Lynn bought 12% municipal bonds and 15% company bonds. The amount invested in the company bonds was $600 greater than that in the municipals. If her total annual income was $390, how much was invested in each type?

7) Puss C. Katt put a sum of money into a money-market certificate yielding 9% interest. She put twice as much into a 12% bond. Her annual income from her investments was $870. How much was invested at each rate?

8) After receiving a large inheritance, Lucy Stiff invested $50,000. Part of it was invested at 8%, and part at 14%. She received $5890 at the end of a year. Find the amount that she invested at each rate.

9) Andre invested $20,000 in two parts. The first part was put into an investment yielding 10%, while the second part went into 13% bonds. The total annual return was $2150. How much was invested at each rate?

10) Joyce bought 12% bonds and 15% debentures. She invested a total of $6000. If the annual interest that she received on both investments was the same, find the amount she invested at each rate.

11) David had two small bank accounts totalling $500. One of them paid 5% interest, while the other paid $6\frac{1}{4}$%. After a year, he received interest from both accounts totalling $30. How much was in each account?

## Solutions

**1.**  a) $5000 × .05 = $250

b) $5000 × .125 = $625

c) $5000 × .13 = $650

d) $5000 × .075 = $375

e) $5000 × .19 = $950

**2.**  a) $12,000 - p$

b) $.155(12,000 - p)$

c) $.12p$

**3.**  $.09x + .12(x + 900) = 1200$
$.09x + .12x + 108 = 1200$
$.21x = 1092$
$x = \$5200$

**4.**  $.14p + .16(10{,}000 - p) = 1520$
$.14p + 1600 - .16p = 1520$
$^-.02p = ^-80$
$p = \$4000$ at 14%
$10{,}000 - p = \$6000$ at 16%

**5.**  $.09p + .18(p - 450) = 162$
$.09p + .18p - 81 = 162$
$.27p = 243$
$p = \$900$ at 9%
$p - 450 = \$450$ at 18%

**6.**  $.12p + .15(p + 600) = 390$
$.12p + .15p + 90 = 390$
$.27p = 300$
$p = \$1111.11$
in municipals
$p + 600 = \$1711.11$
in companys

**7.**  $.09p + .12(2p) = 870$
$.09p + .24p = 870$
$.33p = 870$
$p = \$2636.36$ at 9%
$2p = \$5272.72$ at 12%

**8.**  $.08p + .14(50{,}000 - p) = 5890$
$8p + 14(50{,}000 - p) = 589{,}000$
(Multiplying through by 100 gets rid of the decimals and makes computation easier.)
$8p + 700{,}000 - 14p = 589{,}000$
$^-6p = ^-111{,}000$
$p = \$18{,}500$ at 8%
$50{,}000 - p = \$31{,}500$ at 14%

**9.**  $.10p + .13(20{,}000 - p) = 2150$
$.10p + 2600 - .13p = 2150$
$^-.03p = ^-450$
$p = \$15{,}000$ at 10%
$20{,}000 - p = \$5000$ at 13%

**10.**  $.12p = .15(6000 - p)$
$.12p = 900 - .15p$
$.27p = 900$
$p = \$3333.33$ at 12%
$6000 - p = \$6666.67$ at 15%

**11.**  $.05p + .0625(500 - p) = 30$
$.05p + 31.25 - .0625p = 30$
$^-.0125p = ^-1.25$
$p = \$100$ at 5%
$500 - p = \$400$ at $6\frac{1}{4}$%

## COIN AND STAMP PROBLEMS

Coin and stamp problems are useful in laying the foundation for another class of word-problems — mixture problems. The main thing to bear in mind is that two quantities are being dealt with: the number of coins or stamps, and the value of each. A diagram is most helpful when it comes to organizing the data for each problem. Bear in mind that the number of coins multiplied by the value of each coin gives the total value of the coins. In order to eliminate the need for decimal multiplication and division, it is helpful to express the value of each coin in cents, i.e. a nickel which is .05 dollars would normally have its value expressed as 5 cents. $3.20 would be written as 320 cents.

Since it is necessary to use only one variable in an equation, it is helpful to express the quantity of each type of coin in terms of the coin upon which the other numbers in the problem are based. Examine the model problems, and you'll see what we mean.

*Model Problem 1*

Jason had a collection of dimes, nickels, and quarters in a jar. He had twice as many nickels as dimes, and four more quarters than nickels. Altogether, he had $3.80. How many coins of each type did he have?

First of all, notice that the number of quarters is based upon the number of nickels, but the number of nickels is based upon the number of dimes. Dimes, then, are the coins upon which the situation is based.

Let $x$ = the number of dimes
$2x$ = the number of nickels
$2x + 4$ = the number of quarters

|  | Number of coins | Value of each | Total value |
|---|---|---|---|
| dimes | $x$ | 10 | $10x$ |
| nickels | $2x$ | 5 | $5(2x)$ |
| quarters | $2x + 4$ | 25 | $25(2x + 4)$ |

Notice that a dime is worth 10 cents, a nickel, 5 cents, and a quarter, 25 cents.

Notice too that total value is determined by multiplying the number of each type of coin by the value of each.

The equation is formed primarily from the last column of the diagram. In essence, it states that if you add the total value of dimes to the total value of nickels and the total value of quarters, you end up with the total amount of money in the jar:

$10x + 5(2x) + 25(2x + 4) = 380$      (Note that $3.80 is 380 cents.)

$10x + 10x + 50x + 100 = 380$

$70x + 100 = 380$

$70x = 280$

$x = 4$      Now refer back to the let-statement.

$x = 4$ dimes
$2x = 8$ nickels
$2x + 4 = 12$ quarters

It never hurts to check the answer, so:

4 dimes = .40
8 nickels = .40
12 quarters = 3.00
$3.80      which is what Jason started with.

*Model Problem 2*

The local high school held a carnival and charged 75¢ admission for adults and 30¢ for children under 12. Twice as many children as adults were admitted, with the total receipts coming to $135. How many tickets of each type were sold?

Let $x$ = the number of adult tickets sold
$2x$ = the number of children's tickets

|          | # of tickets | Unit value | Total value |
|----------|:------------:|:----------:|:-----------:|
| adult    | $x$          | 75         | $75x$       |
| children | $2x$         | 30         | $30(2x)$    |

Once more, the total value of the children's tickets combined with the total value of the adult's tickets gives the total receipts:

$$75x + 30(2x) = 13500 \quad (\$135 = 13500¢)$$
$$75x + 60x = 13,500$$
$$135x = 13,500$$
$$x = 100$$

There were 100 adult and 200 children's tickets.

*Check*

$$100 \times .75 = \$75.00$$
$$200 \times .30 = \underline{\phantom{00}60.00}$$
$$\$135.00$$

Solve the following coin and stamp problems.

1) Represent the value of each of the following in cents.

    a) 5 nickels

    b) 6 quarters

    c) 9 dimes

    d) 3 dimes and 7 nickels

    e) 5 quarters and 7 dimes

    f) 3 quarters, 5 dimes, 9 nickels

    g) 6 dollars

    h) 12 dollars

    i) \$5.79

    j) \$6.75

2) Represent the value of each of the following in cents.

    a) $x$ nickels, $3x$ dimes

    b) $y$ quarters, $4y$ nickels

    c) 5 quarters and $9n$ nickels

    d) $r$ nickels and $(r + 3)$ dimes

    e) $(x + 7)$ quarters and $(2x - 3)$ dimes

    f) $5z$ dimes, $2z$ nickels, and $(3 - z)$ quarters

Make a let-statement and a diagram to organize the data for each. Then solve.

3) Anthony has a beer can full of coins. There are six times as many quarters as nickels, and four more dimes than quarters. Altogether, the can contains \$11.15. How many coins of each type are in the can?

4) A vending machine operator is counting the change taken in from a single candy machine. He finds that he has 43 quarters, twice as many nickels, and 4 more than 3 times as many dimes as nickels. How much money was in the machine?

5) A vending machine contains $4.20 in dimes and nickels. Altogether there are 61 coins. How many coins of each type were in the machine?

6) Mary buys 20¢ regular stamps, and 35¢ airmail stamps at the post office. Altogether she spends $6.20 and receives 22 stamps. How many of each denomination did she buy?

7) Marge paid a grocery bill of $9.20 with quarters, dimes, and nickels. The number of nickels were 6 less than the number of dimes, and there were 10 more dimes than quarters. How many of each type of coin were there?

8) A post office clerk sold 75 stamps for $14.40. If some of the stamps were 15¢ ones, and the others were 24¢ stamps, how many of each kind did she sell?

9) Henry has $8.20 in dimes and quarters. He has 16 more quarters than he has dimes. How many coins of each type does he have?

10) Karen put $11.50 into her savings account. There were 15 more dimes than nickels, and 48 fewer quarters than nickels. How many coins of each type did Karen deposit?

11) Alan collected $7.15 for the volunteer fire department. There were 46 coins altogether, some of which were quarters, and some dimes. How many coins of each type did he collect?

12) Mema took $6.30 to the grocery store in nickels, dimes and quarters. She had three more dimes than quarters, and three fewer nickels than dimes. How many coins of each type did she have?

## Solutions

1.    a) 25¢     b) 150¢     c) 90¢     d) 65¢     e) 195¢     f) 170¢

     g) 600¢     h) 1200¢     i) 579¢     j) 675¢

2.    a) $5x + 30x = 35x$¢       b) $25y + 20y = 45y$¢       c) $(125 - 45n)$¢

     d) $5r + 10(r + 3) = 5r + 10r + 30 = 15r + 30$¢

     e) $25(x + 7) + 10(2x - 3) = 25x + 175 + 20x - 30 = (45x + 145)$¢

     f) $10(5z) + 5(2z) + 25(3 - z) = 50z + 10z + 75 - 25z = (35z + 75)$¢

3.      Let $x$ = # of nickels

        $6x$ = # of quarters

   $6x + 4$ = # of dimes

| Type of coin | # of each | Value of each | Total value |
|---|---|---|---|
| nickels | $x$ | 5 | $5x$ |
| dimes | $6x + 4$ | 10 | $10(6x + 4)$ |
| quarters | $6x$ | 25 | $25(6x)$ |

$$5x + 10(6x + 4) + 25(6x) = 1115$$
$$5x + 60x + 40 + 150x = 1115$$
$$215x = 1075$$
$$x = 5 \text{ nickels}$$
$$6x = 30 \text{ quarters}$$
$$6x + 4 = 34 \text{ dimes}$$

**4.**

| Type of coin | # of each | Value of each | Total value |
|---|---|---|---|
| nickels | 2(43) | 5 | 5[2(43)] |
| dimes | 3[2(43)] + 4 | 10 | 10{3[2(43)] + 4} |
| quarters | 43 | 25 | 25(43) |

Let $v$ = total value.

$$v = 5[2(43)] + 10\{3[2(43)] + 4\} + 25(43)$$
$$v = 5(86) + 10[3(86) + 4] + 1075$$
$$v = 430 + 10(258 + 4) + 1075$$
$$v = 430 + 10(262) + 1075$$
$$v = 430 + 2620 + 1075$$
$$v = 4125 = \$41.25$$

**5.** Let $n$ = # of nickels
$61 - n$ = # of dimes

| Type of coin | # of each | Value of each | Total value |
|---|---|---|---|
| nickels | $n$ | 5 | $5n$ |
| dimes | $61 - n$ | 10 | $10(61 - n)$ |

$$5n + 10(61 - n) = 420$$
$$5n + 610 - 10n = 420$$
$$^-5n = ^-190$$
$$n = 38 \text{ nickels}$$
$$61 - n = 23 \text{ dimes}$$

**6.** Let $a$ = # of 35¢ airmail stamps
$22 - a$ = # of 20¢ stamps

| Type of stamp | # of each | Value of each | Total value |
|---|---|---|---|
| regular | $22 - a$ | 20 | $20(22 - a)$ |
| airmail | $a$ | 35 | $35a$ |

$$20(22 - a) + 35a = 620$$
$$440 - 20a + 35a = 620$$
$$15a = 180$$
$$a = 12 \text{ airmail stamps}$$
$$22 - a = 10 \text{ regular stamps}$$

**7.** Let $x$ = # of quarters
$x + 10$ = # of dimes
$x + 4*$ = # of nickels

| Type of coin | # of each | Value of each | Total value |
|---|---|---|---|
| nickels | $x + 4$ | 5 | $5(x + 4)$ |
| dimes | $x + 10$ | 10 | $10(x + 10)$ |
| quarters | $x$ | 25 | $25x$ |

$$5(x + 4) + 10(x + 10) + 25x = 920$$
$$5x + 20 + 10x + 100 + 25x = 920$$
$$40x + 120 = 920$$
$$40x = 800$$
$$x = 20 \text{ quarters}$$
$$x + 4 = 24 \text{ nickels}$$
$$x + 10 = 30 \text{ dimes}$$

$*[(x + 10) - 6] = x + 4$

**8.**     Let $x$ = # of 15¢ stamps
$75 - x$ = # of 24¢ stamps

| Type of stamp | # of each | Value of each | Total value |
|---|---|---|---|
| 15¢ | $x$ | 15 | $15x$ |
| 24¢ | $75 - x$ | 24 | $24(75 - x)$ |

$$15x + 24(75 - x) = 1440$$
$$15x + 1800 - 24x = 1440$$
$$^-9x + 1800 = 1440$$
$$^-9x = ^-360$$
$$x = 40 \text{ 15¢ stamps}$$
$$75 - x = 35 \text{ 24¢ stamps}$$

**9.**     Let $x$ = # of dimes
$x + 16$ = # of quarters

| Type of coin | # of each | Value of each | Total value |
|---|---|---|---|
| dimes | $x$ | 10 | $10x$ |
| quarters | $x + 16$ | 25 | $25(x + 16)$ |

$$10x + 25(x + 16) = 820$$
$$10x + 25x + 400 = 820$$
$$35x + 400 = 820$$
$$35x = 420$$
$$x = 12 \text{ dimes}$$
$$x + 16 = 28 \text{ quarters}$$

**10.**     Let $x$ = # of nickels
$x + 15$ = # of dimes
$x - 48$ = # of quarters

| Type of coin | # of each | Value of each | Total Value |
|---|---|---|---|
| nickels | $x$ | 5 | $5x$ |
| dimes | $x + 15$ | 10 | $10(x + 15)$ |
| quarters | $x - 48$ | 25 | $25(x - 48)$ |

$$5x + 10(x + 15) + 25(x - 48) = 1150$$
$$5x + 10x + 150 + 25x = 1150$$
$$40x - 1050 = 1150$$
$$40x = 2200$$
$$x = 55 \text{ nickels}$$
$$x + 15 = 70 \text{ dimes}$$
$$x - 48 = 7 \text{ quarters}$$

**11.**     Let $x$ = # of quarters
$46 - x$ = # of dimes

| Type of coin | # of each | Value of each | Total value |
|---|---|---|---|
| dimes | $46 - x$ | 10 | $10(46 - x)$ |
| quarters | $x$ | 25 | $25x$ |

$$10(46 - x) + 25x = 715$$
$$460 - 10x + 25x = 715$$
$$15x = 255$$
$$x = 17 \text{ quarters}$$
$$46 - x = 29 \text{ dimes}$$

**12.**     Let $x$ = # of quarters
$x + 3$ = # of dimes
$(x + 3) - 3 = x$ = # of nickels

| Type of coin | # of each | Value of each | Total value |
|---|---|---|---|
| nickels | $x$ | 5 | $5x$ |
| dimes | $x + 3$ | 10 | $10(x + 3)$ |
| quarters | $x$ | 25 | $25x$ |

$$5x + 10(x + 3) + 25x = 630$$
$$5x + 10x + 30 + 25x = 630$$
$$40x + 30 = 630$$
$$40x = 600$$
$$x = 15 \text{ nickels}$$
$$x = 15 \text{ quarters}$$
$$x + 3 = 18 \text{ dimes}$$

# MIXTURE PROBLEMS

At the beginning of the last section it was noted that coin and stamp problems are really a lead-in to mixture problems. After all, very few people are likely to wonder how many quarters, dimes, and nickels they have in a jar or purse. All they are really concerned with is how much they can buy with the total. Nonetheless, coin and stamp problems serve to introduce the notion that the worth of each item times the number of items is a useful way of calculating the total value of purchases. This approach is essential to a successful experience with mixture problems.

The model problems on the next page will serve to acquaint you with the way in which mixture problems are solved, as well as different types of mixture problems. Once more, a diagram is used to organize the data and to help you construct the equation. Let-statements, as always, are essential.

*Model Problem 1*

A supermarket manager wishes to mix raisins worth $1.29 per pound with almonds worth $2.20 per pound in order to make 35 pounds of a mixture worth $1.81 per pound. How many pounds of each must he use?

Let $x$ = the number of pounds of raisins
$35 - x$ = the number of pounds of almonds

| Ingredients | # of pounds | Price/pound (in cents) | Total value |
|---|---|---|---|
| raisins | $x$ | 129 | $129x$ |
| almonds | $35 - x$ | 220 | $220(35 - x)$ |
| mixture | 35 | 181 | $181(35)$ |

Notice that since there are 35 pounds altogether, and we have arbitrarily decided that $x$ would represent the number of pounds of raisins, then $35 - x$ (what is left when $x$ pounds are removed from 35 pounds) represents the number of pounds of almonds.

The equation comes from the total value of the parts of the mixture being added together to find the total value of the mixture itself:

$$129x + 220(35 - x) = 181(35)$$
$$129x + 7700 - 220x = 6335$$
$$^-91x = ^-1365$$
$$x = 15 \text{ pounds of raisins}$$
$$35 - x = 20 \text{ pounds of almonds}$$

*Model Problem 2*

How many kilograms of pretzels worth $1.05 per kilogram must be mixed with 45 kilograms of potato chips worth $1.45 per kilogram, in order to make a mixture which will sell for $1.15 per kilogram?

Let $x$ = # of kilograms of pretzels

| Ingredients | Amt. of each | Price (in ¢) | Total value |
|---|---|---|---|
| pretzels | $x$ | 105 | $105x$ |
| potato chips | 45 | 145 | $145(45)$ |
| mixture | $45 + x$ | 115 | $115(45 + x)$ |

Once more (as always), the equation is derived by combining the total value of the components and setting that equal to the value of the mixture:

$$105x + 145(45) = 115(45 + x)$$
$$105x + 6525 = 5175 + 115x$$
$$10x = 1350$$
$$x = 13.5 \text{ kilograms of pretzels}$$
$$45 - x = 31.5 \text{ kilograms of potato chips}$$

Solve the following mixture problems.

1) A certain type of nut is worth $3 per pound. What is the value of

   a) 6 pounds?   b) 2 pounds?   c) 5 pounds?   d) $x$ pounds?   e) $(5 - x)$ pounds?

2) How many pounds of $2.40 per pound coffee must be mixed together with $3.48 per pound coffee in order for the roaster to sell 360 pounds of the mixture for $2.76 per pound?

3) How many gallons of $1.20 gasoline must be mixed with $1.45 per gallon gasoline to get 500 gallons of gasoline that will sell for $1.35 per gallon?

4) A baker has cookies worth 90¢ per pound, and cookies worth $1.35 per pound. How many pounds of each should he mix together in order to get 30 pounds of a mixture that will sell for $1.05 per pound?

5) How many tons of tea that sells for $345 per ton must be mixed with 15 tons of tea selling for $270 per ton in order to get a blend that can be wholesaled at $295 per ton?

6) How many kilograms of $4.20 per kilogram cattle fodder must be mixed with 310 kilograms of $2.40 per kilogram fodder in order to get a mixture worth $3.33 per kilogram?

7) A candy-maker wishes to make an assortment from $3.89 per pound filled chocolates and $4.38 per pound covered nuts. How many pounds of the filled chocolates must he combine with 13 pounds of the nuts in order to get an assortment that will be valued at $4.19? (Express your answer to the nearest pound.)

8) A landscape supply store owner mixes rye grass seed at $2.07 per ounce with Kentucky blue grass at $3.45 per ounce. He mixes them in the ratio of 4:7. How much should the mixture sell for?

9) A distiller combines 500 gallons of neutral grain spirits worth $3.59 per gallon with 1200 gallons of rye whiskey worth $7.38 per gallon. How much per gallon should he charge the bottler in order to recognize a 20% profit?

10) A canner of fruit cocktail combines pears, peaches, and pineapple in the ratio 5:3:1. If pears cost the canner $.49 per pound, peaches $.65 per pound, and pineapple $1.12 per pound, how much should the canner charge per pound of fruit cocktail in order to recognize a 35% profit?

11) Sesame seeds cost $.76 per ounce, cashews $5.13 per pound, and raisins, $1.68 per pound. A health food store makes a mix of the three by weight in the ratio 1:3:4. How much should the store charge for a $\frac{1}{2}$ pound of the mixture if it is to make a 15% profit on each sale?

## Solutions

**1.**   a) $18          b) $6          c) $15          d) $3x$          e) $15 - 3x$

**2.**     Let $x$ = # of pounds of $2.40 coffee

$360 - x$ = # of pounds of $3.48 coffee

| Ingredients | Amt. of each | Price (¢) | Total value |
|---|---|---|---|
| $2.40 coffee | $x$ | 240 | $240x$ |
| $3.48 coffee | $360 - x$ | 348 | $348(360 - x)$ |
| Mixture | 360 | 276 | $360(276)$ |

$$240x + 348(360 - x) = 360(276)$$
$$240x + 125{,}280 - 348x = 99{,}360$$
$$^-108x + 125{,}280 = 99{,}360$$
$$^-108x = ^-25{,}920$$
$$x = 240 \text{ pounds of } \$2.40 \text{ coffee}$$
$$360 - x = 120 \text{ pounds of } \$3.48 \text{ coffee}$$

**3.**     Let $x$ = # of gallons of $1.20 gasoline

$500 - x$ = # of gallons of $1.45 gasoline

| Ingredients | Amt. of each | Price (¢) | Total value |
|---|---|---|---|
| $1.00 gasoline | $x$ | 120 | $120x$ |
| $1.45 gasoline | $500 - x$ | 145 | $145(500 - x)$ |
| Mixture | 500 | 135 | $135(500)$ |

$$120x + 145(500 - x) = 135(500)$$
$$120x + 72{,}500 - 145x = 67{,}500$$
$$^-25x = ^-5000$$
$$x = 200 \text{ gallons @ } \$1.20$$
$$500 - x = 300 \text{ gallons @ } \$1.45$$

**4.**     Let $x$ = # of pounds of 90¢ cookies

$30 - x$ = # of pounds of $1.35 cookies

| Ingredients | Amt. of each | Price (¢) | Total value |
|---|---|---|---|
| 90¢ cookies | $x$ | $90x$ | $90x$ |
| $1.35 cookies | $30 - x$ | $135(30 - x)$ | $135(30 - x)$ |
| Mixture | 30 | 105 | $30(105)$ |

$$90x + 135(30 - x) = 30(105)$$
$$90x + 4050 - 135x = 3150$$
$$^-45x = ^-900$$
$$x = 20 \text{ pounds of } 90¢ \text{ cookies}$$
$$30 - x = 10 \text{ pounds of } \$1.35 \text{ cookies}$$

**5.** Let $x$ = # of \$345 per ton of tea

Then $x + 15$ = # of tons of mixture

| Ingredients | Amt. of each | Price (¢) | Total value |
|---|---|---|---|
| \$345 per ton of tea | $x$ | 345 | $345x$ |
| \$270 per ton of tea | 15 | 270 | $15(270)$ |
| Mixture | $x + 15$ | 295 | $295(x + 15)$ |

$$345x + 15(270) = 295(x + 15)$$
$$345x + 4050 = 295x + 4425$$
$$50x = 375$$
$$x = 7\tfrac{1}{2} \text{ tons @ \$345}$$

**6.** Let $x$ = # of kilograms of \$4.20 fodder

$x + 310$ = # of kilograms of mixture

| Ingredients | Amt. of each | Price (¢) | Total value |
|---|---|---|---|
| \$4.20 per kilogram of fodder | $x$ | 420 | $420x$ |
| \$2.40 per kilogram of fodder | 310 | 240 | $240(310)$ |
| Mixture | $x + 310$ | 333 | $333(x + 310)$ |

$$420x + 240(310) = 333(x + 310)$$
$$420x + 74,400 = 333x + 103,230$$
$$87x = 28,830$$
$$x = 331.38 \text{ kilograms}$$

**7.** Let $x$ = # of pounds of chocolates

$x + 13$ = # of pounds of assortment

| Ingredients | Amt. of each | Price (¢) | Total value |
|---|---|---|---|
| chocolates | $x$ | 389 | $389x$ |
| nuts | 13 | 438 | $13(438)$ |
| assortment | $x + 13$ | 419 | $419(x + 13)$ |

$$389x + 13(438) = 419(x + 13)$$
$$389x + 5694 = 419x + 5447$$
$$^-30x = {}^-247$$
$$x = 8.23$$
$$x = 8 \text{ pounds}$$

**8.** If the grass seeds are mixed in the ratio 4:7, there are a total of 11 parts to the mixture ($4 + 7 = 11$). $\frac{4}{11}$ is rye @ \$2.07 and $\frac{7}{11}$ is bluegrass @ \$3.45.

Let $x$ = the price of the mixture.

Then $\frac{4}{11}$ of the price of rye plus $\frac{7}{11}$ of the price of bluegrass should be the price of the bluegrass:

$$x = \tfrac{4}{11}(207) + \tfrac{7}{11}(345)$$
$$x = 75.27 + 219.55$$
$$x = 294.82 \text{ cents}$$
$$x = \$2.95 \text{ (rounded to the nearest cent)}$$

9. 500 gallons of neutral grain spirits @ $3.59 per gallon are worth a total of 500 (3.59) = $1795.

   1200 gallons of rye @ $7.38 per gallon are worth a total of 1200 (7.38) = $8856.

   That means that the total value of the goods is $1795 + $8856 = $10,651. 20% of that total is found by multiplying .20 ($10,651) = $2130.20.

   Add that markup to the total value and you will get the amount for which the entire batch must be sold in order to make a 20% profit: $2130.20 + $10,651 = $12,781.20.

   To find what the distiller must charge the bottler, divide the total ($12,781.20) by the total number of gallons (1700).

   $$\frac{\$12,781.20}{1700} = \$7.52 \text{ (to the nearest penny).}$$

10. The ratio of the parts of the fruit cocktail is 5:3:1, which means that there are 9 parts altogether (5 + 3 + 1); $\frac{5}{9}$ are pears, $\frac{3}{9}$ are peaches, and $\frac{1}{9}$ is pineapple. Accordingly, the price of the mix must be

    $$\tfrac{5}{9}(.49) + \tfrac{3}{9}(.65) + \tfrac{1}{9}(1.12)$$

    The mixture therefore cost the canner .2722 + .2167 + .1244 = .6133, or 61¢ per pound.

    A 35% profit on $.61 is calculated by finding 35% of $.61 and then adding it onto the cost:

    .61(.35) = .214, or 21¢. The canner should charge 82¢.

11. Since all units must be the same in order to compare them, we must first either convert the price of sesame seeds to a per pound value, or convert the other two to per ounce prices. The former is easier. Since there are 16 ounces in a pound, one pound of sesame seeds costs 16(.76) or $12.16. If the mixture were prepared with 1 pound of sesame seeds, 3 pounds of cashews, and 4 pounds of raisins, it would cost 12.16(1) + 5.13(3) + 1.68(4), or $34.27 to prepare 8 pounds of the mixture. To find the cost of $\frac{1}{2}$ pound, divide the price of 8 pounds by 16. That gives a cost of $2.14 per half-pound. The price, after 15% was added on, would be $2.46.

# 6. READING GRAPHS AND CHARTS

A graph is a picture of mathematical data. The data usually refers to a single subject or group of subjects. There are many different types of graphs, the most common ones being pictographs, bar graphs, line graphs, and circle graphs (or pie charts). We shall look at each of these in this chapter.

Every graph contains a legend or key, which may be a small inset or may appear along the axes of the graph. It explains the meanings of the graph's markings. Always locate and read the legend or key before attempting to interpret the meaning of the graph itself. Two graphs may look identical, yet have different keys, thereby making the interpretations of the graphs different from one another.

## GRAPHING PRE-TEST

**Small Farms in Mercer County (1985–1990)**
🏠 = 200 farms

| Year | |
|------|---|
| 1990 | 🏠 🏠 🏠 🏠 🏠 🏠 |
| 1989 | 🏠 🏠 🏠 🏠 🏠 🏠 🏠 🏠 🏠 |
| 1988 | 🏠 🏠 🏠 🏠 🏠 🏠 🏠 🏠 🏠 🏠 🏠 🏠 |
| 1987 | 🏠 🏠 🏠 🏠 🏠 🏠 🏠 🏠 🏠 🏠 🏠 🏠 🏠 🏠 |
| 1986 | 🏠 🏠 🏠 🏠 🏠 🏠 🏠 🏠 🏠 🏠 🏠 🏠 🏠 🏠 🏠 |
| 1985 | 🏠 🏠 🏠 🏠 🏠 🏠 🏠 🏠 🏠 🏠 🏠 🏠 🏠 🏠 🏠 🏠 🏠 |

Statements 1 through 5 refer to the graph above.

For each statement answer "A" if the graph agrees with the statement, "B" if the graph contradicts the statement, or "C" if the graph neither agrees nor disagrees with the statement.

1) There were 600 fewer small farms in Mercer County in 1987 than in 1990.

2) In 1991 there will probably be 1000 small farms in Mercer County.

3) In 1989 there were 900 small farms in Mercer County.

4) Mercer County lost 1100 small farms between 1985 and 1990.

5) The loss of small farms in Mercer County was probably due to consolidations into large factory farms and conversion of farm land to housing developments.

## Answers

**1.** B   **2.** C   **3.** A   **4.** A   **5.** C

# PICTURE GRAPHS

Picture graphs are also known as histograms or pictographs. Each picture on a histogram stands for a quantity of something. For example, a little picture of a person may stand for 500 or 1000 people; a little car may stand for 100 automobiles, and so on. There must be a key or legend to tell you what each picture means.

## *Model Problems*

**Repairs Required During First Three Years for Selected TV Brands (per 100)**
📺 = 5 sets

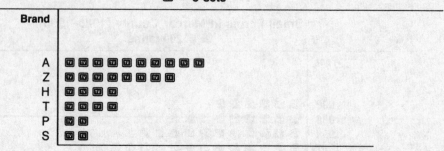

Questions 1 to 4 refer to the graph above.

1) How many more Brand A sets per hundred needed repair during the first three years than Brand T sets per hundred?

   A careful look at the title of the graph and the key tells us that each TV set on the graph stands for 5 per 100 sold. The row for Brand A contains 6 more symbols than the row for Brand T. Multiply 6 (symbols) × 5 (number of sets each symbol stands for) to get 30 more sets per 100.

2) Which brand(s) of TV shown on the graph appear to be the most reliable?

   Those brands that required the fewest repairs would be the most reliable. Two brands, P and S, are tied for that honor, each with 10 repairs per hundred sets.

3) What percent of Brand Z televisions required repair during their first three years?

   Percent is a fraction of 100. Since the graph displays repairs per hundred sets sold, the graph actually shows percent figures, with each picture representing 5%. There are 8 symbols in the Brand Z row. That means that 8 × 5%, or 40%, is the percent of Brand Z sets requiring repair during their first three years.

4) How many more Brand Z televisions were sold compared to Brand P during the three years covered by the graph?

The graph contains no information about sales records. Therefore, there is not enough information given to answer this question.

Questions 1 to 4 refer to the following graph. (Hint: Some questions cannot be answered on the basis of the information given.)

### Blood Samples Taken at Beth David Hospital
Ⓗ = 10 samples

| Day | |
|---|---|
| Sat | Ⓗ Ⓗ Ⓗ Ⓗ Ⓗ Ⓗ Ⓗ Ⓗ |
| Fri | Ⓗ Ⓗ Ⓗ Ⓗ Ⓗ Ⓗ Ⓗ Ⓗ Ⓗ Ⓗ Ⓗ Ⓗ Ⓗ |
| Thu | Ⓗ Ⓗ Ⓗ Ⓗ Ⓗ Ⓗ Ⓗ Ⓗ Ⓗ Ⓗ Ⓗ Ⓗ Ⓗ Ⓗ Ⓗ |
| Wed | Ⓗ Ⓗ Ⓗ Ⓗ Ⓗ Ⓗ Ⓗ Ⓗ Ⓗ Ⓗ Ⓗ Ⓗ Ⓗ Ⓗ Ⓗ Ⓗ Ⓗ |
| Tue | Ⓗ Ⓗ Ⓗ Ⓗ Ⓗ Ⓗ Ⓗ Ⓗ Ⓗ Ⓗ Ⓗ Ⓗ Ⓗ Ⓗ Ⓗ Ⓗ |
| Mon | Ⓗ Ⓗ Ⓗ Ⓗ Ⓗ Ⓗ Ⓗ Ⓗ Ⓗ Ⓗ Ⓗ Ⓗ Ⓗ Ⓗ Ⓗ Ⓗ Ⓗ Ⓗ Ⓗ Ⓗ |

1) How many more samples were taken on Tuesday than on Thursday?

2) How many patients' blood samples revealed an illness?

3) On which two days were the same number of samples taken?

4) On which day were the samples taken half the number taken on Tuesday?

Questions 5 to 8 refer to the following graph.

### Percent of Rejects per Week at ABCO Transmissions
🚗 = 1% of transmissions

| Week | |
|---|---|
| 6 | 🚗 🚗 🚗 🚗 🚗 🚗 🚗 🚗 |
| 5 | 🚗 🚗 🚗 🚗 🚗 🚗 🚗 |
| 4 | 🚗 🚗 |
| 3 | 🚗 🚗 🚗 🚗 🚗 🚗 🚗 🚗 🚗 🚗 🚗 |
| 2 | 🚗 🚗 🚗 🚗 🚗 🚗 🚗 🚗 |
| 1 | 🚗 🚗 🚗 🚗 |

5) In which week was the percentage of rejects half that of week six?

6) What is the difference in the number of transmissions rejected in week three and those rejected in week one?

7) What percentage of transmissions was rejected in week three?

8) How many more transmissions were rejected in week five than in week one?

Questions 9 to 12 refer to the following graph.

**New Telephone Installations Last Week**
☎ = 100 phones

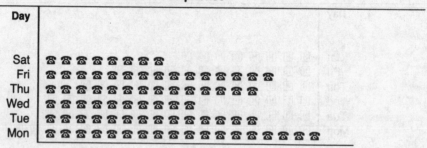

9) How many more phones were installed on Thursday than on Saturday?

10) On which day of the week were the fewest phones installed done?

11) On which day of the week were 1000 installations done?

12) Are any phones installated on Sunday?

Questions 13 to 16 refer to the following graph.

**Survey of Preferred Cookware Materials**
♀ = 100 persons

| Material | | |
|---|---|---|
| Enamel | ♀ ♀ ♀ ♀ ♀ ♀ | |
| Glass | ♀ ♀ ♀ ♀ ♀ ♀ ♀ ♀ | |
| Ceramic | ♀ ♀ ♀ ♀ ♀ ♀ ♀ ♀ ♀ | |
| Steel | ♀ ♀ ♀ ♀ ♀ ♀ ♀ ♀ ♀ ♀ ♀ ♀ ♀ | |
| Iron | ♀ ♀ ♀ ♀ ♀ ♀ ♀ | |
| Aluminum | ♀ ♀ ♀ ♀ ♀ ♀ ♀ ♀ ♀ ♀ ♀ ♀ ♀ ♀ ♀ ♀ ♀ | |

13) Which type of cookware was preferred by fewer than half as many as those preferring aluminum?

14) Which types of cookware were preferred by exactly the same number of people?

15) How many more people preferred steel over glass cookware?

16) Which type of cookware is able to boil water quickest?

## Answers

**1.** 20    **2.** Not enough information    **3.** Tuesday and Wednesday    **4.** Saturday
**5.** Week one    **6.** Not enough information    **7.** 10    **8.** Not enough information    **9.** 500    **10.** Saturday    **11.** Wednesday    **12.** Not enough information
**13.** Enamel    **14.** Iron and glass    **15.** 600    **16.** Not enough information

# BAR GRAPHS

The bar graph is the logical extension of the picture graph. It looks like a rectangle drawn around each row of pictures, with the pictures themselves then erased. Since there are no pictures to count, there are markings along one axis to tell you the quantity being represented. Bar graphs can be horizontal, like most picture graphs, or vertical. Unlike pictographs, bar graphs can be used to compare two or more different things at the same time, as in the graph below.

## *Model Problems*

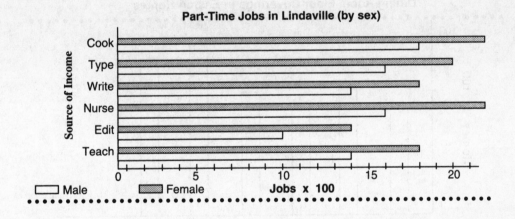

Questions 1 to 4 refer to the graph above.

1) How many more females than males teach part-time in Lindaville?

   To answer the question, we first need to examine the legend. There we find that the shaded bars are for females and the white bars are for males. We also learn that the numbers written along the horizontal axis must be multiplied by 100. Put your finger (or better still, a straightedge) at the right end of the shaded "Teach" bar. Next, look down to the marking on the horizontal axis. It is 18. Multiplied by 100, that's 1800 female part-time teachers. Now do the same thing with the white

"Teach" bar. You should find 1400 male teachers. Subtract to find the difference: 1800 − 1400 = 400 more female teachers.

2) At which job are there as many females as there are males who write?

Follow the white "Write" bar to its right end. While holding your finger or straightedge there, find a shaded bar that ends at the same place. It's the shaded "Edit" bar.

3) Do more females than males hold part-time jobs because more males than females in Lindaville hold full-time jobs?

The graph gives us figures on part-time jobs. It says nothing about full-time jobs, nor does it give us reasons or explanations for the information given. There is not enough information to answer this question.

4) How many females in Lindaville work part-time or in sales as typists?

Find the right end of the shaded "Cook" bar. Square a straightedge with the horizontal axis and move it to the right end of that bar. It ends at the 22 mark. Multiply 22 by 100, the number of jobs each mark stands for: 22 × 100 = 2200. Now repeat the same thing for the shaded "Type" bar and you'll get 2000. Add the two figures together: 2200 + 2000 = 4200 females who work as cooks or typists.

Questions 1 to 4 refer to the following graph.

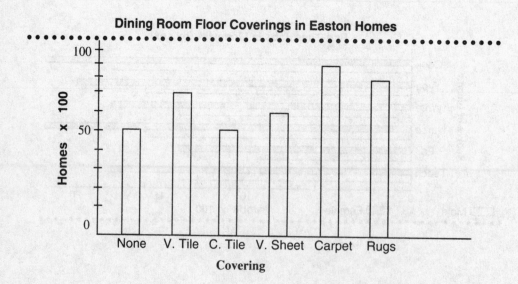

1) How many Easton homes have no floor covering in the dining room?

2) How many more Easton dining room floors have vinyl tile than ceramic?

3) How many Easton homes have carpeted living rooms?

4) How many Easton homes have either rugs or carpet in their dining rooms?

Questions 5 to 8 refer to the following graph.

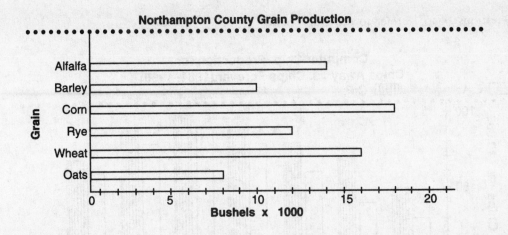

**Northampton County Grain Production**

5) What is the difference between corn and oat production?

6) What is the total amount of grain produced in Northampton County?

7) How much grain is barley or rye?

8) What part of the grain production goes to cattle fodder?

Questions 9 to 13 refer to the graph below.

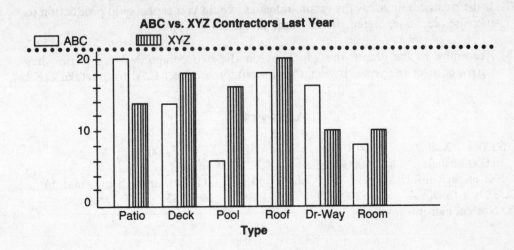

**ABC vs. XYZ Contractors Last Year**

9) ABC contractors installed as many driveways last year as XYZ installed
_____.

10) How many more patios did ABC contractors install last year compared to XYZ?

11) How many more roofs would you expect ABC to install this year compared to XYZ?

12) How many roofs were installed by both companies last year?

13) Which company did more jobs last year?

Questions 14 to 18 refer to the graph below.

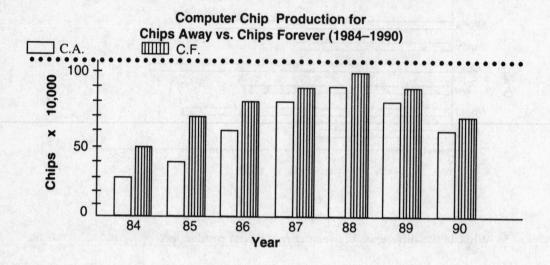

14) What is the difference between C.F.'s (Chips Forever's) production in 1984 and 1990?

15) In what year did C.A.'s (Chips Away's) production peak?

16) In what year was the output of each of the two companies furthest apart?

17) If the trend continues as the graph indicates, would you expect chip production to increase, decrease, or remain the same in 1991?

18) According to the graph, the gap between the two companies' production has narrowed over the years. By what year would you expect C.A. to overtake C.F.?

## Answers

**1.** 5000    **2.** 2000    **3.** Not enough information    **4.** 17,000
**5.** 10,000 bushels    **6.** 78,000 bushels    **7.** 22,000 bushels
**8.** Not enough information    **9.** Pools    **10.** 6    **11.** Not enough information
**12.** 38    **13.** XYZ    **14.** 200,000    **15.** 1988    **16.** 1985    **17.** Decrease
**18.** Not enough information

# LINE GRAPHS

You may think of a line graph as connecting the topmost points of vertical bars on a bar graph and then erasing the bars themselves. Or you may think of a line graph as plotting points at the intersection of the values along the horizontal and vertical axes and then connecting the points. Line graphs can be used to display the same information as bar graphs, but they are better than bar graphs at displaying continuous information, such as a range of temperatures over a period of time, or stock-price variations. It is easier to read peaks and valleys on a line graph than on a bar graph, especially if more than one line is being considered.

## *Model Problems*

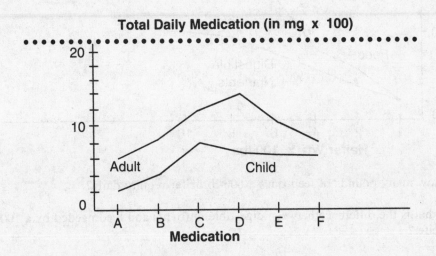

Questions 1 to 4 refer to the graph above.

1) What is the difference in the amounts of a child's and an adult's daily doses of medication C?

It helps to have two straightedges available. Move the first straightedge along the horizontal axis until it is on the medication C mark. Leave it there and bring the second straightedge down until it touches the "adult" line. Now read the dosage on the vertical axis (each mark is 2 from the last). You should get 12. Multiply that 12 by 100 mg (from the legend):

$$12 \times 100 = 1200 \text{ mg}$$

Now move the second straightedge down until it intersects the "child" line. Read 8 on the vertical axis. Multiplied by 100 mg, that's 800 mg. To find the difference, subtract:

$$1200 - 800 = 400 \text{ mg}$$

2) For which medication is the difference between child and adult doses the least?

There is no need to calculate the answer to this question. The two lines are closest together at medication F.

3) For which medication is the difference between the child and adult doses greatest?

Again, no need to measure. The lines are farthest apart at medication D.

4) For which medication(s) is the child's dose greater than the adult dose of medication A?

Bring your straightedge down, keeping it square with the axes (against the vertical axis) until it reaches the adult dose for medication A. The edge is now covering the "child" line for C, D, and E. Hence, those medications have child doses higher than A's adult dose.

Questions 1 to 4 refer to the following graph.

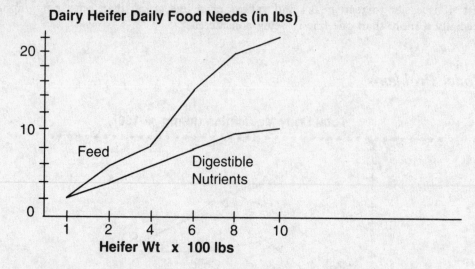

1) How many pounds of feed does a 600-lb heifer require daily?

2) What is the difference between digestible nutrients and feed needed by a 1000-lb heifer?

3) As a heifer increases in weight, does the proportion of its food that must be digestible nutrients increase, decrease, or remain the same?

4) At what weight must all of a heifer's daily feed be digestible nutrients?

Questions 5 to 8 refer to the following graph.

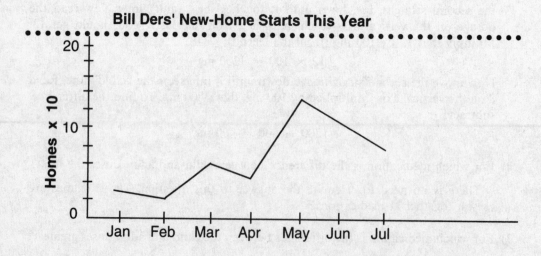

5) What was the difference in new-home starts between the best month and the poorest month?

6) Was the fear of not finishing before winter responsible for no new starts after July?

7) How many new homes were started in March?

8) During what month did the biggest downturn in homestarts occur?

Questions 9 to 12 refer to the following graph.

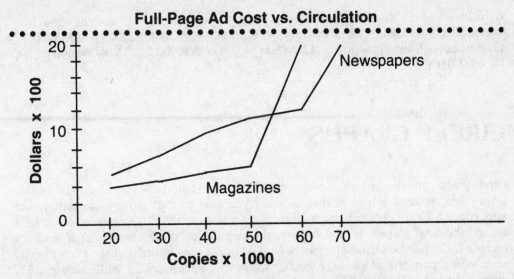

9) At what circulation does magazine advertising become more expensive than newspaper advertising?

10) What is the cost of a full-page ad in a newspaper with a circulation of 70,000?

11) What is the difference in cost between ads in magazines and newspapers with 40,000 circulation?

12) What is the cost of an ad in a newspaper with a circulation of 10,000

Questions 13 to 16 refer to the following graph.

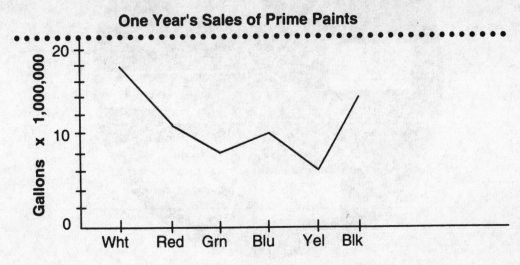

13) What color paint sold three times better than yellow?

14) How many gallons of green paint were sold?

15) How many fewer gallons of blue paint were sold compared to black?

16) How many gallons of paint did Prime Paints sell during the year shown?

## Answers

**1.** 16 lbs  **2.** 12 lbs  **3.** Decrease  **4.** 110 lbs  **5.** 120  **6.** Not enough information  **7.** 60  **8.** May–July  **9.** 55,000+  **10.** $2000  **11.** $400  **12.** Not enough information  **13.** White  **14.** 8,000,000  **15.** 4,000,000  **16.** 68,000,000

# CIRCLE GRAPHS

Circle graphs are also known as pie charts. (One look should tell you why.) They differ from other types of graphs in that they tell you how various parts of something are apportioned. Every pie chart in its entirety represents a whole. That whole could be a dollar, the total income of a company, the population of the world, or a person's income for a specific period of time. Each slice of the pie (segment of the circle) represents how a part of that whole is used or made up. When working with circle graphs, always keep in mind that the whole is 100%.

## *Model Problems*

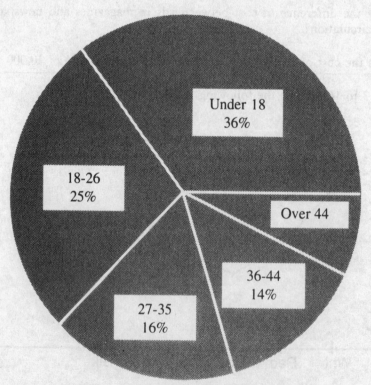

**Rockin' Records' Sales by Age Group**

Questions 1 to 3 refer to the graph above.

1) What percent of Rockin' Records' customers are younger than 27 years of age?

36% are shown as being under age 18, and 25% are shown as being aged 18 to 26. Add those two percentages together:

$$36 + 25 = 61$$

61% are younger than age 27.

2) What percent of Rockin' Records' customers are over age 44?

To find this answer, we must first add up all the percentages that we have from the chart:

$$36 + 25 + 16 + 14 = 91$$

The group we are *not* interested in totals 91% of sales. Subtract that from 100% to get the over-44 group:

$$100 - 91 = 9$$

9% are over age 44.

3) How many of Rockin' Records' clients are aged 27 to 35?

The graph gives percentages, not numbers. If we knew how many clients there were altogether, then 16% of that number would be the answer to the question. With the information we have, however, we can't answer the question.

Questions 1 to 5 refer to the following graph.

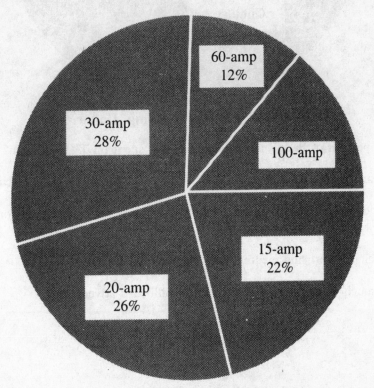

**Circuit Breakers at Napa Industries**

1) What is the difference in the percentages of 30- and 60-amp circuit breakers used at Napa Industries?

2) What percent of the breakers are 100-amp?

3) What percent of Napa breakers are lower than 30-amp?

4) What percent of Napa breakers can handle 220 volts?

5) If Napa used 300 breakers, how many would be 60-amp or higher?

Questions 6 to 10 refer to the following graph.

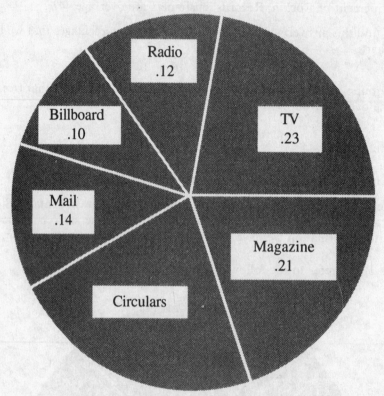

**S.O. Badd's Advertising Dollar**

6) What percent of Badd's advertising dollar is spent on TV and radio?

7) How many cents of each advertising dollar does Badd spend on circulars?

8) If Badd spends $10,000 on advertising, how many dollars are spent on magazine ads?

9) On which advertising medium does Badd spend the most?

10) How much money does Badd spend on billboard advertising?

Questions 11 to 15 refer to the following graph.

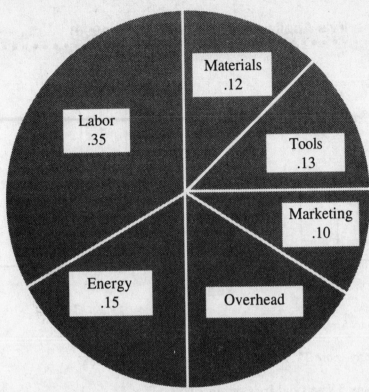

**Where U.R. Manufacturing's Dollar Goes**

11) How much does the average worker at U.R. earn per hour?

12) What percent of U.R.'s expenditures go to energy?

13) How many cents of each dollar does U.R. spend on marketing and overhead combined?

14) What does U.R. spend the least amount per dollar on?

15) If U.R. spends $200,000 per year altogether, how much does it spend on labor?

## Answers

**1.** 16%  **2.** 12%  **3.** 48%  **4.** Not enough information  **5.** 72  **6.** 35%
**7.** $.20  **8.** $2100  **9.** TV  **10.** Not enough information  **11.** Not enough information  **12.** 15%  **13.** $.25  **14.** Marketing  **15.** $70,000

# GRAPHING POST-TEST

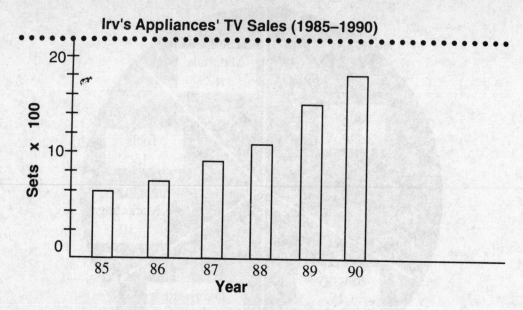

**Irv's Appliances' TV Sales (1985–1990)**

Questions 1 to 5 refer to the graph above.

1) How many more TV sets were sold in 1990 than in 1985?

2) How many TV sets did Irv's sell in 1988?

3) Does Irv's sell other things besides TVs?

4) If the trend shown on the graph continues, is Irv's likely to sell more, fewer, or the same number of sets in 1991?

5) What was the total number of TV sets sold by Irv's from 1985 through 1990?

## Answers

**1.** 1200    **2.** 1100    **3.** Not enough information    **4.** More    **5.** 6600

# 7. GEOMETRY

Geometry is the study of the measurements of different types of figures, and their relationships. As a general rule, all geometric figures occupy space. The points, lines, and line-segments which outline those figures, however, do not occupy any space. This distinction should become clearer in a short while.

Most of this section is concerned with plane geometry. A plane is a flat surface, and so plane geometry concerns those figures which may be drawn on a flat surface. A circle, for example, is a plane figure. A sphere (ball) is not.

Much of our knowledge of geometry we owe to the Greeks of about 2500 years ago. They studied the relationships of angles and sides of all types of plain and solid figures, with an eye toward their aesthetic as well as their practical applications. Much of what they discovered was applied in laying out and constructing buildings — most of which were temples to the gods of Mount Olympus. The person responsible for organizing all of the discoveries into an organized volume of knowledge was a man known as Euclid. It is in honor of his achievement that for thousands of years people have studied "Euclidean Geometry."

## GEOMETRY PRE-TEST

What type of triangle is each marked to be?

1)    2)    3)

Find the total number of degrees of angle measure in each figure.

4)    5)

Find the area of each figure.

6) 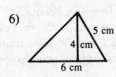   7) 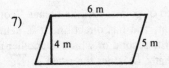   8)

9) Write the equation of a line that has a slope of ⁻3 and a y-intercept of 4.

10) Write the equation of a line that passes through the points (⁻3,2) and (5,11).

11) Find the distance on a graph between (2,4) and (5,8).

225

## Answers

| | | | |
|---|---|---|---|
| **1.** isosceles | **2.** obtuse | **3.** equiangular | **4.** 360° |
| **5.** 540° | **6.** 12 cm² | **7.** 24 m² | **8.** 16π ft² |
| **9.** $y = {}^-3x + 4$ | **10.** $y = \frac{8}{8} \times {}^-5\frac{1}{4}$ | **11.** 5 | |

## *ANALYSIS OF PRE-TEST ITEMS*

# SOME VERY BASIC DEFINITIONS

A **point** is a location in space. It occupies no space itself. Below, you see representations of two points, **A** and **B**. The dot in each case, represents, **but is not actually**, a point. That is because the dots occupy space, and points (as just noted) do not. Note that a single uppercase letter is used to name a point.

A **ray** is an infinite series of points. Infinite means "continuing forever without end." A ray has a single endpoint, and has direction. It is named by two points, the first of which is its endpoint, and the second of which is another point that lies on it. Note from the representation below that $\overrightarrow{CD}$ is not the same as $\overleftarrow{DC}$. Each has a different endpoint and goes in the opposite direction.

The arrowhead on the end of each ray indicates that it continues infinitely in the direction indicated.

A **line** is defined alternately as an infinite series of points (but unlike a ray) having no endpoint, or as two opposite rays. It is represented as indicated below. The line represented below may be called either $\overleftrightarrow{EF}$ or $\overleftrightarrow{FE}$. Unlike the rays on the previous page, both names indicate the same line.

Note that $E$ and $F$ are any two points on the line.

Perhaps the geometric representation with which you have had the most experience is the **line-segment**. A line-segment, as in the two previous figures, is also an infinite series of points. It differs from the previous two, however, in that it has two endpoints. Often, a line is incorrectly defined as the shortest distance between two points. In fact, a line-segment is the shortest distance between two points. A line-segment is named by its endpoints, hence line segment $GH$ ($\overline{GH}$) is illustrated below:

When two rays have the same endpoint, they form an **angle**. That angle is named either by using the letter of the mutual endpoint of the rays, or by naming the three points in order with the mutual endpoint in the center. Hence, below is pictured $\angle C$, $\angle BCD$, or $\angle DCB$.

The mutual endpoint of the two rays, at which the angle, $BCD$, is formed, is known as the **vertex** of the angle. Point $C$ is the vertex of angle $C$. (The plural of vertex is vertices.)

Name each of the figures below. Also give the appropriate symbol and letter names.

1) _____

2) _____

3) _____

4) _____

5) _____

6) _____

7) _____

8) _____

9) _____

10) _____

## Answers

**1.** ray, $\overrightarrow{EW}$

**2.** ray, $\overrightarrow{SR}$

**3.** line, $\overleftrightarrow{PQ}$ or $\overleftrightarrow{QP}$

**4.** point, $M$

**5.** line-segment, $\overline{VR}$ or $\overline{RV}$

**6.** angle, $\angle S$, $\angle TSG$, or $\angle GST$

**7.** angle, $\angle I$, $\angle HIJ$, or $\angle JIH$

**8.** angle, $\angle M$

**9.** line-segment, $\overline{KF}$ or $\overline{FK}$

**10.** line, $\overleftrightarrow{R}$

# TYPES OF ANGLES AND ANGLE MEASUREMENT

Imagine two rays, *OA* and *OB*. At the start, point *A* is lying exactly atop point *B*.

Pivoting at *O*, ray *OA* begins to rotate upward, forming an angle with *OB* at *O*. Before the rotation began (Figure 1) the angle at *O* had a measure of 0°. In Figure 2, that angle is greater than 0° but less than 90°.

Figure 3 shows ray *OA* having rotated through a quarter of a circle. The distance through which it has rotated is measured as an angle of 90°.

In Figure 4, *OA* has rotated through an angle of more than 90° but less than 180°. Figure 5 shows a rotation of 180°, or a half circle.

Figure 1:

Figure 2

Figure 3

Figure 4

Figure 5

Notice that measuring angles is not like measuring distance. That is because the legs of the angle are at different distances from the vertex, different distances apart. Remember that degree measure measures the amount of rotation around a pivotal point. Based upon the amount of rotation, angles may be classified. An angle containing fewer than 90° is known as an **acute** angle. An acute angle is illustrated in Figure 2 (above). An angle containing exactly 90° is a **right** angle (see Figure 3, above). Figure 4 shows an **obtuse** angle — that is one of greater than 90° but less than 180°. An angle of exactly 180° is often referred to as a **straight** angle.

Classify each of the following as an acute, right, obtuse, or straight angle. (It may be helpful in some cases to rotate your book in order to get a true picture.)

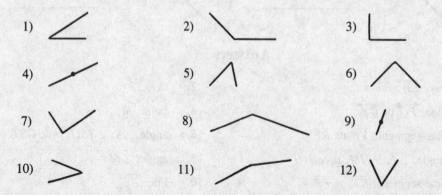

## Answers

| | | | | | | | |
|---|---|---|---|---|---|---|---|
| **1.** | acute | **2.** | obtuse | **3.** | right | **4.** | straight |
| **5.** | acute | **6.** | right | **7.** | right | **8.** | obtuse |
| **9.** | straight | **10.** | acute | **11.** | obtuse | **12.** | acute |

# TRIANGLES

Closed figures made up of line segments are known as **polygons**. The word, polygon, means many sides. The simplest of the polygons is the **triangle** — a closed figure with three sides. It is impossible to have a closed figure containing fewer than three sides. Try to make one, and prove the last statement to yourself.

Triangles may be classified in two ways — by angles, or by sides. When classified according to sides, there are three types of triangles: **Equilateral, isosceles,** and **scalene**.

An equilateral triangle is a triangle which has three sides of equal length.

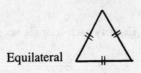

Equilateral

An isosceles triangle has two sides of equal length. Those sides are known as the legs. The non-equal side is known as the base.

Isosceles

A scalene triangle is a triangle which has no two sides equal in length.

Scalene

The markings on the sides of the triangles above are used to indicate equality of length (also known as **congruency**). Sides which are similarly marked are congruent.

When triangles are classified according to their angles, there are also three types: **Acute**, **right**, and **obtuse**.

An acute triangle is one which contains acute angles, and acute angles only.

Acute Triangle

A right triangle is a triangle which contains exactly one right angle. Notice the way in which the right angle is marked. This is a standard marking used to indicate that an angle is a right angle. The corners of this page are right angles.

Right Triangle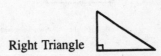

An obtuse triangle is one which contains exactly one obtuse angle. As with the right triangle, those angles other than the one from which the figure gets its name are acute angles.

Obtuse Triangle

You may wish to note at this time that an equilateral triangle is also equiangular. That is to say, all three angles are congruent (contain the same size degree measure). Also, an isosceles triangle contains two congruent angles — those opposite the congruent sides.

The sum of the measures of all the angles of any triangle is equal to 180°. If you wish to prove that to yourself, you may cut out a triangle from a piece of paper, and mark each of the angles in some way (1). Then cut or tear the triangle apart, making sure not to damage any of the original angles (2). Finally piece the three angles together with the vertices touching, and you will see that the angles total up to a straight angle (3). This will be true of any triangle, no matter whether it is acute, right, or obtuse. Try it with as many different types of triangles as you like until you are convinced.

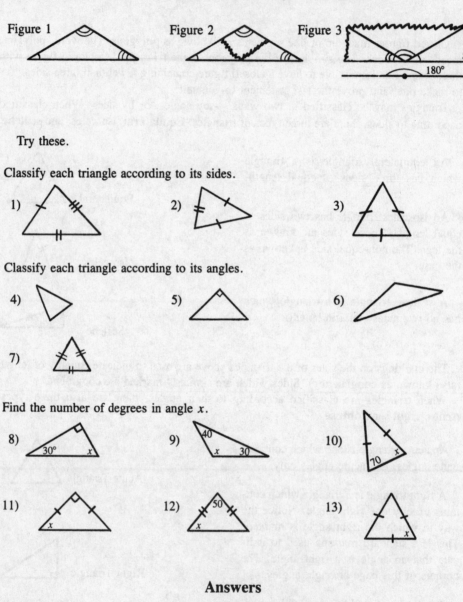

Try these.

Classify each triangle according to its sides.

1)    2)    3)

Classify each triangle according to its angles.

4)    5)    6)

7)

Find the number of degrees in angle $x$.

8)    9)    10)

11)    12)    13)

## Answers

| | | | |
|---|---|---|---|
| **1.** scalene | **2.** isosceles | **3.** equilateral | **4.** acute |
| **5.** right | **6.** obtuse | **7.** equiangular | **8.** 60° |
| **9.** 110° | **10.** 70° | **11.** 45° | **12.** 65° | **13.** 60° |

# QUADRILATERALS

The next polygon in complexity after the triangle is the quadrilateral. A quadrilateral is any four-sided polygon. Quadrilaterals, like triangles, may be classified according to certain features. One with no special features is simply known as a **quadrilateral** (1).

Incorporating one pair of parallel sides into a quadrilateral makes a figure known as a **trapezoid** (2).

If the other pair of legs of a trapezoid are also made parallel, a new quadrilateral is formed which is known as a **parallelogram** (3).

From the basic parallelogram it is possible to go in either of two directions. A right angle may be added, in which case the parallelogram becomes a **rectangle** (4). Otherwise, all sides of the parallelogram may be made equal, in which case the parallelogram is known as a **rhombus** (4a).

If a rectangle is made equilateral, the resulting figure is a **square**. If a right angle is added to a rhombus, the resulting figure is also a **square** (5). Examine the diagram closely, and see how quadrilaterals change.

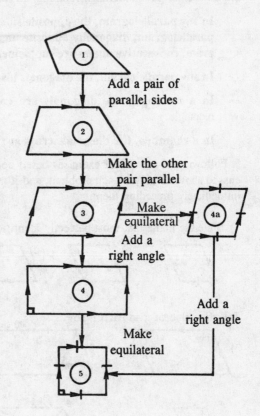

There are certain properties that are shared by all quadrilaterals. All have four sides and four vertices. Each quadrilateral is also capable of being cut by a diagonal into two triangles:

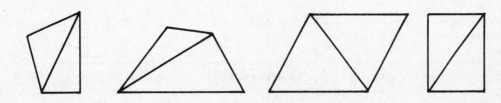

Since we have seen that the total degree measure of a triangle's angles is 180°, and since we have seen that any quadrilateral can be cut into two triangles, it is reasonable to conclude that the total number of degrees in the angles of a quadrilateral is 360°.

## SPECIAL FEATURES OF PARALLELOGRAMS

Bear in mind that as you progress down the chart of quadrilaterals (page 215), each figure incorporates the features of the one before, and then adds a special characteristic of its own. All the figures on the chart are quadrilaterals. The square, rhombus, and rectangle are all special parallelograms, retaining all the characteristics of any parallelogram.

**In any parallelogram, the opposite sides are parallel and congruent. In any parallelogram, diagonally opposite angles are congruent. In any parallelogram, consecutive angles are supplementary — that is, they add up to 180°.**

**In any parallelogram, the diagonals bisect each other** (cut each other in half).

**In a rectangle, the diagonals are congruent.** (Remember a square is a rectangle.)

**In a rhombus, the diagonals cross at right angles.**

Following is a group of exercises based upon the characteristics of quadrilaterals discussed above. Analyze each problem, and if necessary refer to the rules stated above and immediately preceding them.

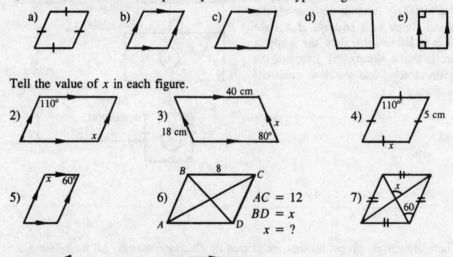

1) State the name that most perfectly identifies each type of figure.

a)    b)    c)    d)    e)

Tell the value of $x$ in each figure.

2)    3)    4)

5)    6) $AC = 12$ $BD = x$ $x = ?$    7)

8)    9)

## Answers

1.  a) rhombus          b) parallelogram          c) trapezoid
    d) quadrilateral     e) rectangle

2.  110°          **3.** 18 cm     **4.** 5 cm     **5.** 120°

6.  not enough information     **7.** 90°     **8.** 85°     **9.** 80°

# OTHER POLYGONS

A five-sided polygon is known as a pentagon, a six-sided polygon is known as a hexagon, and an eight-sided polygon is known as an octagon. It is at least theoretically possible to have a polygon of any number of sides. A polygon of an infinite number of sides is a circle — which is the limit to how many sides a polygon may have. In a circle, each of the infinite number of points making up its circumference (the distance around it) may be thought of as a separate side. Circles will be discussed separately in another section (beginning on page 224).

Any polygon has the same number of sides as it has vertices. That is to say, as a triangle has three sides and three vertices, a quadrilateral four sides and four vertices, and a pentagon five sides and five vertices, so an *n*-gon has *n* sides and *n* vertices. A **regular polygon** is defined as **a polygon whose sides are all congruent**.

To calculate the number of degrees in all the interior angles of a regular polygon, divide the polygon up into triangles by drawing as many diagonals as can be drawn from a single vertex. In the pentagon pictured below, all diagonals drawn originated at vertex *V*.

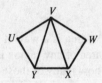

The number of triangles is then multiplied by 180° to find the number of degrees of angle measure in the figure. In this case, $3 \cdot 180° = 540°$. To find the number of degrees in each angle, divide the total by the number of vertices (in this case 5). $\frac{540}{5}$ yields a figure of 108° per interior angle of the pentagon.

# AREA AND PERIMETER

The **perimeter** of a figure is the distance around that figure. A rectangle, as a case in point, may be considered as the fence around a rectangular shaped region. The length of the fence is the perimeter of the rectangle. For a rectangle or a parallelogram the perimeter may readily be computed as twice the length plus twice the width:

$$P = 2L + 2W$$

The perimeter of a square or rhombus is even easier to compute, since its length and width are the same. Simply multiply the length of any side by 4:

$$P = 4s$$

For other figures, however, some figuring may have to be done, based upon the information provided. Try the exercises below, and you should get a pretty good idea of how the process works.

Find the perimeter of each figure.

1)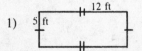

2)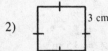

3)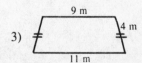

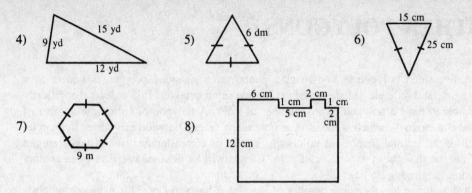

## Answers

| | | | | | | | |
|---|---|---|---|---|---|---|---|
| **1.** | 34 ft | **2.** | 12 cm | **3.** | 28 m | **4.** | 36 yd |
| **5.** | 18 dm | **6.** | 65 cm | **7.** | 54 m | **8.** | 56 cm |

Just as we described perimeter as the fence around a park, area is a way of measuring the part itself — i.e. the region enclosed by the fence. The area of any region is found by dividing that region up into small squares, and then finding how many of those squares fit into the region. For that reason area is always expressed in square units, be they square inches, square feet, square meters, etc.

# AREA OF A RECTANGLE

To find the area of a rectangular region that is 3 meters wide by 5 meters long, we may follow the steps below:

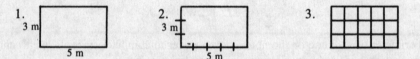

Counting up the little squares, we find that the area is 15 square meters (or 15 m²). Of course, if you look back at step 1, you well might see another way in which we could have found the same result. We could have multiplied the base of the rectangle by the height (we formerly referred to these dimensions as length and width, but will now change to base and height since, as you will see, these names have wider applicability).

$$A = bh$$
$$A = 5 \cdot 3$$
$$A = 15 \text{ m}^2$$

## AREA OF A SQUARE

A square is, as has been previously noted, a special case of the rectangle (that is, a rectangle that happens to be equilateral). Since that is the case, the same formula for finding its area must apply. That is to say, a square's base times its height will give you its area.

Since a square's base is the same length as its height, a new formula is made possible. Examine the square in the diagram, and you will notice that its side has been marked as being $s$ units long. Since the base and the height must each be $s$ units long, then we may substitute $s$ for both $b$ and $h$ in the formula for area. Thus we derive a special formula for the area of the square. While this is a handy formula to be aware of, memorizing it is hardly necessary, since it can always be derived from the rectangle area formula as needed. You will find that the same is true for special formulas for most of the other areas that we shall look

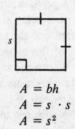

$$A = bh$$
$$A = s \cdot s$$
$$A = s^2$$

at. Most are derived from the basic area formula. If you can clearly see how that derivation takes place, and can understand why it works, then you should be readily able to derive the appropriate formula when the need to use it arises.

## HEIGHT AND PERPENDICULARS DEFINED

We have prior to this point discussed in passing the term "height," without ever bothering to formally define that term. Although it was rather easy to get away with it before, from here on in it will be necessary to have a formal definition of the term before applying it further. Before defining height, it is necessary to examine another term: perpendicular. **Perpendicular** lines and perpendicular line-segments intersect, or cross each other, at right (90°) angles. Figures 1, 3, and 5 below show perpendicular lines and/or segments. Figures 2 and 4 do not.

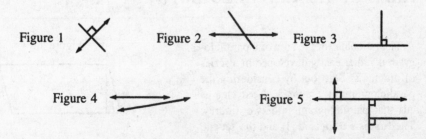

The symbol ⊥ is used to indicate perpendicularity, and is read "is perpendicular to." Now consider the case of point *P* and segment *AB* (6). How far is point *P* from *AB*? Any of an infinite number of segments may be drawn from *P* to *AB* (7). Only one of them, however, would be the shortest distance. The shortest distance from *P* to *AB* is the perpendicular distance from *P* to *AB* (8). This distance, *PQ* is also defined as "the distance" from the point to the line.

The height of a geometric figure is defined as the perpendicular distance from the base of the figure to the opposite vertex. In the case of the rectangle, which we have already discussed, any side qualifies as the height with respect to an adjacent side, since any pair of adjacent sides of a rectangle are adjacent to each other (9). In a parallelogram that is not a rectangle, however, no side is the height to another. Rather, the height must be drawn in, as in Figure 10b.

A triangle may have three different heights, as long as you are aware of the fact that each height refers to a different base. The base of any figure, as you should be able to infer from the diagram (11), does not necessarily refer to the side upon which the figure is resting. Rather, it refers to the side that is perpendicular to the height, and may change according to convenience. (This is not true of an isosceles triangle, in which the base is defined as the non-congruent side (12), or of a trapezoid, in which the bases are defined as the two parallel sides (13) — the other two being the legs.)

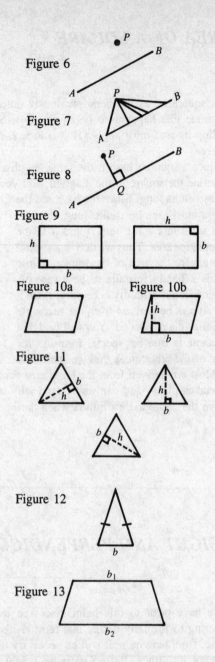

Figure 6

Figure 7

Figure 8

Figure 9

Figure 10a  Figure 10b

Figure 11

Figure 12

Figure 13

# AREA OF A PARALLELOGRAM

The rationale for the area of a parallelogram is rather easily developed in a series of diagrams. Start out by considering the parallelogram in Figure 1. Next, let us cut that parallelogram into two figures: The first is a trapezoid (I) and the second

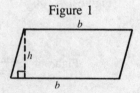

Figure 1

is a right triangle (II). You can see this in Figure 2.

Figure 3 shows the triangle and the trapezoid juxtaposed. Since the hypotenuse (longest side) of the right triangle was originally parallel to the non-perpendicular leg of the trapezoid, it will align perfectly with that leg in its new position. We can therefore put the two figures together (Figure 4) to form a new figure which is identical in area to the original parallelogram. That new figure is, of course, a rectangle. Can you see why the base of the rectangle is identical to the base of the original parallelogram? Can you see why the height of the rectangle is identical to the height of the parallelogram? In that case — since any parallelogram can be reconstructed as a rectangle with the identical base and height — the formula for the area of a parallelogram must be identical to that for a rectangle: $A = bh$.

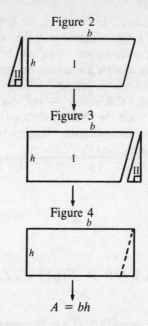

Figure 2

Figure 3

Figure 4

$A = bh$

## *AREA OF A TRIANGLE*

There is a special formula for finding the area of a triangle. It is, however, a formula that you need not memorize, since it is derived, once again, from the rectangle formula. Consider any rectangle. Draw the diagonal of that rectangle, and you will have two triangles:

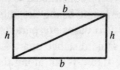

Then, it should be rather obvious that the area of either of the two triangles is half that of the rectangle. Hence, the formula for finding the area of a triangle is:

$$A = \tfrac{1}{2}bh$$

Now, you well might say, that is fine for finding the area of a right triangle, but what about oddly shaped ones — scalene, acute, etc? Well, look at the following:

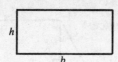

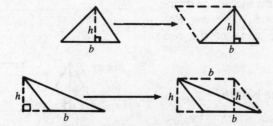

You can readily see from the diagrams on page 221 that any triangle can be made to be half of a parallelogram with the same base and height. But, since we have already seen that a parallelogram's area may be computed by multiplying the base times the height, then any triangle's area may be computed by finding half the parallelogram's area, or half its base times its height. You may also notice from the diagram — and if you have not, make sure that you do — that the height of an obtuse triangle falls outside the triangle itself. Since the shortest distance between a point and a line is the perpendicular distance, by extending the triangle's base (the line that the base is a line-segment of) we can legitimately find that distance.

The height of a triangle is also known as its **altitude**.

## AREA OF A TRAPEZOID

A trapezoid's area can be rather complex to determine. The information required in order to determine a trapezoid's area is the height of the figure as well as the length of both bases. From this information, coupled with the rectangle area formula, it is possible to derive a formula which may be applied to find the area of any trapezoid. If you follow the series of diagrams, you should be able to see how the trapezoid area formula is derived. For openers, we have a trapezoid with an altitude of $h$ units, and the bases respectively designed as $b_1$ and $b_2$.

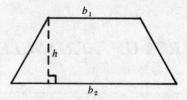

In Figure 1, you will notice that the second altitude has been constructed to the base. It is the same length as the first aitiutde ($h$) since the two bases are parallel, and therefore the same distance apart.

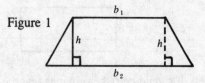

Figure 1

In Figure 2, the figure is cut along the altitudes to form a rectangle and two right triangles. Notice that the rectangle has dimensions $h$ and $b_1$. The triangles both have an altitude $h$, but the bases of the two right triangles are somewhat less obvious.

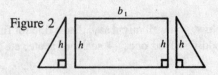

Figure 2

In Figure 3, the two right triangles are combined into a single triangle of altitude $h$. It can now be seen that the base of the new triangle is the difference of the trapezoid's 2 bases ($b_2 - b_1$). We can now proceed to find the areas of the two figures:

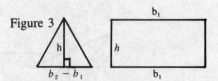

Figure 3

The triangle's area is $\frac{1}{2}h(b_2 - b_1)$.

The rectangle's area is $b_1 h$.

Therefore, the area of the trapezoid is found by combining the area of the rectangle with the area of the triangle:

$$A = \tfrac{1}{2}h(b_2 - b_1) + b_1h$$

| | |
|---|---|
| $2A = h(b_2 - b_1) + 2b_1h$ | (by doubling both sides) |
| $2A = b_2h - b_1h + 2b_1h$ | (clear the parentheses) |
| $2A = b_2h + b_1h$ | (combine $-b_1h + 2b_1h$) |
| $2A = h(b_2 + b_1)$ | (distributive property) |
| $A = \tfrac{1}{2}h(b_2 + b_1)$ | (divide both sides by 2) |

And there's the formula!

Find the area enclosed by each figure.

1)

2)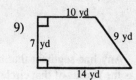

3)

4)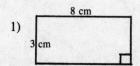

5)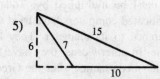

6)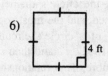

7)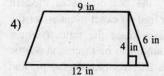

8)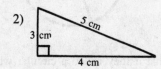

9)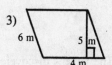

10)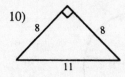

11)

12)

## Answers

| | | | | | | | |
|---|---|---|---|---|---|---|---|
| **1.** | 24 cm² | **2.** | 6 cm² | **3.** | 20 m² | **4.** | 42 in² |
| **5.** | 30 | **6.** | 16 ft² | **7.** | 48 m² | **8.** | 60 |
| **9.** | 84 yd² | **10.** | 32 | **11.** | 92 | **12.** | 40 |

# CIRCLES

The circle is the one figure that GED geometry considers that is not composed of line-segments or rays. Indeed, it is sufficiently unique to merit at least one section all to itself. It was the Greeks who first discovered a relationship between the longest distance across a circle and the distance around the circle. The longest distance across a circle is known as its **diameter**. It is labelled *d* in the circle below. The distance around a circle (labelled *C*) is known as the **circumference**.

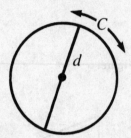

The Greeks discovered that if they rolled a circular wheel along a straight line until one complete turn had been made, the distance covered was a little more than 3 times the diameter. No matter how they tried, 3 and a little bit more was the best they could do for what the circle's diameter must be multiplied by. Today, the best minds of modern science, and the most sophisticated computers have tried to find an exact number for the ratio of a circle's circumference to its diameter. They have found the ratio to equal 3.141592 . . . and then some. In other words, they have found it to be three and a little bit more. This relationship has been named after the Greek letter, $\pi$, known as pi, and is approximated by the decimal 3.14 or by the fraction $\frac{22}{7}$. To all intents and purposes, then, the formula for the circumference of a circle is:

$$C = \pi d$$

Any line-segment that runs from the center of a circle to the circumference is known as the **radius** of that circle (plural is **radii**). A radius is half the size of a diameter, or, conversely, a diameter is the length of two radii. (In case you had not noticed from the diagram above, the diameter passes through the center of the circle.)

There is no limit to the number of radii that there may be in any circle. No matter how many there are, however, there is one thing of which you can be sure: **In the same or equal circles, all radii are congruent.**

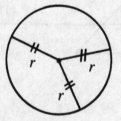

Since a diameter is equal in length to two radii, there is an alternate formula for finding the circumference of a circle:

$$C = 2\pi r$$

Note that both mean the same thing, so that while it is advisable to learn one of them, it is not necessary to learn both. After all, $2r = d$.

Find the circumference of a circle when

1) $r = 2$ inches      2) $d = 7$ centimeters      3) $r = 14$ meters

4) $d = 21$ feet      5) $r = 35$ yards      6) $d = 3.5$ millimeters

(Express your answers in terms of pi.)

## Answers

**1.**   $4\pi$ inches      **2.**   $7\pi$ centimeters      **3.**   $28\pi$ meters

**4.**   $21\pi$ feet      **5.**   $70\pi$ yards      **6.**   $3.5\pi$ millimeters

A circle's area may also be expressed as a formula entailing the use of the quantity, pi. The area of a circle is found by multiplying pi by the square of the circle's radius, hence the formula:

$$A = \pi r^2$$

Remember too, that if two quantities are known, a third may always be found, hence if we know the radius of a circle to be 5, its area is $25\pi$, but if we know the area of a circle to be $49\pi$ then we can determine the radius of that circle to be 7.

For the following exercises, leave the answer in terms of pi (where appropriate).

Find the area of a circle of

1) radius 3      2) radius 9      3) radius 11      4) diameter 12      5) diameter 14

Find the radius of a circle when its

6) area = $64\pi$                    7) area = $100\pi$

8) circumference = $32\pi$             9) circumference = $25\pi$

## Answers

**1.**   $9\pi$      **2.**   $81\pi$      **3.**   $121\pi$      **4.**   $36\pi$      **5.**   $49\pi$

**6.**   8      **7.**   10      **8.**   16      **9.**   $12\frac{1}{2}$

The diameter of a circle has already been mentioned as a measure of the longest distance across a circle. A diameter is also the longest chord in a circle. A chord is a line segment that connects two points on the circle's circumference. In the circle in Figure 1, chords $AB$ and $CD$ are drawn. The endpoints of $AB$ are also the endpoints of arc $AB$ (written $\overset{\frown}{AB}$). Similarly, $C$ and $D$ are the endpoints of $\overset{\frown}{CD}$. What other arcs can you name that are part of Circle $O$?

Figure 1

**In the same or congruent circles, congruent chords cut off congruent arcs. In the same or congruent circles, congruent arcs cut off congruent chords.**

A rather interesting and useful fact about chords concerns chords that intersect within a circle. You will notice that in Circle $P$, the lengths of segments $EI$, $FI$, $GI$, and $HI$ are marked. If you multiply the lengths of the segments of chord $EF$ together, you will get 24. What do you get by multiplying the lengths of the segments of $\overline{GH}$ together?

Figure 2

**When two chords intersect in a circle, the product of the segments of one equals the product of the segments of the other.**

Arcs of a circle are measured in degrees, just as angles are. In fact, there are 360 arc degrees in a circle, just as there are 360 angle degrees. An angle formed by two radii of a circle is known as a **central angle**. It is equal in degree measure to its intercepted arc. Look at angle $POQ$ in circle $O$. It is a central angle, and has a degree measure of 75°. Its intercepted arc, $\overset{\frown}{PQ}$, has a measure of 75°.

A second type of angle in a circle is formed by two chords that share a common endpoint. Witness angle $MVW$ in circle $P$. Angle $MVW$ is known as an **inscribed angle**. It is measured by ½ its intercepted arc. Since arc $\overset{\frown}{MW}$ is shown as containing 140°, angle $MVW$ must contain half of that amount, or 70°.

In circle $Q$, you see several angles. Each of them is formed by two chords with a common endpoint. Therefore, each

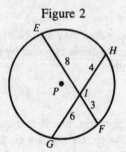

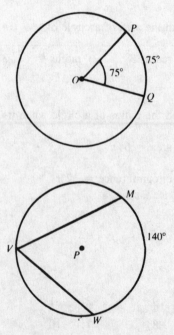

of the angles drawn is an inscribed angle. *GH* is a diameter of circle *Q*. That means that *GH* cuts circle *Q* into two halves. How many arc degrees are there in each arc $\overset{\frown}{GH}$?

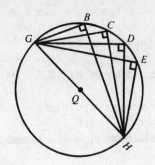

Now look at all the angles inscribed in circle *Q*. Since each of them is cutting off an arc of 180°, and since each of them is an inscribed angle, then each of them must be a right angle.

**Any angle inscribed in a semi-circle is a right angle.**

When two chords cross within a circle, angles are formed at the point of intersection. Angles formed by two intersecting lines or segments which are opposite each other are called **vertical angles**. In or out of a circle, vertical angles are congruent. Angle *MRP* = angle *QRN*. Similarly, angle *MRQ* = angle *PRN*.

Let us now examine the two pairs of angles formed when chords *YZ* and *VW* intersect in circle *O*. Angle *VXY* and its vertical companion, *WXZ*, intercept arcs $\overset{\frown}{YV}$ and $\overset{\frown}{WZ}$. Those arcs contain 70° and 50° respectively. By adding their degree measures together and dividing by 2, we find that each of the angles in question has a measure of 60°.

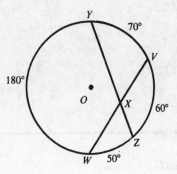

The other pair of angles, *YXW* and *VXZ* intercept arcs of 180° and 60° respectively, for a total of 240°. Divide by 2 and find that each of the angles in question contains 120°. The rule may be stated as follows:

**When two chords intersect in a circle, each angle formed at the point of intersection is measured by $\frac{1}{2}$ of the arcs intercepted by itself and its vertical angle.**

On the next page, you will find a number of questions which will allow you to apply the information discussed in this section. Feel free to refer to the rules and diagrams while working the exercises.

Given circle $O$, with diameter $FM$, $FC = 60°$, $CR = 40°$. Find:

1) The measure of $\angle FOC$.

2) The measure of $\angle CPR$.

3) The measure of $\angle POM$.

4) The measure of $\widehat{MR}$, $\widehat{MP}$, and $\widehat{FP}$.

5) The measure of $\angle MVR$ and $\angle FVR$.

6) $\overline{MV} = 3$, $\overline{FV} = 12$, $\overline{PV} = 4$. Find the length of $\overline{VR}$.

7) In the same circle, draw $\angle FRM$. What is its degree measure?

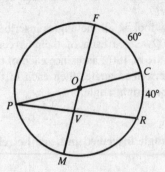

Given circle $Q$ with the angles and arcs as marked, find the measures of:

8) $\widehat{SD}$

9) $\angle EDT$

10) $\angle LXS$

11) $\angle SWX$

12) $\angle TFX$

13) $\overline{WD}$

14) $\angle DZF$

15) $\angle ESF$

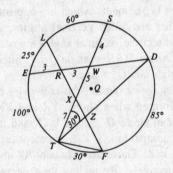

## Answers

1.  60°                    2.  20°                    3.  60°

4.  $\widehat{MR} = 80°$, $\widehat{MP} = 60°$, $\widehat{FP} = 120°$     5.  $\angle MVR = 100°$, $\angle FVR = 80°$

6.  $\overline{VR} = 9$        7.  90°                8.  60°        9.  50°

10. 45°          11. 180°              12. $62\frac{1}{2}°$      13. 8°

14. 105°        15. 65° (when drawn)

A line from outside the circle that touches the circumference at a single point only is known as a **tangent**. *RS* is tangent to circle *O* at point *T*. *PM* and *PV* are not tangents. They touch circle *O* at two points, and, hence are known as **secants**. Secants may be thought of as chords which extend beyond the circumference of the circle. Notice that secant *PM* terminates at *M* on the circle's circumference, while *PV* continues on past the circle to *U*. Both segments are, nonetheless, secants.

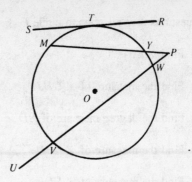

In circle *Q* you can see two tangents drawn to the circle from an outside point. Two tangents drawn to a circle from an outside point are always congruent. A radius drawn to the point of tangency (as is *QC*) is perpendicular to the tangent. That is to say, a right angle is formed at *C*.

When two secants intersect outside a circle, the angle formed may be measured by taking half of the difference of their intercepted arcs. The angle formed by two tangents meeting outside the circle may be found in the same way. The angle formed by the two secants to circle *P* is ½(110 − 20) or 45°. Find *BAC* in the figure containing circle *Q*.

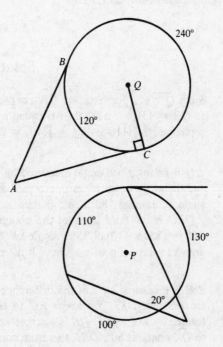

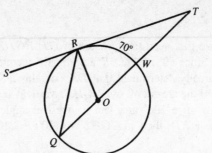

Questions 1 and 2 refer to circle *O* above.

1) The rule that applies to finding the angle formed by two secants or two tangents intersecting outside a circle applies to an angle formed by an intersecting secant and tangent as well. Find angle *STQ* in circle *O*.

2) In circle *O*, find the measure of ∠*QRO*. Also find ∠*SRO*.

Questions 3–7 all refer to circle $P$.

3) Find $\angle E$.

4) Find the measure of $\angle GHJ$.

5) Find the degree measure of $\overset{\frown}{BD}$.

6) Find the measure of $\angle ABD$.

7) Find the measure of $\angle FDP$.

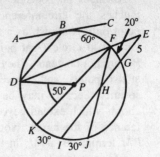

## Solutions

1. Since $\overline{QW}$ is a diameter, arc $\overset{\frown}{QW}$ contains 180°. That means that $\overset{\frown}{QR} + 70° = 180°$, so $\overset{\frown}{QR} = 110°$. $\angle STQ$ then is found by taking half the difference of its two intercepted arcs: $\frac{1}{2}(110 - 70) = \frac{1}{2}(40) = 20°$.

2. $\angle Q$ is an inscribed angle measured by half $\overset{\frown}{RW}$, or 35°. $\angle ROT$ is a central angle, and therefore equal to its intercepted arc, 70°. $\angle ROQ + \angle ROT$ form a straight angle containing 180°. That makes $\angle ROQ$ equal to $180° - 70°$, or 110°. Since $\angle QRO$ is the third angle of the triangle containing angles $ROQ$ and $Q$, it equals $180 - (35 + 110)$ or 35°. Angle $SRO$ is an angle formed by a tangent and a radius drawn to the point of tangency. It therefore contains 90°.

3. $\angle E$ is measured by half the difference of its intercepted arcs. Its intercepted arcs are $\overset{\frown}{FG}$ and $\overset{\frown}{DKI}$. We know $\overset{\frown}{FG}$ to contain 20°, while $\overset{\frown}{KI}$ contains 30°. $\overset{\frown}{DKI}$ is formed by $\overset{\frown}{DK} + \overset{\frown}{KI}$. $\overset{\frown}{DK}$ is intercepted by central angle $DPK$ which contains 50°, so $\overset{\frown}{DK}$ contains 50°. $\overset{\frown}{DKI}$, therefore contains $50 + 30$, or 80°. $m\angle E = \frac{1}{2}(80 - 20) = \frac{1}{2}(60) = 30°$.

4. To find $\angle GHJ$ we first need the measure of $\overset{\frown}{GJ}$. $\overset{\frown}{FGJIK}$ is a semicircle bounded by diameter $\overline{FK}$. Since 80° of $\overset{\frown}{FGJIK}$ are already accounted for, $\overset{\frown}{GJ}$ must contain 100°. We have already determined that $\overset{\frown}{DK}$ contains 50°, and so can readily find $\overset{\frown}{BD}$ which is part of the arc cut off by $\angle GHJ$'s vertical angle, $\angle FHI$. $m\overset{\frown}{BD} = 70°$. Since $\angle GHJ$ cuts off a 100° arc, and its vertical angle cuts off a 210° arc (add $\overset{\frown}{FB} + \overset{\frown}{BD} + \overset{\frown}{DK} + \overset{\frown}{KI}$), then $m\angle GHJ = \frac{1}{2}(100 + 210) = \frac{1}{2}(310) = 155°$.

5. We have already found $\overset{\frown}{BD}$ to contain 70°.

6. $\angle ABD$ is measured by half its intercepted arc, $\overset{\frown}{BD}$, hence is 35°.

7. $\angle FDP$ is an angle of triangle $FDP$. $\angle FPD$ is a central angle measured by $\overset{\frown}{FB} + \overset{\frown}{BD}$, and so is $60 + 70$, or 130°. $\angle DFK$ is an inscribed angle measured by $\frac{1}{2}\overset{\frown}{KD}$, and so is 25°. Adding the measures of the two angles just found together, we find that 155° of the 180° allotted for all the angles of the triangle have been used up. $180 - 155 = 25°$. $m\angle FDP = 25°$.

# COORDINATE AXES

On a plane surface, any point can be located by giving two coordinates, a horizontal and a vertical one. This system assumes that all flat surfaces can be covered by a grid of intersecting lines that form little square boxes. Each point where two lines intersect on that grid is assigned a pair of numbered coordinates. The lines from which all numbering begins are called **axes** (axis is the singular of axes).

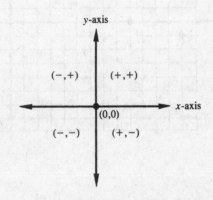

The vertical axis is known as the "*y*-axis." The *y*-axis intersects the horizontal "*x*-axis" at the point with coordinates (0,0). Beginning at that point, known as the origin, all other points on the grid are assigned a pair of coordinates in the form (*x*,*y*). Notice that the coordinate written first is the *x* coordinate. It tells the horizontal distance of a point from the origin, as well as its direction from the origin. A point with a positive *x* coordinate is to the right of the origin, while one with a negative *x* coordinate is to the left of the origin. The *y* coordinate tells the vertical distance of a point above (positive) or below (negative) the origin. The signs written as ordered pairs on the axes above indicate which is positive and which is negative on each portion of the grid. (The four sections of the grid are known as **quadrants**.) In the first quadrant, both *x* and *y* are positive. In the second quadrant (upper left) *x* is negative and *y* is positive. Both *x* and *y* are negative in the third quadrant. The fourth quadrant is positive for *x* and negative for *y*.

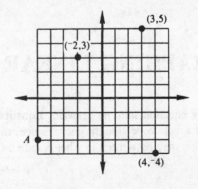

Consider the point with coordinates (3,5). Those coordinates mean that the point is located by counting three spaces to the right of the *y*-axis and then 5 spaces up from the *x*-axis. You can see it marked on the grid at the right. Figure out how (⁻2,3) and (4,⁻4) were arrived at. What are the coordinates of point *A*? Have you actually figured out *A* or are you peeking ahead? Well, in either case, its coordinates are (⁻5,⁻3).

On the next page, there is a grid with a number of points marked off and indicated by letters. Give the coordinates of each lettered point. It may help you to remember that the origin has coordinates (0,0).

Name each lettered point by an ordered pair of coordinates.

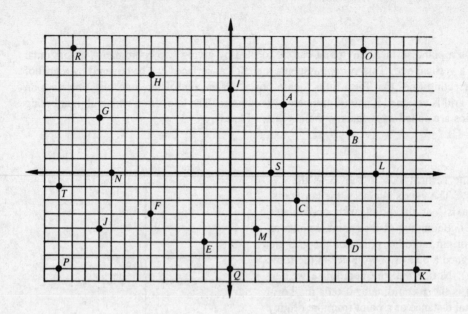

## Answers

| | | | | | | | |
|---|---|---|---|---|---|---|---|
| **A.** | (4,5) | **B.** | (9,3) | **C.** | (5,⁻2) | **D.** | (9,⁻5) |
| **E.** | (⁻2,⁻5) | **F.** | (⁻6,⁻3) | **G.** | (⁻10,4) | **H.** | (⁻6,7) |
| **I.** | (0,6) | **J.** | (⁻10,⁻4) | **K.** | (14,⁻7) | **L.** | (11,0) |
| **M.** | (2,⁻4) | **N.** | (⁻9,0) | **O.** | (10,9) | **P.** | (⁻13,⁻7) |
| **Q.** | (0,⁻7) | **R.** | (⁻12,9) | **S.** | (3,0) | **T.** | (⁻13,⁻1) |

# GRAPHING LINEAR EQUATIONS

Any equation may be graphed. Equations that do not contain any exponents higher than 1 graph to be straight lines. Hence, they are known as linear equations. Any linear equation may be written in what is called the **slope and y-intercept form**:

$$y = mx + b$$

In the equation above, $x$ and $y$ stand for, respectively, the $x$ and $y$ coordinates of any point on the graph of a given equation, $m$ stands for the slope of the graph, and $b$ for its $y$-intercept. The meanings of each of the last two terms, we shall now go into separately.

The **y-intercept** is the name given to the point at which a graph crosses the $y$ (vertical) axis. Where the graph crosses the $y$-axis, the value of the $x$ coordinate must be 0. Think about that for a moment. If the graph (the line) is touching the *y*-axis at a particular point, then it is neither to the right nor to the left of the *y*-axis. Its distance from the *y*-axis, and hence its *x*-coordinate, must be 0. See Figure 1. The *y*-intercepts of the three graphs shown on the grid are, from top to bottom, 3, 0, and ⁻2. Note the co-ordinates of each *y*-intercept (as shown in the figure).

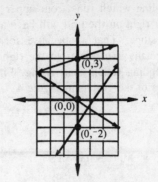

Figure 1

Now, assume that a linear equation has been written in slope and *y*-intercept form ($y = mx + b$). It has already been pointed out that *b* indicates the *y*-intercept. Here is why. Consider the equation, $y = 3x - 4$.

Notice that ⁻4 is in the *b* position, and, hence should be the *y*-intercept — if you are inclined to take what has been said so far on faith. You may recall that the *x* and *y* in the standard form of the linear equation stand for the coordinates of any point on the graph of the equation. But, since we know that at the *y*-intercept the *x* coordinate must be zero, let us substitute 0 for the *x* in the equation and see what happens:

$$y = 3x - 4$$
$$y = 3 \cdot 0 - 4$$
$$y = 0 - 4$$
$$y = {}^-4$$

Well, what do you know? The *y*-intercept is ⁻4 after all!

Now that we have discussed *y*-intercept, it is time to take a look at the meaning of *m* (in $y = mx + b$) — **slope**. A look back at Figure 1 will reveal to you that the graphs of the equations that are pictured are lines which move from left to right at different angles. There are several different ways to calculate the steepness of the incline. One of those ways is known as slope. Slope is a measure of how much a line rises for every space it moves to the right on the grid. The graph in Figure 2 is rising 3 spaces for every 4 it moves to the right. It therefore has a slope of $\frac{3}{4}$.

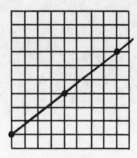

Figure 2

Slope may be figured by referring to any two points on the graph of an equation. It is calculated as the difference in *y* values over the difference in *x* values (sometimes expressed $\frac{dy}{dx}$). While slope may be calculated between any two points on a graph, it is most conveniently computed between two points which clearly are on the intersection between two lines on the grid. Otherwise, the slope would be no more than an approximation. Name the slopes of each of the line graphs in Figure 3.

($A$'s slope is $\frac{1}{5}$, $B$'s is 2, $C$'s is 3, and $D$'s is 1.)

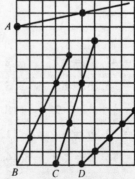

Figure 3

A line which runs from upper left to lower right on the grid will have a negative slope. That is because for every square the line moves to the right, it is descending rather than rising. Find the slopes of the graphs in Figure 4.

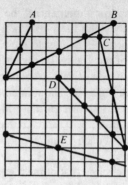

Figure 4

## Answers

**A.** 2    **B.** $\frac{1}{2}$    **C.** $^-4$

**D.** $^-1$    **E.** $^-\frac{1}{4}$

For the exercises below, you are asked to identify the slope and $y$-intercept of the lines that are the graphs of the equations, just by putting each equation into standard slope and $y$-intercept form and then identifying $m$ and $b$.

Name the slope and $y$-intercept for each.

1) $y = 4x - 7$      2) $y = 5x + 8$      3) $y = {}^-9x + 4$

4) $y = {}^-3x + 8$      5) $y = 6 - 4x$      6) $2y = 4x - 8$

7) $3y = x - 27$      8) $5y = 2x + 6$      9) $3x + y = 4$

10) $2x = 5 - y$      11) $7 - x = {}^-y$      12) $y + 7 = {}^-8x$

13) $8x - 7y = 12$      14) $5y + 9 = 3x$      15) $8x = 21 + y$

## Answers

1. $m = 4, \ b = {}^-7$      2. $m = 5, \ b = 8$      3. $m = {}^-9, \ b = 4$

4. $m = {}^-3, \ b = 8$      5. $m = {}^-4, \ b = 6$      6. $m = 2, \ b = {}^-4$

7. $m = \frac{1}{3}, \ b = {}^-9$      8. $m = \frac{2}{5}, \ b = \frac{6}{5}$      9. $m = {}^-3, \ b = 4$

10. $m = {}^-2, \ b = 5$      11. $m = 1, \ b = {}^-7$      12. $m = {}^-8, \ b = {}^-7$

13. $m = \frac{8}{7}, \ b = {}^-\frac{12}{7}$      14. $m = \frac{3}{5}, \ b = {}^-\frac{9}{5}$      15. $m = 8, \ b = {}^-21$

# WRITING AN EQUATION FROM THE SLOPE AND Y-INTERCEPT

If one can tell the slope and $y$-intercept of an equation just from examining it, then it stands to reason that one should be able to determine an equation if the slope and $y$-intercept are known. Consider the model example below, and you will see how easy it is.

*Model Example*

Find the equation of the line with a slope of $^-3$ and a $y$-intercept of 6.

Remember that the standard form for a linear equation is:

$$y = mx + b$$

But we know that $m$ = the slope = $^-3$ and $b$ = the $y$-intercept = 6. By substituting the known values for $m$ and $b$, we get:

$$y = {}^-3x + 6$$

That is the equation of the line with the given slope and $y$-intercept.

Use the above model example to help you to do the exercises below. Once you get the hang of it, you will discover that it becomes almost a mechanical operation.

Find the equation of the line which has a slope and $y$-intercept as indicated.

1) $m = 5$, $b = 7$

2) $m = 9$, $b = \frac{1}{2}$

3) $m = \frac{1}{4}$, $b = {}^-8$

4) $m = {}^-3$, $b = 2$

5) slope is $^-2$, $y$-intercept is $^-6$

6) slope is $\frac{2}{3}$, $y$-intercept is 5

7) $y$-intercept is $^-18$, slope is $\frac{4}{5}$

8) slope is $^-15$, $b = 9$

9) slope is $\frac{4}{7}$, the line passes through (0,9)

10) The line passes through (0,6) and has a slope of $^-\frac{1}{4}$.

## Answers

| | |
|---|---|
| 1. $y = 5x + 7$ | 2. $y = 9x + \frac{1}{2}$ | 3. $y = \frac{1}{4}x - 8$ |
| 4. $y = ^-3x + 2$ | 5. $y = ^-2x - 6$ | 6. $y = \frac{2}{3}x + 5$ |
| 7. $y = \frac{1}{3}x - 18$ | 8. $y = ^-15x + 9$ | 9. $y = \frac{4}{7}x + 9$ |
| 10. $y = ^-\frac{1}{4}x + 6$ | | |

You should have noted that in exercises 9 and 10 the points whose coordinates were given were the $y$-intercepts, since the $x$-coordinate of each was 0. $(0,y)$ for any value of $y$ is a $y$-intercept.

# FINDING AN EQUATION FROM TWO POINTS

It is possible to determine the equation of a line if you know the coordinates of two points on that line. In order to understand how this works, you must consider once more the meaning of slope, and how it is derived. Remember that slope is the difference in $y$ values over the difference in $x$ values ($\frac{dy}{dx}$). Applying that to any two points, by subtracting their $y$-coordinates and then putting the result over the difference in their $x$-coordinates, the slope of that line may be found. Consider a graph which passes through points with coordinates (5,7) and (3,9). By naming those two points as being on the graph, the wherewithal has been provided for you to find the slope of the graph. Beginning with the second point, we can find the difference in $y$ values to be $9 - 7 = 2$. The difference in $x$ values is $3 - 5 = ^-2$. The slope, therefore, is $\frac{2}{^-2} = ^-1$. If the slope had been calculated using the points in different order, we would have found $\frac{7 - 9}{5 - 3} = \frac{^-2}{2} = ^-1$. You see then, that either way we get a slope of $^-1$.

We may now substitute the value that we have found for the slope into the equation, $y = mx + b$:

$$y = ^-1x + b, \text{ or}$$

$$y = ^-x + b$$

Now, for any point on the graph, the $x$ and $y$ coordinates of that point may be substituted into the equation, since any point on the graph must satisfy the equation. We may choose either (5,7) or (3,9). If we choose the point (5,7), then the value of $x$ is 5 and the value of $y$ is 7. Remember, the coordinates of any point are in the order $(x,y)$. That means that the equation now looks like this:

$$7 = ^-1(5) + b$$

It is now possible to solve for $b$ and get the result $b = 12$. Suppose, for a moment, that we had chosen to select $x$ and $y$ from the point (3,9). The equation then would have read:

$$9 = {}^-1(3) + b$$

Solving that equation for $b$ would have yielded a value $b = 12$. You'll notice that $b$ comes out the same regardless of which point's coordinates are used.

Now that we know the value of $m$ to be ${}^-1$ and the value of $b$ to be 12, all that is necessary is to substitute those values into the slope and $y$-intercept form of the equation and we will have the equation that we are looking for:

$$y = mx + b$$
$$y = {}^-1x + 12$$
$$y = {}^-x + 12 \qquad \text{. . . and there you have it.}$$

Follow the model example below, referring to the above if necessary.

*Model Example*

Find the equation of the line that passes through the points (3,5) and (${}^-2$,7).

First find the slope: $\qquad m = \dfrac{dy}{dx} = \dfrac{5 - 7}{3 - ({}^-2)} = \dfrac{{}^-2}{5} = -\dfrac{2}{5}$

Then rewrite the slope and $y$-intercept form including the slope that was found: $\qquad y = -\dfrac{2}{5}x + b$

Now substitute the $x$ and $y$ values from either point. Here, we use (3,5): $\qquad 5 = -\dfrac{2}{5}(3) + b$

Then solve the equation for $b$: $\qquad 5 + \dfrac{6}{5} = b$

$$b = 6\dfrac{1}{5}$$

Finally, substitute the values found for $b$ and for $m$ into the standard form: $\qquad y = mx + b$

$$y = -\dfrac{2}{5}x + 6\dfrac{1}{5}$$

Now you should be ready for some exercises. Use the model above as your guide. After you have done a few you should have the hang of it.

Find the equation of the line that passes through the points named.

1) (3,6) and (5,8)

2) (2,4) and (5,10)

3) (0,7) and (2,11)

4) (2,8) and (6,10)

5) (7,10) and (9,2)

6) (5,6) and (7,4)

7) (4,2) and (8,1)

8) (4,4) and (8,7)

9) (0,1) and (5,2)

10) (2,4) and (4,8)

11) (3,0) and (4,3)

12) (7,2) and (9,4)

13) (4,⁻2) and (⁻1,3)

14) (6,⁻3) and (9,⁻3)

15) (⁻2,⁻3) and (⁻6,⁻8)

## Answers

1. $y = x + 3$

2. $y = 2x$

3. $y = 2x + 7$

4. $y = \frac{1}{2}x + 7$

5. $y = {}^{-}4x + 38$

6. $y = {}^{-}x + 11$

7. $y = {}^{-}\frac{1}{4}x + 3$

8. $y = \frac{3}{4}x + 1$

9. $y = \frac{1}{5}x + 1$

10. $y = 2x$

11. $y = 3x - 9$

12. $y = x - 5$

13. $y = {}^{-}x + 2$

14. $y = {}^{-}3$

15. $y = \frac{5}{4}x - \frac{1}{2}$

# THE PYTHAGOREAN THEOREM

The ancient Greek mathematician, Pythagoras, came up with a fascinating discovery about 2300 years ago (give or take a century). He discovered that the square formed on the hypotenuse of a right triangle is equal in area to the sum of the areas of the squares formed on the other two sides of that triangle. His discovery took the form of the figure that you see. Notice that the sides of the triangle are labelled as having lengths of *a, b,* and *c* units. That means that the areas of the squares may be related as follows:

$$a^2 + b^2 = c^2$$

This formula means that given any right triangle, if the lengths of two sides are known, the length of the third side may be found. Examine the two model examples on the next page, and you will see how it works.

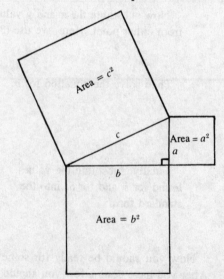

*Model Example 1*

The two legs of a right triangle are 3 inches and 4 inches long respectively. Find the length of the hypotenuse.

$$a^2 + b^2 = c^2 \qquad \text{First write the formula . . .}$$

$$(3)^2 + (4)^2 = c^2 \qquad \text{. . . then substitute into it.}$$

$$9 + 16 = c^2 \qquad \text{Square the 3 and the 4 (raise them to the 2nd power) . . .}$$

$$c^2 = 25 \qquad \text{. . . then add them together.}$$

$$c = 5 \qquad \text{Take the square root of each side.}$$

The hypotenuse is 5 inches long.

*Model Example 2*

Find the length of side $AB$ in the triangle pictured at the right. You may leave the answer in radical form.

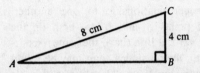

$$a^2 + b^2 = c^2$$

First write the formula. Note, however, that this time we know the length of the hypotenuse, which means that we know the value of $c$! That fact must be taken into account when substituting.

$$(4)^2 + b^2 = (8)^2$$

$$16 + b^2 = 64$$

Now we square the 4 and the 8, and . . .

$$b^2 = 48$$

. . . solve the equation for $b$.

$$b = \sqrt{48} = 4\sqrt{3} \text{ cm}$$

Each exercise below refers to the figure at the right. The lengths of two sides of the triangle are given. Find the length of the third side. You may leave your answer in simplest radical form (where applicable).

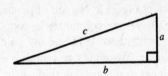

1) $a = 6$, $b = 8$, $c = ?$

2) $a = 5$, $b = 12$, $c = ?$

3) $a = 15$, $c = 25$, $b = ?$

4) $a = 20$, $c = 52$, $b = ?$

5) $a = 7$, $b = 9$, $c = ?$

6) $a = 4$, $b = 11$, $c = ?$

7) $a = 9$, $c = 14$, $b = ?$

8) $a = 4$, $c = 10$, $b = ?$

9) $b = 9$, $c = 12$, $a = ?$

10) $c = 15$, $a = 9$, $b = ?$

11) $c = 16$, $b = 10$, $a = ?$

12) $a = 7$, $b = 10$, $c = ?$

## Answers

| | | | |
|---|---|---|---|
| **1.** 10 | **2.** 13 | **3.** 20 | **4.** 48 |
| **5.** $\sqrt{130}$ | **6.** $\sqrt{137}$ | **7.** $\sqrt{115}$ | **8.** $2\sqrt{21}$ |
| **9.** $3\sqrt{7}$ | **10.** 12 | **11.** $2\sqrt{39}$ | **12.** $\sqrt{149}$ |

# THE DISTANCE BETWEEN POINTS ON A GRAPH

Figure 1 shows a portion of the first quadrant of a grid with three lettered points in proper relationship to one another. Since points $A$ and $B$ are both on the same vertical line (have the same $x$-coordinate), their distance apart may be found by subtracting their $y$-coordinates $(8 - 3)$. $A$ and $B$ are, therefore, 5 units of distance apart. $B$ and $C$ have the same $y$-coordinates, and so their distance apart may be found by subtracting their $x$-coordinates $(10 - 4)$. They are 6 units apart. But how far apart are $A$ and $C$?

If segment $AC$ were drawn, it would form the hypotenuse of right triangle $ABC$. The distance point $A$ is from point $C$ might then be found using the Pythagorean Theorem:

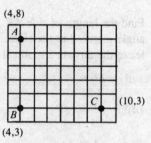

Figure 1

$$\overline{AC}^2 = (5)^2 + (6)^2$$
$$\overline{AC} = \sqrt{61} \text{ units}$$

Now look at Figure 2. No pair of points in Figure 2 have any coordinate in common. Yet the distance between any pair of points in the figure may be found in a manner similar to that used in finding the length of $AC$.

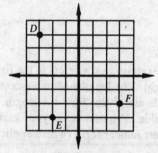

Figure 2

*Model Example*

Find the lengths of the sides of the triangle formed by connecting points $D$, $E$, and $F$ in Figure 2.

First note the coordinates of the points:

$$D: (^-3,3) \quad E: (^-2,^-3) \quad F: (3,^-2)$$

Let us first find segment $DE$. The horizontal distance between $D$ and $E$ is found by subtracting the horizontal coordinates of the two points: $^-3 - (^-2) = ^-1$. Since the minus sign in $^-1$ simply shows direction, we can safely ignore it, and say that the horizontal distance is 1 unit. The vertical distance is found by subtracting their vertical coordinates 3 − (⁻3) which = 6.

For all intents and purposes, we are now seeking to find the hypotenuse of a right triangle with sides 1 and 6. Look at Figure 3, and you just might see that imaginary triangle. In fact, you might even see imaginary right triangles around segments *DF* and *EF*. As long as you are using your imagination, you might as well see them as being shaded.

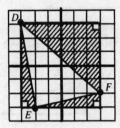

*DE*, then, = $(1)^2 + (6)^2$ if you recall your Pythagorean Theorem. That means that *DE* is $\sqrt{37}$ units long.

Figure 3

To find *DF*, find the difference between the vertical and horizontal coordinates of the two points. They are 5 and 6 respectively.

$$DF^2, \text{ then, } = (5)^2 + (6)^2$$
$$= 25 + 36$$
$$= 61$$
$$DF = \sqrt{61} \text{ units}$$

To find *EF*, find the differences between the vertical coordinates and the horizontal coordinates. Then plug those differences into the Pythagorean formula and find that $EF = \sqrt{26}$.

Find the distance between the points with coordinates as given.

1) (3,7) and (3,⁻9)

2) (5,12) and (5,18)

3) (2,15) and (⁻11,15)

4) (⁻8,⁻5) and (⁻13,⁻5)

5) (4,11) and (7,11)

6) (8,6) and (4,9)

7) (⁻2,10) and (10,5)

8) (3,7) and (5,⁻3)

9) (⁻1,⁻4) and (5,8)

10) (9,6) and (8,1)

11) (0,0) and (10,24)

12) (5,7) and (8,0)

13) (12,3) and (6,5)

14) (⁻3,4) and (5,⁻8)

15) (6,⁻8) and (7,⁻2)

## Answers

| | | | | | | | |
|---|---|---|---|---|---|---|---|
| **1.** | 16 | **2.** | 6 | **3.** | 13 | **4.** | 5 |
| **5.** | 3 | **6.** | 5 | **7.** | 13 | **8.** | $2\sqrt{26}$ |
| **9.** | $6\sqrt{5}$ | **10.** | $\sqrt{26}$ | **11.** | 26 | **12.** | $\sqrt{58}$ |
| **13.** | $2\sqrt{10}$ | **14.** | $4\sqrt{13}$ | **15.** | $\sqrt{37}$ | | |

# GEOMETRY POST-TEST

What type of triangle is each marked to be?

1) 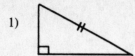  2)   3)

Find the total number of degrees of angle measure in each figure.

4)   5)

Find the area of each figure.

6) 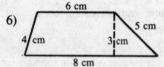  7)   8)

9) Write the equation of a line that passes through the points (⁻4,2) and (6,5).

10) Find the distance between the points (3,6) and (⁻9,11).

## Answers

| | | | | | | | |
|---|---|---|---|---|---|---|---|
| **1.** | right | **2.** | scalene | **3.** | right-isosceles | **4.** | 180° |
| **5.** | 720° | **6.** | 21 cm² | **7.** | 9 m² | **8.** | 9π cm² |
| **9.** | $y + \frac{3}{10}x + 3\frac{1}{5}$ | | | **10.** | 13 | | |

## *ANALYSIS OF POST-TEST ITEMS*

# 8. ADDITIONAL EXERCISES FOR PRACTICE

## WHOLE NUMBERS

### USING ZERO AS A PLACE-HOLDER

Write each number as a place-value numeral. The first is already done.

1) Four thousand twenty ___4020___

2) Three thousand, eight hundred _____

3) Fifty thousand _____

4) Nine million _____

5) Seven million, six thousand _____

6) Fifty-four thousand _____

7) Two hundred five thousand, eighty _____

8) Four million, four hundred _____

9) Seven million, six _____

### Answers

| | | | |
|---|---|---|---|
| **2.** 3800 | **3.** 50,000 | **4.** 9,000,000 | **5.** 7,006,000 |
| **6.** 54,000 | **7.** 205,080 | **8.** 4,000,400 | **9.** 7,000,006 |

### READING LARGE NUMERALS

Write the name (in words) of each numeral.

1) 240,000 _____

2) 6,072,000 _____

3) 41,000,000,062 _____

4) 725,000,002,000 _____ _____

5) 4,312,419 _____

6) 513,245,092,008 _____

## Answers

**1.** Two hundred forty thousand

**2.** Six million, seventy-two thousand

**3.** Forty-one billion, sixty-two

**4.** Seven hundred twenty-five billion, two thousand

**5.** Four million, three hundred twelve thousand, four hundred nineteen

**6.** Five hundred thirteen billion, two hundred forty-five million, ninety-two thousand, eight

## *GROUPING TO TEN IN ADDITION*

1) $6 + 8 = 10 +$ _____     2) $2 + 9 = 10 +$ _____

3) $7 + 5 = 10 +$ _____     4) $9 + 7 = 10 +$ _____

5) $3 + 9 = 10 +$ _____     6) $5 + 5 = 10 +$ _____

7) $8 + 3 = 10 +$ _____     8) $9 + 2 = 10 +$ _____

9) $6 + 5 = 10 +$ _____     10) $8 + 7 = 10 +$ _____

11) $4 + 8 = 10 +$ _____     12) $9 + 7 = 10 +$ _____

### Answers

| **1.** 4 | **2.** 1 | **3.** 2 | **4.** 6 | **5.** 2 | **6.** 0 |
|---|---|---|---|---|---|
| **7.** 1 | **8.** 1 | **9.** 1 | **10.** 5 | **11.** 2 | **12.** 6 |

## *ADDING IN EXPANDED FORM*

1)     346      _____ + _____ + _____
     + 253    + _____ + _____ + _____
              _____ + _____ + _____ = _____

2)    571     \_\_\_\_\_ + \_\_\_\_\_
     +228   + \_\_\_\_\_ + \_\_\_\_\_ + \_\_\_\_\_
              \_\_\_\_\_ + \_\_\_\_\_ + \_\_\_\_\_ = \_\_\_\_\_

3)    238     \_\_\_\_\_ + \_\_\_\_\_ + \_\_\_\_\_
     +560   + \_\_\_\_\_ + \_\_\_\_\_ + \_\_\_\_\_
              \_\_\_\_\_ + \_\_\_\_\_ + \_\_\_\_\_ = \_\_\_\_\_

4)    176     \_\_\_\_\_ + \_\_\_\_\_ + \_\_\_\_\_
     +502   + \_\_\_\_\_ + \_\_\_\_\_ + \_\_\_\_\_ .
              \_\_\_\_\_ + \_\_\_\_\_ + \_\_\_\_\_ = \_\_\_\_\_

## Answers

1.   $500 + 90 + 9 = 599$        2.   $700 + 90 + 9 = 799$
3.   $700 + 90 + 8 = 798$        4.   $600 + 70 + 8 = 678$

## *COLUMN ADDITION*

| 1) H T U | 2) H T U | 3) H T U | 4) H T U | 5) H T U |
|---|---|---|---|---|
| 3 4 5 | 6 7 9 | 2 4 7 | 8 9 | 4 3 7 |
| +2 7 8 | +1 9 6 | 4 8 0 | 6 4 3 | 9 5 |
| | | 5 6 | 5 3 6 | 4 9 3 4 |
| | | | 8 6 8 | 5 3 6 |
| | | | 5 | 5 3 |

6)   435        7) 618        8) 458        9) 807       10) 4315
    +268           278            9           52           914
                   54         867           47           85
                                           633           579
                                                              6802

## Answers

1.   623      2.   875      3.   738      4.   350      5.   1205
6.   703      7.   950      8.   1334      9.   1539      10.   12,695

## *SUBTRACTION WITH RENAMING*

1) $\quad 53 = \qquad 50 \quad + \quad 3 \quad = \qquad 40 \quad + \underline{\qquad}$
   $\quad -28 = -(\quad 20 \quad + \quad 8 \quad) = -(\quad 20 \quad + \quad 8 \quad )$
   $\qquad\qquad\qquad\qquad\qquad\qquad \underline{\qquad} + \underline{\quad} = \underline{\qquad}$

2) $\quad 64 = \underline{\qquad} + \underline{\qquad} = \underline{\qquad} + \underline{\qquad}$
   $\quad -37 = -(\underline{\qquad} + \underline{\qquad}) = -(\underline{\qquad} + \underline{\qquad})$
   $\qquad\qquad\qquad\qquad\qquad\qquad \underline{\qquad} + \underline{\quad} = \underline{\qquad}$

3) $\quad 85 = \underline{\qquad} + \underline{\qquad} = \underline{\qquad} + \underline{\qquad}$
   $\quad -58 = -(\underline{\qquad} + \underline{\qquad}) = -(\underline{\qquad} + \underline{\qquad})$
   $\qquad\qquad\qquad\qquad\qquad\qquad \underline{\qquad} + \underline{\quad} = \underline{\qquad}$

4) $\quad 41 = \underline{\qquad} + \underline{\qquad} = \underline{\qquad} + \underline{\qquad}$
   $\quad -18 = -(\underline{\qquad} + \underline{\qquad}) = -(\underline{\qquad} + \underline{\qquad})$
   $\qquad\qquad\qquad\qquad\qquad\qquad \underline{\qquad} + \underline{\quad} = \underline{\qquad}$

5) $\quad 72 = \underline{\qquad} + \underline{\qquad} = \underline{\qquad} + \underline{\qquad}$
   $\quad -27 = -(\underline{\qquad} + \underline{\qquad}) = -(\underline{\qquad} + \underline{\qquad})$
   $\qquad\qquad\qquad\qquad\qquad\qquad \underline{\qquad} + \underline{\quad} = \underline{\qquad}$

6) $\quad 96 = \underline{\qquad} + \underline{\qquad} = \underline{\qquad} + \underline{\qquad}$
   $\quad -49 = -(\underline{\qquad} + \underline{\qquad}) = -(\underline{\qquad} + \underline{\qquad})$
   $\qquad\qquad\qquad\qquad\qquad\qquad \underline{\qquad} + \underline{\quad} = \underline{\qquad}$

## **Answers**

| | | | | | |
|---|---|---|---|---|---|
| **1.** | $\begin{array}{r} 40 + 13 \\ -(20 + 8) \\ \hline 20 + 5 = 25 \end{array}$ | **2.** | $\begin{array}{r} 50 + 14 \\ -(30 + 7) \\ \hline 20 + 7 = 27 \end{array}$ | **3.** | $\begin{array}{r} 70 + 15 \\ -(50 + 8) \\ \hline 20 + 7 = 27 \end{array}$ |
| **4.** | $\begin{array}{r} 30 + 11 \\ -(10 + 8) \\ \hline 20 + 3 = 23 \end{array}$ | **5.** | $\begin{array}{r} 60 + 12 \\ -(20 + 7) \\ \hline 40 + 5 = 45 \end{array}$ | **6.** | $\begin{array}{r} 80 + 16 \\ -(40 + 9) \\ \hline 40 + 7 = 47 \end{array}$ |

## SUBTRACTION WITH TWO RENAMINGS

1)  $561 =$     $400 + 150 + 11$
   $-285 = -($ $200 + 80 + 5$ $)$
   _____ + _____ + _____ = _____

2)  $485 =$ _____ $+ 170 +$ _____
   $-197 = -($ _____ $+$ _____ $+$ _____ $)$
   _____ + _____ + _____ = _____

3)  $612 =$ _____ $+$ _____ $+$ _____
   $-437 = -($ _____ $+$ _____ $+$ _____ $)$
   _____ + _____ + _____ = _____

4)  $736 =$ _____ $+$ _____ $+$ _____
   $-359 = -($ _____ $+$ _____ $+$ _____ $)$
   _____ + _____ + _____ = _____

5)  $378 =$ _____ $+$ _____ $+$ _____
   $-199 = -($ _____ $+$ _____ $+$ _____ $)$
   _____ + _____ + _____ = _____

6)  $943 =$ _____ $+$ _____ $+$ _____
   $-576 = -($ _____ $+$ _____ $+$ _____ $)$
   _____ + _____ + _____ = _____

7)  $834 =$ _____ $+$ _____ $+$ _____
   $-257 = -($ _____ $+$ _____ $+$ _____ $)$
   _____ + _____ + _____ = _____

8)  $530 =$ _____ $+$ _____ $+$ _____
   $-163 = -($ _____ $+$ _____ $+$ _____ $)$
   _____ + _____ + _____ = _____

## Answers

**1.** 276    **2.** 288    **3.** 175    **4.** 377    **5.** 179    **6.** 367    **7.** 577    **8.** 367

## SUBTRACTION WITH RENAMING IN PLACE-VALUE FORM

1) 67
−38

2) 83
−29

3) 53
−14

4) 91
−62

5) 44
−27

6) 75
−18

7) 55
−36

8) 48
−29

9) 21
− 6

10) 34
−17

11) 57
−19

12) 93
−48

13) 86
−59

14) 17
− 9

### Answers

**1.** 29 **2.** 54 **3.** 39 **4.** 29 **5.** 17 **6.** 57 **7.** 19
**8.** 19 **9.** 15 **10.** 17 **11.** 38 **12.** 45 **13.** 27 **14.** 8

## COMPREHENSIVE SUBTRACTION PRACTICE

1) 589
−267

2) 534
−182

3) 801
−364

4) 582
−259

5) 400
−117

6) 270
−136

7) 810
−346

8) 901
−275

9) 634
−182

10) 5213
−2641

11) 6008
−3384

12) 600
−435

13) 4000
−1082

14) 5030
−2506

15) 6300
−3842

16) 6007
−2562

### Answers

**1.** 322 **2.** 352 **3.** 437 **4.** 323
**5.** 283 **6.** 134 **7.** 464 **8.** 626
**9.** 452 **10.** 2572 **11.** 2624 **12.** 165
**13.** 2918 **14.** 2524 **15.** 2458 **16.** 3445

## *MULTIPLYING TWO DIGITS BY ONE DIGIT*

| 1) 75 | 2) 84 | 3) 64 | 4) 38 | 5) 29 | 6) 97 |
|---|---|---|---|---|---|
| × 8 | × 6 | × 9 | × 7 | × 4 | × 5 |

| 7) 42 | 8) 56 | 9) 67 | 10) 78 | 11) 83 | 12) 94 |
|---|---|---|---|---|---|
| × 3 | × 4 | × 5 | × 6 | × 7 | × 9 |

### Answers

| **1.** 600 | **2.** 504 | **3.** 576 | **4.** 266 | **5.** 116 | **6.** 485 |
|---|---|---|---|---|---|
| **7.** 126 | **8.** 224 | **9.** 335 | **10.** 468 | **11.** 581 | **12.** 846 |

## *MULTIPLYING TWO DIGITS BY TWO DIGITS*

| 1) 82 | 2) 57 | 3) 44 | 4) 73 | 5) 68 | 6) 30 |
|---|---|---|---|---|---|
| × 16 | × 12 | × 11 | × 72 | × 12 | × 20 |

| 7) 70 | 8) 62 | 9) 37 | 10) 68 | 11) 88 | 12) 89 |
|---|---|---|---|---|---|
| × 42 | × 55 | × 26 | × 69 | × 14 | × 30 |

| 13) 44 | 14) 27 | 15) 45 | 16) 97 | 17) 30 | 18) 32 |
|---|---|---|---|---|---|
| × 88 | × 26 | × 21 | × 83 | × 21 | × 12 |

| 19) 87 | 20) 51 | 21) 46 |
|---|---|---|
| × 71 | × 82 | × 27 |

### Answers

| **1.** 1312 | **2.** 684 | **3.** 484 | **4.** 5256 | **5.** 816 |
|---|---|---|---|---|
| **6.** 600 | **7.** 2940 | **8.** 3410 | **9.** 962 | **10.** 4692 |
| **11.** 1232 | **12.** 2670 | **13.** 3872 | **14.** 702 | **15.** 945 |
| **16.** 8051 | **17.** 630 | **18.** 384 | **19.** 6177 | **20.** 4182 |
| **21.** 1242 | | | | |

## MULTIPLYING LARGER NUMBERS

| 1) 925 ×297 | 2) 540 ×343 | 3) 540 ×368 | 4) 767 ×435 | 5) 958 ×446 | 6) 609 ×489 |
|---|---|---|---|---|---|

| 7) 610 ×581 | 8) 953 ×112 | 9) 657 ×629 | 10) 978 ×732 | 11) 717 ×555 | 12) 859 ×429 |
|---|---|---|---|---|---|

| 13) 439 ×141 | 14) 917 ×307 | 15) 937 ×193 | 16) 449 ×211 | 17) 836 ×742 | 18) 728 ×687 |
|---|---|---|---|---|---|

### Answers

| 1. 274,725 | 2. 185,220 | 3. 198,720 | 4. 333,645 |
|---|---|---|---|
| 5. 427,268 | 6. 297,801 | 7. 354,410 | 8. 106,736 |
| 9. 413,253 | 10. 715,896 | 11. 397,935 | 12. 368,511 |
| 13. 61,899 | 14. 281,519 | 15. 180,841 | 16. 94,739 |
| 17. 620,312 | 18. 500,136 | | |

## DIVIDING TWO DIGITS BY ONE DIGIT

1) 2 )15    2) 3 )24    3) 5 )19    4) 6 )39    5) 7 )61    6) 8 )54

7) 4 )23    8) 9 )54    9) 5 )49    10) 7 )51    11) 6 )31    12) 8 )17

### Answers

| 1. 7, R1 | 2. 8 | 3. 3, R4 | 4. 6, R3 |
|---|---|---|---|
| 5. 8, R5 | 6. 6, R6 | 7. 5, R3 | 8. 6 |
| 9. 9, R4 | 10. 7, R2 | 11. 5, R1 | 12. 2, R1 |

## DIVIDING THREE DIGITS BY ONE DIGIT

1) 3 ) 598     2) 6 ) 379     3) 5 ) 842     4) 7 ) 536

5) 7 ) 638     6) 4 ) 742     7) 8 ) 539     8) 3 ) 948

### Answers

**1.** $199\frac{1}{3}$     **2.** 63 R1     **3.** $168\frac{2}{5}$     **4.** 76 R4

**5.** $91\frac{1}{7}$     **6.** 185 R2     **7.** $67\frac{3}{8}$     **8.** 316

## TWO-DIGIT DIVISORS

1) 34 ) 586    2) 27 ) 318    3) 45 ) 269    4) 54 ) 498    5) 46 ) 732    6) 39 ) 267

7) 34 ) 700    8) 63 ) 470    9) 53 ) 389    10) 78 ) 912    11) 61 ) 874    12) 92 ) 653

### Answers

**1.**
```
      17 R8
34 ) 586
     34↓
     246
     238
       8
```

**2.**
```
      11 R21
27 ) 318
     27↓
      48
      27
      21
```

**3.**
```
      5 44/45
45 ) 269
     225
      44
```

**4.**
```
      9 R12
54 ) 498
     486
      12
```

**5.**
```
      15 R42
46 ) 732
     46↓
     272
     230
      42
```

**6.**
```
      6 R33
39 ) 267
     234
      33
```

**7.**
```
      20 R20
34 ) 700
     68↓
      20
```

**8.**
```
      7 29/63
63 ) 470
     441
      29
```

**9.**
```
      7 18/53
53 ) 389
     371
      18
```

**10.**
```
      11 R54
78 ) 912
     78↓
     132
      78
      54
```

**11.**
```
      14 20/61
61 ) 874
     61↓
     264
     244
      20
```

**12.**
```
      7 9/92
92 ) 653
     644
       9
```

## ESTIMATING QUOTIENTS

Estimate quotients by rounding up or down. Solve.

1) 43 ) 5679          2) 37 ) 2891          3) 45 ) 9160          4) 62 ) 8219

5) 79 ) 3540          6) 52 ) 7128          7) 35 ) 4908          8) 64 ) 5191

9) 37 ) 30821         10) 47 ) 13956        11) 23 ) 21530        12) 72 ) 81946

### Answers

| 1. | $132\frac{3}{43}$ | 2. | 78 R5 | 3. | 203 R25 | 4. | $132\frac{35}{62}$ |
|----|----|----|----|----|----|----|----|
| 5. | $44\frac{64}{79}$ | 6. | 137 R4 | 7. | $140\frac{8}{35}$ | 8. | 81 R7 |
| 9. | 833 | 10. | $296\frac{44}{47}$ | 11. | 936 R2 | 12. | 1138 R10 |

## LADDER DIVISION WITH LARGER NUMBERS

1) 53 ) 5692              2) 37 ) 8493              3) 29 ) 7854

4) 27 ) 81,349           5) 32 ) 64,581           6) 49 ) 75,342

7) 19 ) 68,341           8) 234 ) 59,763          9) 418 ) 784,136

### Answers

| 1. | 107 R21 | 2. | 229 R20 | 3. | 270 R24 | 4. | 3012 R25 |
|----|----|----|----|----|----|----|----|
| 5. | 2018 R5 | 6. | 1537 R29 | 7. | 3596 R17 | 8. | 255 R93 |
| 9. | 1875 R386 | | | | | | |

# FRACTIONAL NUMBERS

## EQUIVALENT FRACTIONS

Complete each to form an equivalent fraction.

1) $\frac{3}{5} = \frac{}{30}$      2) $\frac{4}{7} = \frac{12}{}$      3) $\frac{3}{4} = \frac{75}{}$      4) $\frac{5}{9} = \frac{}{81}$

5) $\frac{1}{5} = \frac{}{20}$      6) $\frac{3}{11} = \frac{15}{}$      7) $\frac{5}{8} = \frac{}{32}$      8) $\frac{11}{12} = \frac{}{48}$

9) $\frac{6}{13} = \frac{}{39}$      10) $\frac{2}{3} = \frac{12}{}$      11) $\frac{4}{15} = \frac{}{60}$      12) $\frac{7}{18} = \frac{}{54}$

### Answers

| | | | | | |
|---|---|---|---|---|---|
| **1.** 18 | **2.** 21 | **3.** 100 | **4.** 45 | **5.** 4 | **6.** 55 |
| **7.** 20 | **8.** 44 | **9.** 18 | **10.** 18 | **11.** 16 | **12.** 21 |

## ADDING AND SUBTRACTING FRACTIONS

Solve. Express your answers in lowest terms.

1) $\frac{4}{8} + \frac{2}{6} =$ _____      2) $\frac{11}{15} - \frac{1}{5} =$ _____      3) $\frac{1}{2} + \frac{3}{4} =$ _____

4) $\frac{29}{30} - \frac{1}{6} =$ _____      5) $\frac{7}{8} - \frac{1}{12} =$ _____      6) $\frac{15}{40} - \frac{4}{16} =$ _____

7) $\frac{2}{5} + \frac{3}{8} =$ _____      8) $\frac{2}{6} + \frac{2}{8} =$ _____      9) $\frac{4}{14} + \frac{2}{6} =$ _____

### Answers

| | | | | |
|---|---|---|---|---|
| **1.** $\frac{5}{6}$ | **2.** $\frac{8}{15}$ | **3.** $1\frac{1}{4}$ | **4.** $\frac{4}{5}$ | **5.** $\frac{19}{24}$ |
| **6.** $\frac{1}{8}$ | **7.** $\frac{31}{40}$ | **8.** $\frac{7}{12}$ | **9.** $\frac{13}{21}$ | |

## MULTIPLYING FRACTIONS

Cancel, then multiply.

1) $\frac{4}{9} \times \frac{3}{4} =$ _____      2) $\frac{7}{18} \times \frac{9}{14} =$ _____      3) $\frac{10}{24} \times \frac{8}{15} =$ _____

4) $\frac{12}{17} \times \frac{1}{8} =$ _____      5) $\frac{15}{36} \times \frac{18}{20} =$ _____      6) $\frac{27}{40} \times \frac{12}{27} =$ _____

7) $\frac{35}{42} \times \frac{14}{10} =$ _____      8) $\frac{24}{34} \times \frac{17}{48} =$ _____      9) $\frac{21}{36} \times \frac{9}{14} =$ _____

10) $\frac{15}{24} \times \frac{8}{25} =$ _____      11) $\frac{21}{56} \times \frac{28}{35} =$ _____      12) $\frac{54}{72} \times \frac{45}{63} =$ _____

### Answers

| | | | | | |
|---|---|---|---|---|---|
| **1.** $\frac{1}{3}$ | **2.** $\frac{1}{4}$ | **3.** $\frac{2}{9}$ | **4.** $\frac{3}{34}$ | **5.** $\frac{3}{8}$ | **6.** $\frac{3}{10}$ |
| **7.** $\frac{7}{6}$ | **8.** $\frac{1}{4}$ | **9.** $\frac{3}{8}$ | **10.** $\frac{1}{5}$ | **11.** $\frac{3}{10}$ | **12.** $\frac{15}{28}$ |

## DIVIDING FRACTIONS

1) $\frac{2}{3} \div \frac{1}{4} =$ _____

2) $\frac{5}{8} \div \frac{3}{12} =$ _____

3) $\frac{2}{7} \div \frac{3}{14} =$ _____

4) $\frac{5}{9} \div \frac{1}{3} =$ _____

5) $\frac{4}{7} \div \frac{6}{14} =$ _____

6) $\frac{3}{8} \div \frac{3}{4} =$ _____

7) $\frac{5}{12} \div \frac{10}{18} =$ _____

8) $\frac{1}{2} \div \frac{1}{3} =$ _____

9) $\frac{3}{4} \div \frac{2}{3} =$ _____

10) $\frac{8}{19} \div \frac{4}{38} =$ _____

11) $\frac{4}{38} \div \frac{8}{19} =$ _____

12) $\frac{10}{18} \div \frac{5}{12} =$ _____

### Answers

**1.** $\frac{8}{3}$ or $2\frac{2}{3}$   **2.** $\frac{5}{2}$ or $2\frac{1}{2}$   **3.** $\frac{4}{3}$ or $1\frac{1}{3}$   **4.** $\frac{5}{3}$ or $1\frac{2}{3}$   **5.** $\frac{4}{3}$ or $1\frac{1}{3}$   **6.** $\frac{1}{2}$

**7.** $\frac{3}{4}$   **8.** $\frac{3}{2}$ or $1\frac{1}{2}$   **9.** $\frac{9}{8}$ or $1\frac{1}{8}$   **10.** $4$   **11.** $\frac{1}{4}$   **12.** $\frac{4}{3}$ or $1\frac{1}{3}$

## SUBTRACTING MIXED NUMERALS

Subtract. Express the differences in lowest terms.

1) $\begin{array}{r} 4\frac{3}{5} \\ -2\frac{4}{5} \end{array}$
2) $\begin{array}{r} 5\frac{1}{3} \\ -2\frac{3}{8} \end{array}$
3) $\begin{array}{r} 4\frac{2}{7} \\ -3\frac{7}{8} \end{array}$
4) $\begin{array}{r} 6\frac{1}{16} \\ -2\frac{3}{8} \end{array}$
5) $\begin{array}{r} 9\frac{1}{4} \\ -7\frac{5}{8} \end{array}$
6) $\begin{array}{r} 10\frac{1}{3} \\ -7\frac{2}{3} \end{array}$

7) $8\frac{3}{8} - 4\frac{2}{3} =$ _____

8) $6\frac{1}{5} - 3\frac{5}{6} =$ _____

9) $12\frac{1}{3} - 5\frac{7}{8} =$ _____

10) $7\frac{2}{5} - 3\frac{11}{15} =$ _____

### Answers

**1.** $1\frac{4}{5}$   **2.** $2\frac{23}{24}$   **3.** $\frac{23}{56}$   **4.** $3\frac{11}{16}$   **5.** $1\frac{5}{12}$

**6.** $2\frac{2}{3}$   **7.** $3\frac{17}{24}$   **8.** $2\frac{11}{30}$   **9.** $6\frac{11}{24}$   **10.** $3\frac{2}{3}$

# DECIMAL FRACTIONS

## ADDING DECIMALS

1) $5.3 + 16.48 + .792$

2) $17.3 + 84 + .09$

3) $11.6 + .75 + 2.34 + .357$

4) $86 + .27 + 5.49 + 18.1 + .003$

5) $62.79 + .381 + 5.1 + 87.4$

6) $.17 + .321 + .469 + .008 + 2$

7) $5.94 + 6.38 + 47.3 + .29$

8) $.6531 + 2.4 + .087 + 1.2 + 9$

9) $4.63 + .27 + 5.91 + .34$

10) $17.2 + 126 + .28 + .953 + 15 + .04$

**Answers**

| **1.** 22.572 | **2.** 101.39 | **3.** 15.047 | **4.** 109.863 | **5.** 155.671 |
| **6.** 2.968 | **7.** 59.91 | **8.** 13.3401 | **9.** 11.15 | **10.** 159.473 |

## SUBTRACTING DECIMALS

1) $38.4 - 16.2$    2) $56.9 - 24.7$    3) $82.31 - 64.53$

4) $12.34 - 7.89$    5) $511.31 - 98.520$    6) $76.3 - 48.95$

7) $572.3 - 385.7$    8) $621.4 - 8.374$    9) $38.42 - 9.502$

10) $1.732 - .9$    11) $84.71 - 79.86$    12) $54.82 - 9.634$

13) $47.36 - 18$    14) $75.81 - .3756$    15) $2 - .8461$

**Answers**

| **1.** 22.2 | **2.** 32.2 | **3.** 17.78 | **4.** 4.45 |
| **5.** 412.79 | **6.** 27.35 | **7.** 186.6 | **8.** 613.026 |
| **9.** 28.918 | **10.** .832 | **11.** 4.85 | **12.** 45.186 |
| **13.** 29.36 | **14.** 75.4344 | **15.** 1.1539 | |

## MULTIPLYING DECIMALS

Multiply. Then place the decimal point correctly.

1) $43.8 \times 2.4$    2) $5.7 \times .6$    3) $.69 \times .08$    4) $.58 \times .32$

5) $6.5 \times 3.4$    6) $.75 \times .006$    7) $.27 \times .11$    8) $55 \times 2.7$

9) $.006 \times .0071$    10) $.83 \times 5.611$    11) $.34 \times .00003$    12) $1.8 \times 7$

**Answers**

| **1.** 105.12 | **2.** 3.42 | **3.** .0552 | **4.** .1856 |
| **5.** 22.1 | **6.** .0045 | **7.** .0297 | **8.** 148.5 |
| **9.** .0000426 | **10.** 4.65713 | **11.** .0000102 | **12.** 12.6 |

## DIVIDING DECIMALS

Divide. Where necessary, round the quotient to the nearest hundredth.

1) $.17 \overline{)34.02}$      2) $2.5 \overline{)500}$      3) $.09 \overline{)81}$

4) $.34 \overline{)6.92}$      5) $4.5 \overline{)61.3}$      6) $.004 \overline{).16}$

7) $1.02 \overline{).476}$      8) $3.8 \overline{)97}$      9) $11 \overline{)57.3}$

10) $4.9 \overline{)7.70}$      11) $.52 \overline{)8.16}$      12) $.0014 \overline{)70}$

### Answers

| | | | | | | | |
|---|---|---|---|---|---|---|---|
| **1.** | 200.12 | **2.** | 200 | **3.** | 900 | **4.** | 20.35 |
| **5.** | 13.62 | **6.** | 40 | **7.** | .47 | **8.** | 25.53 |
| **9.** | 5.21 | **10.** | 1.57 | **11.** | 15.69 | **12.** | 50,000 |

# ALGEBRA

## ADDING AND SUBTRACTING WITH VARIABLES

1) $4x + 3x =$ _____      2) $9y - 3y =$ _____      3) $16r - 7r =$ _____

4) $11w + 13p =$ _____      5) $17g + 12g =$ _____      6) $19s - 4s =$ _____

7) $12c + c =$ _____      8) $13v - v =$ _____      9) $12l + 3b =$ _____

10) $f + f + f =$ _____      11) $5x + 5x =$ _____      12) $4q - 3q =$ _____

13) $13w - 13w =$ _____      14) $6n - n =$ _____      15) $5z + 7z =$ _____

### Answers

| | | | | | | | | | |
|---|---|---|---|---|---|---|---|---|---|
| **1.** | $7x$ | **2.** | $6y$ | **3.** | $9r$ | **4.** | $11w + 13p$ | **5.** | $29g$ |
| **6.** | $15s$ | **7.** | $13c$ | **8.** | $12v$ | **9.** | $12l + 3b$ | **10.** | $3f$ |
| **11.** | $10x$ | **12.** | $q$ | **13.** | $0$ | **14.** | $5n$ | **15.** | $12z$ |

## ADDING SIGNED NUMBERS

1) $^+8 + ^-9 =$ _____    2) $^-7 + ^-11 =$ _____    3) $^-5 + ^+12 =$ _____

4) $^+6 + ^+9 =$ _____    5) $^-12 + ^+7 =$ _____    6) $^+9 + ^-15 =$ _____

7) $^-8 + ^+8 =$ _____    8) $^+12 + ^-15 =$ _____    9) $^-13 + ^+20 =$ _____

10) $^+6 + ^+14 =$ _____    11) $^+12 + ^-9 =$ _____    12) $^-15 + ^-13 =$ _____

13) $^-8 + ^-15 =$ _____          14) $^-8 + ^+15 =$ _____

15) $^+8 + ^+15 =$ _____          16) $^+8 + ^-15 =$ _____

17) $^-9 + ^+7 + ^+6 + ^+4 =$ _____          18) $^+11 + ^-5 + ^+3 + ^-8 =$ _____

19) $^-14 + ^+5 + ^-7 + ^+12 =$ _____          20) $^+9 + ^-12 + ^-7 + ^+5 + ^-10 =$ _____

### Answers

| | | | | | | | | | | | | | |
|---|---|---|---|---|---|---|---|---|---|---|---|---|---|
| **1.** $^-1$ | **2.** $^-18$ | **3.** $^+7$ | **4.** $^+15$ | **5.** $^-5$ | **6.** $^-6$ | **7.** 0 |
| **8.** $^-3$ | **9.** $^+7$ | **10.** $^+20$ | **11.** $^+3$ | **12.** $^-28$ | **13.** $^-23$ | **14.** $^+7$ |
| **15.** $^+23$ | **16.** $^-7$ | **17.** $^+8$ | **18.** $^+1$ | **19.** $^-4$ | **20.** $^-15$ | |

## SUBTRACTING SIGNED NUMBERS

1) $^-9 - ^-9 =$ _____    2) $^-6 - ^+8 =$ _____    3) $^+7 - ^-7 =$ _____

4) $^+12 - ^+4 =$ _____    5) $^+18 - ^-5 =$ _____    6) $^-14 - ^+8 =$ _____

7) $^-17 - ^-9 =$ _____    8) $^+13 - ^-15 =$ _____    9) $^-17 - ^+20 =$ _____

10) $^-11 - ^-19 =$ _____    11) $^+10 - ^+14 =$ _____    12) $^-6 - ^-12 =$ _____

### Answers

| | | | | | |
|---|---|---|---|---|---|
| **1.** 0 | **2.** $^-14$ | **3.** $^+14$ | **4.** $^+8$ | **5.** $^+23$ | **6.** $^-22$ |
| **7.** $^-8$ | **8.** $^+28$ | **9.** $^-37$ | **10.** $^+8$ | **11.** $^-4$ | **12.** $^+6$ |

## MULTIPLYING AND DIVIDING SIGNED NUMBERS

1) $^+6 \times ^+8 =$ _____    2) $^-5 \times ^-7 =$ _____    3) $^+16 \div ^-2 =$ _____

4) $^-24 \div ^+6 =$ _____    5) $^-9 \times ^-9 =$ _____    6) $^-60 \div ^-10 =$ _____

7) $^+7 \times ^-8 =$ _____    8) $^-18 \div ^-9 =$ _____    9) $^-6 \times ^+8 =$ _____

10) $^+36 \div {}^-6 = $ _____

11) $^-4 \times {}^-9 = $ _____

12) $^-42 \div {}^+6 = $ _____

13) $^-5 \times {}^-9 = $ _____

14) $^-28 \div {}^+4 = $ _____

15) $^+6 \times {}^-8 = $ _____

16) $^+48 \div {}^-3 = $ _____

17) $^-4 \times {}^-6 = $ _____

18) $^-12 \div {}^-3 = $ _____

### Answers

| | | | | | |
|---|---|---|---|---|---|
| **1.** $^+48$ | **2.** $^+35$ | **3.** $^-8$ | **4.** $^-4$ | **5.** $^+81$ | **6.** $^+6$ |
| **7.** $^-56$ | **8.** $^+2$ | **9.** $^-48$ | **10.** $^-6$ | **11.** $^+36$ | **12.** $^-7$ |
| **13.** $^+45$ | **14.** $^-7$ | **15.** $^-48$ | **16.** $^-16$ | **17.** $^+24$ | **18.** $^+4$ |

## TRANSFORMING EQUATIONS BY MULTIPLE OPERATIONS

Solve for the variable.

1) $5p - 9 = 7p - 11$

2) $7x + 8 = 4x - 16$

3) $^-12 + 5w = {}^-w + 18$

4) $\frac{3}{5}v - 7 = \frac{1}{3}v + 2$

5) $\frac{7}{8}m - 9 = {}^-\frac{1}{8}m + 5$

6) $m + 6 + 3m = 5 - m - 9$

7) $11 - x + 4 = 3x + 5 - 8x$

8) $6n - 3 - 9n = 4 + 2n - 8$

9) $7v - 16 = 5\frac{1}{2}v + 2$

10) $\frac{1}{2}p - \frac{1}{3}p + \frac{1}{4}p = 5$

11) $\frac{1}{3}w - 6 = \frac{2}{5}w + 4$

12) $\frac{7}{8}r - 6 + \frac{1}{3}r = 7 + \frac{1}{2}r$

13) $\frac{4x}{5} = 10$

14) $\frac{7}{2}q = {}^-14$

15) $5s - 8 + 3s + 17 = 11 + 6s - 35$

16) $\frac{3}{4}q + 3 - \frac{1}{2}q + 8 = 11 - \frac{1}{4}q + 6$

### Answers

| | | | | | |
|---|---|---|---|---|---|
| **1.** 1 | **2.** $^-8$ | **3.** 5 | **4.** $\frac{135}{4}$ or $33\frac{3}{4}$ | **5.** 14 | **6.** $^-2$ |
| **7.** $^-2\frac{1}{2}$ | **8.** $\frac{1}{5}$ | **9.** 12 | **10.** 12 | **11.** $^-150$ | **12.** $\frac{312}{17}$ or $18\frac{6}{17}$ |
| **13.** $12\frac{1}{2}$ | **14.** $^-4$ | **15.** $^-16\frac{1}{2}$ | **16.** 12 | | |

## SOLVING PROPORTIONS

1) $\frac{x}{3} = \frac{6}{9}$

2) $\frac{4}{x} = \frac{12}{18}$

3) $\frac{5}{12} = \frac{x}{48}$

4) $\frac{6}{14} = \frac{9}{x}$

5) $\frac{3}{8} = \frac{x}{24}$

6) $\frac{4}{7} = \frac{x}{9}$

7) $\frac{4}{x} = \frac{11}{17}$

8) $\frac{2x}{5} = \frac{9}{50}$

9) $\frac{6}{3x} = \frac{5}{20}$

10) $\frac{5}{8} = \frac{12}{3x}$

11) $\dfrac{x+3}{5} = \dfrac{8}{10}$    12) $\dfrac{3}{x+2} = \dfrac{4}{20}$    13) $\dfrac{x-1}{4} = \dfrac{9}{2}$    14) $\dfrac{6}{9} = \dfrac{6}{x+1}$    15) $\dfrac{4}{7} = \dfrac{x-4}{56}$

## Answers

| | | | | |
|---|---|---|---|---|
| **1.** 2 | **2.** 6 | **3.** 20 | **4.** 21 | **5.** 9 |
| **6.** $\frac{36}{7}$ or $5\frac{1}{7}$ | **7.** $\frac{68}{11}$ or $6\frac{2}{11}$ | **8.** $\frac{9}{20}$ | **9.** 8 | **10.** $\frac{96}{15}$ or $6\frac{2}{5}$ |
| **11.** 1 | **12.** 13 | **13.** 19 | **14.** 8 | **15.** 36 |

# EQUIVALENT FRACTIONS, DECIMALS, AND PERCENTS

Fill in the blanks to write equivalent fractions, decimals, or percents.

| | FRACTION | DECIMAL | PERCENT |
|---|---|---|---|
| 1) | $\frac{10}{17}$ | .58 | _____ |
| 2) | $\frac{10}{11}$ | _____ | 90% |
| 3) | $\frac{1}{20}$ | _____ | 5% |
| 4) | $\frac{6}{23}$ | _____ | 26% |
| 5) | $\frac{8}{25}$ | _____ | 32% |
| 6) | $\frac{7}{23}$ | _____ | 30% |
| 7) | $\frac{6}{19}$ | _____ | _____ |
| 8) | _____ | _____ | 30% |
| 9) | _____ | .62 | 62% |
| 10) | _____ | .05 | 5% |
| 11) | $\frac{4}{23}$ | .17 | _____ |
| 12) | $\frac{2}{7}$ | .28 | _____ |
| 13) | $\frac{6}{20}$ | .3 | _____ |
| 14) | $\frac{7}{10}$ | _____ | 70% |
| 15) | _____ | .83 | 83% |
| 16) | _____ | .08 | 8% |
| 17) | $\frac{4}{7}$ | .57 | _____ |
| 18) | _____ | .8 | 80% |

19) $\frac{10}{24}$ _____ _____

20) $\frac{5}{24}$ _____ 20%

## Answers

1. 58%  2. .9  3. .05  4. .26  5. .32
6. .3  7. .31, 31%  8. $\frac{3}{10}$, .3  9. $\frac{5}{8}$  10. $\frac{1}{20}$
11. 17%  12. 28%  13. 30%  14. .7  15. $\frac{5}{6}$
16. $\frac{1}{12}$  17. 57%  18. $\frac{4}{5}$  19. .41, 41%  20. .2

# EXPRESSING DECIMALS AS PERCENTS

Express each decimal as a percent.

1) .64  2) .45  3) .1  4) .36  5) .5  6) .36  7) .44

8) .5  9) .41  10) .25  11) .27  12) .75  13) .55  14) .35

15) .71  16) .5  17) .3  18) .41  19) .44  20) .58  21) .56

22) .5  23) .07  24) .77  25) .75  26) .38  27) .4  28) .57

29) .36  30) .28  31) .56  32) .37

## Answers

1. 64%  2. 45%  3. 10%  4. 36%  5. 50%
6. 36%  7. 44%  8. 50%  9. 41%  10. 25%
11. 27%  12. 75%  13. 55%  14. 35%  15. 71%
16. 50%  17. 30%  18. 41%  19. 44%  20. 58%
21. 56%  22. 50%  23. 7%  24. 77%  25. 75%
26. 38%  27. 40%  28. 57%  29. 36%  30. 28%
31. 56%  32. 37%

# EXPRESSING FRACTIONS AS PERCENTS

Express each fraction as a percent.

1) $\frac{10}{16}$  2) $\frac{9}{13}$  3) $\frac{3}{11}$  4) $\frac{3}{21}$  5) $\frac{9}{17}$  6) $\frac{7}{25}$  7) $\frac{2}{22}$  8) $\frac{2}{23}$

9) $\frac{9}{13}$  10) $\frac{2}{21}$  11) $\frac{5}{5}$  12) $\frac{9}{15}$  13) $\frac{5}{19}$  14) $\frac{8}{18}$  15) $\frac{2}{18}$  16) $\frac{5}{8}$

17) $\frac{3}{22}$  18) $\frac{2}{19}$  19) $\frac{4}{6}$  20) $\frac{5}{20}$  21) $\frac{5}{15}$  22) $\frac{6}{8}$  23) $\frac{6}{16}$  24) $\frac{6}{10}$

25) $\frac{3}{18}$  26) $\frac{7}{23}$  27) $\frac{1}{23}$  28) $\frac{2}{23}$  29) $\frac{3}{21}$  30) $\frac{5}{23}$  31) $\frac{3}{7}$  32) $\frac{5}{8}$

**Answers**

| | | | | |
|---|---|---|---|---|
| **1.** 62% | **2.** 69% | **3.** 27% | **4.** 14% | **5.** 52% |
| **6.** 28% | **7.** 9% | **8.** 8% | **9.** 69% | **10.** 9% |
| **11.** 100% | **12.** 60% | **13.** 26% | **14.** 44% | **15.** 11% |
| **16.** 83% | **17.** 13% | **18.** 10% | **19.** 66% | **20.** 25% |
| **21.** 33% | **22.** 75% | **23.** 37% | **24.** 60% | **25.** 16% |
| **26.** 30% | **27.** 4% | **28.** 8% | **29.** 14% | **30.** 21% |
| **31.** 42% | **32.** 83% | | | |

## FINDING A PERCENT OF A NUMBER

1) 10% of 737 = _____

2) 61% of 228 = _____

3) 33% of 454 = _____

4) 57% of 907 = _____

5) 85% of 567 = _____

6) 95% of 787 = _____

7) 52% of 764 = _____

8) 28% of 850 = _____

9) 66% of 642 = _____

10) 58% of 601 = _____

11) 56% of 630 = _____

12) 37% of 872 = _____

13) 95% of 659 = _____

14) 39% of 362 = _____

15) 4% of 585 = _____

16) 10% of 939 = _____

17) 39% of 361 = _____

18) 90% of 685 = _____

19) 55% of 958 = _____

20) 12% of 691 = _____

21) 37% of 38 = _____

22) 74% of 606 = _____

23) 15% of 375 = _____

24) 90% of 936 = _____

25) 49% of 28 = _____

26) 12% of 85 = _____

27) 90% of 261 = _____

28) 28% of 157 = _____

29) 14% of 216 = _____

30) 39% of 501 = _____

31) 35% of 335 = _____

32) 99% of 8 = _____

33) 89% of 532 = _____

34) 49% of 157 = _____

35) 100% of 114 = _____

36) 8% of 814 = _____

## Answers

| | | | | | | | |
|---|---|---|---|---|---|---|---|
| **1.** | 73.7 | **2.** | 139.08 | **3.** | 149.82 | **4.** | 516.99 |
| **5.** | 481.95 | **6.** | 747.65 | **7.** | 397.28 | **8.** | 238 |
| **9.** | 423.72 | **10.** | 348.58 | **11.** | 352.8 | **12.** | 322.64 |
| **13.** | 626.05 | **14.** | 141.18 | **15.** | 23.4 | **16.** | 93.9 |
| **17.** | 140.79 | **18.** | 616.5 | **19.** | 526.9 | **20.** | 82.92 |
| **21.** | 14.06 | **22.** | 448.44 | **23.** | 56.25 | **24.** | 842.4 |
| **25.** | 13.72 | **26.** | 10.2 | **27.** | 234.9 | **28.** | 43.96 |
| **29.** | 30.24 | **30.** | 195.39 | **31.** | 117.25 | **32.** | 7.92 |
| **33.** | 473.48 | **34.** | 76.93 | **35.** | 114 | **36.** | 65.12 |

# ANSWER SHEET FOR GED MATHEMATICS TEST I

**Directions:** Take this sample test as though it were the real test. Each problem is followed by five answer choices numbered 1 to 5. Solve each problem, then choose the correct answer from the choices offered. Mark your answers on the answer sheet just as you would have to do on the actual exam. When you have finished the test, check your answers with the solutions on page 293. Allow yourself 90 minutes to complete this test.

1 ① ② ③ ④ ⑤    13 ① ② ③ ④ ⑤    25 ① ② ③ ④ ⑤    37 ① ② ③ ④ ⑤    49 ① ② ③ ④ ⑤
2 ① ② ③ ④ ⑤    14 ① ② ③ ④ ⑤    26 ① ② ③ ④ ⑤    38 ① ② ③ ④ ⑤    50 ① ② ③ ④ ⑤
3 ① ② ③ ④ ⑤    15 ① ② ③ ④ ⑤    27 ① ② ③ ④ ⑤    39 ① ② ③ ④ ⑤    51 ① ② ③ ④ ⑤
4 ① ② ③ ④ ⑤    16 ① ② ③ ④ ⑤    28 ① ② ③ ④ ⑤    40 ① ② ③ ④ ⑤    52 ① ② ③ ④ ⑤
5 ① ② ③ ④ ⑤    17 ① ② ③ ④ ⑤    29 ① ② ③ ④ ⑤    41 ① ② ③ ④ ⑤    53 ① ② ③ ④ ⑤
6 ① ② ③ ④ ⑤    18 ① ② ③ ④ ⑤    30 ① ② ③ ④ ⑤    42 ① ② ③ ④ ⑤    54 ① ② ③ ④ ⑤
7 ① ② ③ ④ ⑤    19 ① ② ③ ④ ⑤    31 ① ② ③ ④ ⑤    43 ① ② ③ ④ ⑤    55 ① ② ③ ④ ⑤
8 ① ② ③ ④ ⑤    20 ① ② ③ ④ ⑤    32 ① ② ③ ④ ⑤    44 ① ② ③ ④ ⑤    56 ① ② ③ ④ ⑤
9 ① ② ③ ④ ⑤    21 ① ② ③ ④ ⑤    33 ① ② ③ ④ ⑤    45 ① ② ③ ④ ⑤
10 ① ② ③ ④ ⑤   22 ① ② ③ ④ ⑤    34 ① ② ③ ④ ⑤    46 ① ② ③ ④ ⑤
11 ① ② ③ ④ ⑤   23 ① ② ③ ④ ⑤    35 ① ② ③ ④ ⑤    47 ① ② ③ ④ ⑤
12 ① ② ③ ④ ⑤   24 ① ② ③ ④ ⑤    36 ① ② ③ ④ ⑤    48 ① ② ③ ④ ⑤

# 9. SAMPLE GED MATHEMATICS TEST I

1) A sporting goods store normally discounts all merchandise 16%. At a special sale, it is taking an additional ⅛ off its discount price. During the special sale, how much would you expect to pay for a baseball glove with a list price of $56?

(1) $47.04
(2) $44.80
(3) $37.63
(4) $50.20
(5) $35.84

2) Dylan wishes to fence in a rectangular garden plot. It is to be 34 feet long, and half as wide as its length. How many feet of fencing will he need?

(1) 51
(2) 102
(3) 578
(4) 68
(5) 120

3)  2.54 centimeters = 1 inch

From the fact stated above, 1 centimeter is about equal to

(1) .4 inches
(2) 1.54 inches
(3) 2.54 inches
(4) .6 inches
(5) .7 inches

4) Bill spent 95 cents for a soda and 35 cents for a newspaper. How much change did he receive from a ten dollar bill?

(1) $ .60
(2) $1.30
(3) $8.05
(4) $8.70
(5) $8.30

5) Roast beef is selling at the local supermarket for $4.80 per pound. Alessandra buys ⅔ of a pound. How much does she pay for it?

(1) $4.13
(2) $5.47
(3) $4.80
(4) $2.40
(5) $3.20

6) A 12-foot tall lamp-post casts an 8-foot long shadow at the same time that a tree nearby casts a 28-foot shadow. How tall is the tree?

    (1) 36 feet
    (2) 42 feet
    (3) 40 feet
    (4) 16 feet
    (5) 48 feet

7) An office ordered 10 dozen pencils. All but four dozen of them were #2 pencils. How many #2 pencils were ordered?

    (1) 120
    (2) 72
    (3) 100
    (4) 48
    (5) 144

8) A lawn mower is on sale for $111.20. That represents a discount of 20% from its normal price. What is the lawn mower's normal price?

    (1) $ 22.24
    (2) $133.44
    (3) $139.00
    (4) $200.16
    (5) $224.00

9) If $x^2 + 5x + 6 = 0$, then $x =$

    (1) $^-2$ and $^-3$
    (2) $^-3$ only
    (3) $^+3$ and $^+2$
    (4) $^+5$ only
    (5) $^+2$ only

10) Which of the following is the radius of the largest ball that will fit into a box that has inside dimensions of 15 centimeters by 8 centimeters by 11 centimeters?

    (1) 11 centimeters
    (2) 8 centimeters
    (3) 15 centimeters
    (4) 4 centimeters
    (5) $5\frac{1}{2}$ centimeters

11) $527(316 + 274)$ has the same value as which of the following?

    (1) $316(527) + 274$
    (2) $316 + 527 + 274$
    (3) $527(316) + 527(274)$
    (4) $316(527) + 316(274)$
    (5) $527(274) + 316(274)$

12) A woman was 72 years old when she died in 1954. In what year was the woman born?

    (1) 1972
    (2) 1902
    (3) 1872
    (4) 1882
    (5) 1892

13) Look at the chart below.

| Time | 7:00 | 8:00 | 9:00 |
|---|---|---|---|
| Distance | 24 km | 48 km | 72 km |

If a ship travelled away from port at a steady speed as shown in the table above, how far from port was it at 8:35?

    (1) 56 kilometers
    (2) 58 kilometers
    (3) 60 kilometers
    (4) 62 kilometers
    (5) Not enough information

14) Melissa withdrew $3487 from her savings account. That left her with a balance of $11,516. What was the balance before the withdrawal?

    (1) $8029
    (2) $15,003
    (3) $6974
    (4) $10,461
    (5) $18,490

15) James plans to cut 58 meters of fencing into 8 pieces of equal length. How long will each piece be?

    (1) 7.25 meters
    (2) 7.5 meters
    (3) 8 meters
    (4) 64 meters
    (5) 464 meters

16) Suzanne bought 4 record albums from Marvin's Music Emporium when it had a "Going Out of Business" sale. Two albums originally sold for $6.95 each; the other two for $8.95 each. Every album in the store was discounted by 30%. How much did Suzanne spend?

    (1) $21.30
    (2) $22.26
    (3) $31.80
    (4) $35.00
    (5) $25.32

17) Mr. Myers' workroom floor measured exactly 7 feet by 6 feet. The vinyl tiles he chose for his flooring came in 1-foot squares, packed 12 to a carton. How many cartons would Mr. Myers need to buy in order to tile his entire floor?

(1) 1 carton
(2) 2 cartons
(3) 3 cartons
(4) 4 cartons
(5) 5 cartons

18) Mrs. Wilson bought a flat of petunias from the garden center. She wanted to plant them in a straight line to border the 22-foot walkway in front of the house. The flat contained 12 plants. How far apart must the plants be placed in order to form an even border from end to end?

(1) 1 foot, 6 inches
(2) 1 foot, 8 inches
(3) 2 feet
(4) 2 feet, 2 inches
(5) 2 feet, 4 inches

19) Penelope saved half of her birthday cake for her grandparents and Aunt Lucy who were coming for a visit. She divided what was left of the cake into 3 equal pieces. What portion of the original cake was each piece?

(1) $\frac{1}{3}$
(2) $\frac{1}{4}$
(3) $\frac{1}{5}$
(4) $\frac{1}{6}$
(5) $\frac{1}{7}$

20) Mrs. Gabaway wants to telephone her friend in Boston. The day rate is $.48 for the first minute and $.34 for each additional minute. The evening rate discounts the day rate by 35%. If Mrs. Gabaway is planning a 45-minute chat, to the nearest penny, how much would she save if she took advantage of the evening rate by calling after 5 PM?

(1) $5.40
(2) $7.55
(3) $5.25
(4) $5.51
(5) $6.30

21) There are 45 children signed up for the class field trip. The number of girls exceeds the number of boys by 7. How many boys are going?

(1) 17
(2) 19
(3) 21
(4) 23
(5) Not enough information is given

22) If a car averages 60 mph on a cross country trip, how long would it take to go 1500 miles?

(1) 20 hours
(2) 25 hours
(3) 30 hours
(4) 35 hours
(5) 40 hours

23) Work O'Holic put in 12 hours per day, Monday through Friday, 8 hours on Saturday and 4 hours on Sunday to produce and package the liniment his factory needed. He is paid $8.40 an hour for a 40 hour week and time and a half for anything over 40 hours. How much did Mr. O'Holic gross for the week?

(1) $436.80
(2) $650.40
(3) $736.80
(4) $739.20
(5) $840.00

24) The Holy Molar Sweet Shoppe sold 10 pounds of jujubes and non pareils to the man who never smiles. The cost of the non pareils was $.77 a pound and the jujubes cost $.49 a pound. The man paid $6.02 for his candy. How much of each type did he buy?

(1) 3 pounds non pareils, 7 pounds jujubes
(2) 4 pounds nonpareils, 6 pounds jujubes
(3) 5 pounds non pareils, 5 pounds jujubes
(4) 6 pounds non pareils, 4 pounds jujubes
(5) 7 pounds non pareils, 3 pounds jujubes

25) The shrew has a heartier appetite than any other animal. A shrew, weighing only $\frac{1}{8}$ of an ounce, is capable of eating $3\frac{1}{4}$ ounces of food in 8 days. How much can the shrew consume in one day?

(1) $\frac{1}{4}$ ounce
(2) $\frac{1}{8}$ ounce
(3) $\frac{7}{16}$ ounce
(4) $\frac{6}{16}$ ounce
(5) $\frac{13}{32}$ ounce

26) Based on the information given in the last problem, how much more or less than its own weight does the shrew consume in one day?

(1) $\frac{3}{8}$ more
(2) $\frac{9}{32}$ more
(3) $\frac{7}{64}$ more
(4) $\frac{1}{8}$ less
(5) $\frac{9}{32}$ less

27) Peter is reading the book *Ivanhoe* which is 436 pages long. He has read 60 pages and it has taken him 1½ hours. How much longer will it take him to finish the book?

    (1) 9.9 hours
    (2) 10.4 hours
    (3) 10.9 hours
    (4) 11.4 hours
    (5) 11.9 hours

28) A piece of rope 40 feet long is cut into two pieces. One piece is 5 feet longer than the other. What is the length of the longer piece?

    (1) 25 feet
    (2) 22.5 feet
    (3) 20 feet
    (4) 17.5 feet
    (5) 23 feet

29) Lefty's Sport Center ran a sale on women's softball gloves at the end of August. The Karen Foster signature mitt sold for $34.95 and the Sue Sims signature mitt sold for $24.00. The store took in $987.00 during the sale. If 32 mitts were sold altogether, how many of the Foster model did Lefty sell?

    (1) 25
    (2) 17
    (3) 30
    (4) 20
    (5) 12

30) If there are 10 millimeters in a centimeter and 10 centimeters in a decimeter, how many millimeters are there in a decimeter?

    (1) 1
    (2) 10
    (3) 100
    (4) 1000
    (5) 10,000

31) The rectangular cardboard backdrop for the Adams Street School play was 16 meters wide and twice as long. To make painting it easier, the students planned to use a roll of heavy white paper to cover it on one side. The paper on the roll was 2 meters wide. Allowing for no overlap, how long a piece of the roll was needed?

    (1) 128 meters
    (2) 256 meters
    (3) 256 sq meters
    (4) 512 meters
    (5) 512 sq meters

32) To convert Fahrenheit to Celsius, use the equation $C = \frac{5}{9}(F - 32)$. A spring day of 68 degrees Fahrenheit would be equal to how many degrees Celsius?

    (1) 20
    (2) 32
    (3) 48
    (4) 55
    (5) 88

33) Nancy wishes to make a macrame wall hanging for her living room. The directions call for 12 pieces of jute 12.5 meters long, 18 pieces 8.25 meters long, and 24 pieces 7 meters long. How much jute will she need for her wall hanging?

    (1) 148.5 meters
    (2) 298.5 meters
    (3) 466.5 meters
    (4) 502.5 meters
    (5) 675 meters

34) If Elaine spends an average of 13 minutes on each interview at her temporary employment agency, approximately how many prospective employees can she interview in an 8-hour workday?

    (1) $\dfrac{8 \times 13}{60}$
    (2) $8 \times 60 \times 13$
    (3) $\dfrac{8 \times 60}{13}$
    (4) $\dfrac{13}{8}(60)$
    (5) $\dfrac{60 \times 13}{8}$

35) Bill and Bert drove 530 miles to a secluded lake for a week of fishing. They drove for 10 hours, alternating between 60 mph on the highways and 40 mph through the towns. For how much of their trip were the men traveling 40 mph?

    (1) $3\frac{1}{2}$ hours
    (2) 4 hours
    (3) $4\frac{1}{2}$ hours
    (4) $5\frac{1}{2}$ hours
    (5) Not enough information is given

36) A cassette box is $2\frac{1}{2}$ inches wide, 4 inches long, and $\frac{3}{4}$ of an inch high. Ogden wants to ship his collection of cassettes to his brother in California. What is the maximum number of cassettes Ogden can put into a carton with a capacity of 180 cubic inches?

    (1) 12
    (2) 18
    (3) 24
    (4) 30
    (5) 36

37) Myra received a chain letter in the mail which warned that failure to send $5.00 to the first name on the list would result in a face full of warts. Myra sent the $5.00, crossed off the receiver's name, and added her name to the bottom of the list which at any given time consists of 5 names. She then sent copies to 10 of her friends who were each instructed to do likewise. Assuming everyone followed directions, by the time Myra's name rose to the first position on the list, how much money would she receive?

(1) $5,000
(2) $50,000
(3) $500,000
(4) $5,000,000
(5) $50,000,000

38) If a record revolves $33\frac{1}{3}$ times per minute, how long will it take for the record to make 2,400 revolutions?

(1) 72 minutes
(2) 66 minutes
(3) 80 minutes
(4) 90 minutes
(5) 84 minutes

39) New York hosted the first World's Fair 111 years before the New York World's Fair of 1964. In what year was that?

(1) 1845
(2) 1853
(3) 1865
(4) 1873
(5) 1884

40) Stock in North American Electric fluctuated in price with a high of $67\frac{3}{4}$ and a low of $27\frac{5}{8}$. Find the difference between the high price and the low price.

(1) $40\frac{1}{4}$
(2) $40\frac{1}{8}$
(3) $40\frac{1}{16}$
(4) $39\frac{1}{8}$
(5) $39\frac{7}{8}$

Graph is from Bureau of Labor Statistics, 1976

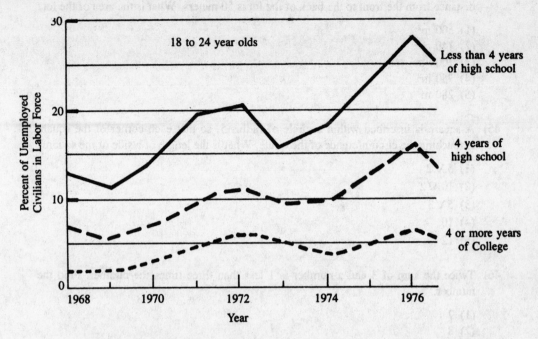

The graph illustrates the unemployment rate by age and amount of education. The next 3 questions refer to the graph above.

41) According to the graph, in which year was unemployment the highest?

(1) 1972
(2) 1973
(3) 1974
(4) 1975
(5) 1976

42) What was the difference in percent of unemployment between high school graduates and those with less than 4 years of high school in 1973?

(1) 6%
(2) 10%
(3) 12%
(4) 15%
(5) 18%

43) What was the greatest difference in unemployment rates for those with less than 4 years of high school?

(1) 5%
(2) 10%
(3) 15%
(4) 20%
(5) 25%

44) A triangular shaped building lot has a front on the road that is 20 meters long. The distance from the front to the back of the lot is 50 meters. What is the area of the lot?

(1) 500 m²
(2) 140 m²
(3) 1000 m²
(4) 750 m²
(5) 280 m²

45) A square is inscribed within a circle of radius 5, so that each corner of the square is touching the circumference of the circle. What is the length of a side of the square?

(1) $5\sqrt{2}$
(2) $10\sqrt{2}$
(3) $5\sqrt{3}$
(4) 10
(5) 12

46) Twice the sum of 3 and a number is 1 less than three times the number. Find the number.

(1) 7
(2) 8
(3) 9
(4) 10
(5) 11

47) A vending machine contains $21 in dimes and nickels. Altogether there are 305 coins. How many of those coins are dimes?

(1) 190
(2) 165
(3) 125
(4) 115
(5) 95

48) A baker has cookies worth $1.80 per pound and cookies worth $2.70 per pound. How many pounds of $1.80 cookies should be in 30 pounds of the assortment that he can sell for $2.10 per pound?

(1) 18 pounds
(2) 20 pounds
(3) 22 pounds
(4) 24 pounds
(5) 10 pounds

49) A can has a lid with a 3-inch radius and is 8 inches tall. How many cubic inches of liquid can it hold?

(1) $48\pi$
(2) $64\pi$
(3) $72\pi$
(4) $96\pi$
(5) $108\pi$

50) Bill invested a sum of money at 9% and a second sum at 18%. The second sum was $450 less than the first. He received an annual return of $162 from his investments. How much was placed at 18%?

(1) $900
(2) $750
(3) $625
(4) $450
(5) $300

51) What is the average height of a player on the 10th Street Basketball Team if the heights of the individual players are 5'8", 6'1", 5'10", 6'3", and 5'9"?

(1) 5'8"
(2) 5'9"
(3) 5'10"
(4) 5'11"
(5) 6'

Questions 52 to 56 refers to the following graph.

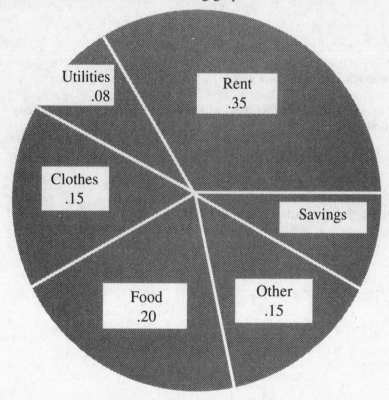

**Karen's Take-Home Dollar**

52) How much of each dollar does Karen spend on food and clothing?

(1) $.35
(2) $.25
(3) $.15
(4) $.20
(5) Not enough information is given

53) Suppose Karen earns $200 per week after taxes. How much money does she save each week?

(1) $7
(2) $.07
(3) $14
(4) $.14
(5) Not enough information is given

54) Suppose Karen brings home $500 per week. How much does she spend per week on entertainment?

(1) $75
(2) $7.50
(3) $.75
(4) $15
(5) Not enough information is given

55) Karen spends $45 per week on clothing. How much money does she take home each week?

(1) $200
(2) $275
(3) $300
(4) $350
(5) Not enough information is given

56) If Karen brings home $450 per week, which of the following *might* she pay weekly for electricity?

(1) $24
(2) $38
(3) $48
(4) $60
(5) Not enough information is given

# Solutions to Sample Test 1

1.  (3) A 16% discount means that you would normally pay 84% of $56 for the glove, or .84 × 56 = $47.04. Now take another $\frac{1}{5}$ off $47.04. That means divide $47.04 by 5, multiply it by $\frac{1}{5}$, or multiply it by .20 to find out how much more to take off, or, if you are taking off another 20% ($\frac{1}{5}$) you are paying 80% of $47.04 = .80 × $47.04 = $37.63.

2.  (2) Half of 34 is 17. Halfway around the garden would be 34 + 17, or 51 feet. Double that and you go all 102 feet around.

3.  (1) Make a proportion: $\dfrac{2.54 \text{ cm}}{1 \text{ inch}} = \dfrac{1 \text{ cm}}{x \text{ inch}}$
$$2.54x = 1$$
$$x = .3937, \text{ or } .4 \text{ inch}$$

4.  (4) Bill spent $.95 + $.35 = $1.30. $10.00 − $1.30 = $8.70.

5.  (5) $\frac{2}{3}$ × $4.80 = $3.20

6.  (2) Make a proportion: $\dfrac{12}{8} = \dfrac{x}{28}$
$$8x = 336$$
$$x = 42 \text{ feet}$$

7.  (2) 10 − 4 = 6 dozen #2 pencils. 12 = 1 dozen.   6 × 12 = 72 pencils.

8.  (3) The sale price is 80% of the list price. Let $x$ = the list price. Then
$$.80x = \$111.20$$
$$.80x = \frac{\$111.20}{\$.80}$$
$$x = \$139$$

9.  (1)    $x^2 + 5x + 6 = 0$
$(x + 3)(x + 2) = 0$
$x + 3 = 0$  or  $x + 2 = 0$
$x = {}^-3$  or      $x = {}^-2$

10. (4) The largest ball will have the same diameter as the smallest dimension of the box. That's 8 centimeters. A radius is half a diameter, hence it must be half of 8, or 4 centimeters.

11. (3) This is an illustration of the distributive property:
$$527(316 + 274) = 527(316) + 527(274)$$

12. (4) Subtract 72 from 1954. 1954 − 72 = 1882.

13. (4) The ship is travelling 24 km/hr. In 35 minutes it will go $\frac{35}{60}$ of 24 kilometers. $\frac{35}{60} \times \frac{24}{1}$ = 14 kilometers. 48 kilometers that the ship was out at 8:00 + 14 = 62 kilometers.

**14.**   (2) $11,516 + $3487 = $15,003.

**15.**   (1) $\frac{58}{8}$ = 7.25 meters

**16.**   (2) 2 × $6.95 = $13.90.  2 × $8.95 = $17.90. Adding them together makes a total list price of $31.80. With a 30% discount, Suzanne pays 70% of list. .70 × $31.80 = $22.26.

**17.**   (4) A 7 × 6 foot area is 42 square feet. $\frac{42}{12}$ = 3$\frac{1}{2}$, but Mr. Myers cannot buy 3$\frac{1}{2}$ boxes, so he must buy 4.

**18.**   (3) The flat contains 12 plants. The first plant is put at the beginning of the walkway, still leaving 22 feet to be covered, but leaving 11 plants with which to cover them. $\frac{22}{11}$ = 2 feet between plants.

**19.**   (4) $\frac{\frac{1}{2}}{3} = \frac{1}{2} \times \frac{1}{3} = \frac{1}{6}$

**20.**   (1) A day call would cost $.34 × 44 minutes + $.48, or $15.44. If the evening rate discounts the day rates by 35%, an evening call would cost 65% of $15.44, or .65 × $15.44 = $10.04. The saving is $15.44 − $10.04, or $5.40.

**21.**   (2)       Let $x$ = the number of boys
         Then $x + 7$ = the number of girls

$$x + x + 7 = 45$$
$$2x + 7 = 45$$
$$2x = 38$$
$$x = 19 \text{ boys}$$

**22.**   (2)     $d = rt$

$$1500 = 60t$$
$$t = 25 \text{ hours}$$

**23.**   (4) 5 × 12 = 60 hours Monday through Friday, + 12 hours for the weekend. That is a total of 72 hours. 72 is 32 more than 40 hours, so the pay is 40($8.40) and 32(1$\frac{1}{2}$ · $8.40)

$$= 336 + 32(12.60)$$
$$= 336 + 403.20$$
$$= \$739.20$$

**24.**   (2)       Let $x$ = # of pounds of jujubes
         Then $10 - x$ = # of pounds of nonpareils

$$49x + 77(10 - x) = 602$$
$$49x + 770 - 77x = 602$$
$$^-28x = {}^-168$$
$$x = 6 \text{ pounds of jujubes} \quad 10 - x = 4 \text{ pounds of nonpariels}$$

**25.**   (5) Divide 3$\frac{1}{4}$ by 8. 3$\frac{1}{4}$ = $\frac{13}{4}$. $\frac{13}{4}$ ÷ $\frac{8}{1}$ = $\frac{13}{4}$ × $\frac{1}{8}$ = $\frac{13}{32}$ ounce

**26.** (2) $\frac{11}{12} - \frac{1}{8} = \frac{11}{12} - \frac{3}{12} = \frac{8}{12}$ more than its own weight. If the amount had been less, the answer would have been negative.

**27.** (3) Form a proportion:

$$\frac{60 \text{ pages}}{90 \text{ min}} = \frac{436 \text{ pages}}{x \text{ minutes}} \text{ (the amount left to be read)}$$

$$\frac{60}{90} = \frac{2}{3}, \text{ therefore } \frac{2}{3} = \frac{436}{x}$$

$$2x = 1308$$

$$x = 654 \text{ minutes}$$

Dividing by 60 we get 10 hours, 54 minutes, or 10.9 hours.

**28.** (2) Let $x$ = the length of one piece.

Then $x + 5$ = the length of the longer piece.

$$x + x + 5 = 40$$

$$2x + 5 = 40$$

$$2x = 35$$

$$x = 17.5$$

$$x + 5 = 22.5 \text{ feet}$$

**29.** (4) Let $F$ = the number of Karen Foster mitts.

Then $32 - F$ = the number of Sue Sims mitts.

$$3495(F) + 2400(32 - F) = 98700$$

$$3495F + 76800 - 2400F = 98700$$

$$1095F = 21900$$

$$F = 20$$

**30.** (3) $10 \times 10 = 100$ millimeters

**31.** (2) If the backdrop is 16 meters wide, it is 32 meters long. $\frac{16}{2}$ or 8 2 meter widths fill it from side to side. Then $8 \times 32$ meters, or 256 meters of paper are needed.

**32.** (1) $C = \frac{5}{9}(F - 32)$

$$C = \frac{5}{9}(68 - 32)$$

$$C = \frac{5}{9}(36)$$

$$C = 20°$$

**33.** (3) $12(12.5) + 18(8.25) + 24(7) = 150 + 148.5 + 168 = 466.5$ meters

**34.** (3) Multiply $8 \times 60$ to find number of minutes in each workday. Then divide by 13 to find number of interviews per day.

$$\frac{8 \times 60}{13}$$

**35.** (1)

$$\text{Let } t = \text{time at 40 mph}$$
$$\text{Then } 10 - t = \text{time at 60 mph}$$
$$d = rt$$
$$530 = 40t + 60(10 - t)$$
$$530 = 40t + 600 - 60t$$
$$20t = 70$$
$$t = 3\tfrac{1}{2} \text{ hours}$$

**36.** (3) The volume of one box is $2.5 \times 4 \times .75 = 7.5 \text{ in}^3$

$$\frac{180}{7.5} = 24 \text{ boxes}$$

**37.** (3) Myra writes 10 letters with her name at the bottom of the list of 5. Each of those 10 writes 10 (100) letters with Myra's name in 4th place. Each of the 100 writes 10 (1000) letters with Myra's name in 3rd place. Each of the 1000 writes 10 letters (10,000) with Myra's name in 2nd place. Each of the 10,000 writes 10 letters (100,000) with Myra's name in 1st place. Now Myra gets 100,000 $5 bills, or $500,000. P.S. This scheme is illegal, but it's fun to think about, isn't it?

**38.** (1) $\dfrac{2400}{33\frac{1}{3}} = 72 \text{ minutes}$

**39.** (2) $1964 - 111 = 1853$

**40.** (2) $67\tfrac{3}{4} - 27\tfrac{5}{8} = 40\tfrac{1}{8}$

**41.** (5) The highest peaks on all three graphs occur in 1976.

**42.** (1) In 1973, the high school graduate line is at about 10%, while the line for those with less than 4 years of high school is at 15%. The difference then is about 5%. 6% is the closest choice given.

**43.** (3) The greatest difference occurs between the low in 1969 and the high in 1976. The low is about 12%, while the high is about 27%. The difference then is found by subtracting 12 from 27 and getting 15%.

**44.** (1) The distance from the long front to the backmost point is the altitude of the triangle. The 20 meter front is the base, and so $A = \tfrac{1}{2}bh = \tfrac{1}{2}(20)(50) = 500 \text{ m}^2$.

**45.**   (1) The diameter of the circle is the diagonal of the square. If a radius is 5, then the diagonal (diameter) is 10. The diagonal of the square forms two isosceles right triangles, each with side $s$. But the diagonal is the hypotenuse of either of those triangles, so by using the Pythagorean Theorem we find that

$$s^2 + s^2 = 10^2$$
$$2s^2 = 100$$
$$s^2 = 50$$
$$s = \sqrt{50} = 5\sqrt{2}$$

**46.**   (1) Let $x$ = the number.

$$\text{Then } 2(3 + x) = 3x - 1$$
$$6 + 2x = 3x - 1$$
$$x = 7$$

**47.**   (4)   Let $d$ = # of dimes

Then $305 - d$ = # of nickels.

The value of the dimes is $10d$, and $5(305 - d)$ is the value of the nickels.

$$10d + 5(305 - d) = 2100$$
$$10d + 1525 - 5d = 2100$$
$$5d = 575$$
$$d = 115 \text{ dimes}$$

**48.**   (2)

| Quantity | Unit price | Total value |
|----------|-----------|-------------|
| $x$ | 180 | $180x$ |
| $30 - x$ | 270 | $270(30 - x)$ |
| 30 | 210 | 6300 |

$$180x + 270(30 - x) = 6300$$
$$180x + 8100 - 270x = 6300$$
$$^-90x = ^-1800$$
$$x = 20 \text{ pounds}$$

**49.**   (3) The volume of any solid may be found by finding the area of one end of the solid (in this case the can) and then multiply that by the height. The area os the circular lid of the can is $\pi r^2$, or $9\pi$. $8 \times 9\pi = 72\pi$.

**50.**   (4) Bill invested $x$ dollars at 9% and $x - 450$ at 18%. His annual return from both investments is represented by the equation:

$$.09x + .18(x - 450) = 162$$
$$9x + 18(x - 450) = 16200$$
$$9x + 18x - 8100 = 16200$$
$$27x = 24300$$
$$x = 900$$

That means that $450 were invested at 18%.

**51.** (4) To find the average, add all the values given, then divide by the number of values. To add the values in this problem, first change all the heights to inches:

$$5'8'' = 68''$$
$$6'1'' = 73''$$
$$5'10'' = 70''$$
$$6'3'' = 75''$$
$$5'9'' = \underline{69''}$$
$$355'' \div 5 = 71'' = 5'11''$$

**52.** (1) Add together the amount spent on food (.20) and the amount spent on clothes (.15):

$$.20 + .15 = \$.35 \text{ spent on food and clothing}$$

**53.** (3) First find out how much of each dollar she saves. To do that, add up all the known amounts on the pie and subtract from $1.00:

$$\$1.00 - (.35 + .08 + .15 + .20 + .15) = \$.07$$

That means she saves 7 cents from each dollar she takes home. Now multiply the amount she saves per dollar by the number of dollars she takes home:

$$\$200 \times .07 = \$14.00$$

She saves $14 per week.

**54.** (5) While the amount Karen spends for entertainment is in the "Other" segment of the pie, we don't know that it's the only thing covered in that segment, hence there is not enough information to answer the question.

**55.** (3) Karen spends $.15 out of each dollar on clothing. If she's spending $45 on clothing in a week, set up a proportion comparing her weekly clothing expense to her clothing expense per dollar:

Weekly clothing: weekly income as clothing expense per dollar: $1
Mathematically, letting x = weekly income, that's:

$$45/x = .15/1$$
$$.15x = 45$$
$$x = 300$$

She takes home $300 per week.

**56.** (1) $.08 of every dollar goes for utilities. Electricity is a utility: $.08 \times 450 = \$36$ means she spends $36 per month on all her utilities. The only possible answer is $24, since she can't spend more on one utility than she spends on all utilities.

# ANSWER SHEET FOR GED MATHEMATICS TEST II

**Directions:** Take this sample test as though it were the real test. Each problem is followed by five answer choices numbered 1 to 5. Solve each problem, then choose the correct answer from the choices offered. Mark your answers on the answer sheet just as you would have to do on the actual exam. When you have finished the test, check your answers with the solutions on page 313. Allow yourself 90 minutes to complete this test.

1 ① ② ③ ④ ⑤      13 ① ② ③ ④ ⑤      25 ① ② ③ ④ ⑤      37 ① ② ③ ④ ⑤      49 ① ② ③ ④ ⑤
2 ① ② ③ ④ ⑤      14 ① ② ③ ④ ⑤      26 ① ② ③ ④ ⑤      38 ① ② ③ ④ ⑤      50 ① ② ③ ④ ⑤
3 ① ② ③ ④ ⑤      15 ① ② ③ ④ ⑤      27 ① ② ③ ④ ⑤      39 ① ② ③ ④ ⑤      51 ① ② ③ ④ ⑤
4 ① ② ③ ④ ⑤      16 ① ② ③ ④ ⑤      28 ① ② ③ ④ ⑤      40 ① ② ③ ④ ⑤      52 ① ② ③ ④ ⑤
5 ① ② ③ ④ ⑤      17 ① ② ③ ④ ⑤      29 ① ② ③ ④ ⑤      41 ① ② ③ ④ ⑤      53 ① ② ③ ④ ⑤
6 ① ② ③ ④ ⑤      18 ① ② ③ ④ ⑤      30 ① ② ③ ④ ⑤      42 ① ② ③ ④ ⑤      54 ① ② ③ ④ ⑤
7 ① ② ③ ④ ⑤      19 ① ② ③ ④ ⑤      31 ① ② ③ ④ ⑤      43 ① ② ③ ④ ⑤      55 ① ② ③ ④ ⑤
8 ① ② ③ ④ ⑤      20 ① ② ③ ④ ⑤      32 ① ② ③ ④ ⑤      44 ① ② ③ ④ ⑤      56 ① ② ③ ④ ⑤
9 ① ② ③ ④ ⑤      21 ① ② ③ ④ ⑤      33 ① ② ③ ④ ⑤      45 ① ② ③ ④ ⑤
10 ① ② ③ ④ ⑤      22 ① ② ③ ④ ⑤      34 ① ② ③ ④ ⑤      46 ① ② ③ ④ ⑤
11 ① ② ③ ④ ⑤      23 ① ② ③ ④ ⑤      35 ① ② ③ ④ ⑤      47 ① ② ③ ④ ⑤
12 ① ② ③ ④ ⑤      24 ① ② ③ ④ ⑤      36 ① ② ③ ④ ⑤      48 ① ② ③ ④ ⑤

# 10. SAMPLE GED MATHEMATICS TEST II

1) The Schlick Oil Company earned $1051 million in sales in 1981. Their net profit for that year was $84.1 million. What percentage of the money Schlick took in became net profit in 1981?

(1) 7%
(2) 8%
(3) 9%
(4) 10%
(5) 11%

2) Mitch needs cord to section off his bean bushes from the rest of his garden. The bean section is 3 feet wide and half again as long. How much cord will he need?

(1) 10½ feet
(2) 10 feet
(3) 7½ feet
(4) 12 feet
(5) 15 feet

3) Mrs. B. Y. Product went to the butcher to purchase link sausages for herself and her neighbor. There were 57 sausages on the chain purchased. When Mrs. Product split the sausage chain into two pieces, one piece had 3 fewer sausages than the other. The chain with the most sausages went to the neighbor. How many sausages in Mrs. Product's chain?

(1) 27
(2) 30
(3) 33
(4) 36
(5) Not enough information is given

4) If there are 25 coins in your bank totaling $3.85 and you only save dimes and quarters, how many quarters do you have?

(1) 7
(2) 9
(3) 11
(4) 13
(5) 16

5) Moose Lodge #142 needs to raise $459.00 for transportation to a chicken ranch in New Mexico. A local greeting card company has offered to give them $1.35 on every box of cards they sell. How many boxes must they sell in order to fund their trip?

(1) 324
(2) 340
(3) 354
(4) 440
(5) 454

301

6) Hans Dishpan can wash approximately 240 dishes in one hour's time. How many dishes would Hans average in 5 minutes?

   (1) 15
   (2) 20
   (3) 24
   (4) 40
   (5) 42

7) The snail can creep at speeds up to 0.03 mph but the snail has also been observed to travel as slowly as 0.00036 mph. Find the difference between the snail's fastest and slowest speeds.

   (1) .033 mph
   (2) .03036 mph
   (3) .02964 mph
   (4) .00108 mph
   (5) .00364 mph

8) Robert and Randy leave the house at 6 AM to go camping. Sam decides to go with them but to his dismay, when he reaches Robert's house, he learns that Robert and Randy had left an hour ago. If Sam drives 65 mph, how long will it take him to overtake his friends who are travelling at 45 mph?

   (1) $3\frac{1}{4}$ hours
   (2) $2\frac{1}{4}$ hours
   (3) 4 hours
   (4) $4\frac{1}{2}$ hours
   (5) Not enough information is given

9) Tung Chap Ping contracted to lick envelopes for a mail order firm. After realizing the enormity of her task, Ms. Ping hired a professional licker who could lick 120 envelopes per hour more than she. If they worked 6 hours on Friday and licked 4,320 envelopes, how much time did Ms. Ping save by employing the professional licker?

   (1) 6 hours
   (2) 14.4 hours
   (3) 8.4 hours
   (4) 10 hours
   (5) 11.6 hours

10) One gallon = 3.785 liters. Phil Rupp bought his gasoline at a station which had recently converted its pumps to measuring gasoline in liters. If the tank took 34.0 liters, how many gallons did it take?

   (1) 8
   (2) 9
   (3) 9.25
   (4) 10
   (5) 11.5

11) Antoinette told Alice that her street was exactly 6.4 miles from the railroad trestle. At the trestle, Alice noticed that her odometer read 5488.9 miles. What will her odometer read once she has reached Antoinette's street?

(1) 5494.13
(2) 5494.3
(3) 5495.3
(4) 5495.4
(5) 5495.14

12) Christine banked the $84.00 she earned over the summer wrapping egg rolls at the shore. The money was deposited at the beginning of an interest period at a simple yearly rate of 6%. If Christine left her money plus her interest in the bank for 4 entire years, how much would she have in her account at the end of that period?

(1) $100.04
(2) $104.16
(3) $106.05
(4) $129.36
(5) $134.16

13) Red E. Dudieu wanted to nourish an acre of his farmland. One acre equals 43,560 square feet. The general store sold only 20-pound bags of fertilizer and each bag covered 5,000 square feet. How many bags would Mr. Dudieu need to purchase to insure coverage of his acre?

(1) 8 bags
(2) 9 bags
(3) 10 bags
(4) 11 bags
(5) 12 bags

14) The heights of Miss America winners from 1921 to 1935 were as follows: 5 feet 1 inch, 5 feet 7 inches, 5 feet 6 inches, 5 feet 8 inches, 5 feet 4 inches, 5 feet 5.5 inches, 5 feet 4.5 inches, and 5 feet 6 inches. What was the average height of Miss America for that period?

(1) 5 feet 3.5 inches
(2) 5 feet 4 inches
(3) 5 feet 4.75 inches
(4) 5 feet 5 inches
(5) 5 feet 5.25 inches

15) A box of animal crackers contained 10 lions, 13 elephants, 6 giraffes, 11 tigers, 8 seals, and 12 bears. Mrs. Kidd gobbled up 8 bears. Her husband decided to "bear" with her and ate the remaining 4 bears. What percentage of cookies remained in the box for the little Kidds?

(1) 20%
(2) 40%
(3) 65%
(4) 75%
(5) 80%

16) Jonathan drove his 66-year-old grandmother and 9-year-old little brother to the movie theater on Saturday afternoon. He treated all three of them to the matinee. The prices read as follows: Adults $3.50, Children Under 12 $1.50, Senior Citizens 20% discount. How much change did Jonathan receive from his $10.00 bill?

   (1) $1.50
   (2) $2.20
   (3) $2.25
   (4) $3.50
   (5) $4.30

17) Sally's Health Spa charged $25.00 for a monthly membership. In March, however, the owner decided to run a monthly special to attract new members. Sally ran a ''2 for the price of 1'' ad in the local newspaper and was delighted when each member brought a friend to registration. Sally's Health Spa made $450.00 on March memberships. How many people registered?

   (1) 16
   (2) 18
   (3) 24
   (4) 32
   (5) 36

18) The Ya Hoos released a new album entitled ''Mud and Sludge.'' Side A contained 4 songs and their times in minutes and seconds were as follows: 'Down and Dirty' 3:20, 'My Kind of Oil' 4:13, 'Port o'Slime' 2:56, 'Love You, Mom' 3:32. How long would it take you to listen to Side A?

   (1) 13:01
   (2) 13:21
   (3) 13:42
   (4) 14:01
   (5) 14:21

19) Using $\frac{22}{7}$ as $\pi$, find the circumference of a circle whose radius is 4 feet 8 inches.

   (1) 14' 10"
   (2) 340"
   (3) 176"
   (4) 29' 4"
   (5) 21' 2"

20) Henry's VW Rabbit Diesel gets 50 mpg. Diesel fuel costs an average of $1.10 per gallon. This summer, Henry and his family drove 1200 miles to Niagara Falls for vacation. How much did Henry pay for fuel?

   (1) $ 26.40
   (2) $ 52.80
   (3) $105.60
   (4) $132.20
   (5) $264.00

21) Find the volume of a rectangular solid with a length of 12 centimeters, a width of 10 centimeters, and a height of 7 centimeters.

(1) 840 cm²
(2) 84 cm³
(3) 840 cm³
(4) 8.4 m³
(5) 8.4 m²

22) Louis bought a locket for his girlfriend at the jewelry store. The original price had been dropped 25%. Louis paid $33.00. How much did the locket originally cost?

(1) $24.75
(2) $32.25
(3) $38.50
(4) $44.00
(5) $47.50

23) Three couples went out to dinner. The check came to $84.80 and to this was added a 15% tip. The couples split the total cost of the meal 3 ways. About how much did each couple pay?

(1) $32.51
(2) $35.84
(3) $65.02
(4) $72.08
(5) $97.52

24) A baseball team had a roster of 12 players. Their batting averages were .220, .242, .204, .333, .514, .187, .442, .208, .287, .318, .301, and .212. What was the team batting average?

(1) .264
(2) .289
(3) .292
(4) .313
(5) .346

25) In 1966, the average salary of a New Jersey teacher was $7647. Ten years later, teachers in New Jersey were averaging $15,252. Find the nearest whole percentage of increase in salary from 1966 to 1976.

(1) 50%
(2) 100%
(3) 99%
(4) 86%
(5) 75%

26) A woman bought $9\frac{1}{2}$ yards of ribbon to decorate curtains. If she cut the ribbon into 9 equal pieces, how long was each piece?

    (1) $1\frac{1}{18}$ yards
    (2) $1\frac{1}{8}$ yards
    (3) $1\frac{1}{6}$ yards
    (4) $1\frac{1}{5}$ yards
    (5) $1\frac{1}{4}$ yards

27) Amanda buys a package of bacon for $1.98, a dozen eggs for $1.29, paper plates for $1.25, and napkins for $.75. There is a 5% sales tax on non-food items. How much change did Amanda receive from a $10.00 bill?

    (1) $3.43
    (2) $3.53
    (3) $4.53
    (4) $4.63
    (5) $4.73

28) The landscaping company ordered 7 dozen evergreen trees from the nursery. With the exception of 30 hemlocks, the rest are blue spruce trees. How many spruce trees were ordered?

    (1) 4 dozen
    (2) $4\frac{1}{3}$ dozen
    (3) $4\frac{1}{2}$ dozen
    (4) $4\frac{3}{4}$ dozen
    (5) 5 dozen

29) Which of the following equations is equal to 82(9) + 82(12)?

    (1) (82 + 9) + (82 + 12)
    (2) 82(9 + 12)
    (3) (82 + 9)(82 + 12)
    (4) 82(108)
    (5) 82(9) + 9(12)

30) A discount toy store generally takes $\frac{1}{5}$ off the list price of their merchandise. During the holiday season, an additional 15% is taken off the list price. Mrs. Johnson bought a sled listed at $62.00 for Joey and a doll house listed at $54.00 for Jill. To the nearest penny, how much did Mrs. Johnson pay?

    (1) $ 75.40
    (2) $ 78.88
    (3) $ 82.64
    (4) $ 92.80
    (5) $112.52

31) The neon sign over McGinty's Bar flashed 480 times in $1\frac{1}{2}$ hours. How far apart did the flashes occur?

   (1) $5\frac{1}{3}$ seconds
   (2) 3 seconds
   (3) $12\frac{1}{2}$ seconds
   (4) $11\frac{1}{4}$ seconds
   (5) 30 seconds

32) Mr. Elliott has a $52 \times 70$ inch rectangular table. He would like to purchase a table cloth which overlaps each of the four sides by 12 inches. What will the perimeter of his new table cloth be?

   (1) 244 inches
   (2) 170 inches
   (3) 340 inches
   (4) 268 inches
   (5) 292 inches

33) The sailfish is built for speed and can swim through the water at a speed of 68 mph. Approximately how many kilometers can he travel in an hour? 1 kilometer = .62 miles.

   (1) 42 km/hr
   (2) 68 km/hr
   (3) 96 km/hr
   (4) 109 km/hr
   (5) 110 km/hr

34) A plane is scheduled to leave the airport at 9:55 PM on a flight to Florida. The flight takes 3 hours and 48 minutes. What would be the estimated time of arrival?

   (1) 12:43 PM
   (2) 1:43 PM
   (3) 2:43 PM
   (4) 12:43 AM
   (5) 1:43 AM

35) One cubic foot of water weighs 62.4 pounds. A swimming pool holds $18\frac{1}{4}$ cubic feet of water. How many pounds of water will the pool hold when full?

   (1) $\dfrac{18.25}{62.4}$
   (2) $62.4 \times (18\frac{1}{4})^3$
   (3) $18.25 \times 62.4$
   (4) $\dfrac{62.4}{3} (18\frac{1}{4})$
   (5) $\dfrac{18.25 \times 62.4}{3}$

36) A knot measures speed — one nautical mile an hour equals 1 knot. An International Nautical Mile is 1852 meters. How many meters can a ship traveling at a speed of 18 knots cover in 15 minutes?

(1) 1852 meters
(2) 463 meters
(3) 4167 meters
(4) 3704 meters
(5) 8334 meters

**Distribution of Income**

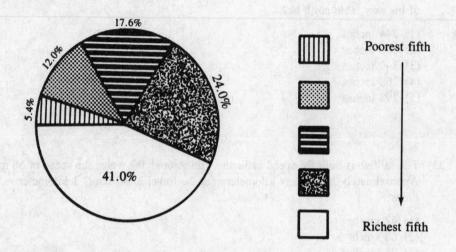

17.6%
12.0%
5.4%
24.0%
41.0%

Poorest fifth

Richest fifth

The following two questions refer to the graph above.

On the circle graph, the distribution of available income in the United States for a particular year is represented. The population has been divided into 5 equal parts, starting from the poorest fifth and ending with the richest.

37) What is the difference between the income available to the poorest ⅗ of the population and that available to the richest ⅕?

(1) 11%
(2) 6%
(3) 18%
(4) 12.9%
(5) 5.6%

38) Which of the following ratios best illustrates the relationship in income distribution between the poorer ⅗ of the population and the richest ⅖?

(1) 34:66
(2) 41:59
(3) 76:24
(4) 6:4
(5) 59:41

39) Eleanor received $5890 each year from her investments which totalled $50,000. Part of the money earned 8% annual interest, while the other part earned 14%. How much money had she invested at 14%?

   (1) $18,500
   (2) $22,500
   (3) $27,500
   (4) $31,500
   (5) $33,500

40) How long is the line-segment that connects the points (3,7) and (9,⁻4) on a graph?

   (1) $4\sqrt{3}$
   (2) $\sqrt{119}$
   (3) $\sqrt{157}$
   (4) $3\sqrt{71}$
   (5) $\sqrt{179}$

41) A coat which lists for $240 is on sale for $180. By what percent had the coat been discounted?

   (1) 40%
   (2) 35%
   (3) 30%
   (4) 25%
   (5) 20%

42) A rectangular parking lot is 200 feet long and 60 feet wide. What is its area?

   (1) 520 ft²
   (2) 1200 ft²
   (3) 12,000 ft²
   (4) 6000 ft²
   (5) 9000 ft²

43) A health food store mixes $1.29 per pound raisins with $2.20 per pound almonds to make 70 pounds of a mixture worth $1.81 per pound. How many pounds of almonds are in the mixture?

   (1) 20
   (2) 25
   (3) 30
   (4) 35
   (5) 40

44) $x^2 - 9x - 22 = 0$. The value of $x$ is

   (1) ⁻2 and 11
   (2) ⁻2 and ⁻11
   (3) 2 and ⁻11
   (4) 11 only
   (5) 2 only

45) George bought a $4.65 notebook, and a $2.15 pen. There was an 8% sales tax. How much change did he receive from a $10 bill?

    (1) $6.80
    (2) $2.66
    (3) $0.54
    (4) $4.05
    (5) $3.12

46) When 9 is added to a certain number, the result is the same as when twice the number is diminished by 6. Find the number.

    (1) 13
    (2) 15
    (3) 17
    (4) 19
    (5) 21

47) How far does a point on the outer rim of a wheel with a 6 inch diameter travel when the wheel rotates one full time?

    (1) $3\pi$ inches
    (2) $6\pi$ inches
    (3) $9\pi$ inches
    (4) $24\pi$ inches
    (5) $36\pi$ inches

48) On a map, 1 inch represents three miles. How many inches are needed to represent a road that is actually 171 miles long?

    (1) 513 inches
    (2) 3 inches
    (3) 121 inches
    (4) 57 inches
    (5) 17 inches

49) At the ballpark, 23,000 customers consumed 630 pounds of hot dogs. At that rate of consumption, how many pounds of hot dogs would be needed for a crowd of 57,500?

    (1) 1175
    (2) 1225
    (3) 1575
    (4) 1625
    (5) 1875

50) Two ships leave the same harbor at the same time and travel in opposite directions, one at 30 km/hr and the other at 50 km/hr. After how many hours will they be 360 kilometers apart?

    (1) $2\frac{1}{2}$ hours
    (2) $3\frac{1}{2}$ hours
    (3) $4\frac{1}{2}$ hours
    (4) $5\frac{1}{2}$ hours
    (5) $6\frac{1}{2}$ hours

51) A plumber completed five jobs yesterday. On the first job she earned $36.45, the second $52.80, the third $42.81, the fourth $49.54, and the fifth $48.90. What was the average amount she earned for each job?

    (1) $38.50
    (2) $39.75
    (3) $40.80
    (4) $42.50
    (5) $46.10

Questions 52 to 56 refer to the following graph.

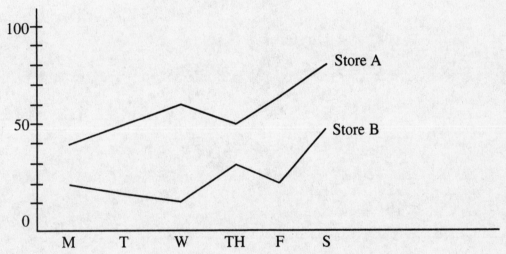

**Sales for Week Ending 8/10**
(in dollars X 1000)

52) On which day was the gap between the two stores' sales greatest?

    (1) Tuesday
    (2) Wednesday
    (3) Thursday
    (4) Friday
    (5) Saturday

53) What was Store B's largest sales volume for a single day?

    (1) $4900
    (2) $8000
    (3) $48,000
    (4) $49,000
    (5) Not enough information is given

54) Sales dipped for Store A between

    (1) Monday and Wednesday
    (2) Tuesday and Thursday
    (3) Wednesday and Thursday
    (4) Wednesday and Friday
    (5) Thursday and Saturday

55) What is the difference between Store A's worst and best days?

    (1) $30,000
    (2) $35,000
    (3) $40,000
    (4) $45,000
    (5) $50,000

56) On which day did store B draw the greatest number of shoppers?

    (1) Monday
    (2) Tuesday
    (3) Thursday
    (4) Saturday
    (5) Not enough information is given

## Solutions to Sample Test 2

**1.** (2) To find out what percent of the $1051 was net profit, set up a proportion:

$$\frac{84.1}{1051} = \frac{x}{100} \quad \text{(Remember, \% means hundredths.)}$$

$$1051x = 8410$$
$$x = 8\%$$

**2.** (5) Half again as long as three is $3 + 1.5$, or $4\frac{1}{2}$. The perimeter of a rectangle 3 by $4\frac{1}{2}$ is found by adding twice the width and twice the length.

$$2 \cdot 3 + 2 \cdot 4\frac{1}{2} = 15 \text{ feet}$$

**3.** (1) Let $x$ = Mrs. Product's sausages.
Then $57 - x$ = the neighbor's

The two amounts are not equal. The neighbor has 3 more. Adding 3 to Mrs. Product's chain would make them equal.

$$x + 3 = 57 - x$$
$$2x = 54$$
$$x = 27 \text{ sausages}$$

**4.** (2) Let $x$ = # of dimes
Then $25 - x$ = # of quarters

$$10x + 25(25 - x) = 385$$
$$10x + 625 - 25x = 385$$
$$^-15x = ^-240$$
$$x = 16$$
$$25 - x = 9 \text{ quarters}$$

**5.** (2) 459 divided by $1.35 = 340 boxes.

**6.** (2) There are 12 5-minute periods in an hour. 240 divided by 12 = 20 dishes.

**7.** (3)
$$\begin{array}{r} .03000 \\ -.00036 \\ \hline \end{array}$$
.02964 mph — and that's a snail's pace.

**8.** (2) $d = r \cdot t$

Sam and his friends travel the same distance, but Sam travels for 1 hour less than his friends:

Let $t$ = Number of hours Robert and Randy travel.
$t - 1$ = Number of hours Sam travels.

$$45t = 65(t - 1)$$
$$45t = 65t - 65$$
$$^-20t = ^-65$$
$$t = 3\frac{1}{4} \text{ hours}$$
$$t - 1 = 2\frac{1}{4} \text{ hours}$$

9. (3) Let Ms. Ping's rate = $x$
   Then $x + 120$ = the professional's rate.

   $$6(x + x + 120) = 4320$$
   $$6(2x + 120) = 4320$$
   $$12x + 720 = 4320$$
   $$12x = 3600$$
   $$x = 300 \text{ per hour that Ms. Ping could lick.}$$

   If she had had to lick 4320 envelopes herself, it would have taken her $\frac{4320}{300} = 14.4$ hours. She therefore saved $14.4 - 6 = 8.4$ hours.

10. (2) Divide 34.0 by 3.785 and get 8.98 which is closest to 9 liters.

11. (3) $5488.9 + 6.4 = 5495.3$

12. (3) $84 \times 1.06 \times 1.06 \times 1.06 \times 1.06 = \$106.05$

13. (2) $\frac{43,560}{5000} = 8 +$ bags. Since he cannot buy 8 and a fraction bags, he must buy 9.

14. (5) Add all the heights together and get 40 feet 42 inches. To find the average height, divide by the number of persons, 8, and get 5 feet $5\frac{1}{4}$ inches, or 5 feet 5.25 inches.

15. (5) There were 60 crackers in the box. They ate 12. $\frac{12}{60}$ is $\frac{1}{5}$, or 20%. That leaves 80% for the little Kidds.

16. (2) If Jonathan drove, he must be an adult, so he paid \$3.50 for his ticket, and \$1.50 for his brother's. His grandmother's ticket cost 80% of \$3.50 = $.8 \times 3.50 = \$2.80$. Add the three ticket prices together and get \$7.80. Jonathan got \$2.20 in change.

17. (5) $\frac{450}{25} = 18$ memberships, but since there are 2 for the price of 1, there are really twice as many, or 36 people registered.

18. (4) $3:20 + 4:13 + 2:56 + 3:32 = 12:121$, but 121 seconds = 2 minutes and 1 second, hence it took 14:01.

19. (4) 4 feet 8 inches is 56 inches $C = 2\pi r = 2(\frac{22}{7})(56) = 352$ inches
    $\frac{352}{12} = 29$ feet 4 inches

20. (1) $\frac{1200 \text{ miles}}{50 \text{ miles}}$ per gallon = 24 gallons used. Then multiply \$1.10 by 24 to get a total cost of \$26.40.

21. (3) length $\times$ width $\times$ height = volume. $12 \times 10 \times 7 = 840 \text{ cm}^3$

22. (4) Let $x$ = the original price.
    Louis paid 75% of the original price. That means:
    $$.75x = 33$$
    $$x = \$44$$

**23.** (1) $84.80 + .15(84.80) = \$97.52 \quad \dfrac{97.52}{3} = \$32.51$

**24.** (2) Adding up the 12 averages we get 3.468. Then, dividing by 12, we find a team average of .289.

**25.** (3) The amount of increase is $7605. To find the % increase, set up a proportion:

$$\frac{7605}{7647} = \frac{x}{100}$$
$$7647x = 760500$$
$$x = 99.45, \text{ or } 99\%$$

**26.** (1) Divide $9\frac{1}{2}$ by 9. $\frac{19}{2} \div \frac{9}{1} = \frac{19}{2} \times \frac{1}{9} = \frac{19}{18} = 1\frac{1}{18}$ yards

**27.** (4) The napkins and paper plates add up to $2.00. 5% tax on $2.00 is $.05 \times 2 =$ $.10. Now add $2.00 + .10 + 1.98 + 1.29 = \$5.37$.
$$\$10.00 - 5.37 = \$4.63 \text{ change}$$

**28.** (3) 7 dozen $= 7 \times 12 = 84$. $84 - 30 = 54$. $\frac{54}{12} = 4\frac{1}{2}$ dozen. Or, $30 = 2\frac{1}{2}$ dozen. 7 dozen $- 2\frac{1}{2}$ dozen $= 4\frac{1}{2}$ dozen.

**29.** (2) Since both numbers are multiplied by 82, it must be $82(9 + 12)$.

**30.** (1) $\frac{1}{5}$ is 20%. If both are taken off the list price, then the discount is actually 35%. The total purchases were $116. If 35% is coming off that, then 65% is being paid. $.65(116) = \$75.40$

**31.** (4) There are 90 minutes in $1\frac{1}{2}$ hours. $\frac{480}{90} = 5\frac{1}{3}$ times per minute. There are 60 seconds in a minute, 60 divided by $5\frac{1}{3} = \frac{60}{1} \times \frac{3}{16} = \frac{45}{4} = 11\frac{1}{4}$ seconds between flashes.

**32.** (3) Add 24 inches to the length and to the width for the overlap. That makes the dimensions 76 inches $\times$ 94 inches. Perimeter of a rectangle is $2L + 2W$, which in this case means $2(76) + 2(94) = 340$ inches.

**33.** (5) Since a kilometer is less than a mile, it will travel more than 68 kilometers. Multiplying by a fraction (.62) will give a smaller number, so we must divide $\frac{68}{.62} = 109.67 = 110$ kilometers.

$$\text{Alternate solution: } \frac{68}{x} = \frac{.62}{1}$$
$$.62x = 68$$
$$x = 109.67 = 110 \text{ kilometers}$$

**34.** (5) $9{:}55 + 3{:}48 = 12{:}103$. But 60 minutes $= 1$ hour, so we have 13:43. That's 1:43 A.M.

**35.** (3) Weight of water in pool = weight of 1 cubic foot (62.4) times number of cubic feet ($18\frac{1}{4}$ or 18.25).

**36.** (5) 15 minutes is $\frac{15}{60}$ or $\frac{1}{4}$ of an hour. A ship travelling 18 knots will travel $\frac{1}{4}$ that distance in 15 minutes. $\frac{1}{4} \times 18 = 4.5$ nautical miles. 4.5 nautical miles $= 4.5 \times 1852 = 8334$ meters.

**37.** (2) To find the income available to the poorest $\frac{3}{5}$, add 5.4 + 12.0 + 17.6 and get 35%. That is 6% less than the 41% available to the richest $\frac{1}{5}$.

**38.** (5) The poorest $\frac{4}{5}$ received 59% while the richest $\frac{1}{5}$ got 41%. In that order, the ratio is 59:41.

**39.** (4) 

Let $x$ = amount at 14%

Then $50{,}000 - x$ = amount at 8%

Her total income is found from the equation

$$.14x + .08(50{,}000 - x) = 5890$$
$$14x + 8(50{,}000 - x) = 589{,}000$$
$$14x + 400{,}000 - 8x = 589{,}000$$
$$6x = 189{,}000$$
$$x = \$31{,}500$$

**40.** (3) To find the vertical distance, subtract the $y$-coordinates and get 11. To find the horizontal distance, subtract the $x$-coordinates and get 6. We are now looking to find the hypotenuse of a right triangle whose legs are 6 and 11.

$$6^2 + 11^2 = c^2$$
$$36 + 121 = c^2$$
$$157 = c^2$$
$$c = \sqrt{157}$$

**41.** (4) Make a proportion:

$$\frac{180}{240} = \frac{x}{100}$$
$$\frac{3}{4} = \frac{x}{100}$$
$$4x = 300$$
$$x = 75\%$$

If the coat is selling for 75% of list, then it must have been discounted 25%.

**42.** (3) The area of a rectangle is $L \times W = 60 \times 200 = 12{,}000 \text{ ft}^2$

**43.** (5)

|  | Quantity | Unit value | Total value |
|---|---|---|---|
| raisins | $x$ | 129 | 129$x$ |
| nuts | $70 - x$ | 220 | $220(70 - x)$ |
| mix | 70 | 181 | 70(181) |

$$129x + 220(70 - x) = 70(181)$$
$$129x + 15{,}400 - 220x = 12{,}670$$
$$^-91x = ^-2730$$
$$x = 30 \text{ pounds}$$
$$70 - x = 40 \text{ pounds}$$

**44.** (1) 

$$x^2 - 9x - 22 = 0$$
$$(x + 2)(x - 11) = 0$$
$$x + 2 = 0 \qquad x - 11 = 0$$
$$x = {}^-2 \qquad x = 11$$

**45.** (2) Adding $4.65 and $2.15, we arrive at a total of $6.80. Next we must find 8% of that total by multiplying .08 × 6.80. The tax comes to .54. Adding that on we find a grand total of $7.34, which means that change from a $10 bill would be $2.66.

**46.** (2)　　　Let $x$ = the number.

Then $x + 9 = 2x - 6$

$x = 15$

**47.** (2) In one full rotation, the point will travel one full circumference of the wheel. Since $C = \pi d$, the point would travel $6\pi$ inches.

**48.** (4) A proportion can be established between the scale of the map in inches and the actual distance in miles:

$$\frac{1}{3} = \frac{x}{171}$$

$$3x = 171$$

$$x = 57 \text{ inches}$$

**49.** (3) This is also a problem for which a proportion will yield a quick solution:

$$\frac{630}{23,000} = \frac{x}{57,500}$$

$$23,000x = 57,500(630)$$

$$23x = 57.5(630)$$

$$23x = 36,225$$

$$x = 1575 \text{ pounds}$$

**50.** (3) $D = rt$

Since the two ships are travelling in opposite directions, we may imagine one ship to be standing still and the other moving away from it at their combined rates of 80 km/hr. In that case,

$$D = rt$$

$$360 = 80t$$

$$t = 4\tfrac{1}{2} \text{ hours}$$

**51.** (5) To find the average, add all the values given, then divide by the number of values.

$ 36.45
$ 52.80
$ 42.81
$ 49.54
48.90
$230.50 ÷ 5 = $46.10

**52.** (2) The gap between the two lines is greatest on Wednesday.

**53.** (4) Keeping a straightedge square with the vertical axis and moving it until the "B" line just touches its right end, we find it comes out between the 48 and 50 markings. Call it 49. But since the sales volume is graphed in terms of thousands of dollars, we must multiply the 49 by 1000: $49 × 1000 = $49,000.

**54.** (3) The graph of "A" dips from Wednesday to Thursday. All other choices are for intervals when the graph dips and rises or rises only.

**55.** (3) Store A did $80,000 in sales on Saturday and $40,000 on Monday: $80,000 − $40,000 = $40,000.

**56.** (5) The graph shows sales for one week in store A and store B. There is no information given about number of shoppers.